| | |
|---|---|
| LBT | Listen Before Talk |
| LCC | Lost Calls Cleared |
| LCD | Lost Calls Delayed |
| LLC | Logical Link Control |
| LWT | Listen While Talk |
| MAC | Medium Access Control |
| NBS | National Bureau of Standards |
| NCC | Network Control Center |
| OSI | Open Systems Interconnection |
| PABX | Private Automatic Branch Exchange |
| PBX | Private Branch Exchange |
| PCM | Pulse Code Modulation |
| PDN | Public Data Network |
| PSK | Phase-Shift Keying |
| SAP | Service Access Point |
| SNS | Secondary Network Server |
| TCP | Transmission Control Protocol |
| TDM | Time-Division Multiplexing |
| TIU | Trusted Interface Unit |
| TMS | Time-Multiplexed Switching |
| TP | Transport Protocol |
| TSI | Time-Slot Interchange |
| VAN | Value-Added Network |
| VTP | Virtual Terminal Protocol |

# LOCAL NETWORKS

## An Introduction

# WILLIAM STALLINGS, Ph.D.

# LOCAL NETWORKS

## An Introduction

**Macmillan Publishing Company**

*New York*

**Collier Macmillan Publishers**

*London*

Macmillan Publishing Company
866 Third Avenue, New York, New York, 10022

Collier Macmillan Canada, Inc.

**Library of Congress Cataloging in Publication Data**
Stallings, William.
  Local networks.

  Bibliography: p.
  Includes index.
  1. Computer networks.  2. Electronic data processing
—Distributed processing.  I. Title.
TK5105.5.S78  1984        001.64′404       83-5423
ISBN 0-02-415460-1


Printing:     3 4 5 6 7 8        Year: 4 5 6 7 8 9 0 1 2

ISBN  0-02-415460-1

To my wife, Tricia

# PREFACE

Perhaps no other major innovation in data processing or data communications has been so widely discussed or so eagerly anticipated before its maturity as local networks. Local networks are attractive for such features as high availability and the ability to support multiple vendor equipment. And, although the technology is rapidly evolving, the principal architectural forms and design approaches have emerged.

## Objectives

This book focuses on the broad and constantly changing field of local networks. The aim of the text is to provide a reasoned balance among breadth, depth, and timeliness. The book emphasizes topics of fundamental importance concerning the technology and architecture of local networks. Certain key areas, such as the network interface and performance, are treated in some detail. Others, such as security and reliability, can only be treated in an introductory fashion.

The book explores the key topics in the field in the following general categories:

- *Technology and architecture:* There is a small collection of ingredients that serves to characterize and differentiate local networks, including transmission medium, network topology, communication protocols, switching technique, and hardware/software interface.
- *Network type:* It is convenient to classify local networks into three types, based partly on technology and partly on application. These are local area network (LAN), high-speed local network (HSLN), and digital switch/computerized branch exchange (CBX).
- *Design approaches:* While not attempting to be exhaustive, the book exposes and discusses important issues related to local network design.

Conspicuously missing from this list is a category with a title such as "typical systems." This book focuses on the common principles underlying the design and implementation of all local networks. It should, therefore, give the reader sufficient background to judge and compare local network products. A description of even a small sample of such systems is beyond the scope of this book. Discussions of specific systems are included herein only when they are the best vehicle for communicating the concepts and principles under discussion.

In terms of style, the book is primarily:

- *Descriptive:* Terms are defined and the key concepts and technologies are discussed in some detail.
- *Comparative:* Wherever possible, alternative or competing approaches are compared and their relative merits, based on suitable criteria, are discussed.

On the other hand, analytic and research-oriented styles are present to a much lesser degree. Virtually all of the mathematical content is confined to the chapters on performance, and even there, the emphasis is on results rather than derivations.

## Intended Audience

This book is intended for a broad range of readers interested in local networks:

- *Students and professionals in computer science and data communications:* The book is intended as both a textbook for study and a basic reference volume for this exciting area within the broader fields of computer science and data communications.
- *Local network designers and implementors:* The book discusses the critical design issues and illustrates alternative approaches to meeting user requirements.
- *Local network customers and system managers:* The book alerts the reader to some of the key issues and tradeoffs, and what to look for in the way of network services and performance.

The book is intended to be self-contained. For the reader with little or no background in data communications, a brief primer is included.

## Plan of the Text

The book is organized to clarify both the unifying and differentiating concepts underlying the field of local networks. The organization of the chapters is as follows:

1. *Introduction:* This chapter defines the term local network and looks at some of the applications and advantages and disadvantages.
2. *Topics in data communications and computer networking:* This necessarily brief survey explains the relevant concepts used throughout the book.
3. *Local network technology:* Focuses on the key characteristics of transmission medium and topology. The classification of local networks used in this book is presented and discussed.
4, 5. *Local area networks:* The term local area network (LAN) is often mistakenly identified with the entire field of local networks. LANs are general-purpose in nature and most of the better-known local networks fall into this class. The major types of LANs—baseband bus, broadband bus/tree, and ring—are described and compared. The important issue of medium access control protocols is explored. The standards currently being developed for LANs are also described.
6. *High-speed local networks:* This chapter focuses on a special purpose high-speed type of local network, examining current technology and standards and possible future directions.
7. *Circuit-switched local networks:* Networks in this category constitute the major alternative to LANs for meeting general local interconnection needs. The category includes the data-only digital switch and the voice/data computerized branch exchange (CBX). This chapter explores the technology and architecture of these devices and examines their pros and cons relative to LANs.
8. *The network interface:* The nature of the interface between an attached device and LAN or HSLN is an important design issue. This chapter explores some alternatives.
9, 10. *Network performance:* The purpose of these chapters is to give some insight into the performance problems and the differences in performance of various local networks.
11. *Internetworking:* In the majority of cases, local networks will be connected in some fashion to other networks. Some alternatives are explored.
12. *Local network design issues:* The purpose of this chapter is to give the reader some feel for the breadth of design issues that must be addressed in implementing and operating local networks.

In addition, the book includes an extensive glossary, a list of frequently-used acronyms, and a bibliography. Each chapter includes problems and suggestions for further reading.

The book is suitable for self-study and can be conveniently covered in a one-semester course.

A final note: a considerable fraction of the material is organized with reference to the Open Systems Interconnection (OSI) model and the local network standards being developed. This structure is suggestive of the certain future direction of local network architecture, and, equally important, it provides a terminology and frame of reference that is becoming universal in networking discourses.

## Related Volumes

Two of my other books may be of interest to students and professionals. *Local Network Technology* (IEEE Computer Society Press, 1983) is a companion to this text, and follows the same topical organization. It contains reprints of many of the key references used herein; these are indicated by an asterisk when mentioned in the recommended reading section of each chapter. The address of the IEEE Computer Society Press is P.O. Box 80452, Worldway Postal Center, Los Angeles, CA 90080; telephone (714) 821-8380.

Another related text is *Data and Computer Communications,* forthcoming from Macmillan. This book covers fundamental concepts in the areas of data transmission, communication networks, and computer-communications protocols.

## Acknowledgments

Many people have helped me during the preparation of this book. I would like particularly to acknowledge and thank the following people. K.C. Houston first introduced me to this fascinating field and provided me with the opportunity to pursue my interest. George Arnovick, Lynn DeNoia, Donald DeVorkin, Harvey Freeman, Kathy Hanson, Mary Loomis, Ira Pohl, Bart Stuck, and Gene Swystun reviewed all or a portion of the manuscript. Dave Carlson, George Jelatis, and Bob Donnan of the IEEE 802 Committee and Dolan Toth of the ANS X3T9.5 Committee reviewed the descriptions of the respective standards; of course, any errors remaining in the text are my responsibility. My editor, Sally Elliott, shepherded the book through all the stages from proposal to printing in as rapid and professional a manner as one could wish for. Alice Wilding-White did an amazingly fast job of typing the manuscript. And, finally, my wife Tricia provided the two ingredients essential to the writing of this book: her patience and encouragement.

W.S.

# CONTENTS

# LOCAL NETWORKS

## An Introduction

# Introduction

## A DEFINITION OF LOCAL NETWORKS

To formulate a definition of the term *local network*, and to characterize the purposes of such networks, it is important to understand the trends that have brought about local networks.

Of most importance is the dramatic and continuing decrease in computer hardware costs, accompanied by an increase in computer hardware capability. Today's microprocessors have speeds, instruction sets, and memory capacities comparable to medium scale minicomputers. This trend has spawned a number of changes in the way information is collected, processed, and used in organizations. There is increasing use of single-function systems and intelligent workstations, to make systems friendlier and more accessible to the users. The decrease in hardware cost correspondingly decreases hardware life cycles, which exacerbates software conversion problems. These conversion costs may be reduced by decomposing large computer systems into smaller, separate components.

All of these factors lead to an increased number of systems at a single site: office building, factory, operations center, and so on. At the same time there is likely to be a desire to interconnect these systems for a variety of reasons, including:

- To exchange data between systems
- To provide backup in realtime applications.
- To share expensive resources

To appreciate this last reason, consider that although the cost of data processing hardware has dropped, the cost of essential electromechanical equipment, such as bulk storage and line printers, remains high. In the past, with a centralized data processing facility, these devices could be attached directly to the central host computer. With the dispersal of computer power, these devices must somehow be shared.

We will elaborate on these and other reasons later in this chapter. For now, the discussion above should be enough to motivate the following definition of a *local network*:

A local network is a communications network that provides interconnection of a variety of data communicating devices within a small area.

There are three elements of significance in this definition. First, a local network is a communications network, not a computer network. In this book we deal primarily with issues relating to the communications network. The network software and protocols that are required for attached computers to function as a network are beyond the scope of this book. As a corollary to this definition, note that a collection of devices interconnected by individual point-to-point links is not included in the definition nor in this book.

Second, we interpret the phrase *data communicating devices* broadly, to include any device that communicates over a transmission medium. Examples:

- Computers
- Terminals
- Peripheral devices
- Sensors (temperature, humidity, security alarm sensors)
- Telephones
- Television transmitter and receivers

Of course, not all types of local networks are capable of handling all of these devices.

Third, the geographic scope of a local network is small. The most common occurrence is a network that is confined to a single building. Networks that span several buildings, such as on a college campus or military base, are also common. A borderline case is a network with a radius of a few tens of kilometers. With appropriate technology, such a system will behave like a local network.

Another element that could be added to the definition is that a local network is generally privately owned rather than a public or commercially available utility. Indeed, typically, a single organization will own both the network and the attached devices.

Some of the typical characteristics of local networks are:

- High data rates (0.1 to 100 Mbps)
- Short distances (0.1 to 25 km)
- Low error rate ($10^{-8}$ to $10^{-11}$)

The first two parameters serve to differentiate local networks from two cousins: multiprocessor systems and long-haul networks. This is illustrated in Figure 1.1. The figure indicates three types of local networks: local area networks, high speed local networks, and computerized branch exchanges. These will be defined in Chapter 3.

Other distinctions can be drawn between local networks and its two cousins, and these have a significant impact on design and operation. Local networks generally experience significantly fewer data transmission errors and significantly lower communications costs than those of long haul networks. Cost-performance tradeoffs are thus significantly different. Also, because local networks are generally owned by the same organization as the attached devices, it is possible to achieve greater integration between the network and the devices; this topic is explored in Chapter 8.

A distinction between local networks and multiprocessors systems is the degree of coupling. Multiprocessor systems are tightly coupled, usually have some central control, and completely integrate the communications function. Local networks tend to exhibit the opposite characteristics.

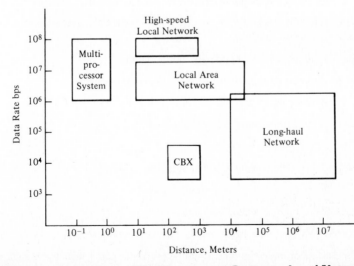

**FIGURE 1–1. Comparison of Multiprocessor Systems, Local Networks, and Long-Haul Networks**

## BENEFITS AND PITFALLS

Table 1.1 lists some of the major benefits of a local network. Whether these are realized or not, of course, depends on the skill and wisdom of those involved in selecting the local network.

Perhaps the most important benefit of a local network relates to system evolution. In a non-networked installation, such as a time-sharing center, all of the data processing power is in one or a few systems. Changes tend to be few and traumatic. By dispersing a site's computer power among a number of systems, it is possible to replace applications or computer systems gradually, avoiding the all-or-nothing approach.

A local network tends to improve the reliability, availability, and survivability of a data processing facility (see Section 12.2). With multiple interconnected systems, the loss of any one system should have minimal impact. Further, key systems can be made redundant so that other systems can quickly take up the load after a failure.

We have already mentioned resource sharing. This includes not only expensive peripheral devices, but data. Data can be housed and controlled from a specific facility but, via the network, be available to many users.

**TABLE 1.1   Benefits and Pitfalls of Local Networks**

Potential Benefits

System evolution: incremental changes with contained impact

Reliability/availability/survivability: multiple interconnected systems disperse functions and provide backup capability

Resource sharing: expensive peripherals, hosts, data

Multivendor support: customer not locked in to a single vendor

Improved response/performance

User needs single terminal to access multiple systems

Flexibility of equipment location

Integration of data processing and office automation

Potential Pitfalls

Interoperability is not guaranteed: software, data

A distributed data base raises problems of integrity, security/privacy

Creeping escalation: more equipment will be procured than is actually needed

Loss of control: more difficult to manage and enforce standards

A local network provides at least the potential of connecting devices from multiple vendors, thus giving the customer greater flexibility and bargaining power. However, a local network will provide only a rather low or primitive level of interconnection. For the network to function properly, higher levels of networking software must be supplied within the attached devices (see Section 2.3 and Chapter 8).

These are, in most cases, the most significant benefits of a local network. Several others are also listed in Table 1.1.

Alas, there are also some pitfalls, or at least potential pitfalls. As we mentioned, a local network does not guarantee that two devices can be used cooperatively, a concept known as *interoperability*. For example, two word processors from different vendors can be attached to a local network, and can perhaps exchange data. But they probably will use different file formats and different control characters, so that it is not possible, directly, to take a file from one and begin editing it on the other. Some sort of format-conversion software is needed.

With a local network, it is likely that data will be distributed or, at least, that access to data may come from multiple sources. This raises questions of integrity (e.g., two users trying to update the data base simultaneously) and security and privacy.

Another pitfall is what Martin refers to as "creeping escalation" [MART81b]. With the dispersal of computer equipment and the ease of incrementally adding equipment, it becomes easier for managers of suborganizations to justify equipment procurement for their department. Although each procurement may be individually justifiable, the totality of procurements throughout an organization may well exceed the total requirements.

There is also a loss of control problem. The prime virtue of networking—distributed systems—is also its prime danger. It is difficult to manage this resource, to enforce standards for software and data, and to control the information available through a network.

We close this discussion with a sobering summary in Table 1.2 based on a recent survey of local network users. While some users noted positive effects from the installation of a local network, a similar number reported negative effects. The conflicting and exaggerated claims of vendors plus the multiplicity of choices has led to confusion and disappointment. Local networks will aid an organization only if they are chosen and managed properly.

## 1.3

# APPLICATIONS

The range of applications for local networks is wide, as indicated by the broad definition given above. Table 1.3 lists some of the potential applications. Again, we emphasize that not all local networks are capable of supporting all applications.

**TABLE 1.2  Organizational Effects of Local Networks**

| Affected Area | Positive Effects | Negative Effects |
|---|---|---|
| Work quality | Wider data accessibility; fewer "lost" items.<br>Wider participation in creating and reviewing work | Indeterminate or mediocre data quality; reduced independence and initiative |
| Productivity | Increased work load handled by more powerful office-systems equipment | Greater resources used to perform inconsequential work |
| Employee changes | Improved skill levels in current staff<br>More challenging work<br>Reduced status distinctions | Fewer jobs for marginal performers<br>Less personal interaction<br>Insufficient status distinctions |
| Decision-making effectiveness | Quicker availability of relevant facts<br>Greater analytic capability<br>More people involved in hypothesis building and testing | Factual component of decision making becomes too high<br>"Forest and trees" problem could encourage "group think" |
| Organizational structure | More effective decentralization | Decentralization can get out of control |
| Costs | Overall cost reduction | Overall cost increase; soft benefits used as justification |
| Total impact | Permits the planning of new business approaches | Creates increased complexity and poorly functioning dependence relationships |

*Source:* [EDN82].

**TABLE 1.3  Local Network Applications**

Data Processing
  Data entry
  Transaction processing
  File transfer
  Inquiry/response
  Batch/RJE

Office automation
  Document/word processing
  Electronic mail
  Intelligent copying/facsimile

Factory automation
  CAD/CAM
  Inventory control/order entry/shipping

Energy management
  Heating
  Ventilation
  Air Conditioning

Process control

Fire and security
  Sensors/alarms
  Cameras and monitors

Telephones

Teleconferencing

Television
  Off-the-air
  Video presentations

To give some feeling for the use of local networks, we discuss in this section four rather different types of potential applications. All of these applications are possible today, although their use is not yet widespread.

## Personal Computer Networks

We start at one extreme, a system designed to support microcomputers, such as personal computers. With the relatively low cost of such systems, individual managers within organizations are independently procuring personal computers for standalone applications, such as VisiCalc and project management tools. Today's personal computers put processor, file storage, high-level languages, and problem-solving tools in an inexpensive, "user-friendly" package. The reasons for acquiring such a system are compelling.

But a collection of standalone processors will not meet all of an organization's needs; central processing facilities are still required. Some programs, such as econometric forecasting models, are too big to run on a small computer. Corporate-wide data files, such as accounting and payroll, require a centralized facility but should be accessible to a number of users. In addition, there are other kinds of files that, although specialized, must be shared by a number of users. Further, there are sound reasons for connecting individual intelligent workstations not only to a central facility but to each other as well. Members of a project or organizational team need to share work and information. By far the most efficient way to do so is electronically.

Figure 1.2 is an example of a local network of personal computers for a hypothetical aerospace engineering group or department [SCHW82]. The figure shows four types of users who have personal computers, each equipped with particular applications.

Each type of user is provided with electronic mail and word processing to improve the efficiency of creating and distributing messages, memos, and reports. Managers are also given a set of program and budget management tools. With the amount of automation that personal computers supply, the role of secretaries becomes less that of a typist and more that of an administrative assistant. Tools such as electronic calendar and graphics support become valuable for these workers. In the same fashion, engineers and technical writers can be supplied with tailored systems.

Certain expensive resources, such as a disk and printer, can be shared by all users of the departmental local network. In addition, the network can tie into larger corporate network facilities. For example, the corporation may have a building-wide local network (see Office Automation below) and a long-haul corporate-wide network using, for example, IBM's SNA. A communications server can provide controlled access to these resources.

A key requirement for the success of such a network is low cost. The cost of attachment to the network for each device should be on the order of one to

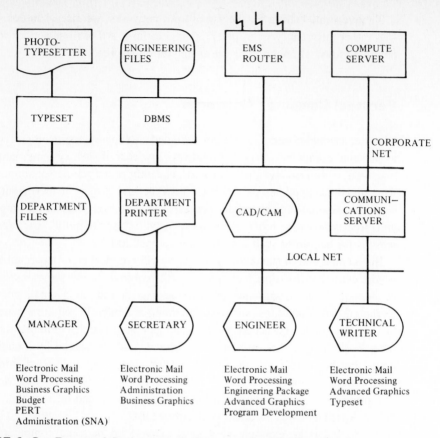

**FIGURE 1–2. Personal Computers in Support of a Working Team**

a few hundred dollars. The capacity and data rate need not be high, so this is a realizable goal. For examples, see [BOSE81], [HAHN81], and [MALO81].

## Computer Room Networks

At the other extreme from a personal computer local network is one designed for use in a computer room containing large, expensive mainframe computers. This is an example of what we will refer to as a *high-speed local network* (HSLN). The HSLN is likely to find application at very large data processing sites. Typically, these sites will be large companies or research installations with large data processing budgets. Because of the size involved, a small difference in productivity can mean millions of dollars. Further, although HSLNs are few in number, the collective cost of the equipment they support is very high. Consequently, the HSLN deserves a close look.

Consider a site that uses a dedicated mainframe computer. This implies a fairly large application or set of applications. As the load at the site grows, the existing model may be replaced by a more powerful one, perhaps a multiprocessor system. At some sites, a single-system replacement will not be able to keep up. We can see this by referring to Tables 1.4 and 1.5. The technology growth rate of IBM mainframes, in terms of millions of instructions per second, correlated closely to 20% per year up to 1981; the introduction of the four-processor 3084 caused a spurt. Similarly, the capacity of a single disk box is growing at about 40% per year.

For a number of sites, these equipment growth rates will be exceeded by demand growth rates. The facility will eventually require multiple independent computers. Again, there are compelling reasons for interconnecting these systems. The cost of system interrupt is high, so it should be possible, easily and quickly, to shift applications to backup systems. It must be possible to test new procedures and applications without degrading the production system. Large bulk storage files must be accessible from more than one computer.

An example of an HSLN installation is the one at the National Center for Atmospheric Research (NCAR), shown in Figure 1.3. The NCAR facility is

**TABLE 1.4   Technology Growth Rate: Computer MIPS**

| Year | 20% Growth[a] (MIPS) | IBM | | |
|------|------|------|------|------|
| | | Model | Number of Processors | MIPS |
| 1967 | 0.72 | 360/65 | 1 | 0.72 |
| 1972 | 1.8 | 370/165 | 1 | 1.8 |
| 1976 | 3.7 | 370/168-3 | 1 | 2.5 |
| 1978 | 5.4 | 3033 | 1 | 5.3 |
| 1981 | 9.3 | 3081 | 2 | 10.4 |
| 1982 | 11.2 | 3084 | 4 | 27 |

[a]Technology limits system growth in terms of MIPS (millions of instructions per second) to 20% per year.

**TABLE 1.5   Technology Growth Rate: Single Disk Box Capacity**

| Year | 40% Growth[a] (megabytes) | IBM | |
|------|------|------|------|
| | | Model | Megabytes |
| 1969 | 36.4 | 2319 | 30 |
| 1972 | 100 | 3330-I | 100 |
| 1974 | 196 | 3330-II | 200 |
| 1976 | 384 | 3350 | 317 |
| 1979 | 1054 | 3375 | 820 |
| 1981 | 2066 | 3380 | 2520 |

[a]Technology limits storage per box to 40% per year.

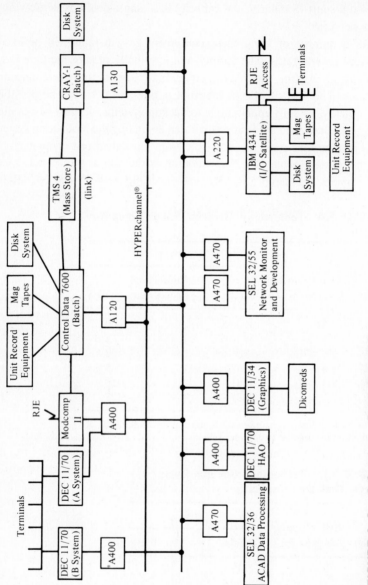

**FIGURE 1–3. A Computer Room Network**

used for atmospheric research. This entails storage of massive amounts of data and the use of huge number-crunching simulation and analysis programs. There is also an extensive on-site graphics facility.

Initially, the NCAR facility consisted of a single mainframe run in batch mode. When it became clear that additional batch machines were needed, NCAR investigated the requirements for a new configuration to meet their needs. The result was four objectives:

- Provide front-end processors to remove job and file preparation tasks from the batch computers.
- Provide an efficient method for interactive processing.
- Design a system architecture which would allow different services for special needs and purposes.
- Provide a system that would allow configuration flexibility without excessive modification to existing resources.

The result of this study was a plan that called for the procurement of front-end processors, special-purpose computers, and bulk storage systems. A network was needed that met two requirements:

- Easy addition and subtraction of equipment
- High sustained data transfer speeds

These requirements were met by an HSLN system [CHRI79].

It can be seen that some key requirements for HSLNs are the opposite of those for personal computer local networks. High data rates are required to keep up with the work. This is expensive but, given the cost of the attached equipment, attachment costs in the tens of thousands of dollars are reasonable.


## Office Automation

Most local network applications will fall between these two extremes. Moderate data rates and moderate attachment costs are requirements. In some cases, the local network will support one or a few types of devices and rather homogeneous traffic. Others will support a wide variety of device and traffic types.

A good generic example of the latter is an office automation system, which can be defined as the incorporation of appropriate technology to help people manage information.

The key motivation for the move to office automation is productivity. As the percentage of white-collar workers has increased, the information and paperwork volume has grown. In most installations secretarial and other support functions are heavily labor intensive. Increased labor costs combined with low productivity and increasing work load have caused employers to seek effective ways of increasing their rather low capital investment in this type of work.

At the same time, principals (managers, skilled "information workers") are faced with their own productivity bind. Work needs to be done faster with less wait time and waste time between segments of a job. This requires better access to information and better communication and coordination with others.

Table 1.6 lists elements of a hypothetical integrated office automation system. A study of this list gives some idea of the range of devices and information types that are part of the system. For this system to work and be truly effective, a local network is needed that can support the various devices and transmit the various types of information. A discussion of the use of local networks to tie together office automation equipment such as this can be found in [DERF83].

### Integrated Voice and Data Local Networks

In virtually all offices today, the telephone system is separate from any local network that might be used to interconnect data processing devices. With the advent of digital voice technology, the capability now exists to integrate the telephone switching system of a building with the data processing equipment, providing a single local network for both.

Such integrated voice/data networks might simplify network management and control. It will also provide the required networking for the kinds of integrated voice and data devices to be expected in the future. An example is an executive voice/data workstation that provides verbal message storage, voice annotation of text, and automated dialing.

### Summary

This section has only scratched the surface of possible applications of local networks. This book focuses on the common principles underlying the design and implementation of all local networks, and so will not pursue the topic of specific applications. Nevertheless, in the course of the book, the reader will gain an appreciation of the variety of uses for local networks.

**1.4**

## RECOMMENDED READING

There have been a number of survey articles on local networks. Examples are [CLAR78], [COTT79], [PARK83a], [STAL83b]*, and [WOOD83a]. Annotated bibliographies can be found in [SHOC80b] and [STAL83a].

There have been several collections of articles. [STAL83a] is a companion to this text and contains many of the key references used herein; these are indicated by an asterisk when mentioned in the recommended reading section

**TABLE 1.6 Elements of an Integrated Office Automation System**

### Basic IOAS Components

Action elements
  Word management (keying and editing)
  Terminal-oriented computer-based message system
  Automated file indexing
  Electronic filing and retrieval
  Off-line connection to computer-operated micrographics (for system purging)
Control elements
  Electronic calendar
  Electronic tickler file
Inquiry elements
  Automated file searching and retrieval
  Directory of users (names, addresses, telephone numbers, etc.)
  Capability for open-loop computer-aided retrieval (CAR) of micrographics
  Capability for input/output control of physical files

### Extended-Application IOAS Components

Action elements
  Automated departmental billing for IOAS usage
  Individual applications
  Personal computing (permits individual to program)
  Unit applications
  Departmental applications
  Divisional applications
  Regional applications
  Line-of-business applications
  Functional applications (mathematical formulas)
Control elements
  System usage monitoring (departmental level)
  Specialized applications (as above)
Inquiry elements: specialized applications (as above)

### Optional IOAS Components

Action elements
  Interconnection to other terminal-oriented, computer-based message systems
  Interconnection to public teletypewriter systems
  OCR (optical character recognition) input
  Digitized, hard-copy input (temporary; for incoming mail)
  Store-and-forward fax
  Soft-copy fax
  Interconnection to external fax devices and networks
  Audio output electronic mail (digital-to-audio conversion)
  Business graphics (black-and-white)
  Electronic calculator
  Sorting capabilities
  Photocomposer output
  On-line output of computer-operated micrographics (COM)
  Computer teleconferencing
Control elements
  COM format previewing
  Project management and control
  Management of multiauthor document preparation
Inquiry elements
  Soft-copy CAR
  Electronic publishing (manuals, price lists, news, etc.)
  Interconnection to other internal systems and data bases
  Interconnection to external research data base services

*Source:* [BARC81].

of each chapter. [THUR81] is a collection of articles about specific systems, most of which are experimental or laboratory systems rather than commercially available products.

[DERF83] is a less technical treatment of the topic than the present text.

# PROBLEMS

**1.1** A computer network is an interconnected set of computers and other devices (terminals, printers, etc.) that can communicate and cooperate with each other to perform certain applications. A subset of a computer network is a communications network (sometimes called a subnetwork) that provides the necessary functions for transferring data between network devices. List functions and capabilities that should be part of the subnetwork and those that should be part of the computer network outside the subnetwork.

**1.2** On what grounds should a collection of devices connected by point-to-point links be excluded from the definition of local network?

**1.3** For each of the items listed in Table 1.2, what factors are key in determining whether the effects will be mostly positive or mostly negative?

**1.4** An alternative to a local network for meeting local requirements for data processing and computer applications is a centralized time-sharing system plus a large number of terminals dispersed throughout the local area. What are the major benefits and pitfalls of this approach compared to a local network?

**1.5** What are the key factors that determine the response time and throughput performance of a local network? Of a centralized system?

**1.6** In what ways is the man-machine interface of a local network likely to differ from that of a centralized system for:
- Application users?
- System operator/manager?

# Topics in Data Communications and Computer Networking

The purpose of this chapter is to make this book self-contained for the reader with little or no background in data communications. For the reader with greater interest, references for further study are supplied at the end of the chapter.

## 2.1

### DATA COMMUNICATIONS CONCEPTS

#### Analog and Digital Data Communications

The terms *analog* and *digital* correspond, roughly, to continuous and discrete, respectively. These two terms are used frequently in data communications in at least three contexts:

- Data
- Signaling
- Transmission

Very briefly, we define *data* as entities that convey meaning. A useful distinction is that data have to do with the form of something; *information* has to do with the content or interpretation of those data. *Signals* are electric or electromagnetic encoding of data. *Signaling* is the act of propagating the signal along some suitable medium. Finally, *transmission* is the communication of data by the propagation and processing of signals. In what follows, we try to make these abstract concepts clear, by discussing the terms "analog" and "digital" in these three contexts.

The concepts of analog and digital data are simple enough. *Analog data* take on continuous values on some interval. For example, voice and video are continuously varying patterns of intensity. Most data collected by sensors, such as temperature and pressure, are continuous-valued. *Digital data* take on discrete values; examples are text and integers.

In a communications system, data are propagated from one point to another by means of electric signals. An *analog signal* is a continuously varying electromagnetic wave that may be transmitted over a variety of media, depending on frequency; examples are wire media, such as twisted pair and coaxial cable, fiber optic cable, and atmosphere or space propagation. A *digital signal* is a sequence of voltage pulses that may be transmitted over a wire medium; for example, a constant positive voltage level may represent binary 1 and a constant negative voltage level may represent binary 0.

The principal advantages of digital signaling are that it is generally cheaper than analog signaling and is less susceptible to noise interference. The principal disadvantage is that digital signals suffer more from attenuation than do analog signals. Figure 2.1 shows a sequence of voltage pulses, generated by a source using two voltage levels, and the received voltage some distance down a conducting medium. Because of the attentuation or reduction of signal strength at higher frequencies, the pulses become rounded and smaller. It should be clear that this attenuation can rather quickly lead to the loss of the information contained in the propagated signal.

Both analog and digital data can be represented, and hence propagated, by either analog or digital signals. This is illustrated in Figure 2.2. Generally, analog data are a function of time and occupy a limited frequency spectrum. Such data can be directly represented by an electromagnetic signal occupying the same spectrum. The best example of this is voice data. As sound waves, voice data have frequency components in the range 20 Hz to 20 kHz. However, most of the speech energy is in a much narrower range. The standard spectrum of voice signals is 300 to 3400 Hz, and this is quite adequate to propagate speech intelligibly and clearly. The telephone instrument does just that. For all

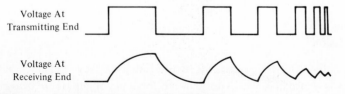

Voltage At
Transmitting End

Voltage At
Receiving End

**FIGURE 2–1. Attentuation of Digital Signals**

Analog Signals – Represent data with continuously varying electromagnetic wave

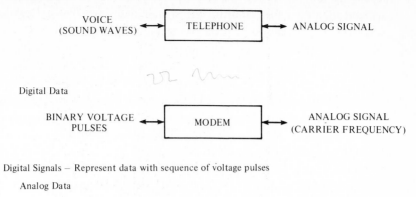

Analog Data

| VOICE (SOUND WAVES) | ←→ | TELEPHONE | ←→ | ANALOG SIGNAL |

Digital Data

| BINARY VOLTAGE PULSES | ←→ | MODEM | ←→ | ANALOG SIGNAL (CARRIER FREQUENCY) |

Digital Signals – Represent data with sequence of voltage pulses

Analog Data

| ANALOG SIGNAL | ←→ | CODEC | ←→ | DIGITAL SIGNAL |

Digital Data
   Direct representation or coded

**FIGURE 2–2.  Analog and Digital Signaling for Analog and Digital Data**

sound input in the range of 300 to 3400 Hz, an electromagnetic signal with the same frequency-amplitude pattern is produced. The process is performed in reverse to convert the electromagnetic energy back into sound.

Digital data can also be represented by analog signals by use of a *modem* (modulator/demodulator). The modem converts a series of binary (two-valued) voltage pulses into an analog signal by modulating a *carrier frequency*. The resulting signal occupies a certain spectrum of frequency centered about the carrier and may be propagated across a medium suitable for that carrier. The most common modems represent digital data in the voice spectrum and hence allow those data to be propagated over ordinary voice-grade telephone lines. At the other end of the line, the modem demodulates the signal to recover the original data. Various modulation techniques are discussed below.

In an operation very similar to that performed by a modem, analog data can be represented by digital signals. The device that performs this function for voice data is a *codec* (coder-decoder). In essence, the codec takes an analog signal that directly represents the voice data and approximates that signal by a bit stream. At the other end of a line, the bit stream is used to reconstruct the analog data.

Finally, digital data can be represented directly, in binary form, by two voltage levels. To improve propagation characteristics, however, the binary data are often encoded, as explained below.

A final distinction remains to be made. Both analog and digital signals may be transmitted on suitable transmission media. The way these signals are treated is a function of the transmission system. Table 2.1 summarizes the methods of data transmission. Analog transmission is a means of transmitting analog signals without regard to their content; the signals may represent analog data (e.g., voice) or digital data (e.g., data that pass through a modem). In either case, the analog signal will attenuate after a certain distance. To achieve longer distances, the analog transmission system includes amplifiers that boost the energy in the signal. Unfortunately, the amplifier also boosts the noise components. With amplifiers cascaded to achieve long distances, the signal becomes more and more distorted. For analog data, such as voice, quite a bit of distortion can be tolerated and the data remain intelligible. However, for digital data, cascaded amplifiers will introduce errors.

Digital transmission, in contrast, is concerned with the content of the signal. We have mentioned that a digital signal can be transmitted only a limited distance before attenuation endangers the integrity of the data. To achieve greater distances, repeaters are used. A repeater receives the digital signal, recovers the pattern of 1's and 0's, and retransmits a new signal. Thus the attenuation is overcome.

The same technique may be used with an analog signal if it is assumed that the signal carries digital data. At appropriately spaced points, the transmission system has retransmission devices rather than amplifiers. The retransmission device recovers the digital data from the analog signal and generates a new, clean analog signal. Thus noise is not cumulative.

For long-haul communications, digital signaling is not as versatile and practical as analog signaling. For example, digital signaling is impossible for

**TABLE 2.1  Analog and Digital Transmission**

(a) Treatment of Signals

|  | **Analog Transmission** | **Digital Transmission** |
|---|---|---|
| **Analog signal** | Is propagated through amplifiers; same treatment for both analog and digital data | Assumes digital data; at propagation points, data in signal are recovered and new analog signal is generated |
| **Digital signal** | Not used | Repeaters retransmit new signal; same treatment for both analog and digital data |

(b) Possible Combinations

|  | **Analog Transmission** | **Digital Transmission** |
|---|---|---|
| **Analog Data** | Analog signal | Digital signal |
| **Digital Data** | Analog signal | Digital signal<br>Analog signal |

satellite and microwave systems. However, digital transmission is superior to analog, both in terms of cost and quality, and long-haul communications systems are gradually converting to digital transmission for both voice and digital data.

We will see that in local networks, the trade-offs do not always lead to the same solutions as for long-haul communications. It is still true, within the local context, that digital techniques tend to be cheaper because of the declining cost of digital circuitry. However, the limited distances of local networks reduce the size of the noise and attenuation problems, and the cost and quality of analog techniques approach that of digital. Consequently, there is a secure place for analog signaling and analog transmission in local networks.

## Data Encoding Techniques

As Figure 2.2 indicates, with the exception of analog signaling of analog data, some form of data representation or encoding is required. This section summarizes the most common techniques.

### Digital Data, Analog Signals

The basis for analog signaling is a continuous constant-frequency signal known as the *carrier signal*. Digital data are encoded by modulating one of the three characteristics of the carrier: amplitude, frequency, or phase, or some combination of these. Figure 2.3 illustrates the three basic forms of modulation of analog signals for digital data:

- Amplitude-shift keying (ASK)
- Frequency-shift keying (FSK)
- Phase-shift keying (PSK)

In all these cases, the resulting signal contains a range of frequencies on both sides of the carrier frequency. That range is referred to as the *bandwidth* of the signal.

In ASK, the two binary values are represented by two different amplitudes of the carrier frequency. In some cases, one of the amplitudes is zero; that is, one binary digit is represented by the presence, at constant amplitude, of the carrier, the other by the absence of the carrier. ASK is susceptible to sudden gain changes and is a rather inefficient modulation technique. On voice-grade lines, it is typically used only up to 1200 bps.

In FSK, the two binary values are represented by two different frequencies near the carrier frequency. This scheme is less susceptible to error than ASK. On voice grade lines, it is typically used up to 1200 bps. It is also commonly used for high frequency (3 to 30 MHz) radio transmission. It can also be used at even higher frequencies on local networks that use coaxial cable.

Figure 2.4 shows an example of the use of FSK for full-duplex operation over a voice-grade line. *Full-duplex* means that data can be transmitted in both

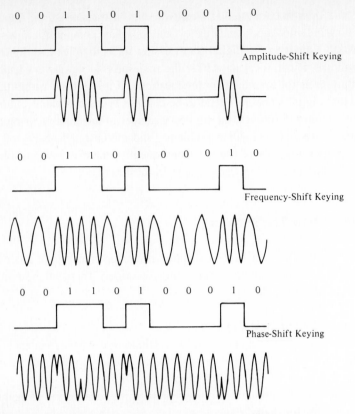

**FIGURE 2–3. Modulation of Analog Signals for Digital Data**

directions at the same time. To accomplish this, one bandwidth is used for sending, another for receiving. The figure is a specification for the Bell System 108 series modems. In one direction (transmit or receive), the modem passes frequencies in the range 300 to 1700 Hz. The two frequencies used to represent 1 and 0 are centered on 1170 Hz, with a shift of 100 Hz on either side. Similarly, for the other direction (receive or transmit) the modem passes 1700 to 3000 Hz and uses a center frequency of 2125 Hz. The shaded area around each pair of frequencies indicates the actual bandwidth of each signal. Note that there is little overlap and thus little interference.

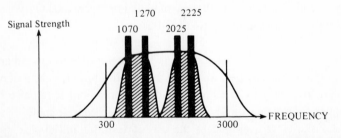

**FIGURE 2–4. Full-Duplex FSK Transmission on a Voice-Grade Line**

In PSK, the phase of the carrier signal is shifted to represent data. Figure 2.3c is an example of a two-phase system. In this system, a 0 is represented by sending a signal burst of the same phase as the previous signal burst sent. A 1 is represented by sending a signal burst of opposite phase to the previous one. PSK can use more than two phase shifts. A four-phase system would encode two bits with each signal burst. The PSK technique is more noise resistant and efficient than FSK; on a voice-grade line, rates up to 9600 bps are achieved.

Finally, the techniques discussed above may be combined. A common combination is PSK and ASK, where some or all of the phase shifts may occur at one of two amplitudes.

### Digital Data, Digital Signals

The most common, and easiest way, to transmit digital signals is to use two different voltage levels for the two binary digits. For example, the absence of voltage (which is also the absence of current) is often used to represent 0, while a constant positive voltage is used to represent 1. It is also common to use a negative voltage (Low) for 0 and a positive voltage (High) for 1. The latter technique, shown in Figure 2.5a, is known as Non-Return to Zero (NRZ).

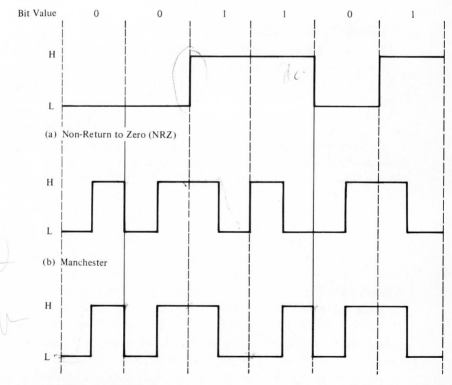

**FIGURE 2–5. Digital Signal Encoding**

There are several disadvantages to NRZ transmission. It is difficult to determine where one bit ends and another begins. There needs to be some means of keeping the transmitter and receiver "clocked" or synchronized. [*Note:* this is true for both synchronous and asynchronous transmission (see discussion below).] Also, there is a direct-current (dc) component during each bit time which will accumulate if 1's or 0's predominate. Thus alternating-current (ac) coupling, which uses a transformer and provides excellent electrical isolation between data communicating devices and their environment (see the discussion of MIL-STD-1553 in Chapter 5), is not possible. Furthermore, the dc component can cause plating or other deterioration at attachment contacts.

An alternative coding scheme, which overcomes these disadvantages, is the *Manchester code* which is commonly used for local network transmission (Figure 2.5b). In the Manchester code, there is a transition at the middle of each bit period. The mid-bit transition serves as a clock and also as data: a high-to-low transition represents a 1, and a low-to-high transition represents a 0. A modified format, known as *Differential Manchester*, is sometimes used (Figure 2.5c). In this case, the mid-bit transition is used only to provide clocking. The encoding of a 0 (1) is represented by the presence (absence) of a transition at the beginning of the bit period. In both cases, because the clock and data are included in a single serial data stream, the codes are known as self-clocking codes.

### Analog Data, Digital Signals

The most common example of the use of digital signals to encode analog data is *pulse code modulation* (PCM), which is used to encode voice signals. This section describes PCM and then looks briefly at a similar, less used scheme, *Delta Modulation* (DM).

PCM is based on the sampling theorem, which states [ITT75]:

If a signal $f(t)$ is sampled at regular intervals of time and at a rate higher than twice the highest significant signal frequency, then the samples contain all the information of the original signal. The function $f(t)$ may be reconstructed from these samples by the use of a low-pass filter.

If voice data are limited to frequencies below 4000 Hz, a conservative procedure for intelligibility, then 8000 samples per second would be sufficient to completely characterize the voice signal. Note, however, that these are analog samples. To convert to digital, each of these analog samples must be assigned a binary code. Figure 2.6 shows an example in which each sample is approximated by being "quantized" into one of 16 different levels. Each sample can then be represented by four bits. Of course, it is now impossible to recover the original signal exactly. By using a 7-bit sample, which allows 128 quantizing levels, the quality of the recovered voice signal is comparable to that achieved via analog transmission. Note that this implies that a data rate of 8000 samples per second $\times$ 7 bits per sample $= 56$ kbps is needed for a single voice signal.

Typically, the PCM scheme is refined using a technique known as *nonlinear*

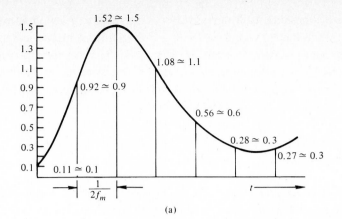

(a)

| Digit | Binary equivalent | Pulse-code waveform |
|-------|-------------------|---------------------|
| 0 | 0000 | |
| 1 | 0001 | |
| 2 | 0010 | |
| 3 | 0011 | |
| 4 | 0100 | |
| 5 | 0101 | |
| 6 | 0110 | |
| 7 | 0111 | |
| 8 | 1000 | |
| 9 | 1001 | |
| 10 | 1010 | |
| 11 | 1011 | |
| 12 | 1100 | |
| 13 | 1101 | |
| 14 | 1110 | |
| 15 | 1111 | |

(b)

**FIGURE 2–6. Pulse Code Modulation**

*encoding*, which means, in effect, that the 128 quantization levels are not equally spaced. The problem with equal spacing is that the mean absolute error for each sample is the same, regardless of signal level. Consequently, lower-amplitude values are relatively more distorted. By using a greater number of quantizing steps for signals of low amplitude, and a small number of quantizing steps for signals of large amplitude, a marked reduction in overall signal distortion is achieved.

PCM can, of course, be used for other than voice signals. For example, a color TV signal has a useful bandwidth of 4.6 MHz, and reasonable quality can be achieved with 10-bit samples, for a data rate of 92 Mbps.

With DM, a bit stream is produced by approximating the derivative of an analog signal rather than its amplitude. A 1 is generated if the current sample is greater in amplitude than the immediately preceding sample; a 0 is generated otherwise. For equal data rates, DM is comparable to PCM in terms of signal quality. Note that for equal data rates, DM requires a higher sampling rate: a 56 kbps voice signal is generated from 8000 PCM samples per second but 56,000 DM samples per second. In general, DM systems are less complex and less expensive than comparable PCM systems. A discussion of these and other encoding schemes can be found in [CROC83].

## Multiplexing

In both local and long-haul communications, it is almost always the case that the capacity of the transmission medium exceeds that required for the transmission of a single signal. To make cost-effective use of the transmission system, it is desirable to use the medium efficiently by having it carry multiple signals simultaneously. This is referred to as *multiplexing*, and two techniques are in common use: frequency-division multiplexing (FDM) and time-division multiplexing (TDM).

FDM takes advantage of the fact that the useful bandwidth of the medium exceeds the required bandwidth of a given signal. A number of signals can be carried simultaneously if each signal is modulated onto a different carrier frequency, and the carrier frequencies are sufficiently separated that the bandwidths of the signals do not overlap. A simple example of FDM is full-duplex FSK transmission (Figure 2.4). A general case of FDM is shown in Figure 2.7a. Six signal sources are fed into a multiplexer, which modulates each signal onto a different frequency ($f_1, \ldots, f_6$). Each signal requires a certain bandwidth centered around its carrier frequency, referred to as a *channel*. To prevent interference, the channels are separated by guard bands, which are unused portions of the spectrum.

An example is the multiplexing of voice signals. We mentioned that the useful spectrum for voice is 300 to 3400 Hz. Thus a bandwidth of 4 kHz is adequate to carry the voice signal and provide a guard band. For both North America (Bell System standard) and internationally [Consultative Committee on International Telegraphy and Telephony (CCITT) standard], a standard voice multiplexing scheme is twelve 4-KHz voice channels from 60 to 108 kHz. For higher-capacity links, both Bell and CCITT define larger groupings of 4-kHz channels.

TDM takes advantage of the fact that the achievable bit rate (sometimes, unfortunately, called bandwidth) of the medium exceeds the required data rate of a digital signal. Multiple digital signals can be carried on a single transmission path by interleaving portions of each signal in time. The interleaving can be at the bit level or in blocks of bytes or larger quantities. For example, the multiplexer in Figure 2.7b has six inputs which might each be, say, 9.6 kbps. A single line with a capacity of 57.6 kbps could accommodate all six sources.

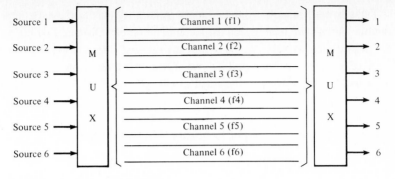

(a) Frequency-Division Multiplexing

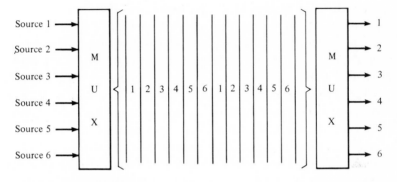

(b) Time-Division Multiplexing

**FIGURE 2–7.  Multiplexing**

Analogously to FDM, the sequence of time slots dedicated to a particular source is called a *channel*. One cycle of time slots (one per source) is called a *frame*.

The TDM scheme depicted in Figure 2.7 is also known as *synchronous TDM*, referring to the fact that time slots are preassigned and fixed. Hence the timing of transmission from the various sources is synchronized. In contrast, asynchronous TDM allows time on the medium to be allocated dynamically. Examples of this will be discussed later. Unless otherwise noted, the term TDM will be used to mean synchronous TDM only.

One example of TDM is the standard scheme used for transmitting PCM voice data, known in Bell parlance as *T1 carrier*. Data are taken from each source, one sample (7 bits) at a time. An eighth bit is added for signaling and supervisory functions. For T1, 24 sources are multiplexed, so there are 8 × 24 = 192 bits of data and control signals per frame. One final bit is added for establishing and maintaining synchronization. Thus a frame consists of 193 bits and contains one 7-bit sample per source. Since sources must be sampled 8000 times per second, the required data rate is 8000 × 193 = 1.544 Mbps. As with voice FDM, higher data rates are defined for larger groupings.

TDM is not limited to digital signals. Analog signals can also be interleaved in time. Also, with analog signals, a combination of TDM and FDM is possible. A transmission system can be frequency-divided into a number of channels, each of which is further divided via TDM. This technique is possible with broadband local networks, discussed in Chapter 4.

## Asynchronous and Synchronous Transmission

A fundamental requirement of digital data communication (analog or digital signal) is that the receiver knows the starting time and duration of each bit that it receives.

The earliest and simplest scheme for meeting this requirement is asynchronous transmission. In this scheme, data are transmitted one character (of 5 to 8 bits) at a time. Each character is preceded by a start code and followed by a stop code (Figure 2.8a). The *start code* has the encoding for 0 and a duration of one bit time; in other words, the start code is one bit with a value of zero. The *stop code* has a value of 1, and a minimum duration, depending on the system, of from one to two bit times. When there are no data to send, the transmitter sends a continuous stop code. The receiver identifies the beginning of a new character by the transition from 1 to 0. The receiver must have a fairly accurate idea of the duration of each bit in order to recover all the bits of the character. However, a small amount of drift (e.g., 1% per bit) will not matter since the receiver resynchronizes with each stop code. This means of communication is simple and cheap, but requires an overhead of 2 to 3 bits per character. This technique is referred to as *asynchronous* because characters are sent independently from each other. Thus characters may be sent at a nonuniform rate.

A more efficient means of communication is synchronous transmission. In this mode, blocks of characters or bits are transmitted without start and stop codes, and the exact departure or arrival time of each bit is predictable. To prevent timing drift between transmitter and receiver, their clocks must somehow

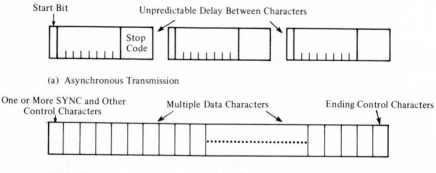

(a) Asynchronous Transmission

(b) Synchronous Transmission (Character-Oriented)

**FIGURE 2–8.   Asynchronous and Synchronous Transmission**

be synchronized. One possibility is to provide a separate clock line between transmitter and receiver. Otherwise, the clocking information must be embedded in the data signal. For digital signals, this can be achieved with Manchester encoding. For analog signals, a number of techniques can be used; the carrier frequency itself can be used to synchronize the receiver based on the phase of the carrier.

With synchronous transmission, there is another level of synchronization required, to allow the receiver to determine the beginning and end of a block of data. To achieve this, each block begins with a *preamble* bit pattern and ends with *postamble* bit pattern. The data plus preamble and postamble is called a *frame*. The nature of the preamble and postamble depends on whether the block of data is character-oriented or bit-oriented.

With *character-oriented* schemes, each block is preceded by one or more "synchronization characters" (Figure 2.8b). The synchronization character, usually called *SYNC*, is chosen such that its bit pattern is significantly different from any of the regular characters being transmitted. The postamble is another unique character. The receiver thus is alerted to an incoming block of data by the SYNC characters and accepts data until the postamble character is seen. The receiver can then look for the next SYNC pattern.

Character-oriented schemes, such as IBM's BISYNC, are gradually being replaced by more efficient and flexible *bit-oriented schemes*, which treat the block of data as a bit stream rather than a character stream. The preamble-postamble principle is the same, with one difference. Since the data are assumed to be an arbitrary bit pattern, there is no assurance that the preamble or postamble pattern will not appear in the data. This event would destroy the higher-level synchronization.

For example, two common bit-oriented schemes, HDLC and SDLC, use the pattern 01111110 (called a *flag*) as both preamble and postamble. To avoid the appearance of this pattern in the data stream, the transmitter will always insert an extra 0 bit after each occurrence of five 1's in the data to be transmitted. When the receiver detects a sequence of five 1's, it examines the next bit. If the bit is 0, the receiver deletes it. This procedure is known as *bit stuffing*.

**2.2**

## COMMUNICATION SWITCHING TECHNIQUES

So far we have discussed how data can be encoded and transmitted over a communication link. In its simplest form, data communication takes place between two devices that are directly connected by some form of transmission medium (many of these media are described in Chapter 3). Often, however, it is impractical for two devices to be directly connected; instead, communication is achieved by transmitting data from source to destination through a network of intermediate nodes. These nodes are not concerned with the content of the data; rather, their purpose is to provide a switching facility that will move the data from node to node until they reach their destination. Figure 2.9 illustrates the situation. We have a collection of devices that wish to communicate; we will refer to them generically as *stations*. The stations may be computers, terminals, telephones, or other communicating devices. We also have a collection of devices whose purpose is to provide communications, which we will refer to as *nodes*. The nodes are connected to each other in some fashion by transmission links. Each station attaches to a node. The collection of nodes is referred to as a *communications network*. If the attached devices are computers and terminals, then the collection of nodes plus stations is referred to as a *computer network*.

Three switching techniques are in common use:

- Circuit switching
- Message switching
- Packet switching

## Circuit Switching

In *circuit switching*, a dedicated communications path is established between two stations through the nodes of the network. The most common example of circuit switching is the telephone system.

Communication via circuit switching implies that there is an actual physical connection between two stations. That connection is a connected sequence of circuits between nodes. On each circuit, a channel is dedicated to the connection.

Communication via circuit switching involves three phases, which can be explained with reference to Figure 2.9.

1. *Circuit establishment:* Before any data can be transmitted, an end-to-end (station-to-station) circuit must be established. For example, station A sends a request to node 4 requesting a connection to station E. Typically, the circuit from A to 4 is a dedicated line, so that part of the connection already exists. Node 4 must find the next leg in a route leading to node 6. Based on routing information and measures of availability and perhaps cost, node 4 selects the circuit to node 5, allocates a free channel (using TDM or FDM) on that circuit and sends a message requesting connection to E. So far, a dedicated path has been established from A through 4 to 5. Since a number of stations may attach to 4, it must be able to establish internal paths from multiple stations to multiple nodes. How this is done is explained in Chapter 7. The remainder of the process proceeds similarly. Node 5 dedicates a channel to node 6 and internally ties that channel to the channel from node 4. Node 6 completes the connection to E. In completing the connection, a test is made to determine if E is busy or is prepared to accept the connection.

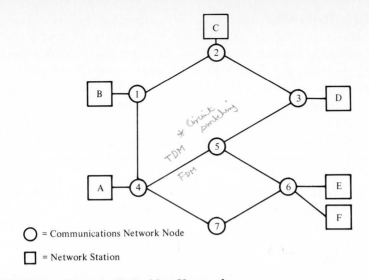

= Communications Network Node

= Network Station

**FIGURE 2–9.  Generic Switching Network**

2. *Data transfer:* Signals can now be transmitted from A through the network to E. The data may be digital (e.g., terminal to host) or analog (e.g., voice). The signaling and transmission may each be either digital or analog. In any case, the path is: A-4 circuit, internal switching through 4, 4-5 channel, internal switching through 5, 5-6 channel, internal switching through 6, 6-E circuit. Generally, the connection is full duplex, and data may be transmitted in both directions.

3. *Circuit disconnect:* After some period of data transfer, the connection is terminated, usually by the action of one of the two stations. Signals must be propagated to 4, 5, and 6 to deallocate the dedicated resources.

Note that the connection path is established before data transmission begins. Thus channel capacity must be available between each pair of nodes in the path, and each node must have internal switching capacity to handle the connection. The switches must have the intelligence to make these allocations and to devise a route through the network.

Circuit switching can be rather inefficient. Channel capacity is dedicated for the duration of a connection, even if no data are being transferred. For a voice connection, utilization may be rather high, but it still does not approach 100%. For a terminal-to-computer connection, the capacity may be idle during most of the time of the connection. In terms of performance, there is a delay prior to data transfer for call establishment. However, once the circuit is established, the network is effectively transparent to the users. Data are transmitted at a fixed data rate with no delay other than the propagation delay through the transmission links. The delay at each node is negligible.

# Message Switching

A very different approach to communication across a network is *message switching*. In this case, it is not necessary to establish a dedicated path between two stations. Rather, if a station wishes to send a message (a logical unit of information) it appends a destination address to the message. The message is then passed through the network from node to node. At each node, the entire message is received, stored briefly, and then transmitted to the next node.

In a circuit-switching network, each node is an electronic or perhaps electromechanical switching device (as described in Chapter 7) which transmits bits as fast as it receives them. A message-switching node is typically a general-purpose minicomputer, with sufficient storage to buffer messages as they come in. A message is delayed at each node for the time required to receive all bits of the message plus a queueing delay waiting for an opportunity to retransmit to the next node.

Again using Figure 2.9, consider a message from A to E. A appends E's address to the message and sends it to node 4. Node 4 stores the message and determines the next leg of the route (say to 5). Then node 4 queues the message for transmission over the 4-5 link. When the link is available, the message is transmitted to node 5, which will forward the message to node 6, and finally to E. This system is also known as a *store-and-forward* message system. In some cases, the node to which the station attaches, or some central node, also files the message, creating a permanent record.

A number of advantages of this approach over circuit switching are listed in [MART76]:

- Line efficiency is greater, since a single node-to-node channel can be shared by many messages over time. For the same traffic volume, less total transmission capacity is needed.
- Simultaneous availability of sender and receiver is not required. The network can store the message pending the availability of the receiver.
- When traffic becomes heavy on a circuit-switched network, some calls are blocked. On a message-switched network, messages are still accepted, but delivery delay increases.
- A message-switching system can send one message to many destinations. This facility is not easily provided by a circuit-switched network.
- Message priorities can be established.
- Error control and recovery procedures on a message basis can be built into the network.
- A message-switching network can carry out speed and code conversion. Two stations of different data rates can be connected since each connects to its node at its proper data rate. The message-switching network can also easily convert format (e.g., from ASCII to EBCDIC). These features are less often found in a circuit-switched system.

- Messages sent to inoperative terminals may be intercepted and either stored or rerouted to other terminals.

The primary disadvantage of message switching is that it is not suited to real-time or interactive traffic. The delay through the network is relatively long and has relatively high variance. Thus it cannot be used for voice connections. Nor is it suited to interactive terminal-host connections.

## Packet Switching

*Packet switching* represents an attempt to combine the advantages of message and circuit switching while minimizing the disadvantages of both. In situations where there is a substantial volume of traffic among a number of stations, this objective is met.

Packet switching is very much like message switching. The principal external difference is that the length of the units of data that may be transmitted is limited in a packet-switched network. A typical maximum length is 1000 to a few thousand bits. Message switching systems accommodate far larger messages. From a station's point of view, then, messages above the maximum length must be divided into smaller units and sent out one at a time. To distinguish the two techniques, the data units in the latter system are referred to as *packets*.

Again using Figure 2.9 for an example, consider the transfer of a single packet. The packet contains data plus a destination address. Station A transmits the packet to 4, which stores it briefly and then passes it to 5, which passes it to 6, and on to E. One difference from message switching is that packets are typically not filed. A copy may be temporarily stored for error recovery purposes, but that is all.

On its face, packet switching may seem a strange procedure to adopt, with no particular advantage over message switching. Remarkably, the simple expedient of limiting the maximum size of a data unit to a rather small length has a dramatic effect on performance. Before demonstrating this, we define two common procedures for handling entire messages over a packet-switched network.

The problem is this. A station has a message to send that is of length greater than the maximum packet size. It breaks the message into packets and sends these packets to its node. Question: How will the network handle this stream of packets? There are two approaches: datagram and virtual circuit.

In the *datagram* approach, each packet is treated independently, just as each message is treated independently in a message-switched network. Let us consider the implications of this approach. Suppose that station A has a 3-packet message to send to E. It pops the packets out, 1-2-3, to node 4. On *each* packet, node 4 must make a routing decision. Packet 1 comes in and node 4 determines that its queue of packets for node 5 is shorter than for node 7, so it queues the packet for node 5. Ditto for packet 2. But for packet 3, node 4 finds that its queue for node 7 is shortest and so queues packet 3 for that node. So the packets, each with the same destination address, do not all follow the same route. Furthermore, it is just possible that packet 3 will beat packet 2 to node 6. Thus it is possible that the packets will be delivered to E in a different sequence from the one in which they were sent. It is up to E to figure out how to reorder them. In this technique each packet, treated independently, is referred to as a "datagram."

In the *virtual circuit* approach, a *logical* connection is established before any packets are sent. For example, suppose that A has one or more messages to send to E. It first sends a Call Request packet to 4, requesting a connection to E. Node 4 decides to route the request *and* all subsequent data to 5, which decides to route the request and all subsequent data to 6, which finally delivers the Call Request packet to E. If E is prepared to accept the connection, it sends out a Call Accept packet to 6. This packet is passed back through nodes 5 and 4 to A. Stations A and E may now exchange data over the logical connection or virtual circuit that has been established. Each packet now contains a virtual circuit identifier as well as data. Each node on the preestablished route knows where to direct such packets; no routing decisions are required. Thus every data packet from A traverses nodes 4, 5, and 6; every data packet from E traverses nodes 6, 5, and 4. Eventually, one of the stations terminates the connection with a Clear Request packet. At any time, each station can have more than one virtual circuit to any other station and can have virtual circuits to more than one station.

So the main characteristic of the virtual circuit technique is that a route between stations is set up prior to data transfer. Note that this does *not* mean that there is a dedicated path, as in circuit switching. A packet is still buffered at each node, and queued for output over a line. The difference from the datagram approach is that the node need not make a routing decision for each packet. It is made only once for each connection.

If two stations wish to exchange data over an extended period of time, there are certain advantages to virtual circuits. They all have to do with relieving the stations of unnecessary communications processing functions. A virtual circuit facility may provide a number of services, including sequencing, error control, and flow control. We emphasize the word "may" because not all virtual circuit facilities will provide all these services completely reliably. With that proviso, we define terms. *Sequencing* refers to the fact that, since all packets follow the same route, they arrive in the original order. *Error control* is a service that assures not only that packets arrive in proper sequence, but that all packets arrive correctly. For example, if a packet in a sequence fails to arrive at node 6, or arrives with an error, it can request a retransmission of that packet from node 4. Finally, *flow control* is a technique for assuring that a sender does not overwhelm a receiver with data. For example, if station E is buffering data from A and perceives that it is about to run out of buffer space, it can request, via the virtual circuit facility, that A suspend transmission until further notice.

One advantage of the datagram approach is that the call setup phase is avoided. Thus if a station wishes to send only one or a few packets, datagram delivery will be quicker. Another advantage of the datagram service is that, because it is more primitive, it is more flexible. A good example of this is the use of the datagram approach for internetworking, a topic explored in Chapter 11. A third advantage is that datagram delivery is inherently more reliable. If a node fails, all virtual circuits that pass through that node are lost. With datagram delivery, if a node is lost, packets may find alternate routes.

We now return to the question of performance, illustrating the techniques discussed in Figure 2.10. This figure intends to suggest the relative performance of the techniques; however, actual performance depends on a host of factors, including:

- Number of stations
- Number and arrangement of nodes
- Total load on system
- Length (in time and data) of typical exchange between two stations

And more. Given the difficulty of comparing these methods, we hazard a few observations.

- For interactive traffic, message switching is not appropriate.
- For light and/or intermittent loads, circuit switching is the most cost effective, since the public telephone system can be used, via dial-up lines.
- For very heavy and sustained loads between two stations, a leased circuit-switched line is the most cost effective.
- Packet switching is to be preferred when there is a collection of devices that must exchange a moderate to heavy amount of data; line utilization is most efficient with this technique.
- Datagram packet switching is good for short messages and for flexibility.
- Virtual circuit packet switching is good for long exchanges and for relieving stations of processing burden.

Table 2.2 summarizes the main features of the four techniques that we have discussed.

As a final point, we mention one common means of making packet-switched networks cost effective, and that is to provide a public connection service. Examples of such networks in the United States are TELENET and TYMNET. The network consists of nodes owned by the network service provider and linked together by leased channels from common carriers such as AT&T. Subscribers pay fees for attaching to the network and for transmitting packets through it. Whereas individual subscribers may not have sufficient traffic to make a packet switched network economically feasible, the total demand of all

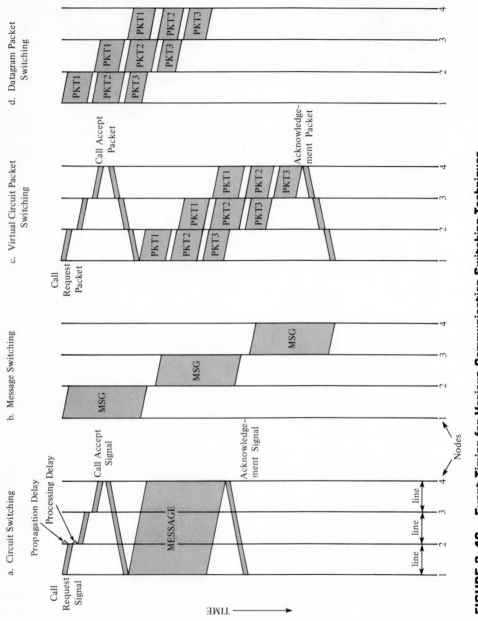

FIGURE 2–10. Event Timing for Various Communication Switching Techniques

**TABLE 2.2 Comparison of Communication Switching Techniques**

| Circut Switching | Message Switching | Datagram Packet Switching | Virtual Circuit Packet Switching |
|---|---|---|---|
| Dedicated transmission path | No dedicated path | No dedicated path | No dedicated path |
| Continuous transmission of data | Transmission of messages | Transmission of packets | Transmission of packets |
| Fast enough for interactive | Too slow for interactive | Fast enough for interactive | Fast enough for interactive |
| Messages are not stored | Messages are filed for later retrieval | Packets may be stored until delivered | Packets stored until delivered |
| Path is established for entire conversation | Route established for each message | Route established for each packet | Route established for entire conversation |
| Call setup delay; negligible transmission delay | Message transmission delay | Packet transmission delay | Call setup delay; packet transmission delay |
| Busy signal if called party busy | No busy signal | Sender may be notified if packet not delivered | Sender notified of connection denial |
| Overload may block call setup; no delay for established calls | Overload increases message delay | Overload increases packet delay | Overload may block call setup; increases packet delay |
| Electromechanical or computerized switching nodes | Message switch center with filing facility | Small switching nodes | Small switching nodes |
| User responsible for message-loss protection | Network responsible for messages | Network may be responsible for individual packets | Network may be responsible for packet sequences |
| Usually no speed or code conversion | Speed and code conversion | Speed and code conversion | Speed and code conversion |
| Fixed bandwidth transmission | Dynamic use of bandwidth | Dynamic use of bandwidth | Dynamic use of bandwidth |
| No overhead bits after call setup | Overhead bits in each message | Overhead bits in each packet | Overhead bits in each packet |

subscribers justifies the network. These networks are referred to as value-added networks (VANs) because they take a basic long-haul transmission service (e.g., AT&T) and add value (the packet-switching logic). In most other countries, there is a single national-monopoly network, called a *public data network* (PDN).

### Switching Techniques for Local Networks

Circuit switching is a widely used switching technique for local networks. The types of networks that use this technique are the digital switch and the *computerized branch exchange* (CBX). These networks are introduced in Chapter 3 and discussed in detail in Chapter 7.

Packet switching is also commonly used for local networking. In many cases, however, there is only a single, direct, path from source to destination. Thus, often, there is no routing or switching function in a local network. As we shall see, packet rather than message switching is used, to facilitate techniques for preventing any source from monopolizing the medium.

Message switching is not used in any of the local networks discussed in this book.

**2.3**

# COMPUTER NETWORKING

## Communications Architecture

### Motivation

In Chapter 1 we discussed some of the motivations for and benefits of local networking. Many of these factors apply equally well to computer networks in general, whether local or long-haul. Indeed, the move to distributed nonlocal computer networks predates the coming of local networks.

When work is done that involves more than one computer, additional elements are needed: the hardware and software to support the communication between or among the systems. Communications hardware is reasonably standard and generally presents few problems. However, when communication is desired among heterogeneous (different vendors, different models of same vendor) machines, the software development effort can be a nightmare. Different vendors use different data formats and data exchange conventions. Even within one vendor's product line, different model computers may communicate in unique ways.

As the use of computer communications and computer networking proliferates, a one-at-a-time special-purpose approach to communications software development is too costly to be acceptable. The only alternative is for computer vendors to adopt and implement a common set of conventions. For this to happen, a set of international or at least national standards must be promulgated by appropriate organizations. Such standards would have two effects:

• Vendors feel encouraged to implement the standards because of an expectation that, because of wide usage of the standards, their products would be less marketable without them.

- Customers are in a position to require that the standards be implemented by any vendor wishing to propose equipment to them.

It should become clear from the ensuing discussion that no single standard will suffice. The task of communication in a truly cooperative way between applications on different computers is too complex to be handled as a unit. The problem must be decomposed into manageable parts. Hence before one can develop standards, there should be a structure or *architecture* that defines the communications tasks.

This line of reasoning led the International Standards Organization (ISO) in 1977 to establish a subcommittee to develop such an architecture. The result was the *Open Systems Interconnection* (OSI) model, which is a framework for defining standards for linking heterogeneous computers. OSI provides the basis for connecting "open" systems for distributed applications processing. The term "open" denotes the ability of any two systems conforming to the reference model and the associated standards to connect.

A widely accepted structuring technique, and the one chosen by ISO, is *layering*. The communications functions are partitioned into a hierarchical set of layers. Each layer performs a related subset of the functions required to communicate with another system. It relies on the next lower layer to perform more primitive functions and to conceal the details of those functions. It provides services to the next higher layer. Ideally, the layer should be defined so that changes in one layer do not require changes in the other layers. Thus we have decomposed one problem into a number of more manageable subproblems.

The task of the ISO subcommittee was to define a set of layers and the services performed by each layer. The partitioning should group functions logically, should have enough layers to make each layer manageably small, but should not have so many layers that the processing overhead imposed by the collection of layers was burdensome. The resulting OSI reference model has seven layers, which are listed with a brief definition in Table 2.3.

Table 2.3 defines, in general terms, the functions that must be performed in a system for it to communicate. Of course, it takes two to communicate, so the same set of layered functions must exist in two systems. Communication is achieved by having the corresponding ("peer") layers in two systems communicate. The peer layers communicate by means of a set of rules or conventions known as a *protocol*. The key elements of a protocol are:

- *Syntax:* Includes such things as data format and signal levels.
- *Semantics:* Includes control information for coordination and error handling.
- *Timing:* Includes speed matching and sequencing.

Figure 2.11a illustrates the OSI model. Each system contains the seven layers. Communication is between applications in the systems, labeled AP X and AP Y in the figure. If AP X wishes to send a message to AP Y, it invokes the application layer (layer 7). Layer 7 establishes a peer relationship with layer 7

**TABLE 2.3 The OSI Layers**

| Layer | Definition |
|---|---|
| 1. Physical | Concerned with transmission of unstructured bit stream over physical link; involves such parameters as signal voltage swing and bit duration; deals with the mechanical, electrical, and procedural characteristics to establish, maintain, and deactivate the physical link (RS-232-C, RS-449, X.21) |
| 2. Data link | Converts an unreliable transmission channel into a reliable one; sends blocks of data (frames) with checksum; uses error detection and frame acknowledgment (HDLC, SDLC, BiSync) |
| 3. Network | Transmits packets of data through a network; packets may be independent (datagram) or traverse a preestablished network connection (virtual circuit); responsible for routing and congestion control (X.25, layer 3) |
| 4. Transport | Provides reliable, transparent transfer of data between end points; provides end-to-end error recovery and flow control |
| 5. Session | Provides means of establishing, managing, and terminating connection (session) between two processes; may provide checkpoint and restart service, quarantine service |
| 6. Presentation | Performs generally useful transformations on data to provide a standardized application interface and to provide common communications services; examples: encryption, text compression, reformatting |
| 7. Application | Provides services to the users of the OSI environment; examples: transaction server, file transfer protocol, network management |

of the target machine, using a layer 7 protocol. This protocol requires services from layer 6, so the two layer 6 entities use a protocol of their own, and so on down to the physical layer, which actually transmits bits over a transmission medium.

Note that there is no direct communication between peer layers except at the physical layer. Even at that layer, the OSI model does not stipulate that two systems be directly connected. For example, a packet-switched or circuit-switched network may be used to provide the communications link. This point should become clearer below, when we discuss the network layer.

The attractiveness of the OSI approach is that it promises to solve the heterogeneous computer communications problem. Two systems, no matter how different, can communicate effectively if they have the following in common.

- They implement the same set of communications functions.
- These functions are organized into the same set of layers. Peer layers must provide the same functions, but note that it is not necessary that they provide them in the same way.
- Peer layers must share a common protocol.

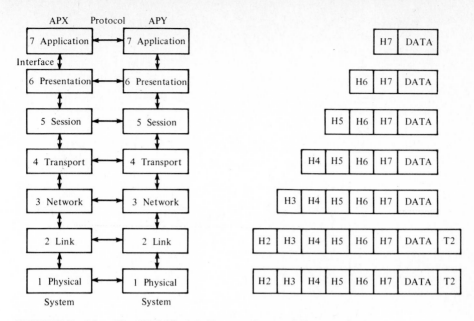

**FIGURE 2–11. The OSI Model: Connection and Encapsulation**

To assure the above, standards are needed. Standards must define the functions and services to be provided by a layer (but not how it is to be done—that may differ from system to system). Standards must also define the protocols between peer layers (each protocol must be identical for the two peer layers). The OSI model, by defining a 7-layer architecture, provides a framework for defining these standards.

### Concepts

Some useful OSI terminology is illustrated in Figure 2.12. For simplicity, any layer is referred to as the *(N) layer*, and names of constructs associated with that layer are also preceded by (N). Within a system, there are one or more active entities in each layer. An *(N) entity* implements functions of the (N) layer and also the protocol for communicating with (N) entities in other systems. An example of an entity is a process in a multiprocessing system. Or it could simply be a subroutine. There might be multiple identical (N) entities, if this is convenient or efficient for a given system. There might also be differing (N) entities, corresponding to different protocol standards at that level. Each (N) entity implements a protocol for communicating with (N) entities in other systems. Each entity communicates with entities in the layers above and below it across an interface. The interface is realized as one or more *service access points* (SAPs). Finally, in order to establish a connection between two (N) entities, a *connection endpoint* (CEP) is defined within an SAP for each of the (N) entities.

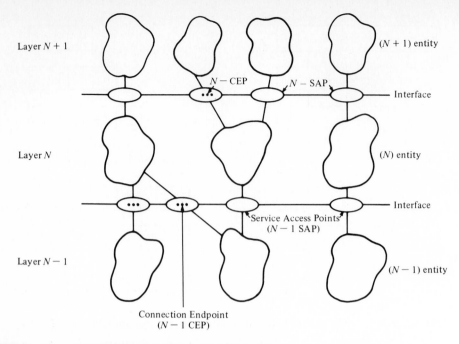

**FIGURE 2–12.  The OSI Model: The Layer Concept**

To clarify these terms as well as some functions common to all layers, refer again to Figure 2.11. The functions we wish to discuss are:

- Encapsulation
- Fragmentation
- Connection establishment
- Flow control
- Error control
- Multiplexing

First, consider the most common way in which protocols are realized, which is by a process of *encapsulation* (Figure 2.11b). When AP X has a message to send to AP Y, it transfers those data to a (7) entity in the application layer. A *header* is appended to the data that contains the required information for the peer layer 7 protocol; this is referred to as an encapsulation of the data. The original data, plus the header, is now passed as a unit to layer 6. The (6) entity treats the whole unit as data, and appends its own header (a second encapsulation). This process continues down through layer 2, which generally adds both a header and a trailer, the function of which is explained below. This layer 2 unit, called a *frame*, is then transmitted by the physical layer onto the transmission medium. When the frame is received by the target system, the reverse process occurs. As the data ascend, each layer strips off the outermost header, acts on the protocol information contained therein, and passes the remainder up to the next layer.

We have already seen several examples of encapsulation. With synchronous communication, a preamble and postamble are appended to each block of data. For packet-switched networks, each packet includes not only data but also (at least) an address.

At each stage of the process, a layer may *fragment* the data unit it receives from the next higher layer into several parts, to accommodate its own requirements. These data units must then be reassembled by the corresponding peer layer before being passed up.

When two peer entities wish to exchange data, this may be done with or without a prior *connection*. We have seen an example of this: virtual circuits versus datagrams. A connection can exist at any layer of the hierarchy. In the abstract, a connection is established between two (N) entities by identifying a connection endpoint, (N-1) CEP, within an (N-1) SAP for each (N) entity. A connection facilitates flow control and error control. *Flow control* is a function performed by an (N) entity to limit the amount or rate of data it receives from another (N) entity. This function is needed to ensure that the receiving (N) entity does not experience overflow. *Error control* refers to mechanisms to detect and correct errors that occur in the transmission of data units between peer entities.

*Multiplexing* can occur in two directions. *Upward* multiplexing means that multiple (N) connections are multiplexed on, or share, a single (N-1) connection. This may be needed to make more efficient use of the (N-1) service or to provide several (N) connections in an environment where only a single (N-1) connection exists. *Downward* multiplexing, or *splitting*, means that a single (N) connection is built on top of multiple (N-1) connections, the traffic on the (N) connection being divided among the various (N-1) connections. This technique may be used to improve reliability, performance, or efficiency.

The preceding discussion has been necessarily abstract. As we proceed in this chapter and the remainder of the book to discuss specific protocols, these concepts should become clear.

## Protocols

In this section we discuss briefly each of the layers and, where appropriate, give examples of standards for protocols at those layers. Table 2.4 shows the relationship to the OSI model of some of the most important standards. Remember that the OSI layers are not standards; they merely provide a framework for standards.

CCITT has developed standards for connecting *data terminal equipment* (DTE) to a packet-switched network that provides *data circuit-terminating equipment* (DCE). These terms correspond to the stations and nodes of Figure 2.9. The standard, X.25, specifically addresses layer 3 and subsumes standards for layers 2 and 1. (Observers are fond of saying that X.25 is an interface, not

**TABLE 2.4   Some Well-Known Layers**

| OSI | CCITT | NBS | DOD | IEEE 802 | ANS X3T9.5 |
|---|---|---|---|---|---|
| 7. Application | | Various | | | |
| 6. Presentation | | Various | | | |
| 5. Session | | Session | | | |
| 4. Transport | | Transport (TP) | TCP | | |
| 3. Network | X.25 | IP | IP | | |
| 2. Link | LAP-B | | | Logical link control | Data link |
| | | | | Medium access control | |
| 1. Physical | X.21 | | | Physical | Physical |

a protocol. This point is discussed under Network Layer below.) Layer 2 is referred to as LAP-B (Link Access Protocol—Balanced) and is almost identical with ISO's HDLC (High-Level Data Link Control) and ANSI's ADCCP (Advanced Data Communication Control Procedures).

The National Bureau of Standards (NBS) is working on a standard for layer 4 and one for layer 5, and multiple standards for layers 6 and 7. They are also developing a special-purpose layer 3 protocol known as the Internet Protocol (IP). The expectation is that, as these standards are published and adopted, they will become mandatory for data processing system procurements throughout the federal government.

An almost identical IP has been developed by the Department of Defense (DOD) for its own needs, plus a Transmission Control Protocol (TCP). TCP subsumes all the functions of layer 4 plus some of layer 5. DOD intends to mandate these standards for its procurements. The mismatch with the NBS protocols is, unfortunately, unresolved.

For the type of local network that we refer to as a *local area network* (LAN), the Institute of Electrical and Electronics Engineers (IEEE), through its 802 committee, has developed a 3-layer architecture that corresponds to layers 1 and 2 of the OSI model. A number of standards have been developed by the committee for these layers. Similarly, a subcommittee responsible to the

American National Standards Institute (ANSI), known as ANS X3T9.5, has developed standards for the type of local network we refer to as a *high-speed local network* (HSLN). These standards, one per layer, correspond nicely to layers 1 and 2 of the OSI model.

Other organizations are active in ways not illustrated in Table 2.4. In addition to the NBS effort, ANSI, ISO, and ECMA (European Computer Manufacturers Association) are working on layers 4 through 7. ECMA is also working on LAN standards.

This narrative may be disheartening, given the alleged benefit of standards, which is to put everyone on the same road. There is certainly room for pessimism. The DOD-NBS disparity makes a uniform federal government position unlikely. For LANs, the 802 committee has produced a number of options and alternatives at each layer, to come up with an astoundingly thick volume for their draft standard.

However, the picture is not as bleak as Table 2.4 makes it seem. With the exception of local networks, which must be treated separately, standards have settled out quite well for layers 1 through 3. Above that, there is considerable cooperation among the various groups, so that uniform or nearly uniform standards are possible in many cases.

### Physical Layer

The *physical layer* covers the physical interface between devices and the rules by which bits are passed from one to another. The physical layer has four important characteristics [BERT80]:

- Mechanical
- Electrical
- Functional
- Procedural

The most common standard in use today is RS-232-C. A typical use of RS-232-C is to connect a digital device to a modem, which in turn connects to a voice-grade telephone line. We will refer to this standard in describing these four characteristics.

The *mechanical characteristics* pertain to the point of demarcation. Typically, this is a pluggable connector. RS-232-C specifies a 25-pin connector, so that up to 25 separate wires are used to connect the two devices.

The *electrical characteristics* have to do with the voltage levels and timing of voltage changes. These characteristics determine the data rates and distances that can be achieved.

*Functional characteristics* specify the functions that are performed by assigning meaning to various signals. For RS-232-C, and for most other physical layer standards, this is done by specifying the function of each of the pins in the connector. For example, pin CA (Request to Send) is used for the device to signal the modem that it has data to send, and that a carrier should be established for modulation. Pin CP (Received Line Signal Detector or Carrier Detect) is used for the modem to alert the device that a carrier is present on the line.

*Procedural characteristics* specify the sequence of events for transmitting data, based on the functional characteristics. For RS-232-C, the use of the various pins is defined. For example, when a device asserts Request to Send, the modem will assert Clear to Send if it is ready to transmit data. The device can then send data from pin BA (Transmitted Data) over that line to the corresponding pin on the modem.

### Data Link Layer

· The physical layer provides only a raw bit stream service. The *data link layer* attempts to make the physical link reliable and provides the means to activate, maintain, and deactivate the link. The asynchronous and synchronous transmission techniques discussed in Section 2.1 are examples.

In this subsection we will spend some time defining HDLC, which is a synchronous bit-oriented protocol. We do so for two reasons:

- HDLC is the ancestor of the link layer protocol standard for LANs (IEEE 802).
- Many of the concepts concerning protocols are illustrated.

HDLC, and bit-oriented protocols in general, are intended to provide the following capabilities [CARL80]:

- *Code-independent operation (transparency):* The protocol and the data it carries are independent.
- *Adaptability to various applications, configurations, and uses in a consistent manner:* For example, point-to-point, multidrop, and loop configurations should be supported.
- *Both two-way alternate and two-way simultaneous (full-duplex) data transfer.*
- *High efficiency:* The protocol should have a minimum of overhead bits. Also, it should work efficiently over links with long propagation delays and links with high data rates.
- *High reliability:* Data should not be lost, duplicated, or garbled.

With these requirements in mind, we turn to a description of HDLC.

Three modes of operation are defined: The *normal response mode* (NRM), *asynchronous response mode* (ARM), and *asynchronous balanced mode* (ABM). Both NRM and ARM can be used in point-to-point or multipoint configurations. For each there is one *primary station* and one or more *secondary stations*. The primary station is responsible for initializing the link, controlling the flow of data to and from secondary stations, recovering from errors, and logically disconnecting secondary stations. In NRM, a secondary station may transmit only in response to a poll from the primary; in ARM, the secondary may initiate a transmission without a poll. NRM is ideally suited for a multidrop line consisting of a host computer and a number of terminals. ARM may be needed for certain kinds of loop configurations.

ABM is used only on point-to-point links and each station assumes the role of both primary and secondary. ABM is more efficient for point-to-point lines since there is no polling overhead and both stations may initiate transmissions.

Data are transmitted in frames which consist of six fields (Figure 2.13).

- FLAG: Used for synchronization, this field indicates the start and end of a frame. The flag pattern, 01111110, is avoided in the data by bit stuffing.
- ADDRESS: This field identifies the secondary station for this transmission.
- CONTROL: This field identifies the function and purpose of the frame. It is described below.
- DATA: This field contains the data to be transmitted.
- CRC: This is a frame check sequence field. It uses a 16-bit *cyclic redundancy check* (CRC). The CRC field is a function of the contents of the address, control, and data fields. It is generated by the sender and again by the receiver. If the receiver's result differs from the CRC field, a transmission error has occurred.

Three types of frames are used, each with a different control-field format. Information frames carry the data. Supervisory frames provide basic link control functions, and unnumbered frames provide supplemental link control functions.

The P/F (poll/final) bit is used by a primary station to solicit a response. More than one frame may be sent in response, with the P/F bit set to indicate the last frame. The P/F may be used with supervisory and unnumbered frames to force a response.

The SEQ and NEXT fields in the information frame provide an efficient technique for both flow control and error control. A station numbers the frames that it sends sequentially modulo 8, using the SEQ field. When a station receives a valid information frame, it acknowledges that frame with its own information frame by setting the NEXT field to the number of the next frame it expects to

Frame Structure:

| 8 bits | 8 | 8 | ⩾ 0 | 16 | 8 |
|--------|------|---------|------|-----|------|
| FLAG | ADDRESS | CONTROL | DATA | CRC | FLAG |

Control Field Structure

| | 1 | 2 | 3 | 4 | 5 | 6 | 7 | 8 |
|-------------|---|---|------|---|-----|----------|---|---|
| Information | 0 | | SEQ | | P/F | NEXT | | |
| Supervisory | 1 | 0 | TYPE | | P/F | NEXT | | |
| Unnumbered | 1 | 1 | TYPE | | P/F | MODIFIER | | |

**FIGURE 2–13.  The HDLC Frame Structure**

receive. This is known as a *piggybacked acknowledgment,* since the acknowledgment rides back on an information frame. Acknowledgments can also be sent on a supervisory frame. This scheme accomplishes three important functions.

- *Flow control:* Once a station has sent seven frames, it can send no more until the first frame is acknowledged.
- *Error control:* If a frame is received in error, a station can send a "NAK" (negative acknowledgment) via a supervisory frame to specify which frame was received in error. This is done in one of two ways. In the *go back n protocol,* the sending station retransmits the NAK'ed frame and all subsequent frames that had already been sent. In the *selective repeat technique,* the sending station retransmits only the frame in error.
- *Pipelining:* More than one frame may be in transit at a time; this allows more efficient use of links with high propagation delay, such as satellite links.

The SEQ/NEXT technique is known as a *sliding-window protocol* because the sending station maintains a window of messages to be sent which gradually moves forward with transmission and acknowledgment. The process is depicted in Figure 2.14.

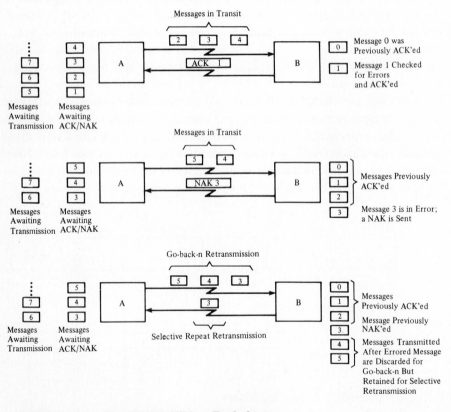

**FIGURE 2–14. The Sliding-Widow Technique**

There are four types of supervisory frames:

- *Receive Ready (RR):* used to acknowledge correct receipt of frames up through NEXT-1. Alternatively, a poll command instructing secondary to begin transmission with sequence number NEXT.
- *Receive Not Ready (RNR):* used to indicate a temporary busy condition. NEXT is used for a possibly redundant acknowledgment.
- *Reject (REJ):* used to indicate an error in frame NEXT and to request retransmission of that and all subsequent frames.
- *Selective Reject (SREJ):* used to request retransmission of a single frame.

The unnumbered frames have no sequence number and are used for a number of special purposes, such as to initialize a station, set the mode, disconnect a station, and reject a command.

### Network Layer

The *network layer* is designed to facilitate communication between systems across a communications network. It is at this layer that the concept of a protocol becomes a little fuzzy. This is best illustrated with reference to Figure 2.15, which shows two systems (DTEs) that are communicating, not via direct link, but via a network. The DTEs have direct links to the network nodes (DCEs). The layer 1 and 2 protocols are DTE-DCE protocols (local). Layers 4 through 7 are clearly protocols between (N) entities in the two DTEs. Layer 3 is a little bit of both.

For X.25, layer 3 has been designed for both virtual circuits and datagrams. The principal dialogue is between the DTE and its DCE; the DTE sends addressed packets to the DCE for delivery across the network. It may also request a virtual circuit connection, use the connection to transmit data, and terminate the connection. The DCE faces toward the DTE for this dialogue, but it must also face inward to the network for routing, virtual circuit establishment, and packet delivery. The X.25 standard refers to itself as an interface between a DTE and a DCE. In the terminology we have been using, it is actually a

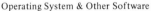

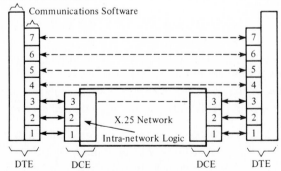

**FIGURE 2–15. Communication Across a Network**

protocol between a DTE and DCE. However, because packets are exchanged and virtual circuits are set up between two DTEs, there are aspects of a DTE-DTE protocol as well.

Nevertheless, the X.25 layer 3 is basically a protocol with local (DTE-DCE) significance. It does not guarantee end-to-end (DTE-DTE) reliability nor does it provide end-to-end flow control. Of course, this is not an inherent limitation of layer 3; it is possible to provide a layer 3 protocol that does have end-to-end significance. We will return to this point in the next subsection.

A brief description of the X.25 layer 3 is given in Chapter 8.

The basic service of the network layer is to provide for the transparent transfer of data between transport entities. It relieves the transport layer of the need to know anything about the underlying communications medium. At one extreme, when there is a direct link between stations, there may be no need for a network layer. Between extremes, the most common use of layer 3 is to handle the details of using a packet-switched network. At the other extreme, two devices might wish to communicate but are not even connected to the same network. Rather, they are connected to networks which, directly or indirectly, are connected to each other. This situation is explored in some detail in Chapter 11. For now it suffices to say that one approach to providing for data transfer in such a case is to use an *Internet Protocol* (IP) that sits on top of a network protocol and is used by a transport protocol. IP is responsible for internetwork routing and delivery, and relies on a layer 3 at each network for intranetwork services. IP is described in Chapter 11; it is sometimes referred to as "layer 3.5."

### Transport Layer

Layers 4 and above of the OSI model are generally referred to as the higher layers [RAUC83]. Protocols at these levels are end-to-end and not concerned with the details of the underlying communications facility.

The purpose of layer 4 is to provide a reliable mechanism for the exchange of data between processes in different systems. The *transport layer* ensures that data units are delivered error-free, in sequence, with no losses or duplications. Typical features of the transport layer are [NBS80b]:

- *Type of service:* It is connection-oriented or connectionless, analogous to virtual circuits and datagrams.
- *Grade of service:* This would allow the (5) entity to specify acceptable error and loss levels, desired delay, priority, and security.
- *Connection management:* Layer 4 will set up and manage connections between (5) entities via (4) CEPs for connection-oriented service.

The size and complexity of a transport protocol depends on the type of service it can get from layer 3. For a reliable layer 3 with a virtual circuit capability, a minimal layer 4 is required. If layer 3 is unreliable and/or only supports datagrams, then the layer 4 protocol should include extensive error detection and recovery. Accordingly, NBS has defined two versions of its Transport Protocol (TP): a basic class for reliable networks and an enhanced class for unreliable networks. The basic class is a subset of the enhanced class. The enhanced class is comparable in capability to DOD's Transmission Control Protocol (TCP), described in Chapter 8. ISO has gone even further and defined five classes of transport protocol, each each oriented toward a different underlying protocol [MIER82].

### Session Layer

The *session layer* provides the mechanism for controlling the dialogue between presentation entities. At a minimum, the session layer provides a means for two presentation entities to establish and use a connection, called a *session*. In addition it may provide some of the following services:

* *Dialogue type:* This can be two-way simultaneous, two-way alternate, or one-way.
* *Quarantining:* A session user (presentation entity) may require that data not be delivered to the destination until a certain amount (quarantine unit) has accumulated. This might be useful if none of the data are significant until a certain point is reached or until after a validation process.
* *Recovery:* The session layer can provide a checkpointing mechanism, so that if a failure of some sort occurs between checkpoints, the session entity can retransmit all data since the last checkpoint.

### Presentation Layer

The presentation layer offers application programs and terminal handler programs a set of data transformation services. Services that this layer would typically provide include:

* *Data translation:* code and character set translation.
* *Formatting:* modification of data layout.
* *Syntax selection:* initial selection and subsequent modification of the transformations used.

Examples of presentation protocols are text compression, encryption, and virtual terminal protocol. A virtual terminal protocol converts between specific terminal characteristics and a generic or virtual model used by application programs. Encryption is discussed in Chapter 12. Virtual terminal protocols are described in Chapter 8.

### Application Layer

The application layer includes applications that are to be run in a distributed environment. It would typically include vendor-provided programs of general utility, such as electronic mail, a transaction server, a file transfer protocol, and a job manipulation protocol.

### Summary

In a few short years, the OSI model has achieved nearly universal acceptance. It provides not only a framework for developing standards but the terms of reference for discussing communications system design. In the latter capacity, we will refer to OSI concepts repeatedly in the remainder of the book.

A question that arises naturally concerns the complexity of the model. Is it efficient to require every communication to undergo seven layers of processing, both to enter the communications process and then to leave it? In one sense, this question is no longer open to debate. Virtually all standards activities for communications are proceeding within the OSI model. Government customers and most private customers will demand OSI compatibility. The industry must conform.

This does not necessarily foreordain inefficiency. Implementers are free to use virtually null layers where appropriate, or at least very streamlined ones. We have mentioned several examples. Where direct connection is possible, layer 3 is not needed. As we will see, it is not really needed for local networks either. When a reliable layer 3 exists, layer 4 can be minimal. And so on.

Another point: much of the communications processing (e.g., layers 1 through 4) can be offloaded from a host computer to a front-end processor. This is an attractive choice, given the increasing speed and declining cost of small computers. We elaborate on this point in Chapter 8.

**2.4**

# RECOMMENDED READING

[STAL84] covers all the topics in this chapter. Martin provides his usual readable treatment in [MART76] which covers most of the topics in Sections 2.1 and 2.2. A thorough treatment of both analog and digital communications can be found in two companion books: [FREE80] and [FREE81]. [FREE81] concentrates on issues involved with the transmission of data. [FREE80] looks at design issues for communications systems, particularly circuit-switched systems. A more electronically oriented treatment can be found in [BELL82]. [MCNA82] also covers the topics of Section 2.1, focusing on digital data communications. [DOLL78] is a good overall survey book, with a particularly good chapter on multiplexing.

A thorough discussion of the OSI model can be found in [TANE81a], which averages about one chapter per layer. A more informal account can be found in [MART81a]. Good articles on the subject are [TANE81b], [FOLT81], and [ZIMM80]. An excellent general discussion of protocols is [POUZ78]. [WOOD83b] discusses a number of specific computer networks.

# PROBLEMS

**2.1** Write a program to do bit stuffing.

**2.2** A user may wish to use a character-oriented synchronous transmission protocol to send arbitrary bit streams. How can the protocol ensure that none of its control characters (e.g., SYNC) appear in the character stream? Write a program to do this.

**2.3** Write a program that implements the sliding window technique for (1) selective repeat and (2) go-back-n.

**2.4** Consider a transmission link between stations A and B with a probability of error in a frame of p.

    **a.** Assume a selective repeat protocol and assume that station A is sending data and station B is sending acknowledgments only (RR, SREJ) and that it individually acknowledges each frame. Assume that acknowledgments are never lost. What is the mean number of transmissions required per frame?

    **b.** Now assume a go-back-n protocol and that the link is such that A will transmit three additional frames before receiving an RR or REJ for each frame. Also assume that acknowledgments are never lost. What is the mean number of transmissions required per frame?

**2.5** Are the modem and the codec functional inverses (i.e., could an inverted modem function as a codec, and vice versa)?

**2.6** List the major disadvantages with the layered approach to protocols.

**2.7** Compare bit-oriented and character-oriented data link protocols in terms of advantages and disadvantages.

**2.8** Among the principles used by ISO to define the OSI layers were [ZIMM80]:

- The number of layers should be small enough to avoid unwieldly design and implementation, but large enough so that separate layers handle functions which are different in process or technology.
- Layer boundaries should be chosen to minimize the number and size of interactions across boundaries.

Based on these principles, design an architecture with eight layers and make a case for it. Design one with six layers and make a case for that.

**2.9** Another form of digital encoding of digital data is known as delay modulation or *Miller coding*. In this scheme, a logic 1 is represented by a midbit transition (in either direction). A logic 0 is represented by a transition at the end of the bit period if the next bit is 0, and is represented by the absence of a transition if the next bit is a 1. Draw a Miller code waveform for the bit stream of Figure 2.5. Why might this technique be preferable to NRZ? To Manchester?

**2.10** What is the percentage of overhead in a T1 carrier (percentage of bits that are not user data)?

**2.11** Define the following parameters for a switching network:

$N$ = number of hops between two given stations
$L$ = message length, in bits
$B$ = data rate, in bps, on all links
$P$ = packet size, in bits
$H$ = overhead (header) bits per packet
$S$ = call setup time (circuit-switched or virtual circuit) in seconds
$D$ = propagation delay per hop in seconds

    **a.** For $N = 4$, $L = 3200$, $B = 9600$, $P = 1024$, $H = 16$, $S = 0.2$, $D = 0.001$, compute the end-to-end delay for circuit switching, message switching, virtual circuit packet switching, and datagram packet switching. Assume that there are no acknowledgments.

    **b.** Derive general expressions for the four techniques, taken two at a time (six expressions in all) showing the conditions under which the delays are equal.

**2.12** What value of $P$, as a function of $N$, $B$, and $H$ results in minimum end-to-end delay on a datagram network? Assume that $L$ is much larger than $P$, and $D$ is zero.

**2.13** Two stations communicate via a 1-Mbps satellite link. The satellite serves merely to retransmit data received from one station to the other, with negligible delay. The up-and-down propagation delay for a synchronous orbit is 270 ms. Using HDLC frames of length 1024 bits, what is the maximum possible data throughput (not counting overhead bits)?

# Local Network Technology

The principal technology alternatives that determine the nature of a local network are the topology and transmission medium of the network. Together, they in large measure determine the type of data that may be transmitted, the speed and efficiency of communications, and even the kinds of applications that a network may support.

This chapter surveys the topologies and transmission media that, within the state of the art, are appropriate for local networks. Based on these two technologies, three classes of local networks are defined. The discussion is brief, with the objective of providing a context for the material in succeeding chapters. In Chapters 4 through 7, we elaborate on the use of the various topologies and media.

**3.1**

## TOPOLOGIES

The term *topology*, in the context of a communications network, refers to the way in which the end points or stations of the network are interconnected. A topology is defined by the layout of communications links and switching elements, and it determines the data paths that may be used between any pair of stations.

To begin this discussion of topology, consider the question of why a communications network is needed at all. According to our definition in Chapter 1, the local network provides a means for interconnecting devices in a small area. Why not provide a direct connection between any pair of devices that need to communicate? Then no intermediate network of communications devices is required.

The problem with this approach is illustrated in Figure 3.1. Each device has a direct, dedicated link, called a *point-to-point link*, with each other device. If there are N devices, then $N(N - 1)$ links are required, and each device requires $(N - 1)$ input/output (I/O) ports. Thus the cost of the system, in terms of cable installation and I/O hardware, grows with the square of the number of devices.

The infeasibility of this approach, sometimes known as the *mesh topology*, was recognized early for wide-area communications. The solution, as shown in Figure 2.9, was to introduce a network of switching nodes with the ability to route messages, creating logical links and eliminating the need for so many direct physical connections. In this approach, each device or station connects directly to a communication network node and communicates to other stations via the network.

This approach—the use of a collection of switching nodes—is not generally used for local networks. Because the distances involved are small, the expense of the switching nodes can be avoided. Topologies have been developed which require no or only one intermediate switching node, and yet avoid the problems of the mesh topology.

Four simple topologies are described below: bus, tree, ring, and star. These are commonly used, as is, to construct local networks. They can also be used

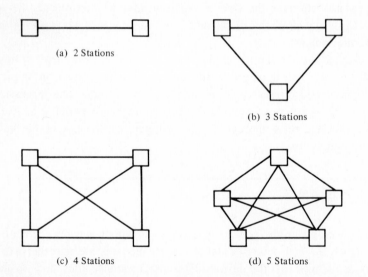

(a) 2 Stations

(b) 3 Stations

(c) 4 Stations

(d) 5 Stations

FIGURE 3–1.   The Problem with Direct Connection or Mesh Topology

as building blocks for networks with more complex topologies. These refinements are discussed in later chapters.

## The Star Topology

In the *star topology*, each station is connected by a point-to-point link to a common central switch (Figure 3.2). Communication between any two stations is via circuit switching. For a station to transmit data, it must first send a request to the central switch, asking for a connection to some destination station. Once the circuit is set up, data may be exchanged between the two stations as if they were connected by a dedicated point-to-point link.

This topology exhibits a centralized communications control strategy. All communications are controlled by the central switch, which must set up and maintain a number of concurrent data paths. Consequently, the central switch node is rather complex. On the other hand, the communications processing burden on the stations is minimal. Other than some rudimentary logic for requesting and accepting connections, the stations need only be concerned with the simple communications requirements of a point-to-point link.

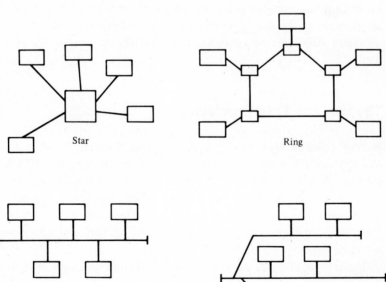

Star    Ring

Bus

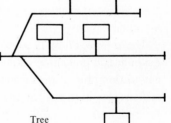

Tree

**FIGURE 3–2.  Local Network Topologies**

## The Ring Topology

In the *ring topology*, the local network consists of a set of *repeaters* joined by point-to-point links in a closed loop. Hence each repeater participates in two links. The repeater is a comparatively simple device, capable of receiving data on one link and transmitting it, bit by bit, on the other link as fast as it is received, with no buffering at the repeater. The links are unidirectional; that is, data are transmitted in one direction only, and all oriented in the same way. Thus data circulate around the ring in one direction (clockwise or counterclockwise).

Each station attaches to the network at a repeater. Data are transmitted in packets. So, for example, if station X wishes to transmit a message to station Y, it breaks the message up into packets. Each packet contains a portion of the data plus some control information, including Y's address. The packets are inserted into the ring one at a time and circulate through the other repeaters. Station Y recognizes its address and copies the packets as they go by.

Since multiple devices share the ring, control is needed to determine at what time each station may insert packets. This is almost always done with some form of distributed control. Each station contains access logic that controls transmission and reception; various techniques are explored in Chapter 5.

Note the contrast between the ring and star topologies. The star topology involves rather complex network processing functions with minimal burden on the stations. In the ring topology, the network devices are the relatively simple repeaters. However, the stations must provide the packetizing and access control logic.

## The Bus and Tree Topologies

A very different approach, compared to ring and star, is taken with the *bus topology*, which is the most common approach in the United States. In this approach the communications network is simply the transmission medium—no switches and no repeaters. All stations attach, through appropriate hardware interfacing, directly to a linear transmission medium, or *bus*. A transmission from any station propagates the length of the medium and can be received by all other stations.

The *tree topology* is a generalization of the bus topology. The transmission medium is a branching cable with no closed loops. Again, a transmission from any station propagates throughout the medium and can be received by all other stations. For both bus and tree topologies, the medium is referred to as *multipoint* or *broadcast*.

Because all nodes share a common transmission link, only one device can transmit at a time. Some form of access control is required to determine which station may transmit next. Typically, but not always, this control is exercised in the form of a protocol shared by all attached nodes (distributed control). A centralized control scheme is sometimes used.

As with the ring, packet transmission is typically used for communication. A station wishing to transmit breaks its message into packets and sends these one at a time, perhaps interleaved on the medium with packets from other stations. The intended destination station will recognize its address as the packets go by, and copy them. There are no intermediate nodes and no switching per se is involved. Nevertheless, from the point of view of the individual station, it is attached to a packet-switching network. Other forms of communication are possible; these are discussed in Chapter 4.

With the bus or tree topology, the trend described for the ring topology is carried to the extreme. The network is relieved of the entire communications processing burden; it is simply a passive (from the point of view of communications) transmission medium. The processing burden on the attached stations is of roughly the same order of magnitude as for ring attachment.

## Choice of Topology

The choice of topology depends on a variety of factors, including reliability, expandability, and performance. This choice is part of the overall task of designing a local network. As the text proceeds, the trade-offs between the various approaches should become clear. A few general observations follow.

The bus/tree topology appears to be the most flexible one. It is able to handle a wide range of devices, in terms of number of devices, data rates, and data types. High bandwidth is achievable. Because the medium is passive, it would appear at first blush to be highly reliable. As we shall see, this is not the case. In particular, a break in the cable can disable a large part or all of the network.

Very high speed links (e.g., optical fiber) can be used between the repeaters of a ring. Hence, the ring has the potential of providing the best throughput of any topology. There are practical limitations, in terms of numbers of devices and variety of data types. Finally, the reliability problem is obvious: a single link or repeater failure could disable the entire network.

The star topology, using circuit switching, readily integrates voice with data traffic. It lends itself well to low-data-rate ($\leq$64 kbps) devices. The star topology is good for terminal-intensive requirements because of the minimal processing burden that it imposes.

**3.2**

# TRANSMISSION MEDIA

The *transmission medium* is the physical path between transmitter and receiver in a communications network. Figure 3.3 shows the basic elements of a

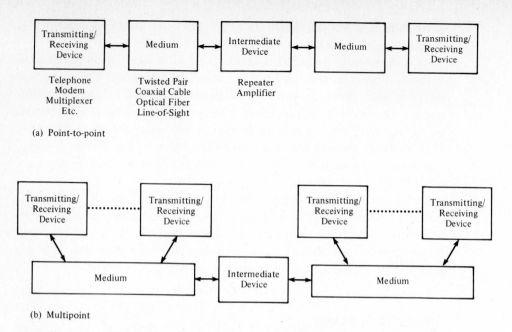

**FIGURE 3—3. Simplified Transmission System Block Diagram (After [BELL 82])**

transmission system. The most common configuration is a point-to-point link between two transmitting/receiving devices, which, through appropriate interfaces, insert analog or digital signals onto the medium. One or more intermediate devices may be used to compensate for attentuation or other transmission impairments. Point-to-point links are used in the ring topology to connect adjacent repeaters, and in the star topology to connect devices to the central switch. Point-to-point links may also be used to connect two local networks in different buildings; we elaborate on this point below. Multipoint links are used to connect multiple devices, as in the bus and tree topologies. Devices attach to the medium at various points; again, repeaters (digital signals) or amplifiers (analog signals) may be used to extend the length of the medium.

The media that have been used in local networks include twisted-pair wire, coaxial cable, and optical fiber. Table 3.1 summarizes some of the important characteristics of the various media. In addition, various forms of electromagnetic propagation through the atmosphere, which we shall refer to as *line-of-sight media*, are employed for building-to-building connections.

In this section, we describe these media using a set of characteristics based on that proposed in [ROSE82]. The characteristics are:

- *Physical description:* the nature of the transmission medium.
- *Transmission characteristics:* include whether analog or digital signaling is used, modulation technique, capacity, and the frequency range over which transmission occurs.
- *Connectivity:* point-to-point or multipoint.

- *Geographic scope:* the maximum distance between points on the network; whether suitable for intrabuilding, interbuilding, and/or intracity use.
- *Noise immunity:* resistance of medium to contamination of the transmitted data.
- *Relative cost:* based on cost of components, installation, and maintenance.

## Twisted Pair

By far the most common transmission medium, for both analog and digital data, is *twisted pair*. The wiring within a building to connect the telephones is twisted pair, as are the "local loops" that connect all of the phones in a limited geographic area to a central exchange.

### Physical Description

A twisted pair consists of two insulated wires arranged in a regular spiral pattern. The wires are copper or steel coated with copper. The copper provides conductivity; steel may be used for strength. A wire pair acts as a single communication link. Typically, a number of these pairs are bundled together into a cable by wrapping them in a tough protective sheath. Over longer distances, cables may contain hundreds of pairs. The twisting of the individual pairs minimizes electromagnetic interference between the pairs. The wires in a pair have thicknesses of from 0.015 to 0.056 inch.

### Transmission Characteristics

Wire pairs may be used to transmit both analog and digital signals. For analog signals, amplifiers are required about every 5 to 6 km. For digital signals, repeaters are used every 2 or 3 km.

The most common use of wire pair is for analog transmission of voice. Although frequency components of speech may be found between 20 Hz and 20 kHz, a much narrower bandwidth is required for intelligible speech reproduction [FREE81]. The standard bandwidth of a full-duplex voice channel is 300 to 3400 Hz. Multiple voice channels can be multiplexed, using FDM, on a single wire pair. A bandwidth of 4 kHz per channel provides adequate separation between channels. Twisted pair has a capacity of up to 24 voice channels using a bandwidth of up to 268 kHz.

Digital data may be transmitted over an analog voice channel using a modem. With a current modem design, speeds of up 9600 bps using phase-shift keying (PSK) are practical. On a 24-channel wire pair, the aggregate data rate is 230 kbps.

It is also possible to use digital or baseband signaling on a wire pair. Bell offers a T1 circuit using twisted pair which handles 24 PCM voice channels, for an aggregate data rate of 1.544 Mbps. Higher data rates, depending on distance, are possible. A data rate of few megabits per second represents a reasonable upper limit.

### Connectivity

Twisted pair can be used for both point-to-point and multipoint applications. As a multipoint medium, twisted pair is a less expensive, lower performance alternative to coax cable but supports fewer stations. Point-to-point usage is far more common.

### Geographic Scope

Twisted pair can easily provide data transmission to a range of 15 km or more. Twisted pair for local networks is typically used within a single building or just a few buildings.

### Noise Immunity

Noise immunity is achieved by proper shielding and by using different twist lengths for nearby pairs in a bundle. These measures are effective for wavelengths much greater than the twist length of the cable. Noise immunity can be as high or higher than for coaxial cable for low frequency transmission. However, above 10 to 100 kHz, coaxial cable is typically superior.

### Cost

Twisted pair is less expensive than either coaxial cable or fiber in terms of cost per foot. However, because of its connectivity limitations, installation costs may approach that of other media.

## Coaxial Cable

The most versatile transmission medium for local networks is *coaxial cable*. Indeed, many people think of coaxial cable as the *only* local network transmission medium, despite the growing use of twisted pair.

In this section we discuss two types of coaxial cable currently in use for local network applications: 75-$\Omega$ cable, which is the standard used in *community antenna television* (CATV) systems, and 50-$\Omega$ cable. As Table 3.1 illustrates, 50-$\Omega$ cable is only used for digital signaling, called *baseband*; 75-$\Omega$ cable is used for analog signaling with FDM, called *broadband*, and for high-speed digital signaling and analog signaling in which no FDM is possible. The latter is sometimes referred to as *single-channel broadband*.

### Physical Description

The coaxial cable, like the twisted pair, consists of two conductors, but it is constructed differently to permit it to operate over a wider range of frequencies. It consists of a hollow outer cylindrical conductor which surrounds a single inner wire conductor. The inner conductor can be either solid or stranded; the outer conductor can be either solid or braided. The inner conductor is held in place by either regularly spaced insulating rings or a solid dialectric material.

**TABLE 3.1  Transmission Media for Local Networks: Multipoint**

| Medium | Signaling Technique | Maximum Data Rate (Mbps) | Maximum Range at Maximum Data Rate (km) | Practical Number of Devices |
|---|---|---|---|---|
| Twisted pair | Digital | 1–2 | Few | 10's |
| Coaxial cable (50 Ω) | Digital | 10 | Few | 100's |
| Coaxial cable (75 Ω) | Digital | 50 | 1 | 10's |
|  | Analog with FDM | 20 | 10's | 1000's |
|  | Single-channel Analog | 50 | 1 | 10's |
| Optical fiber | Analog | 10 | 1 | 10's |

The outer conductor is covered with a jacket or shield. A single coaxial cable has a diameter of from 0.4 to about 1 inch.

### Transmission Characteristics

The 50-Ω cable is used exclusively for digital transmission. A form of Manchester encoding is used. Data rates of up to 10 Mbps can be achieved.

CATV cable is used for both analog and digital signaling. For analog signaling, frequencies up to 300 to 400 MHz are possible. Analog data, such as video and audio, can be handled on CATV cable in much the same way as free-space radio and TV broadcasting. TV channels are each allocated 6 MHz of bandwidth; each radio channel requires much less. Hence a large number of channels can be carried on the cable using FDM.

When FDM is used, the CATV cable is referred to as "broadband." The frequency spectrum of the cable is divided into channels, each of which carries analog signals. In addition to the analog data referred to above, digital data may also be carried in a channel. Various modulation schemes have been used for digital data, including ASK, FSK, and PSK. The efficiency of the modem will determine the bandwidth needed to support a given data rate. A good rule of thumb [STAH82] is to assume 1 Hz per bps for rates at 5 Mbps and above and 2 Hz per bps for lower rates. For example, a 5-Mbps data rate can be achieved in a 6-MHz TV channel, whereas a 4.8-kbps modem might use about 20 kHz. With current technology, a data rate of about 20 Mbps is achievable; at this rate, the bandwidth efficiency may exceed 1 bps/Hz.

To achieve data rates above 20 Mbps, two approaches have been taken. Both require that the entire bandwidth of the 75-Ω cable be dedicated to this data transfer; no FDM is employed. One approach is to use digital signaling on the cable, as is done for the 50-Ω cable. A data rate of 50 Mbps has been achieved with this scheme. An alternative is to use a simple PSK system; using a 150-MHz carrier, a data rate of 50 Mbps has also been achieved. Much lower data rates are achieved using FSK.

### Connectivity
Coaxial cable is applicable to point-to-point and to multipoint configurations. Baseband 50-$\Omega$ cable can support on the order of 100 devices per segment, with larger systems possible by linking segments with repeaters. Broadband 75-$\Omega$ cable can support thousands of devices. The use of 75-$\Omega$ cable at high data rates (50 Mbps) introduces technical problems, discussed in Chapter 6, that limit the number of devices to 20 to 30.

### Geographic Scope
Maximum distances in a typical baseband cable are limited to a few kilometers. Broadband networks can span ranges of tens of kilometers. The difference has to do with the relative signal integrity of analog and digital signals. The types of electromagnetic noise usually encountered in industrial and urban areas are of relatively low frequencies, where most of the energy in digital signals resides. Analog signals may be placed on a carrier of sufficiently high frequency to avoid the main components of noise.

High-speed transmission (50 Mbps), digital or analog, is limited to about 1 km. Because of the high data rate, the physical distance between signals on the bus is very small. Hence very little attenuation or noise can be tolerated before the data are lost.

### Noise Immunity
Noise immunity for coaxial cable depends on the application and implementation. In general, it is superior to that of twisted pair for higher frequencies.

### Cost
The cost of installed coaxial cable falls between that of twisted pair and optical fiber.

## Optical Fiber Cable

The most exciting developments in the realm of local network transmission media are in the area of *fiber optics*. Because the technology is changing rapidly, this section can provide only a current snapshot of fiber optic capability.

### Physical Description
An optical fiber is a thin (50 to 100 μm), flexible medium capable of conducting an optical ray. Various glasses and plastics can be used to make optical fibers [ITT75]. The lowest losses have been obtained using fibers of

ultrapure fused silica. Ultrapure fiber is difficult to manufacture; higher-loss multicomponent glass fibers are more economical and still provide good performance. Plastic fiber is even less costly and can be used for short-haul links, for which moderately high losses are acceptable.

For a single optical fiber, the glass or plastic fiber, having a high index of refraction, is surrounded by a cladding layer of a material with slightly lower index. The cladding layer isolates the fiber and prevents crosstalk with adjacent fibers. Fiber optic cable consists of a bundle of fibers, sometimes with a steel core for stability. Stacked ribbon cable is an alternative method of bundling; the cable consists of a stack of flat ribbons, each with a single row of fibers [MOKH81].

### Transmission Characteristics

Optical fiber transmits a signal-encoded beam of light by means of total internal reflection. Total internal reflection can occur in any transparent medium that has a higher index of refraction than the surrounding medium. In effect, the optical fiber acts as a waveguide for frequencies in the range $10^{14}$ to $10^{15}$ Hz, which covers the visible spectrum and part of the infrared spectrum. As Figure 3.4 shows, light entering the fiber at a shallow angle is reflected along the fiber; rays at more acute angles are simply absorbed.

Two different types of light source are used in fiber optic systems: the *light-emitting diode* (LED) and the *injection laser diode* (ILD). The LED is a solid-state device that emits light when a current is applied. The ILD is a solid-state device that works on the laser principle in which quantum electronic effects are stimulated to produce a superradiant beam of narrow bandwidth. The LED is less costly, operates over a greater temperature range, and has a longer operational life. The ILD is more efficient and can sustain greater data rates.

The detector used at the receiving end to convert the light into electrical energy is a *photodiode*. Two solid-state devices have been used: the PIN detector and the APD detector. The PIN photodiode has a segment of intrinsic (I) silicon between the P and N layers of a diode. The APD, avalanche photodiode, is

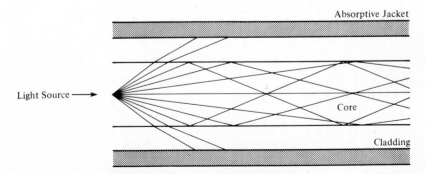

**FIGURE 3—4. Optical Transmission via Internal Reflection**

similar in appearance but uses a stronger electric field. Both devices are basically photon counters. The PIN is less expensive and less sensitive than the APD.

Modulation of the light carrier is a form of ASK called *intensity modulation*. Typically, the two binary digits are represented by the presence or absence of light at a given frequency. Both LED and ILD devices can be modulated in this fashion; the PIN and APD detectors respond directly to intensity modulation.

Data rates as high as a few gigabits per second have been demonstrated in the laboratory. Current practical applications are in the range of a few hundreds of megabits per second over a few kilometers.

Currently, a single carrier frequency is used for optical fiber transmission. Future advance will permit practical FDM systems, also referred to as wavelength division multiplexing or color division multiplexing.

### Connectivity

The most common use of optical fiber is for point-to-point links. Experimental multipoint systems using a bus topology have been built, but are too expensive to be practical today. In principle, however, a single segment of optical fiber could support many more drops than either twisted pair or coaxial cable, due to lower power loss, lower attenuation characteristics, and greater bandwidth potential.

There is one approach to multipoint use of optical fiber that is commercially feasible and that is referred to as a *passive star coupler* [RAWS78, RAWS79, JONE83]. This configuration has a star topology physically, but is logically a bus topology (Figure 3.5). The passive star coupler is fabricated by fusing together a number of optical fibers. Any light input to one of the fibers on one

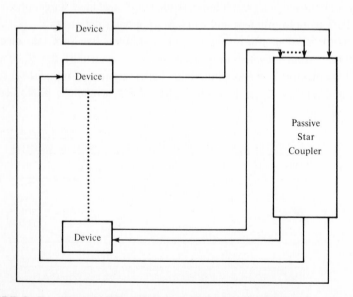

**FIGURE 3–5.  Optical Fiber Passive Star Configuration**

side of the coupler will be equally divided among and output through all the fibers on the other side. Thus each device is connected to the coupler with two fibers. A few tens of devices at a radial distance of up to about 1 km have been supported at a data rate of 10 Mbps.

### Geographic Scope

Present technology supports transmission over distances of 6 to 8 km without repeaters. Hence optical fiber is suitable for linking local networks in several buildings via point-to-point links.

### Noise Immunity

Optical fiber is not affected by electromagnetic interference or noise. This characteristic permits high data rates over long distance and provides excellent security.

### Cost

Fiber optic systems are more expensive than twisted pair and coaxial cable in terms of cost per foot and required components (transmitters, receivers, connectors). While costs of twisted pair and coaxial cable are unlikely to drop, engineering advances should reduce the cost of fiber optics to be competitive with these other media.


## Line-of-Sight Media

In this section we look at three techniques for transmitting electromagnetic waves through the atmosphere: microwave, infrared, and laser. All three require a *line-of-sight path* between transmitter and receiver.

Because of the high frequency ranges at which these devices operate (microwave, $10^9$ to $10^{10}$ Hz; infrared, $10^{11}$ to $10^{14}$ Hz; laser, $10^{14}$ to $10^{15}$ Hz), there is the potential for very high data rates. Practical systems for short links have been built with data rates of several megabits per second.

These transmission techniques are primarily useful for connecting local networks that are in separate buildings. It is difficult to string cable between buildings, either underground or overhead on poles, especially if the intervening space is public property. The line-of-sight techniques only require equipment at each building.

The *infrared* link consists of a pair of transmitter/ receivers (transceivers) that modulate noncoherent infrared light. Transceivers must be within the line of sight, installed on either a rooftop or within a building with data transmitted through adjacent exterior windows. The system is highly directional; it is extremely difficult to intercept, inject data, or to jam such systems. No licensing is required, and the system can be installed in just a few days. Data rates of a few megabits per second over a few kilometers are practical [SEAM82].

**TABLE 3.2 Transmission Media for Local Networks: Point-to-Point Across Public Property**

| Medium | Ease of Installation | Regulatory Licensing (months) | Data Rate (Mbps) | Ease of Maintenance | Cost |
|--------|---------------------|-------------------------------|------------------|---------------------|------|
| Infrared | 1–2 days, easy | None | 1–3 | Excellent | Low |
| Laser | 1–2 days, easy | 2–6 | 1–3 | Excellent | Low |
| Microwave | 1 week, easy | 2–3 | 1–3 | Excellent | Low |
| Underground coax/ optical fiber | 1–18 months, moderate to hard | 6–18 | 10+ | Fair to good | Moderate to high |
| Aerial coax/ optical fiber | 1–6 months, moderate | 6–18 | 10+ | Good | Moderate to high |

*Source:* [CELA82].

A similar system can be installed with *laser* transceivers using coherent light modulation. The major difference is that the Food and Drug Administration (FDA) requires that laser hardware, which emits low-level radiation, be properly shielded. The licensing process takes from 2 to 6 months [CELA82].

Both infrared and laser are susceptible to environmental interference, such as rain and fog. A system with less sensitivity is *microwave*. As with laser and infrared, installation is relatively easy; the major difference is that microwave transceivers can only be mounted externally to a building. Microwave is less directional than either laser or infrared; hence there is a security problem of data eavesdropping, insertion, or jamming. As with all radio-frequency systems, microwave requires Federal Communications Commission (FCC) licensing, which takes about 2 to 3 months. Comparable data rates and distances to laser and infrared can be achieved [RUSH82].

Table 3.2 summarizes the key characteristics of these techniques and includes, for comparison, the use of cable for building-to-building links.

## Choice of Transmission Medium

The choice of transmission medium is determined by a number of factors. It is, we shall see, constrained by the topology of the local network. Other factors come into play, such as:

- *Capacity:* to support the expected local network traffic.
- *Reliability:* to meet availability requirements.
- *Types of data supported:* tailored to the application.
- *Environmental scope:* to provide service over the range of environments required.

And so on. The choice is part of the overall task of designing a local network, which is addressed in a later chapter. Here we can make a few general observations.

Twisted pair is an inexpensive, well-understood medium. Typically, office buildings are wired to meet the anticipated telephone system demand plus a healthy margin. Compared to coax, the bandwidth is limited. Twisted pair is likely to be the most cost effective for a single building, low-traffic, local network installation. An office automation system, with a preponderance of dumb terminals and/or intelligent workstations plus a few minis, is a good example.

Coaxial cable is more expensive than twisted pair, but has greater capacity. For the broad range of local network requirements, and with the exception of terminal-intensive systems, it is the medium of choice. For most requirements, a coaxial-based local network can be designed to meet current demand with plenty of room for expansion, at reasonable cost. Coaxial systems excel when there are a lot of devices and a considerable amount of traffic. Examples include large data processing installations and sophisticated office automation systems, which may include facsimile machines, intelligent copiers, and color graphics devices.

At the current state of the art, fiber optic links are suited for point-to-point communications. Hence they do not compete with coaxial cable. The exception is for ring topology networks. Until multidrop fiber optic cable is cost competitive with coaxial cable, fiber is best considered with the line-of-sight media. However, when the cost of multidrop fiber cable becomes competitive with that of coaxial cable, its advantages—low noise susceptibility, low loss, small size, light weight—will make it a serious contender for many local network applications.

The line-of-sight media are not well suited to local network requirements. They are, however, good choices for point-to-point links between buildings, each of which has a twisted-pair or coaxial-based local network.

## 3.3

## RELATIONSHIP BETWEEN MEDIUM AND TOPOLOGY

The choices of transmission medium and topology are not independent. Table 3.3 illustrates the preferred combinations.

For the bus topology, both twisted pair and the various forms of coaxial cable

**TABLE 3.3   Relationship Between Medium and Topology**

| Medium | Topology | | | |
|---|---|---|---|---|
| | **Bus** | **Tree** | **Ring** | **Star** |
| Twisted pair | × | | × | × |
| Baseband coaxial cable | × | | × | |
| Broadband coaxial cable | × | × | | |
| Optical fiber | | | × | |

are appropriate. At the present time, fiber optic cable is not appropriate, as the multipoint configuration is not cost effective.

The tree topology is used with broadband, CATV coaxial. As we shall see in Chapter 4, the unidirectional nature of broadband signaling allows the construction of a tree architecture. On the other hand, the bidirectional nature of baseband signaling, on either twisted pair or coaxial cable, is not suited to the tree topology. Again, optic fiber is not now cost effective for the multiple access nature of the tree topology.

The ring requires point-to-point links between repeaters. Twisted pair, baseband coaxial, and fiber can all be used to provide the links. Broadband coaxial would not work well in this topology. Each repeater would have to be capable, asynchronously, of receiving and retransmitting data on multiple channels. It is doubtful that the expense of such devices can be justified.

The star topology requires a single point-to-point link between each device and the central switch. Twisted pair is admirably suited to the task. The higher data rates of coaxial cable or fiber would overwhelm the switches of today's technology.

## 3.4

## CLASSES OF LOCAL NETWORKS

This section presents a classification of local networks into three categories: local area network (LAN), high-speed local network (HSLN), and computerized branch exchange (CBX). Table 3.4 summarizes representative characteristics. As with any classification, this one is useful to the extent that it provides a clear differentiation among categories and serves to organize the field in a meaningful way. The three classifications were chosen on the following grounds:

• *Technology:* The architectural and design issues differ significantly for the three classes. This will be seen in such areas as performance, communication protocols, switching technique, and hardware/software interface, as well as transmission media and topologies.
• *Applications:* Although there is some overlap, the three classes of local

**TABLE 3.4  Classes of Local Networks**

| Characteristic | Local Area Network | High Speed Local Network | Computerized Branch Exchange |
|---|---|---|---|
| Transmission medium | Twisted pair, coaxial (both), fiber | CATV coaxial | Twisted pair |
| Topology | Bus, tree, ring | Bus | Star |
| Transmission speed | 1–20 Mbps | 50 Mbps | 9.6–64 kbps |
| Maximum distance | 25 km | 1 km | 1 km |
| Switching technique | Packet | Packet | Circuit |
| Number of devices supported | 100's–1000's | 10's | 100's–1000's |
| Attachment cost | $500–$5000 | $40,000–$50,000 | $250–$1000 |

networks have by and large been developed independently to meet different sets of requirements.

- *Standards:* Communication protocol standards are being developed separately for LANs and HSLNs.

## Local Area Network

The term *local area network* (LAN) is typically used to refer to a general-purpose local network, which can serve a wide variety of devices over a large area. LANs support minis, mainframes, terminals, and other peripherals. In many cases, these networks can carry not only data, but voice, video, and graphics. The office automation example of Chapter 1 falls into this category.

The most common type of LAN is a bus or tree using coaxial cable. Rings using twisted pair, coax, or even fiber are an alternative. The data transfer rates on LANs (1 to 20 Mbps) are high enough to satisfy most requirements and provide sufficient capacity to permit large numbers of devices to share the network.

A subcategory of LANs consists of low-cost networks intended primarily for microcomputers and inexpensive peripherals, such as the personal computer example in Chapter 1. Typically, these networks have data rates of 1 Mbps or less and usually use twisted pair. Because of their low cost, and the growing use of personal computers, these are the most prevalent local networks today and probably will continue to be so [KILL82].

The LAN is probably the best choice when a variety of devices and a mix of traffic types are involved. The LAN, alone or as part of a hybrid local network with one of the other types, will become a common feature of many office buildings and other installations.

Standards for LANs have been developed by a committee of the Institute for Electrical and Electronic Engineers (IEEE), known as the IEEE 802 committee.

## High-Speed Local Network

The *high-speed local network* (HSLN) is designed to provide high end-to-end throughput between expensive, high-speed devices such as mainframes and mass storage devices. The computer room network example of Chapter 1 falls into this category.

Although other media and topologies are possible, work on HSLNs has concentrated on the bus topology using CATV coaxial cable. Very high data rates are achievable—50 Mbps is standard—but both the distance and the number of devices are limited.

The HSLN is typically found in a computer room setting. Its main function is to provide I/O channel connections among a number of devices. Typical uses include file and bulk data transfer, automatic backup, and load leveling. Because of the current high prices for HSLN attachment, they are generally not practical for minicomputers, microcomputers, and less expensive peripherals.

Standards for HSLNs have been developed by a committee sponsored by the American National Standards Institute (ANSI), known as the ANS X3T9.5 committee.

## Computerized Branch Exchange

The *computerized branch exchange* (CBX) is a digital on-premise private branch exchange (PBX) designed to handle both voice and data connections. Typically, these systems have a star or hierarchical star topology using twisted pair wire to connect end points to the switch. In the hierarchical star, high speed trunks of coaxial or fiber may be used to connect satellite switching units to the central switching unit. The integrated voice/data network example of Chapter 1 falls into this category.

In contrast to the LAN and HSLN, which use packet switching, the CBX uses circuit switching. Data rates to individual end points are typically low, but bandwidth is guaranteed and there is essentially no network delay once a connection has been made. The CBX is well suited to voice traffic, and to both terminal-to-terminal and terminal-to-host data traffic.

A related category, best considered as a subcategory of CBX, is the digital switch. Devices in this category are designed to handle data only, not voice, and are typically lower in cost than a CBX of comparable size.

# Choice of Network Type

Because the types of local networks are differentiated, at least partly, by transmission medium and topology, the observations of previous sections apply here. In general, the choice of network type represents a balance between requirements and cost [DERF83].

For applications requiring frequent high throughput between expensive devices, the HSLN currently controls the market. Although the attachment cost is high ($40,000 to $50,000), it is still only a fraction of the cost of the mainframes typically connected to the HSLN. High-speed service on a broadband LAN may, in the future, compete with the HSLN. This topic is explored in Chapter 6.

For most other applications, the choice facing the user is between the CBX and the LAN. Both will handle a wide variety of devices. Currently, the CBX service is limited to about 64 kbps for each attachment. However, this speed is typical of devices that attach to the LAN. Only in certain instances, such as the use of a high-speed graphics device or the need for heavy traffic between minis, are higher data rates required.

Figure 3.6, which is based on a recent study by the Institute of Electrical and Electronic Engineers, gives some idea of relative costs. The ring, not shown on the chart, would be about the same as baseband bus. The study showed that baseband and broadband were very close in price and that the CBX was cheaper than either. Of course, prices are changing rapidly; in general, they are dropping.

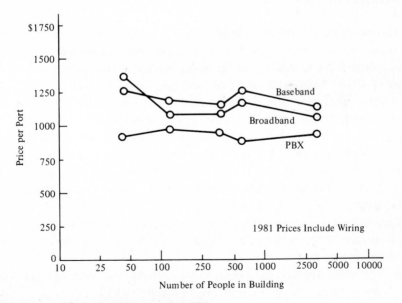

**FIGURE 3–6. Cost of CBX versus LAN**

But the conclusion to be drawn is unlikely to change: for many applications, the CBX is the best choice for a local network because it provides the commonly used capabilities at the lowest cost.

## RECOMMENDED READING

An excellent overview of local network technology is [ROSE82]*; it includes a discussion of the pros and cons of various media and topologies. Detailed description of the transmission characteristics of the media discussed in this section can be found in [FREE81] and [BELL82]; a briefer survey with a good list of references is contained in [CHOU83a]. [THUR79] provides an interesting classification of local networks based on architecture. A commentary along the lines of the classification introduced in this chapter, plus a profile of current products, is given in [LEVY82].

## PROBLEMS

**3.1** What functions should be performed by the network layer (layer 3) in a bus topology local network? Ring topology? Star topology?

**3.2** Could HDLC be used as a link layer for a bus topology local network? If not, what is missing? Answer for ring and star.

**3.3** An asynchronous device, such as a teletype, transmits characters one at a time with unpredictable delays between characters. What problems, if any, do you foresee if such a device is connected to a local network and allowed to transmit at will (subject to gaining access to the medium)? How might such problems be resolved? Answer for ring, bus, and star.

**3.4** Which combination or combinations of medium and topology would be appropriate for the following applications, and why?
  **a.** Terminal intensive: many terminals throughout an office; one or a few shared central computers.
  **b.** Small network: fewer than 50 devices, all low speed ($<56$ kbps).
  **c.** Office automation: a few hundred devices, mostly terminals and minicomputers.

**3.5** Consider the transfer of a file containing one million characters from one station to another. What is the total elapsed time and effective throughput for the following cases:
  **a.** A circuit-switched, star topology local network. Call setup time is negligible, and the data rate on the medium is 64 kbps.
  **b.** A bus topology local network with two stations a distance $D$ apart, a data rate of $B$ bps, and a packet size $P$ with 80 bits of overhead. Each packet is

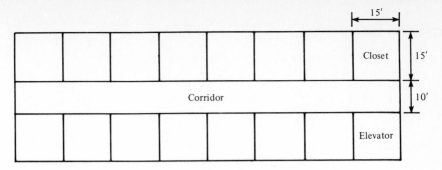

**FIGURE 3–7. Building Layout for a Local Network**

acknowledged with an 88-bit packet before the next is sent. The propagation speed on the bus is 200 m/µsec. Solve for:

(1): $D = 1$ km, $B = 1$ Mbps, $P = 256$ bits
(2): $D = 1$ km, $B = 10$ Mbps, $P = 256$ bits
(3): $D = 10$ km, $B = 1$ Mbps, $P = 256$ bits
(4): $D = 1$ km, $B = 50$ Mbps, $P = 10,000$ bits

   **c.** A ring topology with a total circular length of $2D$, with the two stations a distance $D$ apart. Acknowledgment is achieved by allowing a packet to circulate past the destination station, back to the source station. There are $N$ repeaters on the ring, each of which introduces a delay of one bit time. Repeat the calculation for each of b1 through b4 for $N = 10$; 100; 1000.

**3.6**    A 10-story office building has the floor plan of Figure 3.7 for each floor. A local network is to be installed that will allow attachment of a device from each office on each floor. Attachment is to take place along the outside wall at the baseboard. Cable or wire can be run vertically through the indicated closet and horizontally along the baseboards. The height of each story is 10 ft. What is the minimum total length of cable or wire required for bus, tree, ring, and star topologies?

**3.7**    A tree-topology local network is to be provided that spans two buildings. If permission can be obtained to string cable between the two buildings, then one continuous tree layout will be used. Otherwise, each building will have an independent tree topology network and a point-to-point link will connect a special communications station on one network with a communications station on the other network. What functions must the communications stations perform? Repeat for ring and star.

# Local Area Networks: Characteristics

Local area networks (LANs) are the most general purpose of the three types of local networks. They range from small, inexpensive systems that support personal computers to broadband coaxial cable systems spread over small cities supporting wide ranges of devices.

This chapter focuses on the architecture of bus/tree and ring LANs. Throughout, reference is made to the IEEE 802 LAN standard. This is a draft standard developed by a committee of the Institute of Electrical and Electronic Engineers and discussed more fully in Chapter 5.

## 4.1

## BUS/TREE TOPOLOGY

### Characteristics of Bus/Tree LANs

Of the topologies discussed in the preceding chapter, only the bus/tree topology is a multipoint medium. That is, there are more than two devices connected to and capable of transmitting on the medium.

The operation of this type of LAN can be summarized briefly. Because multiple devices share a single data path, only one may transmit at a time. A

**TABLE 4.1   Bus/Tree Transmission Techniques**

| Baseband | Broadband |
|---|---|
| Digital signaling | Analog signaling (requires RF modem) |
| Entire bandwidth consumed by signal— no FDM | FDM possible—multiple data channels, video, audio |
| Bidirectional | Unidirectional |
| Bus topology | Bus or tree topology |
| Distance: up to a few kilometers | Distance: up to tens of kilometers |

station usually transmits data in the form of a packet containing the address of the destination. The packet propagates throughout the medium and is received by all other stations. The addressed station copies the packet as it goes by.

Two transmission techniques are in use for LANs: baseband and broadband. Baseband, using digital signaling, can be employed on twisted-pair or coaxial cable. Broadband, using analog signaling in the radio-frequency (RF) range, employs coaxial cable. Some of the differences are highlighted in Table 4.1, and this section explores the two methods in some detail. There is also a variant, known as ''single-channel broadband,'' that has the signaling characteristics of broadband but some of the restrictions of baseband. This is also covered below.

The multipoint nature of the bus/tree topology gives rise to several rather stiff problems. First is the problem of determining which station on the medium may transmit at any point in time. With point-to-point links (only two stations on the medium), this is a fairly simple task. If the line is full-duplex, both stations may transmit at the same time. If the line is half-duplex, a rather simple mechanism is needed to ensure that the two stations take turns. Historically, the most common shared access scheme has been the multidrop line, in which access is determined by polling from a controlling station. The controlling station may send data to any other station, or it may issue a poll to a specific station, asking for an immediate response. This method, however, negates some of the advantages of a distributed system and is awkward for communication between two noncontroller stations. A variety of distributed strategies, referred to as medium access control protocols, have now been developed for bus and tree topologies. These are discussed in Chapter 5.

A second problem has to do with signal balancing. When two devices exchange data over a link, the signal strength of the transmitter must be adjusted to be within certain limits. The signal must be strong enough so that, after attenuation across the medium, it meets the receiver's minimum signal strength requirements. It must also be strong enough to maintain an adequate signal to noise ratio. On the other hand, the signal must not be so strong that it overloads the circuitry of the transmitter, which creates harmonics and other spurious signals. Although easily done for a point-to-point link, signal balancing is no easy task for a multiaccess line. If any device can transmit to any other device, then the signal balancing must be performed for all permutations of stations taken two at a time. For $n$ stations that works out to $n \times (n - 1)$ permutations. So for a 200-station network (not a particularly large system), 39,800 signal strength constraints must be satisfied simultaneously. With interdevice distances ranging from tens to thousands of meters, this is an impossible task for any but small networks. In systems that use radio-frequency (RF) signals, the problem is compounded because of the possibility of RF signal interference across frequencies. The solution is to divide the medium into segments within which pairwise balancing is possible, using amplifiers or repeaters between segments.

## Baseband Systems

The principal characteristics of a baseband system are listed in Table 4.1. As mentioned earlier, a baseband LAN is defined as one that uses digital signaling. (This is a restricted use of the word "baseband," which has become accepted in local network circles. More generally, "baseband" refers to the transmission of an analog or digital signal in its original form, without modulation.) Digital signals are inserted on the line as voltage pulses, usually using a form of Manchester encoding. The entire frequency spectrum of the medium is used to form the signal; hence frequency-division multiplexing (FDM) cannot be used. Transmission is bidirectional. That is, a signal inserted at any point on the medium propagates in both directions to the ends, where it is absorbed (Figure 4.1a). The digital signaling requires a bus topology. Unlike analog signals, digital signals cannot easily be propagated through the splitters and joiners required for a tree topology. Baseband systems can extend only a limited distance, about 1 km at most. This is because the attenuation of the signal, which is most pronounced at higher frequencies, causes a blurring of the pulses and a weakening of the signal to the extent that communication over larger distances is impractical.

### Baseband Coax

The most well-known form of baseband bus LAN uses coaxial cable. We concentrate on those systems in this section. Unless otherwise indicated, the discussion is based on the Ethernet system [METC76, SHOC82, DIGI80] and the almost identical IEEE standard [IEEE82].

Most baseband coaxial cable systems use a special 50-$\Omega$ cable rather than the standard CATV 75-$\Omega$ cable. This is because, for digital signals, the 50-$\Omega$ cable suffers less intense reflections from the insertion capacitance of the taps, and provides better immunity against low-frequency electromagnetic noise.

The simplest baseband coaxial LAN consists of an unbranched length of coaxial cable with a terminator at each end to prevent reflections. A maximum

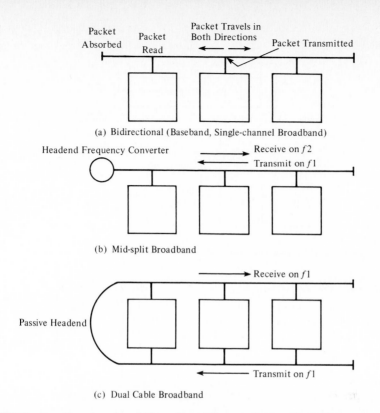

(a) Bidirectional (Baseband, Single-channel Broadband)

Headend Frequency Converter    Receive on $f2$
Transmit on $f1$

(b) Mid-split Broadband

Receive on $f1$

Passive Headend

Transmit on $f1$

(c) Dual Cable Broadband

**FIGURE 4–1.   Baseband and Broadband Transmission Techniques**

length of 500 m is recommended. Stations attach to the cable by means of a tap, with the distance between any two taps being a multiple of 2.5 m; this is to ensure that reflections from adjacent taps do not add in phase. A maximum of 100 taps is recommended.

The specifications given above are for a 10-Mbps data rate. They are based on engineering trade-offs involving data rate, cable length, number of taps, and the electrical characteristics of the transmit and receive components. For example, at lower data rates, the cable could be longer.

Figure 4.2, from the Ethernet specification, illustrates typical components and their functions. The main components are:

- Transceiver
- Transceiver cable
- Controller
- 50-Ω coaxial cable
- 50-Ω terminators

The transceiver taps into the coaxial cable. It transmits signals from the station to the cable, and vice versa. It also contains the electronics necessary to recognize the presence of a signal on the coaxial cable and to recognize a

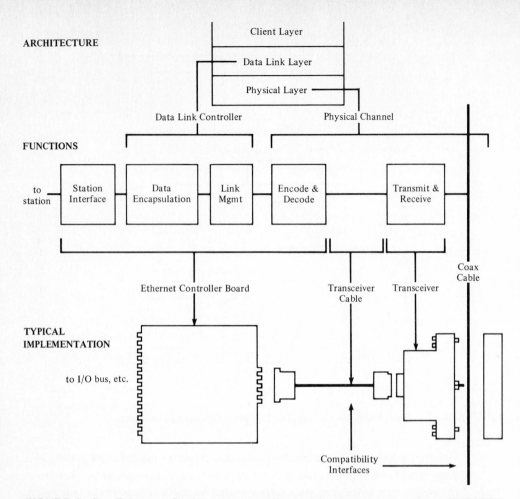

**FIGURE 4–2. Ethernet Architecture and Typical Implementation (From [DIGI80])**

collision of two signals. This last function is needed for Ethernet and 802 because of the CSMA/CD protocol that they use (discussed in Chapter 5). A baseband bus LAN using some other protocol would not require this complexity. The transceiver also provides ground isolation between the signals from the station and the signals on the cable. Since two local grounds may differ by several volts, connection of local grounds to the cable could cause a large current to flow through the cable's shield, introducing noise and creating a safety hazard.

The transceiver cable is a four-pair cable that connects the transceiver to the controller, which contains the bulk of the intelligence required to communicate over the LAN. This split is arbitrary: all of the electronics could be included at the transceiver end. The split is motivated by the assumption that the station will be located some distance from the cable and that the cable tap may be in a relatively inaccessible location. Hence the electronics at the tap should be as simple as possible to reduce maintenance costs. The cable supplies power to the transceiver and passes data signals between the transceiver and the controller as well as control signals. The latter includes a collision presence signal from transceiver to controller. Other signals are possible. For example, the 802 standard has isolate and cease-to-isolate signals, which allow the controller to enable and disable the transceiver.

The controller is an implementation of all the functions (other than those performed by the transceiver) needed to manage access to the coax cable for the purpose of exchanging packets between the coax cable and the attached station. More will be said about the particular functions in Chapter 5.

Finally, the transmission system consists of 50-$\Omega$ coaxial cable and terminators. The terminators absorb signals, preventing reflection from the ends of the bus.

These five types of components are sufficient for building a baseband bus LAN of up to about 1 km with up to about 100 stations. In many cases, this will be enough, but for greater requirements, an additional component is needed: the repeater.

The repeater is used to extend the length of the network. It consists, in essence, of two transceivers joined together and connected to two different segments of coaxial cable. The repeater passes digital signals in both directions between the two segments, amplifying and regenerating the signals as they pass through. A repeater is transparent to the rest of the system; since it does no buffering, it in no sense isolates one segment from another. So, for example, if two stations on different segments attempt to transmit at the same time, their packets will interfere with each other (collide). To avoid multipath interference, only one path of segments and repeaters is allowed between any two stations. The 802 standard allows a maximum of four repeaters in the path between any two stations, extending the effective cable length to 2.5 km. Figure 4.3 is an example of a baseband system with three segments and two repeaters.

### Twisted Pair Baseband

As mentioned in Chapter 1, there is a need for low-cost local networks for hooking together inexpensive devices such as microcomputers. A twisted-pair baseband LAN is an excellent choice in such circumstances. This type of system supports fewer stations at lower speeds than does a coaxial baseband LAN, but at far lower cost.

The components of the system are few and simple:

• Twisted-pair bus
• Terminators
• Controller interface

The latter can simply be a standard two-wire I/O or communications interface. The typical physical layer standard used for the interface is RS-422. This is a common, inexpensive interface.

With this kind of network, the following parameters are reasonable:

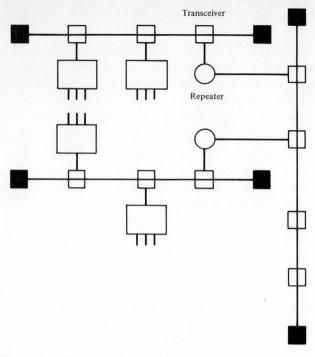

Transceiver

Repeater

**FIGURE 4—3.  Baseband Configuration**

- *Length:* up to 1 km
- *Data rate:* up to 1 Mbps
- *Number of devices:* 10's

Twisted pair is a good medium for several reasons. First, it has lower cost than coaxial cable while providing almost equal noise immunity. Second, virtually anyone can install the network, which consists of laying the cable and connecting the controllers. The task requires only a screwdriver and a pair of pliers, and is similar to hooking up hi-fi speakers.

Examples of these systems can be found in [MALO81], [BOSE81], and [HAHN81].

## Broadband Systems

Like the term "baseband," "broadband" is a word co-opted into the local network vocabulary from the telecommunications world, with a change in meaning. In general, broadband refers to any channel having a bandwidth greater than a voice-grade channel (4 kHz). To local network aficionados, the term is reserved for coaxial cable on which analog signaling is used. A further restriction to transmission techniques that allow frequency-division multiplexing (FDM) on the cable is usually applied. We will generally mean systems capable of

FDM when using the term "broadband." Systems intended to carry only a single analog signal will be referred to as single channel broadband.

### FDM Broadband

Table 4.1 summarizes the key characteristics of broadband systems. As mentioned, broadband implies the use of analog signaling. FDM is possible: the frequency spectrum of the cable can be divided into channels or sections of bandwidth. Separate channels can support data traffic, TV, and radio signals. Broadband components allow splitting and joining operations; hence both bus and tree topologies are possible. Much greater distances—tens of kilometers—are possible with broadband compared to baseband. This is because the analog signals that carry the digital data can propagate greater distances before the noise and attenuation damage the data.

Figure 4.4 shows a typical broadband system. As with baseband, stations attach to the cable by means of a tap. Unlike baseband, however, broadband is inherently a unidirectional medium; signals inserted onto the medium can propagate in only one direction. The primary reason for this is that it is infeasible to build amplifiers that will pass signals of one frequency in both directions. This unidirectional property means that only those stations "downstream" from a transmitting station can receive its signals. How, then, to achieve full connectivity?

Clearly, two data paths are needed. These paths are joined at a point on the network known as the *headend*. For bus topology, the headend is simply one end of the bus. For tree topology, the headend is the root of the branching tree. All stations transmit on one path toward the headend (inbound). Signals received

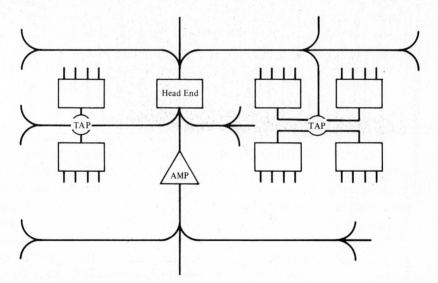

**FIGURE 4—4.  Broadband Configuration**

at the headend are then propagated along a second data path away from the headend (outbound). All stations receive on the outbound path.

Physically, two different configurations are used to implement the inbound and outbound paths (Figure 4.1b and c). On a *dual-cable* configuration, the inbound and outbound paths are separate cables, with the headend simply a passive connector between the two. Stations send and receive on the same frequency.

By contrast, on the *split* configuration, the inbound and outbound paths are different frequencies on the same cable. *Bidirectional amplifiers* pass lower frequencies inbound, and higher frequencies outbound. (Note that this is a different sense of the word "bidirectional.") The headend contains a device, known as a *frequency converter*, for translating inbound frequencies to outbound frequencies.

The frequency converter at the headend can be either an analog or digital device. An analog device simply translates signals to a new frequency and retransmits them. A digital device recovers the digital data from the analog signal and then retransmits the cleaned-up data on the new frequency.

Split systems are categorized by the frequency allocation to the two paths. *Subsplit*, commonly used by the CATV (Community Antenna Television) industry provides 5 to 30 MHz inbound and 40 to 300 MHz outbound. This system was designed for metropolitan area TV distribution, with limited subscriber-to-central office communication. *Midsplit*, more suitable for LANs, provides an inbound range of 5 to 116 MHz and an outbound range of 168 to 300 MHz. This provides a more equitable distribution of bandwidth. Midsplit was developed at a time when the practical spectrum of a CATV cable was 300 MHz. Spectrums surpassing 400 MHz are now available, and "supersplit" or "equalsplit" is sometimes used to achieve even better balance by splitting the bandwidth roughly in half.

The differences between split and dual are minor. The midsplit system is useful when a single cable plant is already installed in a building. Also, the installed system is about 10-15% cheaper than a dual-cable system [HOPK79]. On the other hand, a dual cable has over twice the capacity of midsplit. It does not require the frequency translator at the headend, which on the split system may need to be redundant for reliability.

Broadband systems use standard, off-the-shelf CATV components, including 75-$\Omega$ coaxial cable. All end points are terminated with a 75-$\Omega$ terminator to absorb signals. Broadband is suitable for tens of kilometers radius from the headend and hundreds or even thousands of devices. The main components of the system are [ROMA77, CUNN80]:

- Cable
- Terminators
- Amplifiers
- Directional couplers
- Controller

Cables used in broadband networks are of three types. *Trunk cable*, typically 0.75 to 1.0 inch in diameter with attenuation of 0.7 to 1.2 dB per 100 ft of cable at 300 MHz, might form the spine of a large LAN system. Typically, trunk cables are sheathed in a rigid aluminum shield and range in length from a few kilometers to tens of kilometers. *Distribution cables*, typically 0.4 to 0.5 inch in diameter with attenuation of 1.2 to 2.0 dB per 100 ft, are used for shorter distances and for branch cables. They may be semirigid or rigid. *Drop cables*, typically 0.25 inch in diameter with attenuation of 4 to 6 db per 100 ft, are flexible, short, and used to connect stations to the LAN.

Amplifiers may be used on trunk and distribution cables to compensate for cable attenuation. Amplifiers must have a "slope" to account for the variability of attenuation as a function of frequency; less amplification is needed at lower frequencies. For split systems, amplifiers must be bidirectional, passing and amplifying lower frequencies in one direction and higher frequencies in the other.

Directional couplers or taps provide a means for dividing one input into two outputs and combining two inputs into one output. *Splitters*, used to branch the cable, provide roughly equal attenuation along the split branches. *Taps*, used to connect drop cable and hence stations to the LAN, provide more attenuation to the drop cable. Figure 4.5 illustrates these concepts.

Finally, controllers are needed, as in baseband, to provide the basic LAN service.

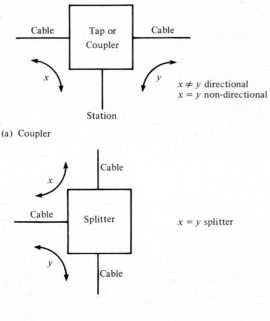

(a) Coupler

(b) Splitter

$x, y$ = attenuation

**FIGURE 4–5. Directional Couplers and Splitters**

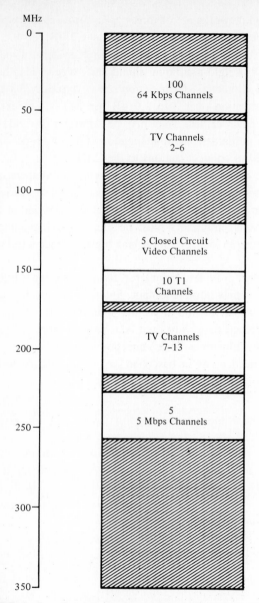

MHz

100
64 Kbps Channels

TV Channels
2–6

5 Closed Circuit
Video Channels

10 T1
Channels

TV Channels
7–13

5
5 Mbps Channels

**FIGURE 4–6.   Dual-Cable Broadband Spectrum Allocation**

As mentioned earlier, the broadband LAN can be used to carry multiple channels, some used for analog signals, such as video and voice, and some for digital. Digital channels can generally carry a data rate of somewhere between 0.25 and 1 bps/Hz. Figure 4.6 shows a possible allocation of a 350-MHz cable.

Three kinds of digital data transfer service are possible on a broadband cable: dedicated, switched, and multiple access (Figure 4.7). For dedicated service, a small portion of the cable's bandwidth is reserved for exclusive use by two

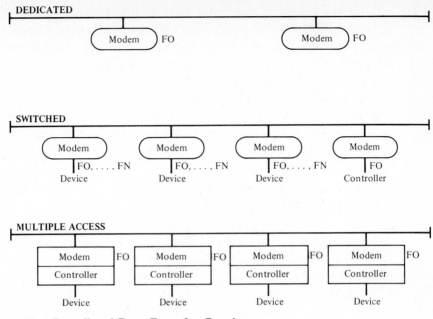

**FIGURE 4–7. Broadband Data Transfer Services**

devices. No special protocol is needed. Each of the two devices attaches to the cable through a modem; both modems are tuned to the same frequency. This technique is analogous to securing a dedicated leased line from the telephone company. Transfer rates of up to 20 Mbps are achievable.

The switched technique requires the use of a number of frequency bands. Devices are attached through *frequency agile modems*, capable of changing their frequency by electronic command. Initially, all attached devices, together with a controller, are tuned to the same frequency. A station wishing to establish a connection sends a request to the controller, which assigns an available frequency to the two devices and signals their modems to tune to that frequency. This technique is analogous to a dial-up line. Because the cost of frequency-agile modems rises dramatically with data rate, rates of 56 kbps or less are typical.

Finally, the multiple-access service allows a number of attached devices to be supported at the same frequency. As with baseband, some form of medium access control protocol is needed to control transmission. These protocols are discussed in Chapter 5.

### Single-Channel Broadband

An abridged form of broadband is one in which the entire spectrum of the cable is devoted to a single transmission path for analog signals. As we shall see, this technique has practical applicability to high speed local networks (HSLNs). It has also been proposed for LANs and is part of the IEEE 802 standard.

In general, a single-channel broadband LAN has the following characteristics. Bidirectional transmission, using a bus topology, is employed. Hence there can be no amplifiers, and there is no need for a headend. Some form of FSK is used, generally at a low frequency (a few MHz). This is an advantage since attenuation is less at lower frequencies.

Because the cable is dedicated to a single task, it is not necessary to take care that the modem output be confined to a narrow bandwidth. Energy can spread over the cable's spectrum. As a result, the electronics are simple and inexpensive. This scheme would appear to give comparable performance, at a comparable price, to baseband.

### Power Line Broadband

A low-cost system that could compete with twisted-pair baseband is a local network based on power-line distribution [ARCH82]. The transmission medium for the network is the ac power distribution system already installed in every home and office building. Touted as a "wireless" network, it involves absolutely no medium installation.

The interface to the medium is simply a standard two- or three-prong outlet plug. Typically, data are FSK modulated in a narrow band at a frequency of 200 to 400 kHz. This signal does not interfere with the 60 Hz power distribution, and presents a sufficiently low-level RF signal to avoid interference with office equipment. Using such techniques, data rates of up to 9600 bps on up to 10 or 20 separate channels are possible.

One of the key advantages of this system is portability. A workstation can be moved into an office, plugged into the wall via a controller, and immediately be part of the network.

## Baseband versus Broadband

One of the silliest aspects of the intense coverage afforded local networks in the trade and professional literature is the baseband versus broadband debate. A *Datamation* article captured the spirit [KLEE82]:

You almost expect to find cabbies talking about it: you've just hopped into the back seat of a Checker at O'Hare, say, and the driver turns around and offers: "Yeah, so me and the wife talked it over and we decided baseband is the way to go. None of this CSMA/CD line access, though; it won't do the job if the net gets busy. We're working on token passing. We'll probably announce it by late second quarter. It looks very promising."

At this point the dispatcher sticks his head in the window. "Oh yeah?" he says, "What are you going to do about voice, then? What are you going to do five years down the pike when you wanna videoconference? You can go ahead and lock yourself into the office of the past if you want, but count me out. My money's on broadband."

The fact is that there is room for both technologies in the local network field. Potential customers will find themselves faced with a lot of other, more complex, decisions than this one. For the interested reader, thoughtful discussions may be found in [HOPK82] and [KRUT81].

Table 4.2 summarizes the pros and cons of the two technologies. Baseband has the advantage of simplicity, and, in principle, lower cost. The layout of a baseband cable plant is simple; there are just five rules for trunk layout in the Ethernet specification. A relatively inexperienced local network engineer should be able to cope.

The potential disadvantages of baseband include the limitations in capacity and distance—disadvantages only if your requirements exceed those limitations. Another concern has to do with grounding. Because dc components are on the cable, it can be grounded in only one place. Care must be taken to avoid potential shock hazards and antenna effects.

Broadband's strength is its tremendous capacity; it can carry a wide variety of traffic on a number of channels. With the use of amplifiers, broadband can achieve very wide area coverage. Also, the system is based on a mature CATV technology. Components are reliable and readily available.

Broadband systems are more complex than baseband to install and maintain. The layout design must include cable type selection, and placement and setting of all amplifiers and taps. Maintenance involves periodic testing and alignment of all network parameters. These are jobs for experienced RF engineers. Finally, the average propagation delay between stations for broadband is twice that for a comparable baseband system. This reduces the efficiency and performance of the system, as discussed below.

As with all other network design choices, the selection of baseband or

**TABLE 4.2   Baseband versus Broadband**

| Advantages | Disadvantages |
|---|---|
| *Baseband* | |
| Cheaper—no modem | Single channel |
| Simpler technology | Limited capacity |
| Easy to install | Limited distance |
| | Grounding concerns |
| *Broadband* | |
| High capacity | Modem cost |
| Multiple traffic types | Installation and maintenance complexity |
| More flexible configurations | Doubled propagation delay |
| Large area coverage | |
| Mature CATV technology | |

broadband must be based on relative costs and benefits. It is likely that some installations will have both types. Neither is likely to win the LAN war.

## RING TOPOLOGY

### Description

The ring consists of a number of repeaters, each connected to two others by unidirectional transmission links to form a single closed path (Figure 4.8). Data are transferred sequentially, bit by bit, around the ring from one repeater to the next. Each repeater regenerates and retransmits each bit.

For a ring to operate as a communications network, three functions are required: message insertion, message reception, and message removal. These functions are provided by the repeaters. Each repeater, in addition to serving as an active element on the ring, serves as a device attachment point for message insertion. Messages are transmitted in packets, each of which contains a destination address field. As a packet circulates past a repeater, the address field

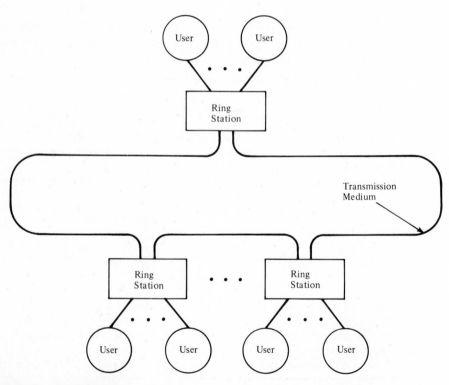

**FIGURE 4–8.   Ring System**

is copied to the attached station. If the station recognizes the address, then the remainder of the packet is copied.

Repeaters perform the message insertion and reception functions in a manner not unlike that of taps, which serve as device attachment points on a bus or tree. Message removal, however, is another story. For a bus or tree, signals inserted onto the line propagate to the end points and are absorbed by terminators. Hence, shortly after transmission ceases, the bus or tree is clear of data. However, because the ring is a closed loop, data will circulate indefinitely unless removed. A packet may be removed by the addressed repeater. Alternatively, each packet could be removed by the transmitting repeater after it has made one trip around the loop. The latter approach is more desirable because (1) it permits automatic acknowledgment, and (2) it permits multicast addressing: one packet sent simultaneously to multiple stations.

A variety of strategies can be used for determining how and when packets are added to and removed from the ring. The strategy can be viewed, at least conceptually, as residing in a medium access control layer, discussed in Chapter 5.

The repeater, then, can be seen to have two main purposes in life: (1) to contribute to the proper functioning of the ring by passing on all the data that comes its way, and (2) to provide an access point for attached stations to send and receive data. Corresponding to these two purposes are two states (Figure 4.9): the listen state and the transmit state.

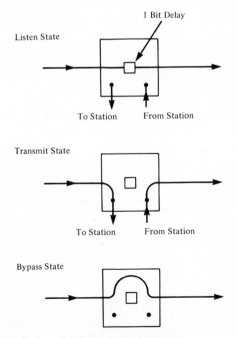

**FIGURE 4–9.   Ring Repeater States**

In the *listen state*, each bit that is received is retransmitted with a small delay, required to allow the repeater to perform necessary functions. Ideally, the delay should be on the order of one bit time (the time it takes for a repeater to transmit one complete bit onto the outgoing line). These functions are:

- Scan passing bit stream for pertinent patterns. Chief among these is the address or addresses of attached devices. Another pattern, used in the token control strategy explained later, indicates permission to transmit. Note that to perform the scanning function, the repeater must have some knowledge of packet format.
- Copy each incoming bit and send it to the attached station, while continuing to retransmit each bit. This will be done for each bit of each packet addressed to this station.
- Modify a bit as it passes by. In certain control strategies, bits may be modified to, for example, indicate that the packet has been copied. This would serve as an acknowledgment.

When a repeater's station has data to send and when the repeater, based on the control strategy, has permission to send, the repeater enters the *transmit state*. In this state, the repeater receives bits from the station and retransmits them on its outgoing link. During the period of transmission, bits may appear on the incoming ring link. There are two possibilities, and they are treated differently:

- The bits could be from the same packet that the repeater is still sending. This will occur if the "bit length" of the ring is shorter than the packet. In this case, the repeater passes the bits back to the station, which can check them as a form of acknowledgment.
- For some control strategies, more than one packet could be on the ring at the same time. If the repeater, while transmitting, receives bits from a packet it did not originate, it must buffer them to be transmitted later.

These two states, listen and transmit, are sufficient for proper ring operation. A third state, the *bypass state*, is also useful. In this state, a bypass relay can be activated, so that signals propagate past the repeater with no delay other than medium propagation. The bypass relay affords two benefits: (1) it provides a partial solution to the reliability problem, discussed later, and (2) it improves performance by eliminating repeater delay for those stations that are not active on the network.

## Ring Benefits

Until recently the ring-topology LAN was little known in the United States. Although much work had been done in Europe, the emphasis in the United States was on the bus/tree topologies. The strengths of the bus/tree approach, discussed in the preceding section, are well known. The benefits of the ring have been less well known, but interest is beginning to build. A good deal of research into overcoming some of the weaknesses of the ring has been done at M.I.T. [SALT79, SALT81]. Ring-based LAN products have begun to appear: examples are those of Prime [GORD79] and Apollo. Most important, IBM has evidenced considerable interest [DIXO82, MARK82, ANDR82, BUX82].

Like the bus and tree, the ring is a shared-access or multiaccess network (although the medium itself is a collection of point-to-point links). Hence the benefits of this type of medium obtain, including ability to broadcast and incremental cost growth. There are other benefits provided by the ring that are not shared by the bus/tree topology.

The most important benefit or strength of the ring is that it uses point-to-point communication links. There are a number of implications of this fact. First, because the transmitted signal is regenerated at each node, transmission errors are minimized and greater distances can be covered than with baseband bus. Broadband bus/tree can cover a similar range, but cascaded amplifiers can result in loss of data integrity at high data rates. Second, the ring can accommodate optical fiber links, which provide very high data rates and excellent electromagnetic interference (EMI) characteristics. Finally, the electronics and maintenance of point-to-point lines are simpler than for multipoint lines.

Another benefit of the ring is that fault isolation and recovery are simpler than for bus/tree. This is discussed in more detail later in this section and in Chapter 12.

With the ring, the "duplicate address" problem is easily solved. If, on a bus or tree, two stations are by accident assigned the same address, there is no easy way to sort this out. A relatively complex algorithm must be incorporated into the LAN protocol. On a ring, the first station with an address match that is encountered by a packet can modify a bit in the packet to acknowledge reception. Subsequent stations with the same address will easily recognize the problem.

Finally, there is the potential throughput of the ring. Under certain conditions, the ring has greater throughput than a comparable bus or tree LAN. This topic is explored in Chapter 9.

## Potential Ring Problems

The potential problems of a ring are, at first blush, more obvious than the benefits. We list here six problems identified by Saltzer [SALT79, SALT81].

1. *Cable vulnerability:* A break on any of the links between repeaters disables the entire network until the problem can be isolated and a new cable installed. The ring may range widely throughout a building and is vulnerable at every point to accidents.
2. *Repeater failure:* As with the links, a failure of a single repeater disables

the entire network. In many networks, it will be common for many of the nodes not to be in operation at any time; yet all repeaters must always operate properly.

3. *Perambulation:* When either a repeater or a link fails, locating the failure requires perambulation of the ring, and thus access to all rooms containing repeaters and cable. This is known as the "pocket full of keys" problem.

4. *Installation headaches:* Installation of a new repeater to support new devices requires the identification of two nearby, topologically adjacent repeaters. It must be verified that they are in fact adjacent (documentation could be faulty or out of date), and cable must be run from the new repeater to each of the old repeaters. These are several unfortunate consequences. The length of cable driven by the source repeater may change, possibly requiring retuning. Old cable, if not removed, accumulates. In addition, the geometry of the ring may become highly irregular, exacerbating the perambulation problem.

5. *Initialization and recovery:* To avoid designating one ring node as a controller (negating the benefit of distributed control), a strategy is required to assure that all stations can cooperate smoothly when initialization and recovery is required. This need arises, for example, when a packet is garbled by a transient line error; in that case, no repeater may wish to assume the responsibility of removing the circulating packet.

6. *Closed-loop clock coordination:* There is a subtle problem of distributed agreement on data transmission rate. Not only must the repeaters all agree on a common clock rate, but that clock rate must result in an integral number of bit times of delay around the ring.

Problems 1 and 2 are reliability problems, which are dealt with in Chapter 12. However, these two problems, together with problems 3 and 4, can be ameliorated by a refinement in the ring architecture, explained in the next section. Problem 5 is a software problem, to be dealt with by the various LAN protocols discussed in Chapter 5.

Finally, problem 6 can be dealt with in several ways [SALT81]. A simple way is to open the ring when a repeater originates a message; all other repeaters track the originator. A more sophisticated approach is to have a phase-locked loop in each repeater tracking its preceding neighbor.

## The Star-Ring Architecture

Two observations can be made about the basic ring architecture described above. First, there is a practical limit to the number of stations on a ring. This limit is suggested by the reliability and maintenance problems cited earlier and by the accumulating delay of large numbers of repeaters. A limit of a few hundred stations seems reasonable. Second, the cited benefits of the ring do not depend on the actual routing of the cables that link the repeaters.

These observations have led to the development of a refined ring architecture, the star-ring, which overcomes some of the problems of the ring and allows the construction of large local networks. This architecture is the basis of IBM's proposed local network product [RAUC82] and grows out of research done at IBM [BUX82] and M.I.T. [SALT79]. At least one commercial product using this architecture is now available [SALW83].

As a first step, consider the rearrangement of a ring into a star. This is achieved by having the interrepeater links all thread through a single site (Figure 4.10). This ring wiring concentrator has a number of advantages. Because there is access to the signal on every link, it is a simple matter to isolate a fault. A message can be launched into the ring and tracked to see how far it gets without mishap. A faulty segment can be disconnected—no pocket full of keys needed—and repaired at a later time. New repeaters can easily be added to the ring: simply run two cables from the new repeater to the site of ring wiring concentration and splice into the ring.

The bypass relay associated with each repeater can be moved into the ring wiring concentrator. The relay can automatically bypass its repeater and two links for any malfunction. A nice effect of this feature is that the transmission path from one working repeater to the next is approximately constant; thus the

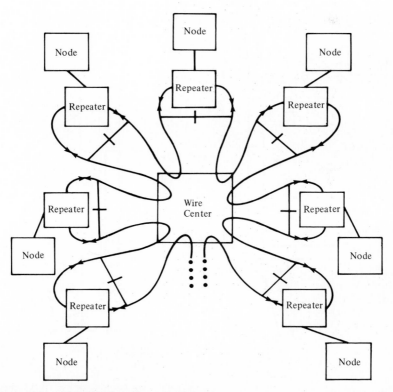

**FIGURE 4–10.  Ring Wiring Concentrator**

range of signal levels to which the transmission system must automatically adapt is much smaller.

The ring wiring concentrator greatly alleviates the perambulation and installation problems mentioned earlier. It also permits rapid recovery from a cable or repeater failure. Nevertheless, a single failure could, at least temporarily, disable the entire network. Furthermore, throughput consideration still places a practical upper limit on the number of stations in a ring. Finally, in a spread-out network, a single wire concentration site dictates a lot of cable.

To attack these remaining problems, consider a local network consisting of multiple rings. Each ring consists of a connected sequence of wiring concentrators, and the set of rings is connected by a bridge (Figure 4.11). The bridge routes data packets from one ring subnetwork to another based on addressing

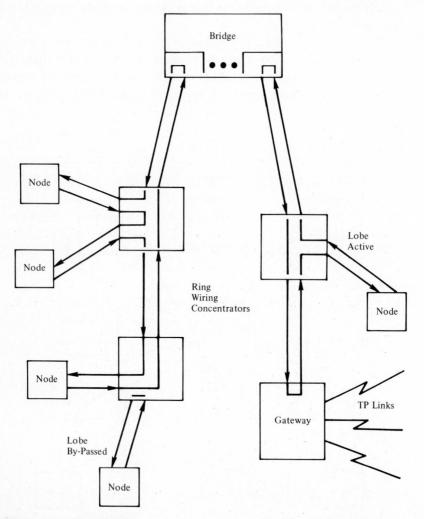

**FIGURE 4–11.  Ring Bridge**

information in the packet so routed. From a physical point of view, each ring operates independently of the other rings attached to the bridge. From a logical point of view, the bridge provides transparent routing among the rings.

The bridge must perform five functions:

- *Input filtering:* For each ring, the bridge monitors the traffic on the ring and copies all packets addressed to other rings on the bridge. This function can be performed by a repeater programmed to recognize a family of addresses rather than a single address.
- *Input buffering:* Received packets may need to be buffered, either because the interring traffic is peaking, or because the target output buffer is temporarily full.
- *Switching:* Each packet must be routed through the bridge to its appropriate destination ring.
- *Output buffering:* A packet may need to be buffered at the threshold of the destination ring, waiting for an opportunity to be inserted.
- *Output transmission:* This function can be performed by an ordinary repeater.

For a small number of rings, a bridge can be a reasonably simple device. As the number of rings on a bridge grows, the switching complexity and load on the bridge also grow. For very large installations, multiple bridges, interconnected by high-speed trunks, may be needed (Figure 4.12).

Three principal advantages accrue from the use of a bridge. First, the closed loop clock coordination problem becomes more difficult as the number of repeaters on a ring grows; this problem is bounded by restricting the size of the ring. Second, the failure of a ring for whatever reason, will disable only a portion of the network; failure of the bridge does not prevent intraring traffic. Finally, multiple rings may be employed to obtain a satisfactory level of performance when the throughput capability of a single ring is exceeded.

There are several pitfalls to be noted. First, the automatic acknowledgment feature of the ring is lost; higher level protocols must provide acknowledgment. Second, performance may not significantly improve if there is a high percentage of interring traffic. If it is possible to do so, network devices should be judiciously allocated to rings to minimize interring traffic.

**4.3**

---

# RECOMMENDED READING

[SHOC82]* is a good description of a baseband system. The original Ethernet article [METC76] is also informative. [DINE80]* is a comprehensive discussion of the broadband approach; [DINE81] is also useful. A detailed exposition on broadband components and their use is in [ROMA77]. A summary of the baseband versus broadband debate can be found [KRUT81]*. [COOP83] compares midsplit and dual broadband.

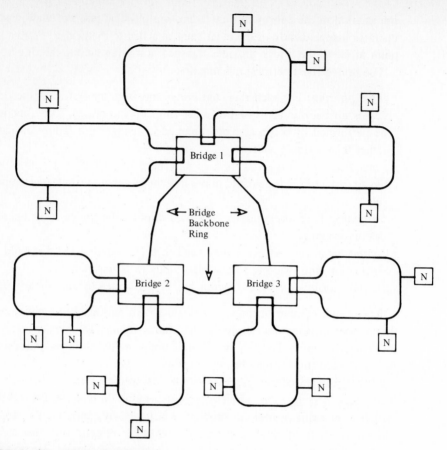

**FIGURE 4–12.   Multiple Bridges**

[ANDR82]* presents IBM's ring LAN approach. [SALT81]* makes a case for the ring as compared to the bus.

**4.4**

---

## PROBLEMS

**4.1**   Consider a baseband bus with a number of equally spaced stations. As a fraction of the end-to-end propagation delay, what is the mean delay between stations? What is it for broadband bus? Now, rearrange the broadband bus into a tree with N rays emanating from the headend; what is the mean delay?

**4.2**   Give examples of appropriate applications of the broadband dedicated service, and the switched service.

**4.3**   Consider a baseband bus with a number of equally spaced stations with a data rate of 10 Mbps and a bus length of 1 km. What is the average time to send a packet of 1000 bits to another station, measured from the beginning of transmission to the end of reception? Assume a propagation speed of 200 m/μs. If two stations begin to transmit at exactly the same time, their packets will interfere with each other. If each transmitting station monitors the bus during transmission, how long before it notices an interference, in seconds? In bit times?

**4.4** Repeat Problem 4.3 for a data rate of 1 Mbps.

**4.5** Repeat Problems 4.3 and 4.4 for broadband bus.

**4.6** Repeat Problems 4.3 and 4.4 for a broadband tree consisting of ten cables of length 100 m emanating from a headend.

**4.7** Reconsider Problem 3.6. Can a baseband bus following the IEEE 802 rules (500-m segments, maximum of four repeaters in a path) span the building? If so, what is the total cable length?

**4.8** Reconsider Problem 3.6 for a broadband tree. Can the total length be reduced compared to the broadband bus?

**4.9** Reconsider problem 3.6, but now assume that there are two rings, with a bridge on floor 5 and a ring wiring concentrator on each floor. The bridge and concentrators are located in closets along the vertical shaft.

**4.10** At a propagation speed of 200 m/μs, what is the effective length added to a ring by a bit delay at each repeater:
   **a.** At 1 Mbps?
   **b.** At 40 Mbps?

**4.11** System A consists of a single ring with 300 stations, one per repeater. System B consists of three 100-station rings linked by a bridge. If the probability of a link failure is $P_l$, a repeater failure is $P_r$, and a bridge failure is $P_b$, derive an expression for parts (a) through (d):
   **a.** Probability of failure of system A.
   **b.** Probability of complete failure of system B.
   **c.** Probability that a particular station will find the network unavailable, for systems A and B.
   **d.** Probability that any two stations, selected at random, will be unable to communicate, for systems A and B.
   **e.** Compute values for 4a through 4d for $P_l = P_b = P_r = 10^{-2}$.

**4.12** Consider two rings of 100 stations each joined by a bridge. The data rate on each link is 10 Mbps. Each station generates data at a rate of ten packets of 2000 bits each per second. Let $F$ be the fraction of packets on each ring destined for the other. What is the minimum throughput of the bridge required to keep up?

# Local Area Networks: Protocols

The preceding chapter examined some key issues relating to the architecture and physical properties of LANs. Because of its scope and importance, the subject of communications architecture or protocols was deferred and is presented here in its own chapter.

This chapter begins with an overall discussion of LAN protocols, and seeks to determine what layers of functionality are required. Then the specific areas of link control and medium access control are explored. Throughout, reference is made to the IEEE 802 standard. This is for two reasons:

- The standard is well thought out, providing a framework for exposing and clarifying LAN communication architectural issues.

- The standard will heavily influence forthcoming LAN products.

A brief rationale and summary of the IEEE 802 standard is contained in an appendix to this chapter. A second appendix introduces another LAN standard, MIL-STD-1553.

## LAN PROTOCOLS

### A LAN Reference Model

Chapter 2 summarized an architecture for communications, the OSI reference model, based on seven layers of protocols. We saw in that discussion (see Figure 2.15) that layers 1 through 3 were required for the functioning of a packet-switched network. To recall, these layers were described as follows:

1. *Physical layer:* concerned with transmission of unstructured bit stream over physical link. Involves such parameters as signal voltage swing and bit duration. Deals with the mechanical, electrical, and procedural characteristics to establish, maintain, and deactivate the physical link.
2. *Data link layer:* converts unreliable transmission channel into reliable one. Sends blocks of data (frames) with checksum. Uses error detection and frame acknowledgment.
3. *Network layer:* transmits packets of data through a network. Packets may be independent (datagram) or traverse a preestablished network connection (virtual circuit). Responsible for routing and congestion control.

We now turn to the question of what layers are required for the proper operation of the LAN. For the sake of clarity, we examine the question in the context of the OSI reference model. Two characteristics of LANs are important in this context. First, data are transmitted in addressed frames. Second, there is no intermediate switching, hence no routing required (repeaters are used in rings and may be used in baseband bus LANs, but do not involve switching or routing). One exception to the second characteristic is the ring bridge. A discussion of that and other exceptions is deferred until Chapter 11.

These two characteristics essentially determine the answer to the question: What OSI layers are needed? Layer 1, certainly. Physical connection is required. Layer 2 is also needed. Data transmitted across the LAN must be organized into frames and control must be exercised. But what about layer 3? The answer is yes and no. If we look at the functions performed by layer 3, the answer would seem to be no. First, there is routing. With a direct link available between any two points, this is not needed. The other functions—addressing, sequencing, flow control, error control, and so on—are, we learned, also performed by layer 2. The difference is that layer 2 performs these functions across a single link, whereas layer 3 may perform them across the sequence of links required to traverse the network. But since only one link is required to traverse the LAN, these layer 3 functions are redundant and superfluous!

From the point of view of an attached device, the answer would seem to be yes, the LAN must provide layer 3. The device sees itself attached to an access point into a network supporting communication with multiple devices. The layer for assuring that a message sent across that access point is delivered to one of a number of end points would seem to be a layer 3 function. So we can say that although the network provides services up through layer 3, the characteristics of the network allow these services to be implemented on two OSI layers. We shall explore this topic more fully in Chapter 8. For the purpose of this chapter it is sufficient to understand that the minimum essential communications functions that must be performed by the LAN correspond to layers 1 and 2 of the OSI model.

With the points above in mind, let us now think about the functional requirements for controlling a local network and examine these from the top down. We follow the reasoning, illustrated in Figure 5.1, used by the IEEE 802 committee [IEEE82, App. E].

At the highest level are the functions associated with accepting transmissions from and delivering receptions to attached stations. These functions include:

- Provide one or more service access points. A service access point (SAP), recall, is a logical interface between two adjacent layers.
- On transmission, assemble data into a frame with address and CRC fields.
- On reception, disassemble frame, perform address recognition and CRC validation.
- Manage communication over the link.

These are the functions typically associated with layer 2, the data link layer. The first three, and related functions, are grouped into a logical link control (LLC) layer by IEEE 802. The last function is treated as a separate layer, called *medium access control* (MAC). This is done for the following reasons:

- The logic required to manage access to a multiple-source, multiple-destination link is not found in traditional layer 2 link control.

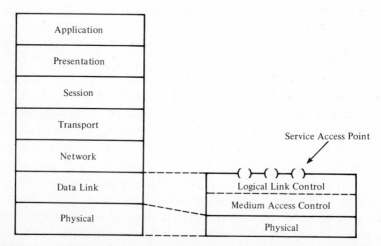

**FIGURE 5–1. LAN Protocol Layers Compared to OSI (From [IEEE82, App. E])**

• For the same LLC, several MAC options may be provided, as we shall see.

Finally, at the lowest layer, are the functions generally associated with the physical layer. These include:

• Encoding/decoding of signals
• Preamble generation/removal (for synchronization)
• Bit transmission/reception

As with the OSI model, these functions are assigned to a physical layer in the IEEE 802 standard.

In the remainder of this section, we touch briefly on two aspects of LAN protocols. First, since the MAC layer is not found in the traditional OSI model, and to provide a context for later discussions, the characteristics and types of medium access control techniques are discussed. Then the structure for LAN frames is discussed briefly, using the IEEE 802 standard as an example.

We are then prepared to get more specific about LAN protocols. Section 5.2 discusses link control. Sections 5.3 and 5.4 provide details for various LAN medium access control techniques. Physical layer functions were discussed in Chapter 4.

## Medium Access Control for Local Networks

All local networks (LAN, HSLN, CBX) consist of collections of devices that must share the network's transmission capacity. Some means of controlling access to the transmission medium is needed so that, when required, two particular devices can exchange data.

The key parameters in any medium access control technique are where and how. "Where" refers to centralized or distributed. A centralized scheme has certain advantages, such as:

• It may afford greater control over access for providing such things as priorities, overrides, and guaranteed bandwidth.
• It allows the logic at each station to be as simple as possible.
• It avoids problems of coordination.

Its principal disadvantages include:

• It results in a single point of failure.
• It may act as a bottleneck, reducing efficiency.

The pros and cons for distributed control are mirror images of the points made above.

The second parameter, how, is constrained by the topology and is a trade-off among competing factors: cost, performance, and complexity.

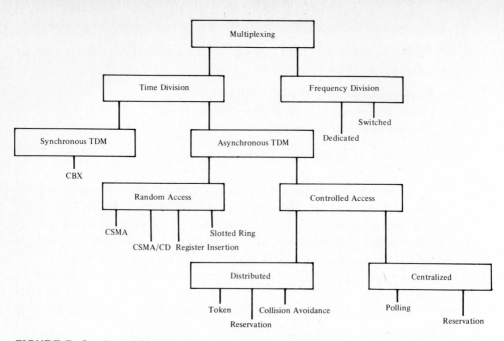

**FIGURE 5—2. Local Network Access Control Schemes**

Figure 5.2 categorizes the most common access control techniques used for local networks. In all cases, multiple data transfers share a single transmission capacity. This always implies some sort of multiplexing, either in the time or the frequency domain. The dedicated and switched services on a broadband network, discussed earlier, are examples of frequency division multiplexing. In fact, any technique on a multiple-channel broadband system is by definition based on FDM. Within a single channel, however, some other form of multiplexing may be required.

In the time domain, synchronous TDM, using circuit switching, is employed by the CBX. This is discussed in Chapter 7. All other TDM techniques of interest are asynchronous; that is, stations are not assigned regular, repetitive time slots. Access to the medium using asynchronous TDM may be random, that is, stations attempt to access the medium at will and at random times, or regulated, that is, some algorithm is used to regulate the sequence and time of station access. The random access category includes two common bus techniques, CSMA and CSMA/CD, and two common ring techniques, register insertion and slotted ring. All of these are discussed later in this chapter. Regulated access techniques can be categorized accordingly as the control is centralized or distributed. Both token bus and token ring, described later in this chapter, are examples of distributed techniques. Distributed reservation has been proposed for HSLNs and is discussed in Chapter 6. That chapter also includes a discussion of collision avoidance, the technique currently used for HSLN systems. Finally, centralized techniques include centralized reservation, discussed in Section 5.3, and polling, a technique commonly used on multidrop lines.

### IEEE 802 Frame Format

This section presents the formats used for frames in the IEEE 802 standard. These formats are similar to those used by most proprietary networks. They are the basis for the LLC, MAC, and physical layer functionality.

At this point it is worth reviewing the HDLC format presented in Chapter 2. The requirements for a local network frame are very similar. There must, of course, be a data or information field. A control field is needed to pass control bits and identify frame type. Starting and ending patterns are usually required to serve as delimiters. Addressing is required. Here is the main difference. Because LAN links are multiple-source, multiple-destination, both source and destination addresses are required. Further, unlike HDLC and virtually all other layer 2 protocols, the IEEE 802 LAN protocols support a form of multiplexing common in layer 3 protocols. As we shall see, this is accomplished in IEEE 802 by identifying service access points at each station.

Figure 5.3 shows the IEEE 802 formats. As can be seen, a separate format is used at the LLC level, and this is then embedded in the appropriate MAC frame. IEEE 802 supports three MAC alternatives: CSMA/CD, token bus, and token ring.

The individual fields will be described in the appropriate section, but one aspect is worth commenting on here: The address information has been split between the LLC frame and the MAC frame. This has been done for the following reason. The source and destination access points need be known only at the LLC level, in order to transfer data to and from attached stations. However, as we shall see, the source and destination addresses are a critical part of the MAC function.

## 5.2

---

# LINK LAYER PROTOCOL FOR LANS

In this section we look first at the general link level requirements for a local area network, then examine the IEEE 802 specification.

### Principles

The link layers for LANs should bear some resemblance to the more common link layers extant. Like all link layers, the LAN link layer is concerned with

Logical Link Control (LLC)

| 1 | 1 | 1 | N | bytes or octets |
|---|---|---|---|---|
| DSAP | SSAP | Control | DATA | |

CSMA/CD

| 8 | 1 | 2, 6 | 2, 6 | 2 | 0–1500 | | 4 |
|---|---|---|---|---|---|---|---|
| Preamble | SFD | DA | SA | Length | LLC | PAD | FCS |

Token Bus

| $\geqslant 1$ | 1 | 1 | 2, 6 | 2, 6 | $\geqslant 0$ | 4 | 1 |
|---|---|---|---|---|---|---|---|
| Preamble | SD | FF | DA | SA | LLC | FCS | ED |

Token Ring

| 1 | 1 | 1 |
|---|---|---|
| SD | AC | ED |

| 1 | 1 | 1 | 6 | 6 | $\geqslant 0$ | 4 | 1 | 1 |
|---|---|---|---|---|---|---|---|---|
| SD | AC | FC | DA | SA | LLC | FCS | ED | FS |

AC   = Access Control
DA   = Destination Address
DSAP = Destination Service Access Point
ED   = Ending Delimiter
FC   = Frame Control
FCS  = Frame Check Sequence
FF   = Frame Format
FS   = Frame Status
SA   = Source Address
SD   = Starting Delimiter
SFD  = Start Frame Delimiter
SSAP = Source Service Access Point

**FIGURE 5–3.   IEEE 802 Frame Formats**

the transmission of a frame of data between two stations, with no intermediate switching nodes.

It differs from traditional link layers in three ways:

• It must support the multiaccess nature of the link (this differs from multidrop in that there is no primary node).
• It is relieved of some details of link access by the Medium Access Control (MAC) layer.
• It must provide some layer 3 functions.

Figure 5.4 will help clarify the requirements for the link layer. We consider two stations or systems that communicate via a LAN (bus or ring). Higher

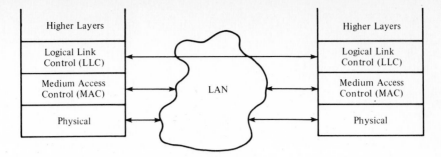

**FIGURE 5–4. LAN Communication Architecture**

layers (the equivalent of transport and above) provide end-to-end services between the stations. Below the link layer, a medium access control (MAC) layer provides the necessary logic for gaining access to the network for frame transmission and reception.

At a minimum, the link layer should perform those functions normally associated with that layer:

- *Error control:* End-to-end error control and acknowledgment. The link layer should guarantee error-free transmission across the LAN.
- *Flow control:* End-to-end flow control.

These functions can be provided in much the same way as for HDLC and other point-to-point link protocols—by the use of sequence numbers (NEXT and SEQ).

It has already been mentioned that because of the lack of intermediate switching nodes, a LAN does not require a separate layer 3; rather, the essential layer three functions can be incorporated into layer 2:

- *Datagram:* Some form of connectionless service is needed for efficient support of highly interactive traffic.
- *Virtual circuit:* A connection-oriented service is also usually needed.
- *Multiplexing:* Generally, a single physical link attaches a station to a LAN; it should be possible to provide data transfer with multiple end points over that link.

Because there is no need for routing, the above functions are easily provided. The datagram service simply requires the use of source and destination address fields, as discussed previously. The station sending the datagram must designate the destination address, so that the frame is delivered properly. The source address must also be indicated so that the recipient knows where the frame came from.

Both the virtual circuit and multiplexing capabilities can be supported with the concept of the service access point (SAP), introduced in Chapter 2. An example may make this clear. Figure 5.5 shows three stations attached to a LAN. Each station has an address. Further, the link layer supports multiple

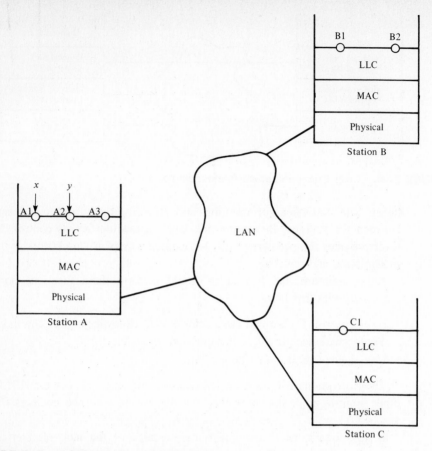

**FIGURE 5–5. LAN Link Control Scenario**

SAPs, each with its own address. The link layer provides communication between SAPs. Assume that a process or application X in station A wishes to send a message to a process in station C. X may be a report generator program in minicomputer A. C may be a printer and a simple printer driver. X attaches itself to SAP 1 and requests a connection to station C, SAP 1 (station C may have only one SAP if it is a single printer). Station A's link layer then sends to the LAN a "connection-request" frame which includes the source address (A,1), the destination address (C,1), and some control bits indicating that this is a connection request. The LAN delivers this frame to C, which, if it is free, returns a "connection-accepted" frame. Henceforth, all data from X will be assembled into a frame by A's LLC, which includes source (A,1) and destination (C,1) addresses. Incoming frames addressed to (A,1) will be rejected unless they are from (C,1); these might be acknowledgment frames, for example. Similarly, station C's printer is declared busy and C will only accept frames from (A,1).

Thus a connection-oriented service is provided. At the same time, process Y could attach to (A,2) and exchange data with (B,1). This is an example of multiplexing. In addition, various other processes in A could use (A,3) to send datagrams to various destinations.

One final function of the link layer should be included, to take advantage of the multiple access nature of the LAN:

• *Multicast, broadcast:* The link layer should provide a service of sending a message to multiple stations or all stations.

With these requirements in mind, we turn to the 802 specification.


## IEEE 802 Logical Link Control

The IEEE 802 Logical Link Control (LLC) is a good example of a LAN link control layer. It is well thought out, and offers a variety of services. This section summarizes the proposed features of LLC.

Figure 5.3 depicts the LLC frame. As can be seen, it specifies the source and destination service access points (thus allowing link multiplexing), a 1-byte control field, and a data field. The source and destination address fields are needed by the LLC, but are also used by MAC, and are included in the outer MAC frame. The LLC can be specified in three parts:

• The interface with the station, specifying the services that LLC (and hence the LAN) provides to the network subscriber.
• The LLC protocol, specifying the LLC functions.
• The interface with MAC, specifying the services that LLC requires to perform its function.

### LLC Services
LLC provides two services:

• *Unacknowledged connectionless service:* This is a datagram service that simply allows for sending and receiving frames. It supports point-to-point, multipoint, and broadcast.
• *Connection oriented service:* This provides a virtual-circuit-style connection between service access points. It provides flow control, sequencing, and error recovery.

Two additional services are currently under study:

• *Acknowledged connectionless service:* This is also a datagram service, but provides for acknowledgment, relieving higher layers of this burden. It also supports point-to-point, multipoint, and broadcast.
• *Management service:* This provides control functions.

These services are specified in terms of primitives which can be viewed as

**TABLE 5.1   Logical Link Control Primitives**

Unacknowledged connectionless service
  L-DATA.request
  L-DATA.indication

Connection-oriented service
  L-DATA-CONNECT.request
  L-DATA-CONNECT.indication
  L-DATA-CONNECT.confirm
  L-CONNECT.request
  L-CONNECT.indication
  L-CONNECT.confirm
  L-DISCONNECT.request
  L-DISCONNECT.indication
  L-DISCONNECT.confirm
  L-RESET.request
  L-RESET.indication
  L-RESET.confirm
  L-CONNECTION-FLOWCONTROL.request
  L-CONNECTION-FLOWCONTROL.indication

commands or procedure calls with parameters. Table 5.1 summarizes the LLC primitives.

The Unacknowledged Connectionless Service provides for only two primitives across the interface between the next highest layer and LLC (not counting management service primitives). L-DATA.request is used to pass a frame to LLC for transmission. L-DATA.indication is used to pass a frame up from LLC upon reception.

The Connection Oriented Service includes L-DATA-CONNECT.request and L-DATA-CONNECT.indication, with meanings analagous to those above, plus L-DATA-CONNECT.confirm, which conveys the result (acknowledged, failure) of the previous associated L-DATA-CONNECT.request. In addition a station, through an SAP, must be able to establish and tear down a connection and receive an acknowledgment of this action from the remote SAP. The primitives that accomplish these tasks are L-CONNECT.request, L-CONNECT.indication, L-CONNECT.confirm, L-DISCONNECT.request, L-DISCONNECT.indication, and L-DISCONNECT.confirm. In addition, link resetting and flow control are provided with L-RESET.request, L-RESET.indication, L-RESET.confirm, L-CONNECTION-FLOWCONTROL.request, and L-CONNECTION-FLOWCONTROL.indication.

The next two categories of service are, at the time of this writing, still under study. The current version of the draft standard does not discuss them, but an earlier draft did propose specific primitives. These are included here to give an idea of what could be done.

For the Acknowledged Connectionless Service, L-DATA-ACK.request and

L-DATA-ACK.indication correspond to the commands for the unacknowledged service. In addition, there is an L-DATA-ACK.confirm.

Finally, there are a variety of management service commands. First, to regulate the flow of data and control frames between the LLC and its higher layer, there are L-SAP-FLOWCONTROL.request and L-SAP-FLOWCON-TROL.indication. Various test and status data may be requested by the higher layer; the appropriate primitives are L-TEST.request, L-TEST.indication, L-STATUS.request, L-STATUS.confirm, and L-STATUS.indication. Finally, the higher layer (and therefore the station) must be able to activate and deactivate SAPs and activate and deactivate the entire node from the LAN. The primitives are L-SAP-ACTIVATE.request, L-SAP-ACTIVATE.confirm, L-SAP-DEACTIVATE.request, L-SAP-DEACTIVATE.confirm, L-SAP-DEACTIVATE.indication, L-LAYER-ACTIVATE.request, L-LAYER-ACTI-VATE.confirm, L-LAYER-DEACTIVATE.request, L-LAYER-DEACTI-VATE.confirm, and L-LAYER-DEACTIVATE.indication.

## LLC Protocol

The LLC protocol is modeled after the HDLC balanced mode, and has similar formats and functions. These are summarized briefly in this section. The reader should be able to see how this protocol supports the LLC services defined above.

First are the address fields. Both the DSAP and SSAP fields actually contain 7-bit addresses. The least significant bit of DSAP indicates whether this is an individual or group address. The least significant bit of SSAP indicates whether this is a command or response frame.

Figure 5.6 shows the format for the LLC control field (compare Figure 2.13).

LLC PDU Control Field Bits

| | 1 | 2 | 3 | 4 | 5 | 6 | 7 | 8 |
|---|---|---|---|---|---|---|---|---|
| Information Transfer Command/Response (I-Format PDU) | 0 | | N(S) | | P/F | | N(R) | |
| Supervisory Commands/Responses (S-Format PDUs) | 1 | 0 | S | S | P/F | | N(R) | |
| Unnumbered Commands/Responses (U-Format PDUs) | 1 | 1 | M | M | P/F | M | M | M |

where
N(S) = Transmitter send sequence number (Bit 2 = low-order bit)
N(R) = Transmitter receive sequence number (Bit 6 = low-order bit)
S    = Supervisory function bit
M    = Modifier function bit
P/F  = Poll bit - command LLC PDU transmissions
       Final bit - response LLC PDU transmissions
       (1 = Poll/Final)

**FIGURE 5—6.  IEEE 802 Control Field Format**

Three types of frames are defined: information transfer, supervisory, and unnumbered. The information transfer frames are used to send data (as opposed to control information). N(S) and N(R) are frame sequence numbers that support error control and flow control. A station sending a sequence of frames will number them, modulo 8, and place the number in N(S). N(R) is a piggybacked acknowledgment. It enables the sending station to indicate which number frame it expects to receive next. These numbers support flow control since, after sending seven frames without an acknowledgment, a station can send no more. The numbers support error control, as explained below. The P/F field is set to 1 only on the last frame in a series, to indicate that the transmission is over.

The supervisory frame is used for acknowledgment and flow control. The 2-bit SS field is used to indicate one of three commands: Receive Ready (RR), Receive Not Ready (RNR), and Reject (REJ). RR is used to acknowledge the last frame received by indicating in N(R) the next frame expected. This frame is used when there is no reverse traffic to carry a piggybacked acknowledgment. RNR acknowledges a frame, as with RR, but also asks the transmitting station to suspend transmission. When the receiving station is again ready, it sends an RR frame. REJ is used to indicate that the frame with number N(R) is rejected and must be sent again.

Unnumbered frames are used for connectionless information transfer and control purpose. The bit pattern defines one of the following commands:

- UI (unnumbered information): used to send a connectionless data frame.
- SABM (set asynchronous balanced mode): used by a station
  to request logical connection with another station.
- DISC (disconnect): used to terminate a logical connection; the sending station is announcing that it is suspending operations.
- XID (exchange identification): used to convey station class (Class I, only connectionless; Class II, connection-oriented and connectionless, plus window size).
- TEST (test): used to request a TEST frame in response, to test the LLC-to-LLC path.

The foregoing frames are all commands, initiated by a station at will. The following frames are responses:

- UA (unnumbered acknowledgment): used to acknowledge SABM and DISC commands.
- DM (disconnected mode): used to respond to a frame in order to indicate that the station's LLC is logically disconnected.
- FRMR (frame reject): used to indicate that an improper frame has arrived—one that somehow violates the protocol.
- XID (exchange identification): response to XID command. Also used to set window to 7 or less.
- TEST (test): response to Test Command.

The P/F bit is used to indicate that a response is requested to a command frame.

### LLC—MAC Interface

The IEEE 802 LLC is intended to operate with any of the three MAC protocols (CSMA/CD, token bus, token ring). A single logical interface to any of the MAC layers is defined. The 802 standard does not define an explicit interface, but provides a "model." The basic primitives are:

- MA-DATA.request: to request transfer of an LLC frame from local LLC to destination LLC. This includes information transfer, supervisory, and unnumbered frames.
- MA-DATA.confirm: response from local MAC layer to LLC's MA-DATA.request. It indicates the success or failure of the request, but has only *local* significance (i.e., it is not an end-to-end acknowledgment).
- MA-DATA.indicate: to transfer incoming LLC frame from local MAC to local LLC.

## 5.3

# MEDIUM ACCESS CONTROL – BUS/TREE

Of all the local network topologies, the bus/tree topologies present the greatest challenges, and the most options, for medium access control. This section will not attempt to survey the many techniques that have been proposed; good discussions can be found in [LUCZ79] and [FRAN81]. Rather, emphasis is placed on the two techniques that seem likely to dominate the marketplace: CSMA/CD and token bus. Preliminary standards for these techniques have been developed by the IEEE 802 committee.

A third technique, centralized reservation, is reviewed briefly. This is for the sake of completeness; virtually all access techniques for bus/tree are related to one of these three techniques.

Table 5.2 compares the three techniques on a number of characteristics. The ensuing discussion should clarify their significance.

### CSMA/CD

The most commonly used medium access control technique for bus/tree topologies is carrier sense multiple access with collision detection (CSMA/CD). The original baseband version of this technique was developed and patented by Xerox [METC77] as part of its Ethernet local network [METC76]. The original broadband version was developed and patented by MITRE [HOPK80] as part of its MITREnet local network [ROMA77, HOPP77].

**TABLE 5.2  Bus/Tree Access Methods**

|                        | CSMA/CD                                   | Token Bus             | Centralized Reservation          |
|------------------------|-------------------------------------------|-----------------------|----------------------------------|
| Access determination   | Contention                                | Token                 | Reservation                      |
| Packet length restriction | Greater than twofold propagation delay | None                  | No greater than slot size        |
| Principal advantage    | Simplicity                                | Regulated/fair access | Regulated/fair access            |
| Principal disadvantage | Performance under heavy load              | Complexity            | Requires central controller      |

Before examining this technique, we look at some earlier schemes from which CSMA/CD evolved.

### Precursors

All of the techniques discussed in this section, including CSMA/CD, can be termed *random access* or *contention* techniques. They are designed to address the problem of how to share a common broadcast transmission medium—the "Who goes next?" problem. The techniques are random access in the sense that there is no predictable or scheduled time for any station to transmit; station transmissions occur randomly. They are contention in the sense that no control is exercised to determine whose turn it is—all stations must contend for time on the network.

The earliest of these techniques, known as *ALOHA*, was developed for ground-based packet radio broadcasting networks [ABRA70]. However, it is applicable to any transmission medium shared by uncoordinated users. ALOHA, or *pure ALOHA* as it is sometimes called, is a true free-for-all. Whenever a station has a frame to send, it does so. The station then listens for an amount of time equal to the maximum possible round-trip propagation time on the network (twice the time it takes to send a frame between the two most widely separated stations). If the station hears an acknowledgment during that time, fine; otherwise, it resends the frame. After repeated failures, it gives up. A receiving station determines the correctness of an incoming frame by examining the checksum. If the frame is valid, the station acknowledges immediately. The frame may be invalid, due to noise on the channel or because another station transmitted a frame at about the same time. In the latter case, the two frames may interfere with each other so that neither gets through; this is known as a *collision*. In that case, the receiving station simply ignores the frame. ALOHA is as simple as can be, and pays a penalty for it. Because the number of collisions rises so rapidly with increased load, the maximum utilization of the channel is only about 18%.

To improve efficiency, a modification of ALOHA [ROBE75] was developed in which time on the channel is organized into uniform slots whose size equals the frame transmission time. Some central clock or other technique is needed to synchronize all stations. Transmission is permitted only to begin at a slot boundary. Thus frames that do overlap will do so totally. This increases the maximum utilization of the system to about 37%. The scheme is known as *slotted ALOHA*.

Both ALOHA and slotted ALOHA are well suited to packet satellite systems, in which the propagation delay between stations is significant compared to frame transmission time. It is hard to see how one could do better for random access over such distances. However, for the smaller distances, found in bus/tree topologies, greater efficiencies can be achieved. Consider the following observations. If the station-to-station propagation time is large compared to the frame transmission time, then, after a station launches a frame, it will be a long time before other stations know about it. During that time, one of the other stations may transmit a frame; the two frames may interfere with each other, and neither gets through. Indeed, if the distances are great enough, many stations may begin transmitting, one after the other, and none of their frames gets through unscathed. Suppose, however, that the propagation time is extremely small compared to frame transmission time. In that case, when a station launches a frame, all the other stations know it almost immediately. So, if they had any sense, they would not try transmitting until the first station was done. Collisions would be rare since they would occur only when two stations began to transmit almost simultaneously. Another way of looking at it is that the short delay time provides the stations with better feedback about the state of the system; this information can be used to improve efficiency.

The foregoing observations led to the development of a technique known as carrier sense multiple access (CSMA) or listen before talk (LBT). A station wishing to transmit first listens to the medium to determine if another transmission is in progress. If the medium is idle, the station may transmit. Otherwise, the station backs off some period of time and tries again, using one of the algorithms explained below. After transmitting, a station waits a reasonable amount of time for an acknowledgment, taking into account the maximum round-trip propagation delay, and the fact that the acknowledging station must also contend for the channel in order to respond.

One can see how this strategy would be effective for systems in which the frame transmission time is much longer than the propagation time. Collisions can occur only when more than one user begins transmitting within a short time (within the period of propagation delay). If a station begins to transmit, and there are no collisions during the time it takes for the leading edge of the frame to propagate to the farthest station, then the station has seized the channel and the remainder of the frame will be transmitted without collision.

Maximum utilization achievable using CSMA can far exceed ALOHA or slotted ALOHA. The maximum utilization depends on the length of the frame and on the propagation time; the longer the frames or the shorter the propagation time, the higher the utilization. This subject will be explored in Chapter 9.

With CSMA, an algorithm is needed to specify what a station should do if the medium is found to be busy. Three approaches are depicted in Figure 5.7. One algorithm is *nonpersistent* CSMA. A station wishing to transmit listens to the medium and obeys the following rules:

1. If the medium is idle, transmit.
2. If the medium is busy, wait an amount of time drawn from a probability distribution (the retransmission delay) and repeat step 1.

The use of random retransmission times reduces the probability of collisions. The drawback is that even if several stations have a frame to send, there is likely to be some wasted idle time following a prior transmission.

To avoid channel idle time, the *1-persistent protocol* can be used. A station wishing to transmit listens to the medium and obeys the following rules:

1. If the medium is idle, transmit.
2. If the medium is busy, continue to listen until the channel is sensed idle; then transmit immediately.
3. If there is a collision (determined by a lack of acknowledgment), wait a random amount of time and repeat step 1.

Whereas nonpersistent stations are deferential, 1-persistent stations are selfish. If two or more stations are waiting to transmit, a collision is guaranteed. Things only get sorted out after the collision.

A compromise that attempts to reduce collisions, like nonpersistent, and reduce idle time, like 1-persistent, is *p-persistent*. The rules are:

1. If the medium is idle, transmit with probability $p$, and delay one time unit

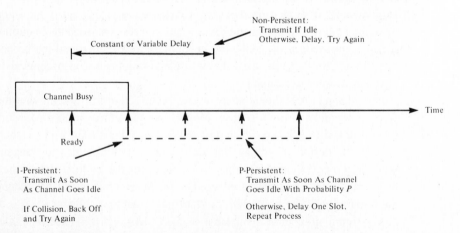

**FIGURE 5—7. CSMA Persistence and Back-off**

with probability $(1-p)$. The time unit is typically equal to the maximum propagation delay.

2. If the medium is busy, continue to listen until the channel is idle and repeat step 1.
3. If transmission is delayed one time unit, repeat step 1.

The question arises as to what is an effective value of $p$. The main problem to avoid is one of instability under heavy load. Consider the case in which $n$ stations have frames to send while a transmission is taking place. At the end of that transmission, the expected number of stations that will attempt to transmit is $np$. If $np$ is greater than 1, multiple stations will attempt to transmit and there will be a collision. What is more, as soon as all these stations realize that they did not get through, they will be back again, almost guaranteeing more collisions. Worse yet, these retries will compete with new transmissions from other stations, further increasing the probability of collision. Eventually, all stations will be trying to send, causing continuous collisions, with throughput dropping to zero. To avoid this catastrophe $np$ must be less than one for the expected peaks of $n$. As $p$ is made smaller, stations must wait longer to attempt transmission but collisions are reduced. At low loads, however, stations have unnecessarily long delays.

### Description of CSMA/CD

All of the techniques described above could be used in a bus/tree topology with an electrical conductor medium or in a packet radio scheme. We now introduce *carrier sense multiple access with collision detection* (CSMA/CD), which, because of the CD part, is appropriate only for a bus/tree topology [it is also referred to as *listen while talk* (LWT)]. CSMA/CD can be used with either baseband or broadband systems. Where details differ between baseband and broadband, we will use Ethernet and MITREnet as examples for comparison.

CSMA, although more efficient than ALOHA or slotted ALOHA, still has one glaring inefficiency. When two frames collide, the medium remains unusable for the duration of transmission of both damaged frames. For long frames, compared to propagation time, the amount of wasted bandwidth can be considerable. This waste can be reduced if a station continues to listen to the medium while it is transmitting. In that case, these rules can be added to the CSMA rules:

1. If a collision is detected during transmission, immediately cease transmitting the frame, and transmit a brief jamming signal to assure that all stations know that there has been a collision.
2. After transmitting the jamming signal, wait a random amount of time, then attempt to transmit again using CSMA.

Now the amount of wasted bandwidth is reduced to the time it takes to detect a collision. Question: How long does that take? Figure 5.8 illustrates the answer

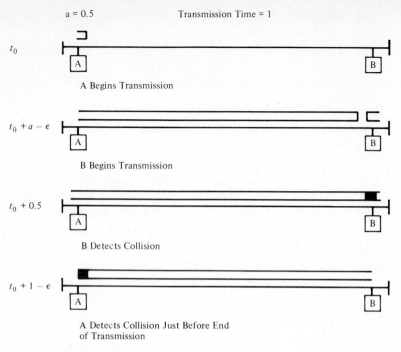

$t_0$

A

B

A Begins Transmission

$t_0 + a - \epsilon$

A

B

B Begins Transmission

$t_0 + 0.5$

A

B

B Detects Collision

$t_0 + 1 - \epsilon$

A

B

A Detects Collision Just Before End
of Transmission

**FIGURE 5–8.   Baseband Collision Detection Timing**

for a baseband system. Consider the worst case of two stations that are as far apart as possible. As can be seen, the amount of time it takes to detect a collision is twice the propagation delay. For broadband bus, the wait is even longer. Figure 5.9 showed a dual-cable system. This time, worst case is two stations close together and as far as possible from the head end. In this case the time required to detect a collision is four times the propagation delay from the station to the head end. The results would be the same for a midsplit system.

Both figures indicate the use of frames long enough to allow CD prior to the end of transmission. In most systems that use CSMA/CD, it is required that all frames be at least this long. Otherwise, the performance of the system is the same as the less efficient CSMA protocol, since collisions are detected only after transmission is complete.

Now let us look at a few details of CSMA/CD. First, which persistence algorithm should we use: non-, 1-, or p-? You may be surprised to learn that the most common choice is 1-persistent. It is used by both Ethernet and MITREnet, and in the IEEE 802 standard. Recall that both nonpersistent and p-persistent have performance problems. In the nonpersistent case, capacity is wasted because the medium will generally remain idle following the end of a transmission even if there are stations waiting to send. In the p-persistent case, $p$ must be set low enough to avoid instability, with the result of sometimes atrocious delays under light load. The 1-persistent algorithm, which after all means $p = 1$, would seem to be even more unstable than p-persistent due to

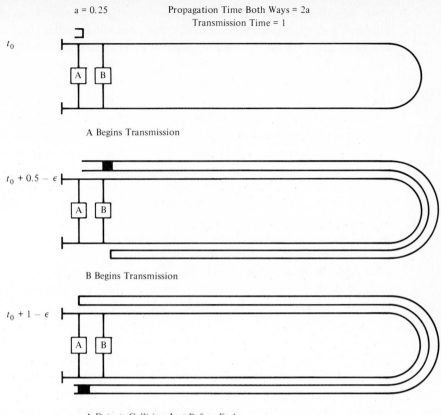

a = 0.25

Propagation Time Both Ways = 2a
Transmission Time = 1

$t_0$

A Begins Transmission

$t_0 + 0.5 - \epsilon$

B Begins Transmission

$t_0 + 1 - \epsilon$

A Detects Collision Just Before End
of Transmission

**FIGURE 5–9.   Broadband Collision Detection Timing**

the greed of the stations. What saves the day is that the wasted time due to collisions is mercifully short (if the frames are long relative to propagation delay!), and with random backoff, the two stations involved in a collision are unlikely to collide on their next tries. To ensure that back-off maintains stability, Ethernet uses a technique known as binary exponential back-off. A station will attempt to transmit repeatedly in the face of repeated collisions, but after each collision, the mean value of the random delay is doubled. After 16 unsuccessful attempts, the station gives up and reports an error.

The beauty of the 1-persistent algorithm with binary exponential back-off is that it is efficient over a wide range of loads. At low loads, 1-persistence guarantees that a station can seize the channel as soon as it goes idle, in contrast to the non- and p-persistent schemes. At high loads, it is at least as stable as the other techniques. However, one unfortunate effect of the Ethernet back-off algorithm is that it has a last-in, first-out effect; stations with no or few collisions will have a chance to transmit before stations that have waited longer.

Although CSMA/CD is substantially the same for baseband and broadband, there are differences. One example is the means for performing carrier sense. For baseband systems using Manchester phase encoding, carrier is conveniently sensed by detecting the presence of transitions on the channel. Strictly speaking, there is no carrier to sense with digital signaling; the term was borrowed from the radio lexicon. With broadband, carrier sense is indeed performed. The station's receiver listens for the presence of a carrier on the outbound channel.

Collision detection also differs for the two systems. In a baseband system, a collision should produce substantially higher voltage swings than those produced by a single transmitter. Accordingly, Ethernet dictates that a transmitting transceiver will detect a collision if the signal on the cable at the transceiver exceeds the maximum that could be produced by the transceiver alone. Because a transmitted signal attenuates as it propagates, there is a potential problem with collision detection. If two stations far apart are transmitting, each station will receive a greatly attenuated signal from the other. The signal strength could be so small that when it is added to the transmitted signal at the transceiver, the combined signal does not exceed the CD threshold. For this reason, among others, Ethernet restricts the maximum length of cable to 500 m. Because frames may cross repeater boundaries, collisions must cross as well. Hence if a repeater detects a collision on either cable, it must transmit a jamming signal on the other side. Since the collision may not involve a transmission from the repeater, the CD threshold is different for a nontransmitting transceiver: A collision is detected if the signal strength exceeds that which could be produced by two transceiver outputs in the worst case.

There are several possible approaches to collision detection in broadband systems. The most common of these is to perform a bit-by-bit comparison between transmitted and received data. When a station transmits on the inbound channel, it begins to hear its own transmission on the outbound channel after a propagation delay to the headend and back. In the MITRE system, the first 16 bits of the transmitted and received signals are compared, and a collision is assumed if they differ. There are several problems with this approach. The most serious is the danger that differences in signal level between colliding signals will cause the receiver to treat the weaker signal as noise and fail to detect a collision. The cable system, with its taps, splitters, and amplifiers, must be carefully tuned so that attenuation effects and differences in transmitter signal strength do not cause this problem. Another problem, for dual cable systems, is that a station must simultaneously transmit and receive on the same frequency. Its two RF modems must be carefully shielded to prevent crosstalk.

An alternative approach for broadband is to perform the CD function at the headend. This is most appropriate for the midsplit system, which has an active component at the headend anyway. This reduces the tuning problem to one of making sure that all stations produce approximately the same signal level at the headend. The headend would detect collisions by looking for garbled data or higher-than-expected signal strength.

### IEEE 802 CSMA/CD

The IEEE 802 CSMA/CD standard is very close to that of Ethernet. Indeed, most of the differences between the two were resolved prior to the latest issuance of the standard and many observers expect the two schemes to merge, due to changes in one or the other.

Figure 5.3 shows the MAC CSMA/CD frame structure. The individual fields are as follows:

- *Preamble:* an 8-byte pattern used by the receiver to establish bit synchronization and then locate the first bit of the frame.
- *Start frame delimiter (SFD):* indicates the start of a frame.
- *Destination address (DA):* specifies the station(s) for which the frame is intended. It may be a unique physical address (one destination transceiver), a multicast-group address (a group of stations), or a global address (all stations on the local network).
- *Source address (SA):* specifies the station that sent the frame.
- *Length:* specifies the number of LLC bytes that follow.
- *LLC:* field prepared at the LLC level.
- *Pad:* a sequence of bytes added to assure that the frame is long enough for proper CD operation.
- *Frame check sequence (FCS):* a 32-bit cyclic redundancy check value. Based on all fields, starting with destination address.

### Token Bus

This is a relatively new technique for controlling access to a broadcast medium, inspired by the token ring technique discussed later. We will first provide a general description, then look at some of the IEEE 802 details.

#### Description

The token bus technique is more complex than CSMA/CD. For this technique, the stations on the bus or tree form a logical ring; that is, the stations are assigned logical positions in an ordered sequence, with the last member of the sequence followed by the first. Each station knows the identity of the stations preceding and following it. The physical ordering of the stations on the bus is irrelevant and independent of the logical ordering (Figure 5.10).

A control frame known as the *token* regulates the right of access. The token frame contains a destination address. The station receiving the token is granted control of the medium for a specified time. The station may transmit one or more frames and may poll stations and receive responses. When the station is done, or time has expired, it passes the token on to the next station in logical sequence. This station now has permission to transmit. Hence steady-state

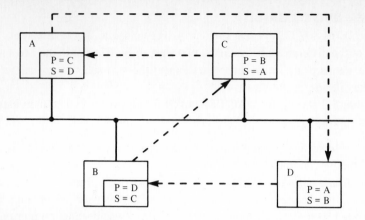

**FIGURE 5–10. Token Bus**

operation consists of alternating data transfer and token transfer phases. Non-token-using stations are allowed on the bus. These stations can only respond to polls or requests for acknowledgment.

This scheme requires considerable maintenance. The following functions, at a minimum, must be performed by one or more stations on the bus:

- *Ring initialization:* When the network is started up, or after the logical ring has broken down, it must be initialized. Some cooperative, decentralized algorithm is needed to sort out who goes first, who goes second, and so on.
- *Addition to ring:* Periodically, nonparticipating stations must be granted the opportunity to insert themselves in the ring.
- *Deletion from ring:* A station must be able to remove itself from the ring by splicing together its predecessor and successor.
- *Recovery:* A number of errors can occur. These include duplicate address (two stations think it is their turn) and broken ring (no station thinks that it is its turn).

### IEEE 802 Token Bus

The IEEE 802 token bus protocol follows the general principles outlined above. In general, token-passing and data-passing phases alternate.

Figure 5.3 shows the MAC frame structure for token bus. The individual fields are as follows:

- *Preamble:* a one or more byte pattern used by receivers to establish bit synchronization and locate the first bit of the frame.
- *Start delimiter (SD):* indicates start of frame.
- *Frame format (FF):* indicates whether this is an LLC data frame. If not, bits in this field control operation of the token bus MAC protocol. An example is a token frame.
- *Destination address (DA):* as with CSMA/CD.
- *Source address (SA):* as with CSMA/CD.

- *LLC:* field prepared by LLC.
- *Frame check sequence (FCS):* as with CSMA/CD.
- *End delimiter (ED):* indicates end of frame.

The details of the protocol can be grouped into the following categories, which will be considered in turn:

- Addition of a node
- Deletion of a node
- Fault management by token holder
- Ring initialization
- Classes of service

First, let us consider how *addition of a node* is accomplished, using a controlled contention process called *response windows*. Each node in the ring has the responsibility of periodically granting an opportunity for new nodes to enter the ring. While holding the token, the node issues a *solicit-successor* frame, inviting nodes with an address between itself and the next node in logical sequence to demand entrance. The transmitting node then waits for one response window or slot time (equal to twice the end-to-end propagation delay of the medium). Three events can occur.

1. *No response:* Nobody wants in. The token holder transfers the token to its successor as usual.
2. *One response:* One node issues a *set-successor* frame. The token holder sets its successor node to be the requesting node and transmits the token to it. The requestor sets its linkages accordingly and proceeds.
3. *Multiple responses:* The token holder will detect a garbled response if more than one node demands entrance. The conflict is resolved by an address-based contention scheme. The token holder transmits a *resolve-contention* frame and waits four demand windows. Each demander can respond in one of these windows based on the first two bits of its address. If a demander hears anything before its window comes up, it refrains from demanding. If the token-holder receives a valid set-successor frame, it is in business. Otherwise, it tries again, and only those nodes that responded the first time are allowed to respond this time, based on the second pair of bits in their address. This process continues until a valid set-successor frame is received, no response is received, or a maximum retry count is reached. In the latter two cases, the token holder gives up and passes the token.

*Deletion of a node* is much simpler. If a node wishes to drop out, it waits until it receives the token, then sends a set-successor frame to its predecessor, instructing it to splice to its successor. If a node fails, it will not pick up the token when the token is passed to it, and this will be detected by the token sender, as explained below.

*Fault management* by the token holder covers a number of contingencies (Table 5.3). First, while holding the token, a node may hear a frame indicating

**TABLE 5.3  Token Bus Error Handling**

| Condition | Action |
|---|---|
| Multiple token | Defer/drop to 1 or 0 |
| Unaccepted token | Retry |
| Failed station | "Who follows" process |
| Failed receiver | Drop out of ring |
| No token | Initialize after time-out |

that another node has the token. If so, it immediately drops the token by reverting to listener mode. In this way, the number of token holders drops immediately to 1 or 0, thus overcoming the multiple-token problem (which could be caused by two nodes having the same address). Upon completion of its turn, the token holder will issue a token frame to its successor. The successor should immediately issue a data or token frame. Therefore, after sending a token, the token issuer will listen for one slot time to make sure that its successor is active. This precipitates a sequence of events:

1. If the successor node is active, the token issuer will hear a valid frame and revert to listener mode.
2. If the issuer does not hear a valid frame, it reissues the token to the same successor one more time.
3. After two failures, the issuer assumes that its successor has failed and issues a *who-follows* frame, asking for the identity of the node that follows the failed node. The issuer should get back a set-successor frame from the second node down the line. If so, the issuer adjusts its linkage and issues a token (back to step 1).
4. If the issuing node gets no response to its who-follows frame, it tries again.
5. If the who-follows tactic fails, the node issues a solicit-successor frame with the full address range (i.e. every node is invited to respond). If this process works, a two-node ring is established and life goes on.
6. If two attempts of step 5 fail, the node assumes that a catastrophe has occurred; perhaps the node's receiver has failed. In any case, the node ceases activity and listens to the bus.

Logical *ring initialization* occurs when one or more stations detect a lack of bus activity of duration longer than a time-out value: the token has been lost. This can be due to a number of causes, such as the network has just been powered up, or a token-holding station fails. Once its time-out expires, a node will issue a *claim-token* frame. Contending claimants are resolved in a manner similar to the response-window process. Each claimant issues a claim-token frame padded by 0, 2, 4, or 6 slots based on the first two bits of its address. After transmission, a claimant listens to the medium and if it hears anything, drops its claim. Otherwise, it tries again, using the second pair of its address bits. The process repeats. With each iteration, only those stations who transmitted the longest on the previous iteration try again, using successive pairs of address bits. When all address bits have been used, a node that succeeds on the last iteration considers itself the token holder. The ring can now be rebuilt by the response window process described previously.

As an option, a token bus system can include *classes of service* that provide a mechanism of prioritizing access to the bus. Four classes of service are defined, in descending order:

- Synchronous (6)
- Asynchronous urgent (4)
- Asynchronous normal (2)
- Asynchronous time-available (0)

Any station may have data in one or more of these classes to send. The object is to allocate network bandwidth to the higher priority frames and only send lower priority frames when there is sufficient bandwidth. To explain, let us define the following variables:

- THT = token holding time: the maximum time that a station can hold the token to transmit class 6 (synchronous) data.
- TRT4 = token rotation time for class 4: maximum time that a token can take to circulate and still permit class 4 transmission.
- TRT2 = token rotation time for class 2: as above.
- TRT0 = token rotation time for class 0: as above.

When a station receives the token, it can transmit classes of data according to the following rules.

1. It may transmit class 6 data for a time THT. Hence for an $n$-station ring, during one circulation of the token, the maximum amount of time available for class 6 transmission is $n \times$ THT.
2. After transmitting class 6 data, or if there were no class 6 data to transmit, it may transmit class 4 data only if the amount of time for the last circulation of the token (including any class 6 data just sent) is less than TRT4.
3. The station may next send class 2 data only if the amount of time for the last circulation of the token (including any class 6 and 4 data just sent) is less than TRT2.
4. The station may next send class 0 data only if the amount of time for the last circulation of the token (including any class 6, 4, and 2 data just sent) is less than TRT0.

This scheme, within limits, gives preference to frames of higher priority. More definitively, it guarantees that class 6 data may have a certain portion of the bandwidth. Two cases are possible. If $n \times$ THT is greater than MAX[TRT4, TRT2, TRT0], the maximum possible token circulation time is $n \times$ THT, and

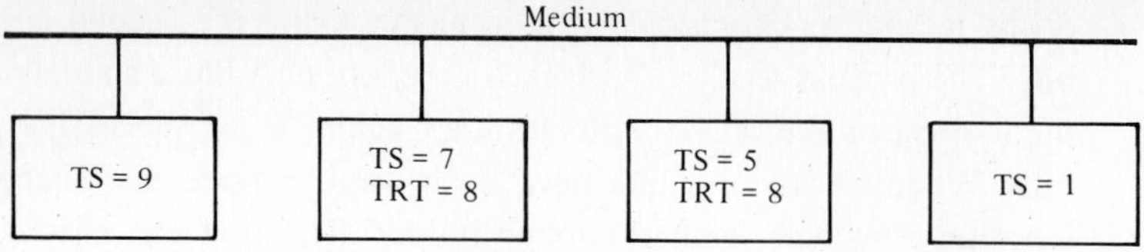

FIGURE 5–11. Operation of a Multiclass Token Bus Protocol

| Token Rot. | TS = 9 TRTC | XMIT | TS = 7 TRT = 8 TRTC | XMIT | TS = 5 TRT = 8 TRTC | XMIT | TS = 1 TRTC | XMIT |
|---|---|---|---|---|---|---|---|---|
| 1 | 0 | 3 | 3 | 5 | 8 | 0 | 8 | 3 |
| 2 | 11 | 3 | 11 | 0 | 6 | 2 | 8 | 3 |
| 3 | 8 | 3 | 8 | 0 | 8 | 0 | 6 | 3 |
| 4 | 6 | 3 | 6 | 2 | 8 | 0 | 8 | 3 |
| 5 | 8 | 3 | 8 | 0 | 6 | 2 | 8 | 3 |
| 6 | 8 | 3 | 8 | 0 | 8 | 0 | 6 | 3 |
| 7 | 6 | 3 | 6 | 2 | 8 | 0 | 8 | 3 |
| 8 | 8 | 3 | 8 | 0 | 6 | 2 | 8 | 1 |
| 9 | 6 | 3 | 6 | 2 | 8 | 0 | 6 | 1 |
| 10 | 6 | 3 | 6 | 2 | 6 | 2 | 8 | 1 |
| 11 | 8 | 3 | 8 | 0 | 6 | 2 | 6 | 1 |
| 12 | 6 | 3 | 6 | 2 | 8 | 0 | 6 | 1 |

TS = Token Station
TRT = Token Rotation Time
TRTC = Amount of Time for Last Circulation of Token
XMIT = Number of Frames Transmitted

class 6 data may occupy the entire cycle to the exclusion of other classes. If $n \times$ THT is less than MAX[TRT4, TRT2, TRT0], the maximum circulation time is MAX[TRT4, TRT2, TRT0], and class 6 data are guaranteed $n \times$ THT amount of that time.

Figure 5.11 is a simplified example of a 4-station ring with THT = 3 and TRT4 = TRT2 = TRT0 = 8. For the first seven token cycles, stations 9 and 1 send as many class 6 frames as possible, and stations 7 and 5 send as many class 4 frames as possible. For cycles 8 through 12, station 1 reduces its output to one frame of class 6 per cycle.

Note that under constant offered traffic, a stable 3-cycle pattern is established. Under the initial load, over any three rotations, class 6 frames occupy 82% (18/22) of the bandwidth, and class 4 frames occupy the remaining 18%. When station 1 reduces its output, the allocation becomes 60 to 40%.

## CSMA/CD Versus Token Bus

At present, CSMA/CD and token bus are the two principal contenders for medium access control technique on bus/tree topologies. Table 5.4 attempts to summarize the pros and cons of the two techniques. A brief discussion follows. See also [STIE81] and [MILL82].

Let us look at CSMA/CD first. On the positive side, the algorithm is simple; good news for the VLSI folks, and also good news for the user, in terms of cost and reliability. The protocol has been widely used for a long time, which

**TABLE 5.4  CSMA/CD versus Token Bus**

| Advantages | Disadvantages |
|---|---|
| *CSMA/CD* | |
| Simple algorithm | Collision detection requirement |
| Widely used | Fault diagnosis problems |
| Fair access | Minimum packet size |
| Good performance at low to medium load | Poor performance under very heavy load |
| | Biased to long transmissions |
| *Token Bus* | |
| Excellent throughput performance | Complex algorithm |
| Tolerates large dynamic range | Unproven technology |
| Regulated access | |

also leads to favorable cost and reliability. The protocol provides fair access—all stations have an equal chance at the bandwidth; good if you require only fair access. As we shall see in a later chapter, CSMA/CD exhibits quite good delay and throughput performance, at least up to a certain load, around 5 Mbps under some typical conditions.

There are, unfortunately, quite a few "cons" for CSMA/CD. From an engineering perspective, the most critical problem is the collision detection requirement. In order to detect collisions, the differences in signal strength from any pair of stations at any point on the cable must be small; this is no easy task to achieve. Other undesirable implications flow from the CD requirement. Since collisions are allowed, it is difficult for diagnostic equipment to distinguish expected errors from those induced by noise or faults. Also, CD imposes a minimum frame size, which is wasteful of bandwidth in situations where there are a lot of short messages, such as may be produced in highly interactive environments.

There are some performance problems as well. For certain data rates and frame sizes, CSMA/CD performs poorly as load increases. Also, the protocol is biased toward long transmissions.

For token bus, perhaps its greatest positive feature is its excellent throughput performance. Throughput increases as the data rate increases and levels off but does not decline as the medium saturates. Further, this performance does not degrade as the cable length increases. A second "pro" for token bus is that, because stations need not detect collisions, a rather large dynamic range is possible. All that is required is that each station's signal be strong enough to be heard at all points on the cable; there are no special requirements related to relative signal strength.

Another strength of token bus is that access to the medium can be regulated.

If fair access is desired, token bus can provide this as well as CSMA/CD. Indeed, at high loads, token bus may be fairer: it avoids the last-in, first-out phenomenon mentioned earlier. If priorities are required, as they may be in an operational or real-time environment, these can be accommodated. Token bus can also guarantee a certain bandwidth; this may be necessary for certain types of data, such as voice, digital video, and telemetry.

An advertised advantage of token bus is that it is "deterministic"; that is, there is a known upper bound to the amount of time any station must wait before transmitting. This upper bound is known because each station in the logical ring can hold the token for only a specified time. In contrast, with CSMA/CD, the delay time can only be expressed statistically. Furthermore, since every attempt to transmit under CSMA/CD can in principle produce a collision, there is a possibility that a station could be shut out indefinitely. For process control and other real time applications, this "nondeterministic" behavior is undesirable. Alas, in the real world, there is always a finite possibility of transmission error, which can cause a lost token. This adds a statistical component to token bus.

The main disadvantage of token bus is its complexity. The reader who made it through the description above can have no doubt that this is a complex algorithm. A second disadvantage is the overhead involved. Under lightly loaded conditions, a station may have to wait through many fruitless token passes for a turn.

Which to choose? That is left as an exercise to the reader, based on requirements and the relative costs prevailing at the time. The decision is also influenced by the baseband versus broadband debate. Both must be considered together when comparing vendors.

## Centralized Reservation

The CSMA/CD technique was developed to deal with bursty traffic, such as is typically produced in interactive applications (query response, data entry, transactions). In this environment, stations are not transmitting most of the time; hence, a station with data to transmit can generally seize the channel quickly and with a minimum of fuss. Token bus, on the other hand, incurs the overhead of passing the token from one idle station to another.

For applications that have a stream rather than bursty nature (file transfer, audio, facsimile), token bus can perform quite well, especially if some priority scheme is used. If the collective load is great enough, CSMA/CD has difficulty keeping up with this kind of demand.

A number of schemes have been proposed, based on the use of reservations, that appear to offer the strengths of both CSMA/CD and token bus. In this section we look at a technique that requires a centralized control. This is a likely candidate for a broadband system, with the control function performed at the headend. In Chapter 6 we will examine a decentralized control technique specifically designed for the high data rates of HSLNs.

The centralized scheme described in this section was developed by AMDAX for its broadband LAN [KARP82]. (Other centralized reservation schemes for bus systems have been described in [WILL73] and [MARK78].) Fixed-size frames of 512 bits are used, of which 72 are overhead bits. Time is organized into cycles, each cycle consisting of a set of equal-size time slots, and each time slot is sufficient for transmitting one frame. At the conclusion of one cycle, another cycle begins. The central controller at the headend may allocate slot or frame positions, within one or more future cycles, to particular stations. Frame positions not assigned to any station are referred to as *unallocated frames*. All stations must remain informed as to which frames are allocated to them and which are unallocated.

From the point of view of the station, communication is as follows. If a station has a small message to send, one that will fit in a single frame, it sends it in the next available unallocated frame on the inbound channel. The frame contains the message, source and destination addresses, and control information indicating that this is a data frame. Because the frame position used by the station is unallocated, it may also be used by another station, causing a collision. Hence the transmitting station must listen to the outbound channel for its transmission. If the station does not see its frame within a short defined time, it continues to send the frame at random times until it gets through.

To send messages too big to fit into a single frame, a station may reserve time on the bus. It does this by sending a reservation request to the central controller on the inbound channel. The request uses an unallocated frame and contains an indication that this is a request frame, the source address, and the number of frames to be sent. The station then listens to the outbound channel a short defined time, expecting to get a reservation confirmation frame containing its address and the number and order of frames in future cycles it has been allocated (if the line is too heavily loaded, it may not get all the bandwidth requested). When confirmation is received, the station may transmit its data in the frames allocated to it. If confirmation is not received, the station assumes that its reservation suffered a collision and tries again.

From the point of view of the central controller, communication is as follows. Frames are received one at a time on the inbound channel. Allocated frames are repeated on the outbound channel with no further processing. Unallocated frames must be examined. If the frame is garbled or contains an error, it is ignored. If it is a valid data frame, it is repeated on the outbound channel. If it is a valid reservation frame, the controller fills the reservation within the limits of its available frames in future cycles and sends a confirmation.

It should be clear that this technique exhibits the strengths of both CSMA/CD and token bus. Its principal disadvantage is that it requires a rather complex central controller, with the attendant reliability problems.

# MEDIUM ACCESS CONTROL—RING

Over the years, a number of different algorithms have been proposed for controlling access to the ring. The three most common access techniques are discussed in this section: register insertion, slotted ring, and token ring. The first two will be briefly described; the token ring is discussed in some detail, as this is on its way to becoming the ring LAN standard.

Table 5.5 compares these three methods on a number of characteristics:

- *Transmit opportunity:* When may a repeater insert a packet onto the ring?
- *Packet purge responsibility:* Who removes a packet from a ring to avoid its circulating indefinitely?
- *Number of packets on ring:* This depends not only on the "bit length" of the ring relative to the packet length, but on the access method.
- *Principal advantage*
- *Principal disadvantage*

The significance of the table entries will become clear as the discussion proceeds.

## Register Insertion

This strategy was originally proposed in [HAFN74] and has been developed by researchers at Ohio State University [REAM75, LIU78]. It is also the technique used in the IBM Series 1 product [IBM82]. It derives its name from the shift register associated with each node on the ring. The shift register, equal in size

**TABLE 5.5  Ring Access Methods**

| Characteristic | Register Insertion | Slotted Ring | Token Ring |
|---|---|---|---|
| Transmit opportunity | Idle state plus empty buffer | Empty slot | Token |
| Packet purge responsibility | Receiver or transmitter | Transmitter | Transmitter |
| Number of packets on ring | Multiple | Multiple | One |
| Principal advantage | Maximum ring utilization | Simplicity | Regulated/fair access |
| Principal disadvantage | Purge mechanism | Bandwidth waste | Token maintenance |

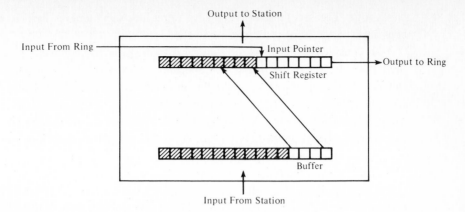

**FIGURE 5—12. Register Insertion Ring**

to the maximum frame length, is used for temporarily holding frames that circulate past the node. In addition, the node has a buffer for storing locally produced frames.

The register insertion ring can be explained with reference to Figure 5.12. When the ring is idle, the input pointer points to the rightmost position of the shift register, indicating that it is empty. When data arrive from the ring they are inserted bit by bit in the shift register, with the input pointer shifting left for each bit. The frame begins with an address field. As soon as the entire address field is in the register, the station can determine if it is the addressee. If not, the frame is forwarded by shifting one bit out on the right as each new bit arrives from the left, with the input pointer stationary. After the last bit of the frame has arrived, the station continues to shift bits out to the right until the frame is gone. If, during this time, no additional frames arrive, the input pointer will return to its initial position. Otherwise, a second frame will begin to accumulate in the register as the first is shifted out.

Two observations are in order. First, the last few sentences imply that more than one frame may be on the ring at a time. How this can be is described below. Second, picture a series of frames, with gaps in between, passing a station. The effect of the actions described in the preceding paragraph is to compress the gaps between the earlier arrivers, and stretch them out for later arrivers. As we shall see, the widening gaps provide an opportunity for new frames to be inserted into the ring.

Returning to the main line of our discussion: If an arriving frame is addressed to the station in question, the station has two choices. First, it can divert the remainder of the frame to itself and erase the address bits from the register, thus purging the frame from the ring. This is the approach taken by IBM. A moment's thought will reveal that such a strategy can result in a total bandwidth utilization that at times exceeds actual bit transmission rate. However, this may be false economy since, if the receiver rather than the transmitter purges the ring, some other means of acknowledgment must be employed, thus wasting bandwidth. The second alternative is to retransmit the frame as before, while copying it to the local station.

Now consider output from the station. A frame to be transmitted is placed in the output buffer. If the line is idle and the shift register is empty, the frame can be transferred immediately to the shift register. If the frame consists of some length $n$ bits, less than the maximum frame size, and if at least $n$ bits are empty in the shift register, the $n$ bits are parallel-transferred to the empty portion of the shift register immediately adjacent to the full portion; the input pointer is adjusted accordingly.

We can see that there is a delay at each station, whose minimum value is the length of the address field and whose maximum value is the length of the shift register. This is in contrast to slotted ring and token ring, where the delay at each station is just the repeater delay—typically one or two bit times. To get a feeling for the effect, consider a station transmitting a 1000-bit frame on a 10-Mbps register insertion ring. The time it takes the station to transmit the frame is $1000/10^7 = 0.10$ ms. If the frame must pass 50 stations to reach its destination and if the address field is 16 bits, then the minimum delay, exclusive of propagation time, is $(16 \times 50)/10^7 = 0.08$ ms. This is a substantial delay compared to transmission time. Worse, if each station has a 1000-bit shift register, the maximum delay the frame could experience is $(1000 \times 50)/10^7 = 5$ ms.

The register insertion technique enforces an efficient form of fairness. As long as the ring is idle, a station with a lot of data to be sent can send frame after frame, utilizing the entire bandwidth of the ring. If the ring is busy, however, a station will find that, after sending a frame, the shift register will not accommodate another frame right away. The station will have to wait until enough intermessage gaps have accumulated before sending again. As a refinement, certain high-priority nodes can be given shift registers whose length is greater than the minimum shift register length (which is equal to the maximum frame length).

The principal advantage of the register insertion technique is that it achieves the maximum ring utilization of any of the methods. There are several other favorable features. Like the token system, it allows variable-length frames, which is efficient from the point of view of both the stations and the ring. Like the slotted ring, it permits multiple frames to be on the ring; again, an efficient use of bandwidth.

The principal disadvantage is the purge mechanism. Allowing multiple frames on the ring requires the recognition of an address prior to removal of a frame, whether it be removed by sender or receiver. If a frame's address field is damaged, it could circulate indefinitely. One possible solution is the use of an error-detecting code on the address field; IBM's Series 1 employs a parity bit. The requirement for address field recognition also dictates that each frame be delayed at each node by the length of that field. No such requirement exists in the other two methods.

## Slotted Ring

For the slotted ring (Figure 5.13), a number of fixed-length slots circulate continuously on the ring. This strategy was first developed by Pierce [PIER72] and is sometimes referred to as the *Pierce loop*. Most of the development work on this technique was done at the University of Cambridge in England [WILK79], and a number of British firms market commercial versions of the *Cambridge ring* [HEYW81].

In the slotted ring, each slot contains a leading bit to designate the slot as empty or full (Figure 5.13). All slots are initially marked empty. A station with data to transmit must break the data up into fixed-length frames. It then waits until an empty slot arrives, marks the slot full, and inserts a frame of data as the slot goes by. The station cannot transmit another frame until this slot returns. The slot also contains two response bits, which can be set on the fly by the addressed station to indicate accepted, busy, or rejected. The full slot makes a complete round trip, to be marked empty again by the source. Each station knows the total number of slots on the ring and can thus clear the full/empty bit as it goes by. Once the now-empty slot goes by, the station is free to transmit again.

In the Cambridge ring, each slot contains room for one source address byte, one destination address byte, two data bytes, and five control bits, for a total length of 37 bits.

Typically, there will be very few slots on a ring. Consider, for example, a 100-station ring with an average spacing of 10 m between stations and a data rate of 10 Mbps. A typical propagation velocity for signals is $2 \times 10^8$ m/s. A moment's thought should reveal that the "bit length" of the link between two stations is $(10^7 \text{ bps} \times 10 \text{ m})/(2 \times 10^8 \text{ m/s}) = 0.5$ bit. Say that the delay at each repeater is one bit time. Then the total "bit length" of the ring is just $1.5 \times 100 = 150$ bits. This is enough for four slots.

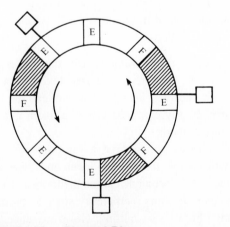

**FIGURE 5–13.  Slotted Ring**

The principal disadvantage of the slotted ring is that it is wasteful of bandwidth. First, each frame contains only 16 bits of data out of 37 bits total, a tremendous amount of overhead. Second, a station may send only one frame per round-trip ring time. If only one or a few stations have frames to transmit, many of the slots will circulate empty.

The principal advantage of the slotted ring appears to be its simplicity. The interaction with the ring at each node is minimized, improving reliability.

## Token Ring

This is probably the oldest ring control technique, originally proposed in 1969 [FARM69] and referred to as the *Newhall Ring*. It has become the most popular ring access technique in the United States. Prime Computer [GORD79] and Apollo both market token ring products, and IBM seems committed to such a product [RAUC82]. This technique is the one ring access method selected for standardization by the IEEE 802 Local Network Standards Committee [GRAU82].

### Description

The token ring technique is based on the use of a single token that circulates around the ring when all stations are idle (Figure 5.14). A typical example of a token is an 8-bit pattern such as '01111111'. A station wishing to transmit must wait until it detects a token passing by. It then changes the token from "free token" to "busy token." This can be done by changing the last bit of the token (e.g., from '01111111' to '01111110'). The station then transmits a frame immediately following the busy token.

There is now no free token on the ring, so other stations wishing to transmit must wait. The frame on the ring will make a round trip and be purged by the transmitting station. The transmitting station will insert a new free token on the ring when both of the following conditions have been met:

• The station has completed transmission of its frame.
• The busy-token has returned to the station.

If the bit length of the ring is less than the frame length, the first condition implies the second. If not, a station could release a free token after it has finished transmitting but before it receives its own busy token; the second condition is not strictly necessary. In any case, the use of a token guarantees that only one station at a time may transmit.

When a transmitting station releases a new free token, the next station downstream with data to send will be able to seize the token and transmit.

Several implications of the token ring technique can be mentioned. Note that under lightly loaded conditions, there is some inefficiency since a station must wait for the token to come around before transmitting. However, under heavy loads, which is where it matters, the ring functions in a round-robin fashion,

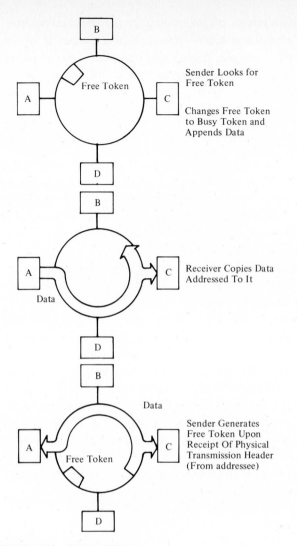

FIGURE 5–14. Token Ring

which is both efficient and fair. To see this, refer to Figure 5.14. Note that after station A transmits, it releases a token. The first station with an opportunity to transmit is D. If D transmits, it then releases a token and C has the next opportunity, and so on. Also, note that the free-token pattern must not appear anywhere in the data. This is avoided by using bit stuffing. Finally, the ring must be long enough to hold the token. If stations are temporarily bypassed, their delay may need to be supplied artificially.

The principal advantage of token ring is the control over access that it provides. In the simple scheme described above, the access is fair. As we shall see, schemes can be used to regulate access to provide for priority and guaranteed bandwidth services.

The principal disadvantage of token ring is the requirement for token maintenance. Loss of the free token prevents further utilization of the ring. Duplication of the token can also disrupt ring operation. One station must be elected monitor to assure that exactly one token is on the ring and to reinsert a free token if necessary.

### IEEE 802 Token Ring

The IEEE 802 token ring specification is a refinement of the scheme just outlined. The key elements are as follows:

1. *Single-token protocol:* A station that has completed transmission will not issue a new token until the busy token returns. This is not as efficient, for small frames, as a multiple-token strategy of issuing a free token at the end of a frame. However, the single-token system simplifies priority and error-recovery functions.
2. *Priority bits:* These indicate the priority of a token and therefore which stations are allowed to use the token. In a multiple-priority scheme, priorities may be set by station or by message.
3. *Monitor bit:* It may be used if a central ring monitor is employed. The operation of the monitor is not covered in the standard.
4. *Reservation indicators:* They may be used to allow stations with high priority messages to indicate in a frame that the next token be issued at the requested priority.
5. *Token-holding timer:* Started at the beginning of data transfer, it controls the length of time a station may occupy the medium before transmitting a token.
6. *Acknowledgment bits:* There are three: error detected (E), address recognized (A), and frame copied (C). These are reset to 0 by the transmitting station. Any station may set the E bit. Addressed stations may set the A and C bits.

Figure 5.3 shows the two frame formats for token ring. The individual fields are as follows

- *Starting delimiter (SD):* a unique 8-bit pattern used to start each frame.
- *Access control (AC):* has the format 'PPPTMRRR', where PPP and RRR are 3-bit priority and reservation variables, M is the monitor bit, and T indicates whether this is a token or data frame. In the case of a token frame, the only additional field is ED.
- *Frame control (FC):* indicates whether this is an LLC data frame. If not, bits in this field control operation of the token ring MAC protocol.
- *Destination address (DA):* as in CSMA/CD and token bus.
- *Source address (SA):* as in CSMA/CD and token bus.
- *LLC:* as in CSMA/CD and token bus.
- *FCS:* as in CSMA/CD and token bus.
- *Ending delimiter (ED):* contains the error detection (E) bit.
- *Frame status (FS):* contains the address recognized (A) and frame copied (C) bits.

Let us first consider the operation of the ring when only a single priority is used. In this case the priority and reservation bits are not used. A station wishing to transmit waits until a free token goes by, as indicated by a token bit of 0 in the AC field. The station seizes the token by setting the token bit to 1. It then transmits one or more frames, continuing until either its output is exhausted or its token-holding timer expires. After the busy token returns, the station transmits a free token.

Stations in the receive mode listen to the ring. Each station can check passing frames for errors and set the E bit if an error is detected. If a station detects its own address it sets the A bit to 1; it may also copy the frame, setting the C bit to 1. This allows the originating station to differentiate three conditions:

- Station nonexistent/nonactive.
- Station exists but frame not copied.
- Frame copied.

The foregoing operation can be supplemented by a multiple-priority scheme. For example, bridges could be given higher priority than ordinary stations. The 802 specification provides three bits for eight levels of priority. For clarity, let us designate three values: $P_m$ = priority of message to be transmitted by station; $P_r$ = received priority; and $R_r$ = received reservation. The scheme works as follows:

1. A station wishing to transmit must wait for a free token with $P_r \leq P_m$.
2. While waiting, a station may reserve a token at its priority level ($P_m$). If a busy token goes by, it may set the reservation field to its priority ($R_r \leftarrow P_m$) if the reservation field is less than its priority ($R_r < P_m$). If a free token goes by, it may set the reservation field to its priority ($R_r \leftarrow P_m$) if $R_r < P_m$ and $P_m < P_r$. This has the effect of preempting any lower-priority reservations.
3. When a station seizes a token, it sets the token bit to 1, the reservation field to 0, and leaves the priority field unchanged.
4. Following transmission, a station issues a new token with the priority set to the maximum of $P_r$, $R_r$, and $P_m$, and a reservation set to the maximum of $R_r$ and $P_m$.

The effect of the above steps is to sort out competing claims and allow the waiting transmission of highest priority to seize the token as soon as possible. A moment's reflection reveals that, as is, the algorithm has a ratchet effect on priority, driving it to the highest used level and keeping it there. To avoid this, two stacks are maintained, one for reservations and one for priorities. In essence, each station is responsible for assuring that no token circulates indefinitely because its priority is too high. By remembering the priority of earlier transmissions, a station can detect this condition and downgrade the priority to a previous, lower priority or reservation.

We are now in a position to summarize the priority algorithm. A station having a higher priority than the current busy token can reserve the next free token for its priority level as the busy token passes by. When the current transmitting station is finished, it issues a free token at that higher priority. Stations of lower priority cannot seize the token, so it passes to the requesting station or an intermediate station of equal or higher priority with data to send.

The station that upgraded the priority level is responsible for downgrading it to its former level when all higher-priority stations are finished. When the station sees a free token at the higher priority, it can assume that there is no more higher-priority traffic waiting, and it downgrades the token before passing it on.

### Token Maintenance

Two approaches can be taken to overcome various error situations such as no token circulating and persistent busy token: decentralized and centralized.

The *decentralized* approach, suggested by the IEEE 802 Committee, employs two timers: a relatively long no-token timer (TNT) and a shorter valid frame timer (TVX). If a station has a frame to transmit and has not seen a token for a time TNT, it assumes that the token is lost, purges the ring, and issues a token. A station also keeps track of the amount of time since the last valid data frame or token. When this exceeds TVX, it assumes that the token is lost and issues a token.

IBM prefers a *centralized* approach, using a station designated as active token monitor [RAUC82]. The monitor detects the lost-token condition by using a time-out greater than the time required for the longest frame to completely traverse the ring. To recover, the monitor purges the ring of any residual data and issues a free token. To detect a circulating busy token, the monitor sets the monitor bit to 1 on any passing busy token. If it sees a busy token with a bit already set, it knows that the transmitting station failed to purge its frame. The monitor changes the busy token to a free token.

Other stations on the ring have the role of passive monitor. Their primary job is to detect failure of the active monitor and assume that role. A contention-resolution algorithm is used to determine which station takes over.

**5.5**

## RECOMMENDED READING

A survey of bus/tree protocols can be found in [LUCZ78], and a survey of ring protocols in [PENN79]. [TROP81], which is concerned with performance, describes most bus and ring protocols. The rationale behind the IEEE 802 standard is contained in [CLAN82]. An opposing viewpoint is expressed in [DAHO83]. The LAN reference model is described in [IEEE82, App. E]. A concise but thorough description of the standard can be found in [MYER82]*.

## PROBLEMS

**5.1** What arguments or parameters are required for each of the LLC primitives in Table 5.1?

**5.2** Why is there not an LLC primitive L-CONNECTION-FLOWCONTROL.confirm?

**5.3** Show, with an example, how the LLC protocol provides the LLC services as defined by the LLC primitives.

**5.4** A simple medium access control protocol would be to use a fixed assignment time-division multiplexing (TDM) scheme, as described in Section 2.1. Each station is assigned one time slot per cycle for transmission. For the bus and tree, the length of each time slot is the time to transmit 100 bits plus the end-to-end propagation delay. For the ring, assume a delay of one bit time per station, and assume that a round-robin assignment is used. Stations monitor all time slots for reception. What are the limitations, in terms of number of stations and throughput per station, for:

   **a.** A 1-km, 10-Mbps baseband bus?
   **b.** A 1-km (headend to farthest point), 10-Mbps broadband bus?
   **c.** A 10-Mbps broadband tree consisting of a 0.5-km trunk emanating from the headend and five 0.1-km branches from the trunk at the following points: 0.05 km, 0.15 km, 0.25 km, 0.35 km, 0.45 km?
   **d.** A 10-Mbps ring with a total length of 1 km?
   **e.** A 10-Mbps ring with a length of 0.1 km between repeaters?
   **f.** Compute throughput per station for all of the above for 10 and 100 stations.

**5.5** The binary exponential back-off algorithm is defined by IEEE 802 thus: "The delay is an integral multiple of slot time. The number of slot times to delay before the $n$th retransmission attempt is chosen as a uniformly distributed random integer $r$ in the range $0 < r < 2**K$, where $K = \min(n,10)$." Slot time is, roughly, twice the round-trip propagation delay. Assume that two stations always have a frame to send. After a collision, what is the mean number of retransmission attempts before one station successfully transmits? What is the answer if three stations always have frames to send?

**5.6** Consider two stations on a baseband bus at a distance of 1 km from each other. Let the data rate be 1 Mbps, the packet length be 100 bits, and the propagation velocity be $2 \times 10^8$ m/s. Assume that each station generates packets at an average rate of 1000 packets per second. For the ALOHA protocol, if one station begins to transmit a packet at time $t$, what is the probability of collision? Repeat for slotted-ALOHA. Repeat for ALOHA and slotted-ALOHA at 10 Mbps.

**5.7** Repeat Problem 5.6 for a broadband bus. Assume that the two stations are 1 km apart and that one is very near the headend.

**5.8** For a p-persistent CSMA, what is the probability that the next transmission after a successful transmission will be successful for $np = 0.1, 1.0$, and 10?

**5.9** In what sense are the slotted ring and token ring protocols the complement of each other?

**5.10** A promising application of fiber optics for local networks is in the ring topology. Which, if any, of the three ring protocols is inappropriate for this medium?

**5.11** For a token ring system, suppose that the destination station removes the data frame and immediately sends a short acknowledgment frame to the sender, rather than letting the original frame return to sender. How will this affect performance?

**5.12** Consider a Cambridge ring of length 10 km with a data rate of 10 Mbps and 500 repeaters, each of which introduces a 1-bit delay. How many slots are on the ring?

**5.13** For the ring in Problem 5.12, assume a constant user data load of 4 Mbps. What is the mean number of slots that a station must wait to insert a packet?

**5.14** Write a program that implements the token ring priority mechanism.

**5.15** For the decentralized token ring maintenance approach, it is possible that two stations will time-out and transmit a new token. Suggest an algorithm for overcoming this problem.

**5.16** The IEEE 802 refers to the token bus service class scheme as a "bandwidth allocation" scheme rather than a priority scheme. A priority scheme would provide that all frames of higher priority would be transmitted before any lower-priority frames would be allowed on the bus. Show by counterexample that the 802 scheme is not a priority scheme.

**5.17** Compare the token bus service class scheme with token ring timer and priority schemes. What are the relative pros and cons? Is it possible, with appropriate parameter settings, to achieve the same behavior from both?

---

## APPENDIX 5A IEEE 802 STANDARD

The key to the development of the LAN market is the availability of a low cost interface. The cost to connect equipment to a LAN must be much less than the cost of the equipment alone. This requirement, plus the complexity of the LAN protocols, dictate a VLSI solution. However, chip manufacturers will be reluctant to commit the necessary resources unless there is a high-volume market. A LAN standard would assure that volume and also enable equipment of a variety of manufacturers to intercommunicate.

This is the rationale of the IEEE 802 committee [CLAN82], which has produced a draft set of standards for LANs [IEEE82]. The standards are in the form of a 3-layer communications architecture with a tree-like expansion of options from top to bottom (Figure 5.15). The three layers encompass the

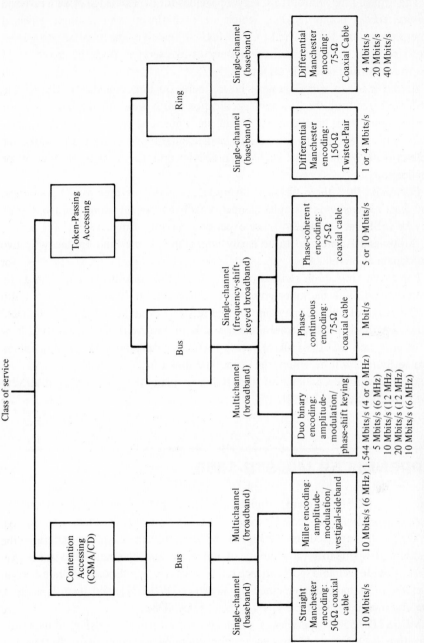

**FIGURE 5–15.** The IEEE 802 LAN Standard

functionality of the lowest two layers (data link and physical) of the OSI Reference model.

The logical link control (LLC) layer provides for the exchange of data between service access points (SAPs), which are multiplexed over a single physical connection to the LAN. The LLC provides for both a connectionless, datagram-like, and connection-oriented, virtual-circuit-like service. Both the protocol and the frame format resemble HDLC.

At the medium access control layer, there are three standards. CSMA/CD has converged with the Ethernet specification and is well suited to typical office applications. Both baseband and broadband options exist at several data rates. Two forms of token access have also been standardized. These are provided for time-critical applications, such as process control, as well as the office applications.

For token bus, three physical layers are provided as options. The simplest and least expensive is a single-channel broadband system using frequency-shift keying (FSK) at 1 Mbps. A more expensive version of this system runs at 5 or 10 Mbps and is intended to be easily upgradable to the final option, which is multichannel broadband.

For token ring, both twisted-pair and baseband coaxial cable options have been defined, with the latter going up to a data rate of 40 Mbps.

The range of options may surprise the reader, given the IEEE 802 rationale. However, the IEEE 802 committee has at least narrowed the alternatives. It is to be expected that the bulk of future LAN development work, at least in the United States, will be within the scope laid down by IEEE 802.

More detail discussions of the standard may be found in [GRAU82], [ALLA82], and [MYER82].

## APPENDIX 5B MIL-STD-1553

The earliest LAN standard, originally released in 1973 by the Department of Defense, is MIL-STD-1553 [SAND82, ILC82]. The current standard is version B. Originally intended for the high-noise environment of military aircraft, the standard is applicable to a variety of industrial and commercial systems that must provide reliable performance under adverse conditions. A number of manufacturers have implemented the interface [WILL82], and there is at least one commercially available LAN product [MAND82].

MIL-STD-1553B specifies a shielded twisted-pair bus using Manchester encoding at 1 Mbps. Under one option, stations are coupled to the bus via transformer; there is no direct connection. This physical isolation ensures that a fault or failure on either the bus or an attached device will not affect the other. A further option is the specification of a redundant backup bus that can be used automatically if the primary bus fails.

The medium access control protocol is two-level. At any time, one station is designated as controller and data are exchanged by means of polling. At a higher level, the controller designation is dynamically reassigned via a form of token passing.

# High-Speed Local Networks

In this chapter we explore the nature of the high-speed local network. HSLNs, recall, are intended to satisfy user requirements for high-speed data transfer among hosts and mass storage devices.

Briefly, the key characteristics of an HSLN are:

- *High data rate:* Both extant products and a draft standard have a 50 Mbps data rate, higher than found with LANs.
- *High-speed interface:* HSLNs are intended to provide high throughput among computer room equipment—mainframes and high-speed peripherals. Thus the physical link between station and network must be high-speed.
- *Distributed access:* As with LANs, it is desirable for reliability and efficiency reasons to have distributed access control.
- *Limited distance:* Generally, an HSLN will be used in a computer room or a small number of rooms; hence great distances are not required.

At present the HSLN field is dominated by the CATV bus architecture. This is reviewed first. Then we look at issues related to link and medium access control. Emphasis will be on a draft standard developed by the ANS X3T9.5 committee of ANSI. Then, some architectural issues and the overlap between LANs and HSLNs are discussed. An appendix contains a brief summary of the X3T9.5 standard.

# COAXIAL CABLE SYSTEMS

Coaxial-cable based HSLNs use a bus topology. As such, they share a number of characteristics with bus-based LANs. In particular, a packet-switching technique is used and, because the medium is multiaccess, a medium access control technique is needed to determine who goes next. The key difference between a bus LAN and a bus HSLN is the higher data rate of the latter. Thus this section will concentrate on highlighting the features of bus HSLNs that result from that difference.

We look at two types of systems: single-channel broadband and baseband. The single-channel broadband is the basis for a pending ANSI standard being drafted by the X3T9.5 committee [ANSI82]; it is also the technique used in CDC's Loosely Coupled Network product [HOHN80]. The baseband technique is used in the oldest and most widely used HSLN, Network Systems Corporation's HYPERchannel [CHRI79].

The approaches have much in common. Among the common characteristics:

- *Data rate of 50 Mbps:* With today's technology, this is about the highest cost-effective speed achievable.
- *Maximum length of about 1 km:* This limit is dictated by the data rate, but should be adequate for many HSLN requirements.
- *Maximum number of stations in the 10's:* Again, this is dictated by the data rate. Since HSLNs are primarily intended for expensive high-speed devices, this restriction is usually not burdensome.
- *Provisions for multiple (up to four) cables:* This increases throughput and reliability.

## Single-Channel Broadband

In this section we describe the system proposed by the ANS X3T9.5 committee. The CDC product is very similar.

As with the single-channel broadband systems described in Chapter 4, the single-channel broadband HSLN consists of the following components:

- Cable
- Terminators
- Taps
- Controllers

The cable used is 75-$\Omega$ CATV cable. Hence 75-$\Omega$ terminators are required to absorb the signal. Transmission on the cable is bidirectional, requiring the use of a nondirectional coupler or tap. Finally, a controller is needed for transmission/reception and to perform medium access control functions.

Several features of the system warrant elaboration. First, let us consider the problem of how many taps can be attached to the cable. The number is more limited with HSLNs than LANs because the higher data rates make low-error reception more difficult. To see this, consider that each bit of transmission at the higher data rate of the HSLN occupies less time and space on the cable. Therefore, a relatively small amount of attenuation or distortion can cause errors.

The draft ANSI standard provides some guidelines for number of taps based on the concept of power budget. This quantity is the ratio in decibels (dB) between the minimum signal power available at a station's transmitter and the minimum acceptable signal power at a station's receiver. For example, if the transmitter power is 1 mw and the receiver operates reliably over a signal range of 1 mw to 1 nw, then the power budget, $Bp$, is

$$B_p = 10 \times \log_{10} \frac{P_0}{P_I} = 10 \times \log_{10} \frac{10^{-3}}{10^{-9}} = 60 \, \text{dB}$$

This says that the loss incurred between the output of one tap and the input of another must not exceed 60 dB for reliable transmission. With greater loss, it will be difficult to separate the signal from the noise.

The sources of loss are the cable and the taps, and the total loss is a function of the length of the cable and the number of taps. The relationship can be expressed as

$$B_p = L_M + L_I(N-2) + 2L_D + L_C \tag{6.1}$$

where $L_M$ = main trunk (cable) loss

$L_I$ = insertion loss per tap: due to the amount of power diverted to the port

$N$ = number of taps

$L_D$ = isolation loss in end couplers: wasted power due to coupler

$L_C$ = cable loss in drop cables (one transmitter, one receiver)

This equation can be solved for $N$, and with coupler losses and the acceptable power budget known, expressed as a function of cable length. This is done in Figure 6.1. The diagram shows how few stations can be accommodated at the 60 dB level (which is a reasonable goal). For less sensitive receivers, the number of devices that can be accommodated drops.

Equation (6.1) can also be used to determine the maximum length of the cable given the number of taps. As was mentioned, this works out to about 1 km for a few tens of devices.

Finally, let us consider the modulation scheme to be used. The technique specified by ANS X3T9.5 is to use 180 degree phase-shift-key (PSK) modulation. For a 50-Mbps data rate, this technique uses a carrier at 150 MHz and a clock signal at 50 MHz. Figure 6.2 indicates the steps in preparing a transmission. A bit stream is encoded at two voltage levels using a "change on zero" convention;

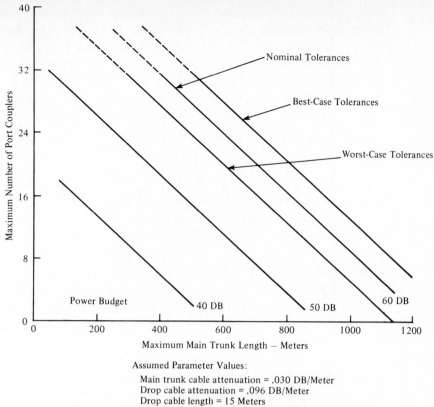

Assumed Parameter Values:

Main trunk cable attenuation = .030 DB/Meter
Drop cable attenuation = .096 DB/Meter
Drop cable length = 15 Meters
Port coupler insertion loss = 0.8 ± 0.2 DB
Port coupler isolation loss = 11 ± 1 DB

**FIGURE 6–1. Number of Port Couplers Versus Main Trunk Length**

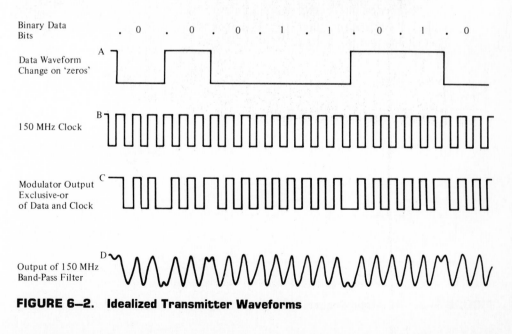

**FIGURE 6–2. Idealized Transmitter Waveforms**

that is, at the beginning of each 0 bit, the voltage level is changed. This encoded bit stream is generated using a 50 MHz clock. To achieve phase encoding, the bit stream is modulated on a 150 MHz digital pulse stream by taking the exclusive-or of the two signals. The result is a 150-MHz digital stream that changes phase at the beginning of each 0 bit. The modulated output is passed through a 150 MHz analog bandpass filter to produce the analog signal on the line. The 50-MHz clock is also sent out to provide synchronization. A simplified block diagram is shown in Figure 6.3.

An inverse process takes place at the receiver. The 50-MHz signal is received and used to recover the clock. The 150-MHz signal is digitized. Two copies are produced: an inverted signal and a signal delayed by one bit time. A disagreement between these two signals corresponds to a transition from 0 to 1 or 1 to 0. A sample is shown in Figure 6.4.

## Baseband

There is little to say about a baseband HSLN that has not already been covered under the baseband LAN. Again, the main components are cable, terminators, taps, and controllers.

The only baseband system commercially available is HYPERchannel. Like the single-channel broadband, it uses a 75-Ω CATV bus with nondirectional taps. The data rate is 50 Mbps using Manchester encoding. HYPERchannel recommends a maximum length of 1.2 km and no more than about 30 stations.

It is difficult to assess the relative advantages of this scheme compared to the single-channel broadband. The broadband adherents claim that the analog signal exhibits better attenuation and distortion characteristics, but there is little empirical evidence to support this. In general, the two approaches should give comparable performances at comparable cost.

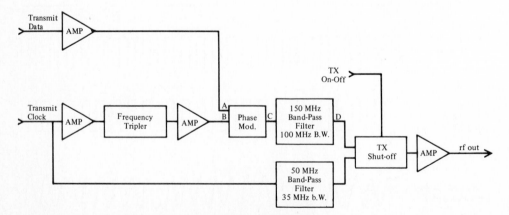

**FIGURE 6–3.  50-Mbps Transmitter Block Diagram**

Received Data
Waveform   E

| 20 NS |

Amplifed, Shaped
and Inverted
Waveform   F

Amplifed, Shaped
and Delayed (20 NS)
Waveform   G

Phase Detector
Output*   H

Binary Data
Bits-NRZ   . 0 . 0 . 0 . 1 . 1 . 0 . 1 . 0 .

*The phase detector develops a negative output voltage for two input voltages in phase and a positive output voltage for two input voltages which are out of phase with each other.

**FIGURE 6–4.   Idealized Receiver Waveform**

## 6.2

## HSLN LINK CONTROL

The general comments concerning link control made in Chapter 5 are equally applicable here. This section first attempts to address the unique requirements for HSLN link control and then presents the ANS X3T9.5 draft standard as an example.

### Requirements

As we mentioned in the beginning of this chapter, the characteristics that distinguish an HSLN from a LAN include fewer devices, shorter distance, and higher speed. More important, in terms of application, the HSLN is more likely to see file transfer application as opposed to interactive usage.

How do these differences manifest themselves in terms of traffic characteristics? With interactive traffic one expects to see frequent short bursts of data transfer; the HSLN is more likely to see infrequent long bursts of traffic.

We can relate this to the requirements for link control. A connection-oriented capability is desirable for the LAN, since a terminal-host interchange may extend over a long period of time. This seems less important for an HSLN. Long bulk transfers of data occur after which the connection is not needed for some time. Hence a connectionless service may be adequate.

For efficient use of the HSLN medium, the link control layer should permit sustained use of the medium either by permitting transmissions of unbounded length or permitting a pair of devices to seize the channel for an indefinite period. In the latter case, the link control layer permits a multiframe dialogue between two devices, with no other data allowed on the medium for the duration of the dialogue. This permits a long sequence of data frames and acknowledgments to be interchanged. An example of the utility of this feature is the use of the HSLN to read or write to high-performance disks. Without the ability to seize the bus temporarily, only one sector of the disk could be accessed per revolution—a totally unacceptable performance. As we shall see, the ANS X3T9.5 standard provides this feature at the link layer and supports it with a mechanism in the medium access control protocol.

## ANS X3T9.5 Data Link Layer

The ANSI committee has come up with a remarkably concise specification for a data link layer, using a convention of signals and interfaces rather than procedure calls.

The features of this layer are simply explained. It is assumed that there is a network layer, not part of the HSLN, above the data link layer (DLL). The DLL exchanges packets of data with the network layer. It provides a reliable connectionless service, with a provision for sustained dialogue. The functions of the DLL are, simply, to accept from the physical layer frames with its address, and to generate during transmission and check during reception a CRC field. The services required by the DLL from the physical layer are that it send and receive data, signal when the medium is available, and signal when the physical layer is operational.

The DLL frame has the following fields:

- D (2 bytes): destination address; may be broadcast.
- S (2 bytes): source address.
- L (2 bytes): length of I field.
- I (variable): data from the network layer, up to 64 kbytes long.
- FCS (4 bytes): frame check sequence field, containing a cyclic redundancy check code.

Figure 6.5 shows the conceptual organization of both the DLL and physical layer. Signal and data interfaces between layers are indicated. The designation conforms to the following conventions. The name of a signal or interface originating in the network, link, or physical layer begins with N, L, or P, respectively. Interface names end with an I. Table 6.1 lists the names of all the signals and interfaces in the standard.

For transmission the network layer uses four signals to the DLL and receives one from the DLL:

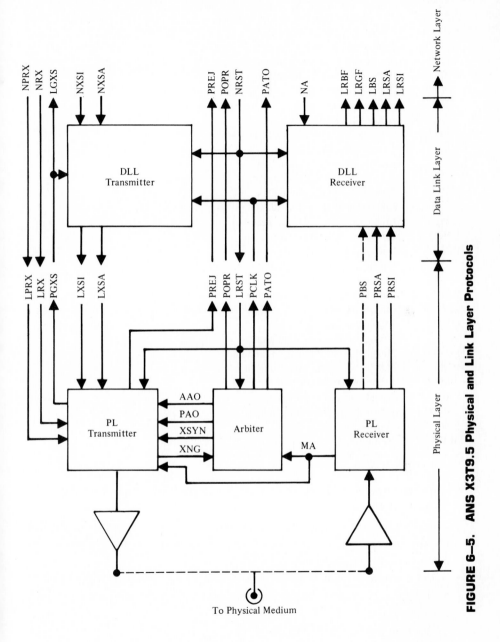

**FIGURE 6–5. ANS X3T9.5 Physical and Link Layer Protocols**

**TABLE 6.1  ANS X3T9.5 Signals and Interfaces**

| Signal | Meaning |
| --- | --- |
| NPRX | Network priority request to transmit |
| NRX | Network request to transmit |
| LGXS | Link grant to transmit stream |
| NXSI | Network transmit stream interface |
| NXSA | Network transmit stream available |
| PREJ | Physical reject |
| POPR | Physical operating |
| NRST | Network reset |
| PATO | Physical acknowledgment time-out |
| NA | Network accept |
| LRBF | Link receive bad frame |
| LRGF | Link receive good frame |
| LBS | Link bad signal (optional) |
| LRSA | Link receive stream available |
| LRSI | Link receive stream interface |
| LPRX | Link priority request to transmit |
| LRX | Link request to transmit |
| PGXS | Physical grant to transmit stream |
| LXSI | Link transmit stream interface |
| LXSA | Link transmit stream available |
| LRST | Link reset |
| PCLK | Physical clock |
| PBS | Physical bad signal (optional) |
| PRSA | Physical receive stream available |
| PRSI | Physical receive stream interface |
| AAO | Arbitrated access opportunity |
| PAO | Priority access opportunity |
| XSYN | Transmit synchronizing frame |
| XNG | Transmitting |
| MA | Medium active |

*Source:* ANS X3T9.5.

- NRX: asserted by network when it wishes to transmit. Transmission will be delayed until the medium is captured.
- NPRX: as above, except that this transmission follows a reception and has priority in capturing the medium. Its use is explained in the context of the medium access control protocol.
- NXSA: asserted when a frame is available for or being transmitted. If a malfunction is sensed during transmission, NXSA is unasserted to abort transmission.
- NXSI: data path for transmission.
- LGXS: grants permission to network to transmit.

The DLL-physical layer interaction uses the following signals:

- LRX: passed down by DLL when NRX is asserted.

- LPRX: as above, for priority transmissions.
- LXSA: asserted when a frame is available; unasserted to abort a transmission.
- LXSI: data path for transmission.
- PGXS: grants permission; medium has been seized.

The operation of the DLL, based on the above, is almost self-explanatory. The DLL accepts the D field, inserts an S field, accepts the L and I fields, and calculates and appends an FCS field. The physical layer is responsible for medium access control and seizes the medium by transmitting a preamble.

The DLL receiver function can be explained almost as consisely. The DLL–physical layer interaction uses the following signals:

- PRSA: asserted when data are available for the DLL.
- PRSI: data path for transmission.
- PBS: asserted if received signal is bad (e.g., a collision, poor signal quality).

The network–DLL interaction consists of:

- LRSA: asserted when data are available for network. Then unasserted to inform network that the complete received frame has been transferred and LRGF and LRBF should be examined.
- LRSI: data path for transmission.
- LRGF: asserted when received FCS indicates that a valid frame has been received.
- LRBF: as above, for invalid frame.
- NA: asserted to signal that the last frame has been received and that network is ready for a new frame.
- LBS: used by DLL to pass the PBS signal up to network.

Again, little more needs to be said. DLL receives all frames from physical and does address recognition. If the destination address is valid for this port, then DLL transfers the D, S, L, and I fields to network. Note there is at least a 2-byte delay.

Several other signals are defined which are needed for various DLL functions:

- NRST: asserted to reset lower layers to known state; any messages in process may be lost.
- LRST: asserted when it is necessary to reinitialize the port; may be precipitated by NRST.
- PREJ: asserted when an invalid physical layer operation is detected.
- PATO: asserted when the Arbitrated Access Timer expires.
- POPR: asserted whenever the physical layer is powered on and operating.
- PCLK: physical clock.

The simplicity of this description is in part due to the lack of a connection-oriented service, which is left to higher layers to provide. But it is, in part, also due to the conciseness of the signal/interface convention.

## HSLN MEDIUM ACCESS CONTROL

In this section we first review the only technique that has so far gained favor for HSLNs, known as CSMA with collision avoidance. It is also referred to as prioritized CSMA. The technique will be described in terms of the ANSI draft standard; the MAC algorithm for HYPERchannel is very similar.

Following this we look briefly at another technique that holds promise for high-speed local networks—distributed reservation.

### ANS X3T9.5 MAC

In devising a MAC algorithm for the type of system described in Section 6.1, a number of objectives suggest themselves. These are briefly described next. As we shall see, these objectives are reflected in the X3T9.5 algorithm.

- Allow equal, almost immediate, access under light loading. The objective is to avoid unnecessary delay; CSMA/CD behaves in this fashion.
- Provide fair (round-robin) access with no throughput falloff under heavy loads. The objective is to avoid the instability of contention-based protocols; token bus behaves in this fashion.
- Allow uninterrupted multiframe dialogue between two stations. The necessity for this feature was described in Section 6.2.

With these objectives in mind, we now turn to a description of the ANS X3T9.5 MAC protocol.

The ANS MAC protocol is based on CSMA. That is, a station wishing to transmit listens to the medium and defers if a transmission is in progress. In addition, an algorithm is used that specifically seeks to avoid collisions when the medium is found idle by multiple stations.

The scheme is remarkably similar to token bus. In both cases, the stations or ports form a logical ring (PORT0, PORT1, . . .PORTN, PORT0,. . .). In the case of token bus, at network initialization PORT(0) has the opportunity to transmit. PORT(I + 1) waits to transmit until it receives the token from PORT(I). With the number of stations equal to N + 1, PORT(0) gets its next opportunity to transmit after PORT(N). In the ANS scheme, the network reinitializes after each transmission by any port. Each station, in turn, may transmit if none of the stations before it has done so. So PORT(I + 1) waits until after PORT(I) has had a chance to transmit. The waiting time consists of:

- The earliest time at which PORT(I) could begin transmitting [which depends on the transmission opportunity for PORT(I-1)].
- Plus a port delay time, during which PORT(I) has the opportunity to transmit.
- Plus the propagation delay between the two ports.

As we shall see, this rather simple concept becomes complex as we consider all of its refinements.

The basic rule can be described as follows. After any transmission, PORT(0) has the right to transmit. If it fails to do so in a reasonable time, then PORT(1) has the chance, and so on. If any port transmits, the system reinitializes.

The first refinement is that we would like to permit multiframe dialogues. To accommodate this, an additional rule is added: after any transmission, the port receiving that transmission has the first right to transmit. If that port fails to transmit, then it is the turn of PORT(0), and so on. This will permit two ports to seize the medium, with one port sending data frames and the other sending acknowledgment frames.

Second refinement: What happens if nobody has a frame to transmit? HYPERchannel solves this by entering a free-for-all period, in which collisions are allowed. The ANS protocol has a more elegant solution: If none of the stations transmits when it has an opportunity, then reinitialize the network and start over.

With these two refinements, we can depict the MAC protocol as a simple sequence of events:

1. Medium Is Active.
2. Medium Goes Idle.
     If Receiver Transmits, Then Go To 1
          Else Go To 3.
3. If PORT(0) Transmits, Then Go To 1
          Else Go To 4.

        ·
        ·
        ·

N + 4. If No Port Transmits, Then Go To 1.

Third refinement: Note that this scheme is biased to the lower-number ports. PORT(0) *always* gets a shot, for example. To make the scheme fair, a port that has just transmitted should not try again until everyone else has had a chance.

To define the algorithm concisely, with these three refinements, we need to define some quantities:

• *Priority access opportunity:* a period of time granted to a port after it receives a frame. May be used to acknowledge frame and/or continue a multiframe dialogue.
• *Priority access timer (PAT):* used to time priority access opportunities—64 bit times.
• *Arbitrated access opportunity:* a period of time granted to each port in sequence, during which it may initiate a transmission—16 bit times. Assigned to individual ports to avoid collisions.
• *Arbitrated access timer (AAT):* used to provide each port with a unique, nonoverlapping, arbitrated access opportunity.

- *Resynchronization timer (RT):* time by which the latest possible arbitrated transmission should have been received. Used to reset all timers.
- *Arbiter wait flag (WF):* used to enforce fairness. When a port transmits, its WF is set, so that it will not attempt another arbitrated transmission until all other ports have an opportunity.

For the timers listed, we use the convention that uppercase letters refer to the variable name, and lowercase letters to a specific value. A timer that reaches a specified maximum value is said to have expired.

Now we are in a position to describe the operation of the algorithm, which is depicted in Figure 6.6. Each port on the medium has three timers (PAT, AAT, RT), which keep "local time" (i.e., time with respect to that port). When the medium is active, all timers on all ports are set to zero. When the medium goes idle, all three timers are started. Note that this event occurs at slightly different times for the various ports due to propagation delay.

When the medium goes idle, the port that just received a frame is granted a priority access opportunity, and may initiate a transmission until PAT expires. Of course, if the port in question chooses to transmit, then all timers on all ports are reset and the operation begins again at the beginning.

Each port is assigned a specific value of AAT which signals the beginning of its arbitrated access opportunity. These values are ordered to give PORT(0) the first opportunity, and so on (aat0 < aat1 . . . < aatN). When the AAT of PORT(0) expires (AAT0 = aat0), and if its WF is not set, and if it has something to transmit, then PORT(0) may transmit. It has 16 bit times to do so, which is the duration of its arbitrated access opportunity. If PORT(0) transmits, it sets its WF. The flag will not be cleared until the port's RT expires. The implication of this, as we shall see, is that the port may not transmit again during an arbitrated access opportunity until all other ports have had an opportunity to do so. However, the port may still transmit during a priority access opportunity when it receives a frame.

If PORT(0) does not transmit during its arbitrated access opportunity, either because it has nothing to send or because its WF prohibits transmission, then it is the turn of PORT(1). PORT(1) will recognize this condition as occurring

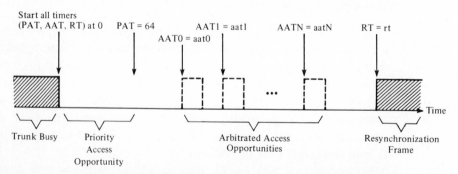

**FIGURE 6–6. Operation of the ANS X3T9.5 Medium-Access Protocol**

when AAT1 expires (AAT1 = aat1). The general condition can be stated as follows. Following any transmission, PORT(I) may transmit when AATI expires. This will occur if and only if both of the following occur:

- The receiving port fails to transmit during its priority access opportunity.
- PORT(J) fails to transmit during its arbitrated access opportunity, for all J, $0 \leq J < I$.

Eventually, a transmission will occur following which the priority access opportunity is not used and none of the ports takes advantage of its arbitrated access opportunity. The latter will occur because each of the ports has nothing to send or its WF is set. At this point, the ordered transmission scheme has broken down and the system must be reinitialized or resynchronized. The easiest way to do this is to have somebody, anybody, transmit a frame, which resets all timers to zero.

The reinitialization function is facilitated by RT. When a port's RT expires, it resets its WF and AAT. If the AAT then expires, the port must send a frame, with or without data. This resets all timers at all ports.

The expiration values for the three timers at each port must be set with due regard for propagation delay. The general strategy is:

- *pat* is the same for all ports—64 bit times.
- *aat0* is set to wait until after a priority transmission from any other port would have reached PORT(0).
- *aatI*, for $I > 0$, is set to wait until after an arbitrated transmission from PORT(I-1) would have reached PORT(I).
- *rt* is the same for all ports, and is set to wait until after an arbitrated transmission from PORT(N) would have reached every port.

A simple technique for satisfying the foregoing conditions is to set each timer to a value greater than the previous timer by an amount equal to 2T + DP, where T equals the end-to-end propagation delay and DP equals a port delay sufficient to allow a port to do the processing required prior to transmission. This technique is less than optimal, and the ANSI draft standard suggests a scheme based on the actual propagation delay between any pair of ports.

To explain this scheme, consider the layout of Figure 6.7. When it hears idle, PORT(0) must wait until the recipient of the last transmission has an opportunity for a priority transmission. The worse case for this is if the last transmission were addressed to PORT(2). Now, PORT(2) may not hear idle until a time later than when PORT(0) hears it by an amount equal to the propagation delay between the two, $t_{0,2}$. PORT(2) then has 64 bit times (*pat*) to transmit, and the start of that transmission will not be heard by PORT(0) until $t_{0,2}$ later. Hence when PORT(0) hears idle, it must wait until after the priority access opportunity plus twice the maximum propagation delay between it and any other port.

Next, PORT(1) must wait until after the duration of PORT(0)'s arbitrated

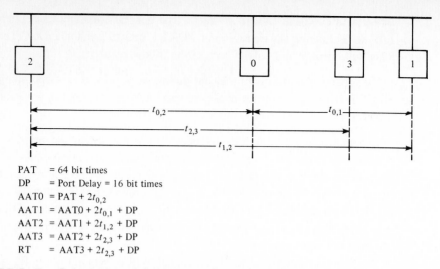

PAT = 64 bit times
DP = Port Delay = 16 bit times
AAT0 = PAT + $2t_{0,2}$
AAT1 = AAT0 + $2t_{0,1}$ + DP
AAT2 = AAT1 + $2t_{1,2}$ + DP
AAT3 = AAT2 + $2t_{2,3}$ + DP
RT = AAT3 + $2t_{2,3}$ + DP

**FIGURE 6–7. Calculation of Arbitration Timer Settings**

access opportunity. Recognize, however, that the timers at the two ports differ. PORT(1) may not have heard idle until $t_{0,1}$ after PORT(0). Further, if PORT(0) chooses to transmit, PORT(1) will not hear it for $t_{0,1}$. So, PORT(1) must wait until after the arbitrated access opportunity for PORT(0) plus twice the propagation delay between the two ports.

The same means of computation is used for PORT(2) and PORT(3). Finally, there is RT. For simplicity, we set it the same for all ports. It is set to wait until after the arbitrated access opportunity for PORT(3) plus twice the propagation delay between PORT(3) and the port most distant from it, PORT(2).

From the above reasoning, we may derive the following general formulas:

$$pat = 64$$
$$aat0 = 64 + 2\,t_{0,f}$$
$$aatI = aat(I - 1) + 2t_{I,I-1} + DP, \qquad 1 \le I \le N$$
$$rt = aatN + 2\,t_{N,f}$$

where $t_{i,f}$ is the propagation delay between PORT(I) and the port most distant from it.

Note that the example in Figure 6.7 is not optimal. That is, the ordering assigned to the ports will not produce the minimum waiting times. If the ports are numbered sequentially in physical order, the waiting times will be less.

There are several strengths to the ANS MAC approach. Collisions are avoided; this reduces overhead. The priority access opportunity permits lengthy multiframe transfers. Finally, fairness is enforced.

There are some weaknesses as well. In general, this approach yields longer waiting times than CSMA/CD. This is so because PORT(I) must wait AATI to transmit when no earlier port wishes to do so. However, because the total number of ports is small, this delay has a reasonably small upper bound. Also, unlike token bus and token ring, this scheme has no concept of an inactive station. Therefore, the greater the number of ports on the network, active or not, the greater the overhead.

The HYPERchannel algorithm is very similar to the ANS scheme just described. There are two major differences:

- HYPERchannel does not use a wait flag. Hence the higher priority ports can easily dominate the medium's capacity.
- If no port transmits during an arbitration cycle, a "free for all" period is entered during which any station may transmit, as in CSMA. This permits collisions to occur.

## Distributed Reservation

The MAC algorithm described above is, in most respects, well suited to the HSLN application. There are, of course, some limitations. Two in particular are of some concern. First, there is a practical limitation on the number of devices. As the number of devices increases, so does the number of arbitrated access opportunities, increasing the system overhead. Second, a long duration transmission can utilize the multiframe dialogue feature to lock the bus and prevent any other station from gaining access.

With current technology, these limitations may not be too serious. A 50-Mbps coaxial system accommodates only a limited number of devices anyway, and the cost of such systems dictates that most stations will be expensive high-speed devices for which long duration transmissions are the most important.

Down the line, however, these limitations may be unsatisfactory. The advent of wider bandwidth technologies (e.g., fiber optic bus) will allow integrated networks with a wide variety of traffic types. For example, some of the stations may generate short, bursty traffic with modest throughput requirements but a need for a short delay time. Other stations may generate long streams of traffic that require high throughput, but they may be able to tolerate moderate delays prior to the start of a transmission.

A fair random access scheme, such as the one described earlier, will not function well in these circumstances. For example, a stream transmission can cause intolerable delays for bursty traffic. If stream traffic load is stable, one solution is to dedicate certain portions of the bandwidth to various traffic types. This can be done using FDM on a broadband LAN, or by dedicating certain time slots on a TDM HSLN system. However, if the stream traffic load varies, as when file transfers are made primarily at night and interactive traffic is high during the day, then a fixed-allocation scheme lacks flexibility and is wasteful of bandwidth.

For a single-channel HSLN, a distributed reservation scheme that can dynamically allocate bandwidth to streams and bursty traffic seems well suited to the type of environment we have been describing. Such a scheme would provide, on demand, adequate bandwidth to meet the stream traffic load, and leave the rest of the bandwidth available for bursty traffic. A number of such schemes have been proposed. We will examine one in particular [HANS81] that was designed specifically for the HSLN context. Similar approaches can be found in [CHU82], [PROT82], and [SUDA83]. But first, we look at the reservation schemes that were its precursors.

### Precursors

All of the schemes to be discussed in this subsection share several features in common. For one, all were originally designed for a satellite network. Such a network consists of a set of ground stations and a satellite in synchronous orbit. All ground stations transmit data to the satellite, which repeats the transmission in broadcast fashion back down to all ground stations. Note the similarity to broadband LAN.

An interesting feature of satellite networks is that while carrier sensing is not practical, collision detection is. This is because of the long round trip propagation delay of 270 ms. With such delays, carrier sense is useless because packets will typically be very short compared to propagation time. Enormous packets would be needed for ground stations to hear a transmission while the originating station was still sending. For example, at a rate of 1.5 Mbps, the "bit length" of the medium is 405,000 bits. On the other hand, because of the delay, a station can easily listen to its own transmission to detect a collision.

Other features in common: They are all based in some sense on the slotted ALOHA (S-ALOHA) protocol. Also, time on the network is organized into an indefinite sequence of fixed-length "frames" (not to be confused with a link layer frame). Each frame, with a duration at least as long as the round-trip propagation delay, is divided into slots. Actual transmission is at the slot level. Because of the minimum frame length constraint, stations are aware of the usage status of time slots in the previous frame. The significance of this will be seen shortly.

Finally, all of these schemes are reservation schemes: Slots in future frames are reserved in some dynamic fashion for specific stations. They differ primarily in the way in which the reservations are made and released.

The simplest of these schemes is one proposed in [CROW73], called R-ALOHA. Reservations are implicit: Successful transmission in a slot serves as a reservation for the corresponding slot in the next frame. By repeated use of that slot position, a station can transmit a long stream of data. A station wishing to transmit one or more packets (one packet per slot) of data monitors the slots in the current frame. Any slot that is empty or contains a collision is available for the next frame; the station may contend for that slot using S-ALOHA. This approach allows a dynamic mixture of stream and bursty traffic.

The scheme described above will work with an unknown or dynamically varying number of stations. A scheme proposed in [BIND75] requires a fixed number of stations less than or equal to the number of time slots in a frame.

Each station owns a particular slot position. If there are any extra slots, these are contended for by all stations using S-ALOHA. The owner may use its slot to transmit continuously. If the owner has no data to send, its slot will become empty. This is a signal to the other stations that they may contend for that slot via S-ALOHA. The owner gets its slot back simply by using it. If the transmission is successful, fine; if not, the collision causes other stations to defer and the station reclaims the slot in the next frame. This technique is superior to R-ALOHA for stream-dominated traffic, since each station is guaranteed one slot of bandwidth. However, when there are a large number of stations, this scheme can lead to a very large average delay because of the required number of slots per frame.

A different approach, proposed in [ROBE73], is to use explicit reservations. For this scheme, a frame is divided into $N + 1$ equal-length slots, one of which is further subdivided into "minislots." The minislots, acquired via S-ALOHA, function as a common queue for all users. A station wishing to transmit must send a request packet in a minislot specifying the number of slots desired, up to some maximum number. If the reservation is successful (no collision), the station then determines which future slots it has acquired and transmits in them. For this to work, each station must keep track of the queue length—the number of slots reserved but not yet used. Figure 6.8 illustrates the operation. For lengthy streams, this scheme requires a user to contend for slots repeatedly, which results in significant delivery delay variances if there is much traffic. If the maximum reservation size is set high enough to allow complete stream transmissions, delays to begin transmission of other traffic become long.

A sophisticated scheme that combines elements of the other schemes just described is referred to as *priority-oriented demand assignment* (PODA). This approach has been implemented in SATNET, a prototype packet satellite network [JACO78]. Each frame consists of a data subframe, divided into data slots, and a control subframe divided into smaller reservation slots. A station with one or more packets to send must reserve data slots by transmitting in a reservation slot. A stream reservation is for one or more data slots per frame for the indefinite future. Further, once a station begins transmitting, additional reservations may be piggybacked onto a data packet.

If the number of stations is small, the control subframe consists of a fixed number of slots equal to the number of stations, and each station owns a reservation slot. For larger networks, the reservation slots are contended for using S-ALOHA. Also, the size of the control subframe decreases as the number of outstanding reservations increases, so that backlog can be cleared out.

All stations must keep track of all outstanding reservations. Each takes into account user-specified delay class and priority according to the same algorithm. For stream reservations, interpacket time is also specified. Each station automatically schedules future stream packets based on the single reservation. Additional reservations can be piggybacked on any transmission in the information subframe. These will be scheduled like reservations in the control

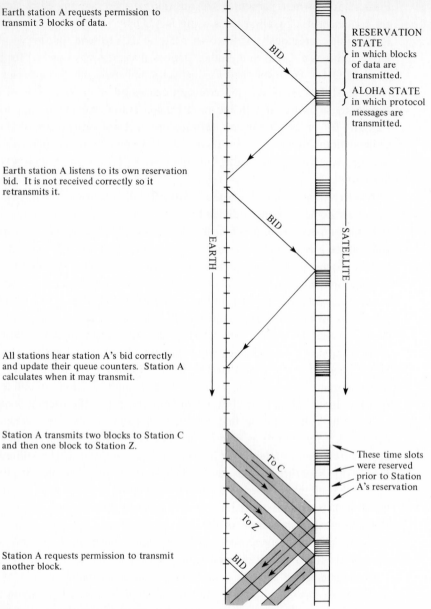

Earth station A requests permission to transmit 3 blocks of data.

BID

RESERVATION STATE in which blocks of data are transmitted.

ALOHA STATE in which protocol messages are transmitted.

Earth station A listens to its own reservation bid. It is not received correctly so it retransmits it.

BID

EARTH

SATELLITE

All stations hear station A's bid correctly and update their queue counters. Station A calculates when it may transmit.

Station A transmits two blocks to Station C and then one block to Station Z.

To C

These time slots were reserved prior to Station A's reservation

To Z

Station A requests permission to transmit another block.

BID

**FIGURE 6—8. ALOHA Scheme with Explicit Reservations**

subframe. Thus both reservation and information subframe messages must be monitored for content by every user. This places a heavy processing burden on each node.

### Hybrid Access Method

Hanson et al. [HANS81] have proposed (but not yet implemented) a distributed reservation MAC protocol for high-speed local networks called the *hybrid access method* (HAM). We examine HAM in some detail because it is representative of the kind of protocol that will be needed for future HSLNs with large numbers of stations and a variety of traffic.

The protocol is designed with the following constraints in mind.

1. Stream transmissions require assurance of bandwidth without interruption.
2. Bursty traffic requires fast response time, and the number of users is large.
3. Simple user stations must have access without the burden of a heavy processing load.
4. A dynamically varying mixture of traffic must be supported.
5. Stream traffic must be restricted to ensure that it does not monopolize the bandwidth.

Constraint 1 can be satisfied with a reservation scheme. Constraint 2 suggests that decentralized control is needed to avoid a bottleneck. Constraint 3 may imply the need for a simple contention scheme for bursty traffic access control; certainly, a simple contention scheme satisfies this constraint. Constraint 4 requires a high bandwidth channel, such as optical fiber. The constraint further implies the need for a dynamic allocation technique. Finally, constraint 5 implies that some guaranteed minimum portion of the channel bandwidth must be dedicated to bursty traffic. HAM is designed to satisfy these constraints; a typical system for which it would be suited would consist of a 0.5- to 1.5-km bus and a 100- to 200-Mbps data rate.

As with the satellite networks, HAM makes use of a frame consisting of a set of slots. Each frame consists of three subframes. The *reservation subframe* consists of a set of reservation minislots. The *reserved subframe* consists of data slots that may be reserved for future use; these are intended for stream traffic. The remainder is an *unreserved subframe* of slots intended for bursty traffic. The boundary between the reserved and unreserved subframes is movable to allow up to a certain maximum number of stream slots with a certain minimum number of bursty slots.

The bursty traffic algorithm is simply explained. Any station may transmit in any bursty slot using S-ALOHA. A station needs timing and synchronization information; it must also know the location of the movable boundary.

To acquire slots in the reserved subframe, a station contends for a minislot to transmit a reservation specifying the requested number of slots per frame. Once a minislot is acquired, the requesting station continues to transmit on the minislot to hold the reservation until the stream transmission is completed. The minislots serve as a queue for the slots available to satisfy stream requests. Requests are met on a first-come, first-served basis.

The sum of the requests in all of the minislots in one frame indicates the number of slots requested for the next frame. If the number requested is less than or equal to the maximum allowable number of stream slots, then all requests are filled and the frame boundary is adjusted so that all unused slots are available for bursty transmission. Otherwise, the maximum number of stream slots is filled and remaining requests are held over. Because all of this is done without centralized control, a station needing to reserve stream slots requires quite a bit of state information. It must know which minislots are in use, to avoid colliding with an ongoing reservation. Once it has the reservation, it must have a count of requests, and it must know what stream slots are available. An example of frame use over time is shown in Figure 6.9.

Slot size selection and frame duration are interrelated with each other and with the traffic mix and load. Longer frames result in greater initial delay for stream transmissions, but can handle more simultaneous streams. Too large a slot size wastes capacity if the stream traffic is not great enough to fill one slot per frame. Too small a slot size reduces effective utilization because a constant overhead for synchronization and addressing is required per slot.

The frame must be at least twice as long as the maximum propagation delay, so the reservations in one frame can be acted on in the next frame. This

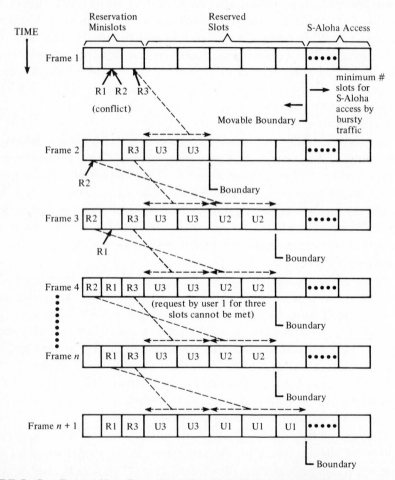

**FIGURE 6–9. Frame Use Over Time for Hybrid Access Method**

condition is easily met because, for synchronization, it seems advisable to require that all slots, including minislots, be as long as the propagation time plus the request or data transmission time. This allows all stations to synchronize on the leading edge of each slot, much as in the ANS technique. Otherwise, a separate clock channel will be needed.

Finally, note that the collision detection function, which is required for the minislots, forces a listen-while-talk capability.

In summary, this scheme meets the different requirements of stream and bursty traffic. Bursty requirements are met with a simple algorithm. For stream traffic, HAM provides for zero delivery time variance unless preemptions are allowed for higher priorities. The use of minislots reduces capacity waste due to collisions.

**6.4**

## HSLN ARCHITECTURE

The special-purpose nature of an HSLN introduces some unique architectural considerations. Some of these we have already considered:

- The high-speed requirement imposes some constraints with current systems, in particular, limited distance and limited number of devices.
- The need to support lengthy file transfers imposes the requirement that multiframe transmissions without interruption be supported.

In this section we look at several additional features of an HSLN architecture. One of these is the use of multiple buses, as depicted in Figure 6.10. Both HYPERchannel and CDC's Loosely Coupled Network offer this configuration, with up to a maximum of four buses allowed. Each controller or adapter may attach to all the buses. Hence a transmission between two devices may take place over any available bus. This configuration has several advantages over a single-bus system.

- *Elimination of a single point of failure:* If one trunk fails, others are available for transmission.

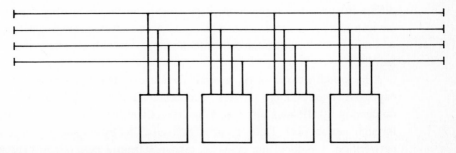

**FIGURE 6–10.   Multiple-Bus HSLN**

- *Reduction of timing delays:* A port must wait for its AAT to expire before transmitting. However, this timer would be kept separately for each bus. Hence a port may transmit when any of its AATs expires.
- *Increased capacity:* Multiple simultaneous transmissions may be accommodated. This is particularly important if multiframe transmissions are common, since a pair of stations can seize one of the buses for an extended period.

It is interesting to note the actual deployment of this feature by customers. Franta [FRAN82] reports statistics on HYPERchannel customers as follows: 60% of networks employ only a single trunk, 35% employ two trunks, 4% contain three, and only 2% contain four trunks. The implication is that most customers feel that they have adequate capacity and availability with a single trunk.

Another implication of the HSLN requirements is that devices must be able to interface to the HSLN at computer channel speeds (on the order of tens of Mbps). These speeds are not met by most standard hardware communications interfaces. Furthermore, many large or mainframe computers do not even have direct communications interfaces; these are usually provided by a front-end processor. A front-end processor off-loads the communications functions from the mainframe and provides a communications interface for low-speed devices such as terminals. For high-speed requirements, such as disk read/write operation, there is a direct connect to the mainframe via an I/O channel. For the HSLN, which is touted as a means of supporting host-to-host and host-to-store file transfers, a direct I/O channel connect to the mainframe is indicated.

This is, in fact, the approach taken by HYPERchannel, which offers a family of HSLN "adapters." Each adapter contains the physical and link layer logic for HSLN operation, plus an interface to the HSLN bus. In addition, each type of adapter offers an I/O channel interface compatible with a particular mainframe or other high-speed data processing device. Building such interfaces is neither simple nor cheap, and the cost accounts in part for the high price tag on an adapter (currently about $40,000). One pays for performance.

Finally, the HSLN is well suited for supporting what has come to be called a *back-end network*. The concept is illustrated in Figure 6.11. This term is in contrast to the term *front-end network*. The latter refers to a LAN or digital switch used to connect terminals to front end processors. A back-end network differs in speed and application. It provides a means for sharing mass storage devices among systems, with high-speed access. More sophisticated systems will relieve the host of some data base functions, providing a data base processor facility.

A back-end network offers several advantages. First, it allows the sharing of expensive mass storage devices. Second, it facilitates distributed data base processing by allowing any host to get directly at the data base, without going through another host. Third, it enhances availability by eliminating "tennis shoe networking": Without the network, recovery from a host failure may require the movement of disk packs or cables.

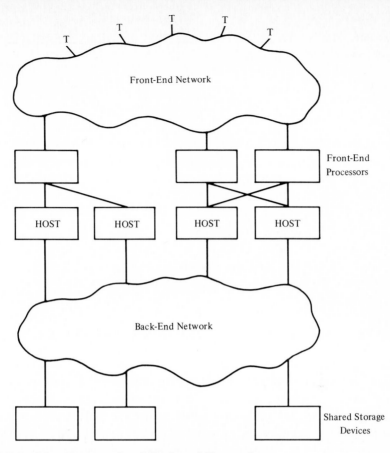

**FIGURE 6–11. Front-end and Back-end Networks**

Statistics reported in [FRAN82] and [ARCH81] indicate that the concept of a back-end network is not yet a dominant one in HSLN installations. The histogram of Figure 6.12 shows that about 90% of installed adapters provide host rather than peripheral interfaces. This suggests that host-to-host applications are currently the most important; it is here that efforts to develop networking services should be directed.

## 6.5

## HSLN versus LAN

We have seen that there are differences in the objectives of the HSLN and the LAN. The HSLN is a special-purpose network, designed for high-speed host-to-host and host-to-storage applications. The LAN is a general-purpose network, designed to support a variety of devices generating a mix of traffic types.

Consider a site that has both a substantial computer room installation plus building-wide office automation requirements. Are two separate local networks necessary? Desirable?

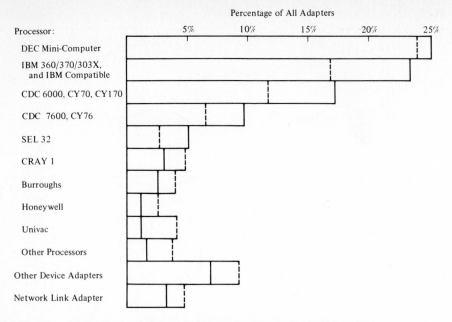

**FIGURE 6—12.  Histogram of Adapter Types in Operational Networks**

The case for two separate networks is clear. The HSLN is tailored to the computer room requirement, the LAN to the office automation requirement. But it is worth considering whether a single broadband LAN, with one or more channels devoted to HSLN-style traffic, might not provide a better solution. With current technology, the broadband LAN can provide a single-channel data rate of up to 15 to 20 Mbps. This is certainly less than 50 Mbps, but as we shall see in Chapter 9, the medium is not the bottleneck in high-speed transfer. An efficient LAN protocol at 20 Mbps should provide throughput of the same order of magnitude as the HSLN. This approach permits the integration of a variety of network requirements on a single network. Which approach is better depends on the trade-offs of the particular situation.

**6.6**

# RECOMMENDED READING

There is not much literature on high-speed local networks, and most of it is concerned with performance, which is discussed in Chapter 9. [THOR80]* provides an overall rationale and describes HYPERchannel. [HOHN80] describes CDC's approach. [ANSI82, App. A]* is a concise and readable description of the ANS X3T9.5 approach. [PARK 83b]* places the standard in the context of a variety of ANSI I/O standards. [HANS81] summarizes the HAM protocol. [KUO80] is a thought-provoking look at the characteristics and applications of future HSLNs in the range 100 to 200 Mbps.

## PROBLEMS

**6.1**    Explain by example how the bit information from the 150 MHz-broadband signal can be recovered by comparing an inverted output to a delayed output.

**6.2**    The 150-MHz carrier has a frequency three times the bit rate of 50 Mbps. Would it be possible to use 50-MHz or 100-MHz carrier?

**6.3**    Using the ANS X3T9.5 signal and interface conventions, develop state transition diagrams for transmission and reception of frames.

**6.4**    For HSLN link control, why is uninterrupted multiframe dialogue preferable to one very long frame to accommodate a long transmission?

**6.5**    Figure 6.5 shows a combined physical and data link diagram for the ANSI standard. Describe the role of each signal and interface, in order to achieve the operation of the ANS scheme described.

**6.6**    Write a program that implements the MAC algorithm in the ANS scheme.

**6.7**    Consider Figure 6.7. Assume propagation delays of 30 bit times between 0 and 2, 15 bit times between 0 and 3, and 5 bit times between 1 and 3. What are the values of the timers? What are the values if the ports are ordered left to right? Right to left?

**6.8**    Derive the formulas for the ANS timers for a unidirectional tree network.

**6.9**    Write a program that calculates the ANS timers for each port on an HSLN, given the appropriate inputs. Assume a propagation velocity of $0.9c$.

**6.10**    Assess token bus, CSMA/CD, and the ANS scheme as MAC algorithms for the HSLN. Which is best suited to the nature and requirements of the HSLN?

**6.11**    Compare the various satellite reservation schemes to HAM when used on an HSLN. Is HAM superior to these other schemes, and why?

**6.12**    In the description of HAM, it was pointed out that to transmit in a bursty slot, a station needs only timing and synchronization information plus the location of the movable boundary. If a station transmits only in bursty slots, can the required information, and hence algorithm complexity, be reduced?

**6.13**    Suggest a bandwidth allocation scheme for HAM. Suggest a priority scheme.

## APPENDIX 6A: ANS X3T9.5 STANDARD

Unlike the situation with LANs, the need for a standard for HSLNs seems less compelling. Because of the high-data-rate requirement, the HSLN vendor must provide a high-throughput interface to the attached device. Such an interface is in the tens of thousands of dollars range, and a VLSI protocol implementation will not significantly affect the price.

In any case, a committee sponsored by the American National Standards Institute (ANSI), known as ANS X3T9.5, has prepared a draft HSLN standard

[ANSI82, PARK83b]. The committee uses a two-layer model, corresponding to the data link and physical layers of the ISO model. The data link layer specifies a simple connectionless service. The physical layer includes the collision-avoidance protocol discussed earlier. It also specifies a single-channel phase-shift-key (PSK) scheme operating at 50 Mbps.

The National Bureau of Standards has announced plans to make the ANS X3T9.5 proposal a federal standard, to be mandatory on future federal government procurements [NBS82].

# CHAPTER 7

# Circuit-Switched Local Networks

Up until now, we have been looking at local networks that use packet switching. For many observers, this is the only kind of local network there is. But there is an alternative, based on the older circuit-switched approach. As we shall see, the differences in architecture and design issues are striking. We will also learn, perhaps to your surprise, that underneath, the similarities are equally striking.

The chapter begins by summarizing the characteristics of a star topology local network. Then we look at the digital switching concepts that underlie this type of network. Next we look at the devices most commonly used to build local networks (although these are rarely thought of as "true" local networks)—digital data switches. We are at last ready to look at the computerized branch exchange (CBX). Finally, the CBX and LAN are compared.

## 7.1

## STAR TOPOLOGY NETWORKS

A star topology network, as described in Chapter 3, consists in essence of a collection of devices or stations attached to a central switching unit. Circuit switching is used; the central switch establishes a dedicated path between any two devices that wish to communicate.

Figure 7.1 depicts the major elements of a star topology network. The heart of a modern system is a digital switch. The advent of digital switching technology has dramatically improved the cost, performance, and capability of circuit-switched networks. Key to the operation of such systems are that (1) all signals are represented digitally, and (2) synchronous time-division multiplexing (TDM) techniques are used.

The network interface element represents the functions and hardware needed to connect digital devices, such as data processing devices and digital telephones, to the network. Analog telephones can also be attached if the network interface contains the logic for converting to digital signals. Trunks to external systems may also be attached. These may include analog voice trunks and digital TDM lines.

The control unit performs three general tasks. First, it establishes connections. This is generally done on demand, that is, at the request of an attached device. To establish the connection, the control unit must handle and acknowledge the request, determine if the intended destination is free, and construct a path through the switch. Second, the logic must maintain the connection. Since the digital switch uses time-division principles, this may require ongoing manipulation of the switching elements. However, the bits of the communication are transferred transparently. This is in contrast to the packet switching used on LANs and HSLNs, which are sensitive to the transmission protocol and can be considered content dependent. Third, the logic must tear down the connection, either in response to a request from one of the parties or for its own reasons.

Star networks may be either one-sided or two-sided. In a one-sided system, all attachment points are viewed the same: A connection can be established between any two devices. In a two-sided system, attachment points are grouped into two classes and a connection can be established only between two devices from different classes. A typical application of the latter is the connection of a

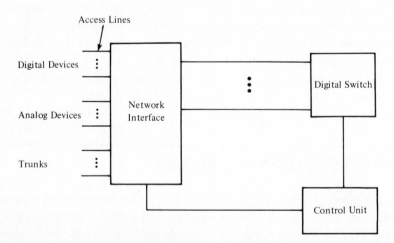

**FIGURE 7–1. Star Topology Elements**

set of terminals to a set of computer ports; in many cases, only terminal-to-port connections are allowed.

An important characteristic of a star topology network is whether it is blocking or nonblocking. Blocking occurs when the network is unable to connect two stations because all possible paths between them are already in use. A blocking network is one in which such blocking is possible. Hence a nonblocking network permits all stations to be connected at once and grants all possible connection requests as long as the called party is free.

## 7.2

## DIGITAL SWITCHING CONCEPTS

The technology of switching has a long history, most of it covering an era when analog signal switching predominated. With the advent of PCM and related techniques, both voice and data can be transmitted via digital signals. This has led to a fundamental change in the design and technology of switching systems. Instead of dumb space-division systems, modern digital switching systems rely on intelligent control of space- and time-division elements.

This section looks at the concepts underlying contemporary digital switching (good discussions can be found in [SKAP79], [JOEL77], [JOEL79a], [JOEL79b], and [FLEM79]). Later sections discuss how these concepts are implemented in data switching devices and CBXs.

### Space-Division Switching

The *space-division switch* is, as its name implies, one in which paths between pairs of devices are divided in space. Each connection requires the establishment of a physical path through the switch that is dedicated solely to the transfer of signals between the two end points. The basic building block of the switch is an electronic crosspoint or semiconductor gate that can be opened and closed by a control unit.

Figure 7.2a shows a simple crossbar matrix with $n$ inputs and $m$ outputs. Interconnection is possible between any input line and any output line by engaging the appropriate crosspoint. The crossbar depicts a bilateral arrangement: there is a distinction between input and output. For example, input lines may connect to terminals, while output lines connect to computer ports. The crossbar switch is said to perform concentration, distribution, or expansion according as $n > m$, $n = m$, or $n < m$.

The crossbar matrix makes a distinction between input and output: Any input can connect to any output. It requires $n \times m$ crosspoints. However, if the inputs and outputs are the same, then $n = m$ and the requirement is that any end point can connect to any other end point. This requires only a triangular

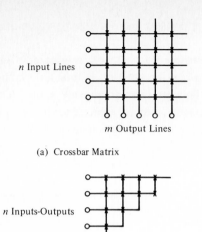

n Input Lines

m Output Lines

(a) Crossbar Matrix

n Inputs-Outputs

(b) Triangular Switch

**FIGURE 7–2.    Single-Stage Space-Division Switch**

array of $n(n - 1)/2$ crosspoints (Figure 7.2b) and is referred to as a ''folded'' configuration.

The crossbar switch has a number of limitations or disadvantages:

- The number of crosspoints grows with $n^2$. This is costly for large $n$, and results in high capacitive loading on any message path.
- The loss of a crosspoint prevents connection between the two devices involved.
- The crosspoints are inefficiently utilized.

To overcome these limitations, multiple stage switches are employed. The $N$ input lines (inlets) are broken up into $N/n$ groups of $n$ lines. Each group of lines goes into a first-stage matrix. The outputs of the first stage matrices become inputs to a group of second-stage matrices, and so on. Figure 7.3a depicts a 3-stage network of switches that is symmetric; that is, the number of inlets to the first stage equals the number of outlets from the last stage. There are $k$ second-stage matrices, each with $N/n$ inlets and $N/n$ outlets. Each first-stage matrix has $k$ outlets so that it connects to all second-stage matrices. Each second-stage matrix has $N/n$ outlets so that it connects to all third-stage matrices.

This type of arrangement has several advantages over the simple crossbar switch:

- The number of crosspoints is reduced (see below), increasing crossbar utilization.
- There is more than one path through the network to connect two endpoints, increasing reliability.

Of course, a multistage network requires a more complex control scheme.

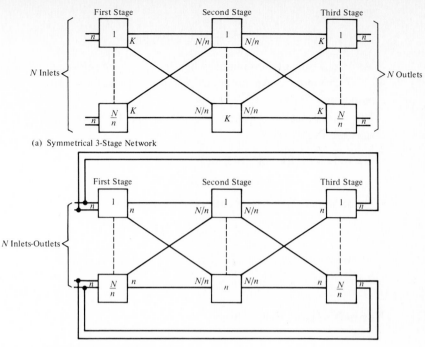

(a) Symmetrical 3-Stage Network

(b) Folded Non-blocking 3-Stage Network

**FIGURE 7–3.   Three-Stage Space-Division Switch**

To establish a path in a single-stage network, it is only necessary to open a single gate. In a multistage network, a free path through the stages must be determined and the appropriate gates opened.

We quote now some of the analytic results for multiple-stage networks. A discussion may be found in [ITT75].

- The number of crosspoints required for a symmetric three-stage network is

$$X = k\left(2N + \frac{N^2}{n^2}\right)$$

- The condition for nonblocking is

$$k = 2n - 1$$

- A minimum number of crosspoints is obtained when $n$ satisfies

$$N = \frac{2n^3}{n - 1}$$

For large $N$, beyond the range of practical 3-stage networks, we have

$$n \cong \sqrt{\frac{N}{2}}$$

This yields:

$$X_{min} = 4N(\sqrt{2N} - 1)$$

As an example of the savings, when $N = 200$, a single-stage network requires 40,000 crosspoints. An optimum 3-stage network ($n = 10$) requires 15,200 crosspoints.

For folded networks (inlets and outlets are the same; see Figure 7.3b) the results are even better:

• The condition for nonblocking is

$$k = n$$

• The minimum number of crosspoints satisfies

$$X_{min} = 2N(\sqrt{2N})$$

A further discussion of this topic can be found in [JASJ83].

## Time-Division Switching

In contrast to space-division switching, in which dedicated paths are used, *time-division switching* involves the partitioning of a lower-speed data stream into pieces that share a higher-speed data stream with other message pieces. The individual pieces or slots are manipulated by the control logic to route data from input to output. Three concepts comprise the technique of time-division switching:

• Time-division multiplexing (TDM)
• Time-slot interchange (TSI)
• Time-multiplex switching (TMS)

### Time-Division Multiplexing

As discussed in Chapter 2, TDM is a technique that allows multiple signals to share a single transmission line by separating them in time. In this chapter we are concerned primarily with synchronous TDM, that is, a situation in which time slots are preassigned so that little or no overhead bits are required.

As shown in Figure 7.4a, synchronous TDM was designed to permit multiple low-speed streams to share a high-speed line. This permits multiple channels of data to be handled efficiently both within and outside switching systems. A set of inputs is sampled in turn. The samples are organized serially into slots (channels) to form a recurring frame of $n$ slots. A slot may be a bit, a byte, or some longer block. An important point to note is that with synchronous TDM, the source and destination of the data in each time slot are known. Hence there is no need for address bits in each slot.

The mechanism for synchronous TDM may be quite simple. For example, each input line deposits data in a buffer; the multiplexer scans these buffers

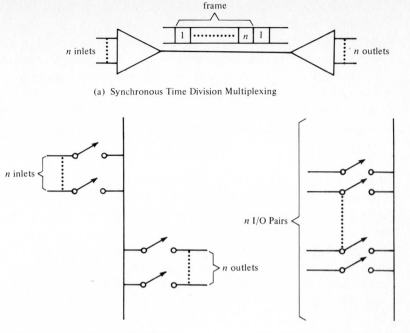

(a) Synchronous Time Division Multiplexing

(b) A Simple Time-Division Switch

(c) A Simple Folded Time-Division Switch

**FIGURE 7—4. TDM Bus Switching**

sequentially, taking fixed size chunks of data from each buffer and sending it out on the line. One complete scan produces one frame of data. For output to the lines, the reverse operation is performed, with the multiplexer filling the output line buffers one by one.

The I/O lines attached to the multiplexer may be synchronous or asynchronous; the multiplexed line between the two multiplexers is synchronous and must have a data rate equal to the sum of the data rates of the attached lines. Actually, the multiplexed line must have a slightly higher data rate, since each frame will include some overhead bits—headers and trailers—for synchronization.

The time slots in a frame are assigned to the I/O lines on a fixed, predetermined basis. If a device has no data to send, the multiplexer must send empty slots. Thus the actual data transfer rate may be less than the capacity of the system.

Figure 7.4b shows a simple way in which TDM can be used to achieve switching. A set of buffered input and output lines are connected through controlled gates to a high-speed digital bus. Each input line is assigned a time slot. During that time, that line's gate is opened, allowing a small burst of data onto the bus. For that same time slot, one of the output line gates is also opened. Since the opening and closing of gates is controlled, the sequence of input and output line activations need not be in the same order. Hence a form of switching is possible. Curiously, this technique has no specific name; we shall refer to it as TDM bus switching.

Of course, such a scheme need not be two-sided. As shown in Figure 7.4c, a "folded" switch can be devised by attaching $n$ I/O pairs to the bus. Any attached device achieves full duplex operation by transmitting during one assigned time slot and receiving during another. The other end of the connection is an I/O pair for which these time slots have the opposite meanings.

The TDM bus switch has an advantage over a crossbar switch in terms of efficient use of gates. For $n$ devices, the TDM bus switch requires $2n$ gates or switchpoints, whereas the most efficient multistage crossbar network requires requires on the order of $n\sqrt{n}$ switchpoints.

Let us look at the timing involved a bit more closely. First, consider a nonblocking implementation of Figure 7.4c. There must be $n$ repetitively occurring time slots, each one assigned to an input and an output line. We will refer to one iteration for all time slots as a frame. The input assignment may be fixed; the output assignments vary to allow various connections. When a time slot begins, the designated input line may insert a burst of data onto the line, where it will propagate to both ends past all other lines. The designated output line will, during that time, copy the data if any as they go by. The time slot, then, must equal the transmission time of the input line plus the propagation delay between input and output lines. In order to keep the successive time slots uniform, time slot length should be defined as transmission time plus the end-to-end bus propagation delay. For efficiency, the propagation delay should be much less than the transmission time. Note that only one time slot or burst of data may be on the bus at a time.

To keep up with the input lines, the slots must recur sufficiently frequently. For example, consider a system connecting full-duplex lines at 19.2 kbps. Input data on each line are buffered at the gate. The buffer must be cleared, by opening the gate, fast enough to avoid overrun. So if there are 100 lines, the capacity of the bus must be at least 1.92 Mbps. Actually, it must be higher than that to account for the wasted time due to propagation delay.

These considerations determine the traffic-carrying capacity of a blocking switch as well. For a blocking switch, there is no fixed assignment of input lines to time slots; they are allocated on demand. The data rate on the bus dictates how many connections can be made at a time. For a system with 200 devices at 19.2 kbps and a bus at 2 Mbps, about half of the devices can be connected at any one time.

The TDM bus switching scheme can accommodate lines of varying data rates. For example, if a 9600 bps line gets one slot per frame, a 19.2-kbps line would get two slots per frame. Of course, only lines of the same data rate can be connected.

Several questions may occur to you. For one, is this circuit switching? Circuit switching, recall, was defined as a technique in which a dedicated communications path is established between devices. This is indeed the case for Figure 7.4. To establish a connection between an input and output line, the controller dedicates a certain number of time slots per frame to that connection. The appropriate input and output gates are opened during those time slots to allow data to pass. Although the bus is shared by other connections, it is nevertheless used to create a dedicated path between input and output. Another question: Is this synchronous TDM? Synchronous TDM is generally associated with creating permanent dedicated time slots for each input line. The scheme depicted in Figure 7.4 can assume a dynamic character, with the controller allocating available time slots among connections. Nevertheless, at steady state—a period when no connections are made or broken—a fixed number of slots is dedicated per channel and the system behaves as a synchronous time-division multiplexer.

The control logic for the system described above requires the opening of two gates to achieve a connection. This logic can be simplified if the input burst into a time slot contains destination address information. All output devices can then always connect to the bus and copy the data from time slots with their address. This scheme blurs the distinction between circuit switching and packet switching.

This point bears further comment. In the bus reservation schemes described in Chapters 5 and 6, a device with a quantity of data to send reserves sufficient future slots to handle that data. After the data are sent, the reservation goes away until the station again wants to send. In the TDM bus switching scheme, a station reserves one or more time slots per frame for the indefinite future by requesting a connection. The reservation lasts until a disconnect is requested. The logic of the two schemes is very close.

Another point: The LAN/HSLN bus and the TDM bus switch differ only in geometry, not topology. The LAN or HSLN bus involves a relatively long bus with stations attached via relatively short lines. The "star topology" of the TDM bus switch actually involves a relatively short bus with stations attached via relatively long lines. This difference is crucial, of course: The timings on the shorter bus are amenable to greater control because of the much shorter propagation delay. Also, as we shall see, not all digital switch architectures use a pure TDM bus switch. Nevertheless, the implication of the preceding discussion is valid: The differences between the technologies and architectures of the various types of networks discussed in this book are less than one might think.

### Time-Slot Interchange

The basic building block of many time-division switches is the *time-slot interchange* (TSI) mechanism. A TSI unit operates on a synchronous TDM stream of time slots, or channels, by interchanging pairs of slots to achieve full duplex operation. Figure 7.5a shows how the input line of device I is connected to the output line of device J, and vice versa.

We should note several points. To achieve interconnection, the input lines of $N$ devices are passed through a synchronous multiplexer to produce a TDM stream with $N$ slots. To allow the interchange of any two slots, the incoming data in a slot must be stored until they can be sent out on the right channel in the next frame cycle. Hence the TSI introduces a delay and produces output

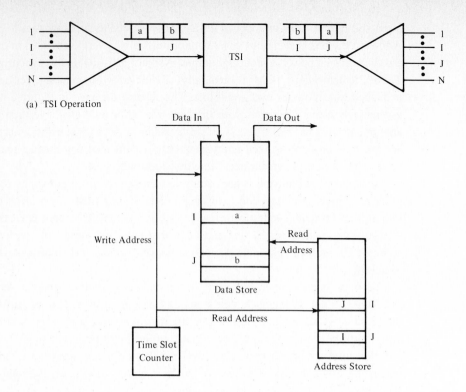

(a) TSI Operation

(b) TSI Mechanism

**FIGURE 7–5. Time-Slot Interchange (TSI)**

slots in the desired order. These are then demultiplexed and routed to the appropriate output line. Since each channel is provided a time slot in the frame, whether or not it transmits data, the size of the TSI unit must be chosen for the capacity of the TDM line, not the actual data transfer rate.

Figure 7.5b depicts a mechanism for TSI. A data store whose width equals one time slot of data and whose length equals the number of slots in a frame is used. An incoming TDM frame is written sequentially, slot by slot, into random access memory. An outgoing TDM frame is created by reading slots from the memory in an order dictated by an address store that reflects the existing connections. In the figure, the data in channels I and J are interchanged, creating a full-duplex connection between the corresponding stations.

TSI is a simple, effective way of switching TDM data. However, the size of such a switch, in terms of number of connections, is limited by the memory access speed. It is clear that, in order to keep pace with the input, data must be read into and out of memory as fast as they arrive. So, for example, if we have 24 sources operating at 64 kbps each, and a slot size of 8 bits, we would have an arrival rate of 192,000 slots per second (this is the structure of the

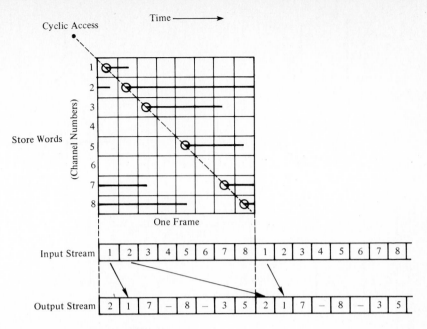

**FIGURE 7–6. Operation of TSI Store**

PCM T1 carrier). Memory access time would need to be 1/192,000, or about 5 μs.

Let us look more closely at the operation of the data store; in particular, we need to view it as a function of time. As an example [DAVI73], consider a system with eight input/output lines, in which the following connections exist: 1–2, 3–7, and 5–8. The other two stations are not in use. Figure 7.6 depicts the contents of the data store over the course of one frame (eight slots). During the first time slot, data are stored in location 1 and read from location 2. During the second time slot, data are stored in location 2 and read from location 1. And so on.

As can be seen, the write accesses to the data store are cyclic, that is, accessing successive locations in sequential order, whereas the read accesses are acyclic, requiring the use of an address store. The figure also depicts two frames of the input and output sequences and indicates the transfer of data between channels 1 and 2. Note that in half the cases, data slots move into the next frame.

As with the TDM bus switch, the TSI unit can handle inputs of varying data rates. Figure 7.7 suggests a way in which this may be done. Instead of presenting the input lines to a synchronous multiplexer, they are presented to a selector device. This device will select an input line based on a channel assignment provided from a store controlled by the time slot counter. Hence, instead of sampling equally from each input, it may gather more slots from some channels than others.

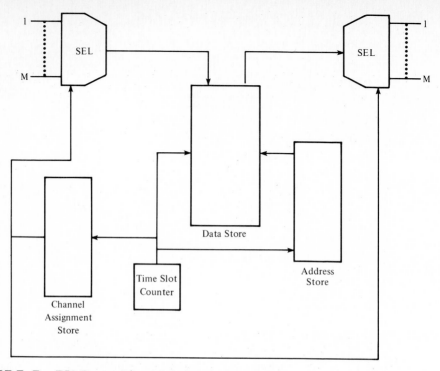

**FIGURE 7—7.  TSI Operation with Variable-Rate Input**

### Time-Multiplexed Switching

As we have seen, a TSI unit can support only a limited number of connections. Further, as the size of the unit grows, for a fixed access speed, the delay at the TSI grows. To overcome both of these problems, multiple TSI units are used. Now, to connect two channels entering a single TSI unit, their time slots can be interchanged. However, to connect a channel on one TDM stream (going into one TSI) to a channel or another TDM stream (going into another TSI), some form of space division multiplexing is needed. Naturally, we do not wish to switch all of the time slots from one stream to another; we would like to do it one slot at a time. This technique is known as *time-multiplexed switching* (TMS).

Multiple-stage networks can be built up by concatenating TMS and TSI stages. TMS stages, which move slots from one stream to another, are referred to as S, and TSI stages are referred to as T. Systems are generally described by an enumeration of their stages from input to output, using the symbols T and S. Figure 7.8 is an example of a 2-stage TS network. Such a network is blocking. For example, if one channel in input stream 1 is to be switched to the third channel in output stream 1, and another channel in input stream 1 is to be switched to the third channel in output stream 2, one of the connections is blocked.

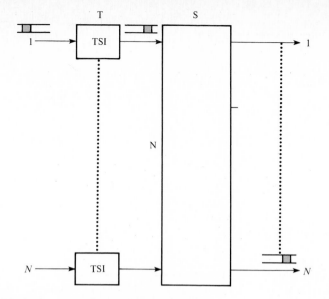

**FIGURE 7–8. Two-Stage Digital Switch**

To avoid blocking, three or more stages are used. Some of the more common structures used in commercially available systems are [SKAP79]:

- TST
- TSSST
- STS
- SSTSS
- TSTST

The requirements on the TMS unit are stringent. The unit must provide space-division connections between its input and output lines, and these connections must be reconfigured for each time slot. This requires, in effect, a control store whose width is sufficient to handle the number of ingoing and outgoing lines and whose length equals the number of time slots in a frame.

One means of implementing the TMS stage is the crossbar switch discussed earlier. This requires that the crosspoints be manipulated at each time slot. More commonly, the TMS stage is implemented by digital selectors (SEL) which select only one input at a time on a time slot basis. These SEL devices are the same as those described in the preceding section, except that here each of their inputs is a TDM stream rather than a single line. Figure 7.9 shows STS and TST networks implemented with the SEL units.

In an STS network, the path between an incoming and outgoing channel has multiple possible physical routes equal to the number of TSI units. For a fully nonblocking network, the number of TSI units must be double the number of incoming and outgoing TDM streams. On the other hand, the multiple routes

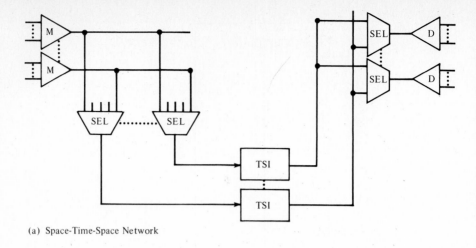

(a) Space-Time-Space Network

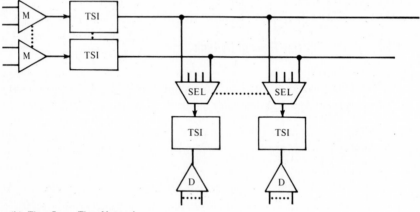

(b) Time-Space-Time Network

## FIGURE 7—9. Three-Stage TDM Switches

between two channels in a TST network are all in the time domain; there is only one physical path possible. Here, too, blocking is a possibility. One way to avoid blocking is by expanding the number of time slots in the space stage. In all multistage networks, a path-search algorithm is needed to determine the route from input to output.

It is interesting to compare the TDM bus switch with TSI and TMS. It does not exactly fit into either category. Compare it to a space switch. The TDM bus switch does connect any input with any output, as in a crossbar or SEL switch. The space switch operates simultaneously on all inputs, whereas the TDM bus switch operates on the inputs sequentially. However, because the frame time on the bus is less than the slot time of any input, the switching is effectively simultaneous. On the other hand, a comparison of Figures 7.5 and 7.4b reveals the similarity between TSI and TDM bus switching.

# DIGITAL DATA SWITCHING DEVICES

The techniques discussed in the preceding section have been used to build a variety of digital switching products designed for data-only applications. These devices do not provide telephone service and are generally cheaper than a CBX for comparable capacity.

The variety of devices is wide and the distinction between types is blurred. For convenience, we categorize them as follows:

• Terminal/port-oriented switch
• Data switch
• Switching statistical multiplexer

In what follows we will look at the functions performed by each type of device, and suggest an architecture that supports those functions. Keep in mind that usually any of the techniques in Section 7.2, or any combination, may be used to implement any of these switches. The discussion here is intended only to give examples.

Before turning to the specific device types, let us look at the requirements for data switching.

## Data Switching Requirements

For any circuit-switching system used to connect digital data transmitting devices, certain generic requirements can be defined. These requirements apply both to pure digital data switching devices and to CBX systems. We begin first by looking briefly at the data transmission techniques that must be supported by a data switch, and then look at the functions to be performed.

The devices attached to a data switch will use either asynchronous or synchronous transmission. Asynchronous transmission, recall, is character-at-a-time. Each character consists of a start bit, 5 to 8 data bits, a parity bit, and a stop signal, which may be 1, 1.5, or 2 bit times in length. Logic is available which can automatically determine character length, parity, and even bit rate. Hence it is a relatively easy matter for a data switch to handle asynchronous transmission. On input, data are accumulated a character at a time, and transmitted internally using synchronous transmission. At the other end of the connection, they are buffered and transmitted a character at a time to the output line. This applies to any switch using time-division switching techniques. Of course, a pure space-division switch need not concern itself with such matters! A dedicated physical path is set up and bits are transmitted transparently.

Synchronous transmission represents a greater challenge. Synchronous communication requires either a separate clock lead from the transmission point to the reception point or the use of a self-clocking encoding scheme, such as Manchester. The latter technique is typical. With synchronous communication, the data rate must be known ahead of time, as well as the synchronization pattern (bits or characters used to signal the beginning of a frame). Thus there can be no universal synchronous interface.

Of course, for either synchronous or asynchronous transmission, full duplex operation is required. Typically, this requires two twisted pairs (known as a *twin pair*) between a device and the switch, one for transmission in each direction. This is in contrast to the case with analog signaling where a single twisted-pair suffices (see Figure 2.4). Recently, however, some vendors have begun to offer full-duplex digital signaling on a single twisted pair, using a *ping-pong protocol*. In essence, data are buffered at each end and sent across the line at double the data rate, with the two ends taking turn. So, for example, two devices may communicate, full duplex, at 56 kbps if they are attached to a 112-kbps line and the line drivers at each end buffer the device data and transmit, alternately, at 112 kbps.

We turn now to the functions to be provided by a data switch. The most basic, of course, is the making of a connection between two attached lines. These connections can be pre-configured by a system operator, but more dynamic operation is often desired. This leads to two additional functions: port contention and port selection. *Port contention* is a function that allows a certain number of designated ports to contend for access to a smaller number of ports. Typically, this is used for terminal to host connection to allow a smaller number of host ports to service a larger number of terminal ports. When a terminal user attempts to connect, the system will scan through all the host ports in the contention group. If any of the ports is available, a connection is made.

*Port selection* is an interactive capability. It allows a user (or an application program in a host) to select a port for connection. This is analogous to dialing a number in a phone system. Port selection and port contention can be combined by allowing the selection, by name or number, of a contention group. Port selection devices are becoming increasingly common. A switch without this capability only allows connections that are preconfigured by a system operator. If one knows in advance what interconnections are required, fine. Otherwise, the flexibility of port selection is usually worth the additional cost.

An interactive capability carries with it an additional responsibility: the control unit of the switch must be able to talk to the requesting port. This can be done in two ways. In some cases, the manufacturer supplies a simple keypad device that attaches to and shares the terminal's line. The user first uses the keypad to dial a connection; once the connection is made, communication is via the terminal. As an alternative, the connection sequence can be effected through the terminal itself. A simple command language dialogue is used. However, this technique requires that the system understand the code and protocol being used by the terminal. Consequently, this feature is generally limited to asynchronous ASCII devices.

## Terminal/Port-Oriented Switches

The devices discussed in this section were designed to address a specific problem: the connection of interactive terminals to computer ports. In many computer sites with one or more time-sharing systems and a population (usually growing) of terminals, means must be found for interconnection.

One means of connection is simply to assign each terminal to a specific computer port, even when not active. This is expensive in terms of computer ports, since generally only a fraction of the terminals are logged on. Further, the user cannot change to a different computer without making cable changes. Another approach is to use multiple dial-up telephone rotaries, for each computer and each transmission speed. The rotary allows a user to call a single number and gain access to one of several autoanswer modems; if all modems are busy, the rotary returns a busy signal. The approach ties up telephones lines for extended periods and requires the use of modems.

One early solution that avoids some of the expenses mentioned above was the patch panel. This device enabled manual connection of two lines and could also provide some system monitoring and diagnostics. The addition of intelligence to this type of device to eliminate the manual connection function has resulted in a variety of intelligent terminal/port-oriented switches. A variety of names are used, depending partly on function, including intelligent patch panel, port selector, and port contention device.

At a minimum, these devices permit a set of connections to be set up and periodically updated by a system operator. Port selection and port contention functions are also provided on many products.

Figure 7.10 is an example of a noninteractive (without port selection) system. The system allows connection of one I/O port to any other I/O port on the same or a different port card. Connections are set up at system intialization time and may be changed dynamically by the system operator (not the user). The means of establishing connections is simple. Each port has associated with it a destination address register. To connect two ports, the address of each is placed in the other. To transmit data, the sending device puts its data (8 bits) and the destination address (8 bits) on the bus. All devices continually monitor the bus for their own address. The switch is nonblocking, allowing the preassignment of time slots to transmitting devices. Receiving devices need not know the time slot for reception since they are looking for an address. Thus, at the cost of 100% overhead, the control logic is greatly simplified.

Figure 7.11 is an example of a port selection system. A collection of line modules are scanned to produce a TDM stream which is passed over a bus to a switch module. The output of the switch module is a switched set of time

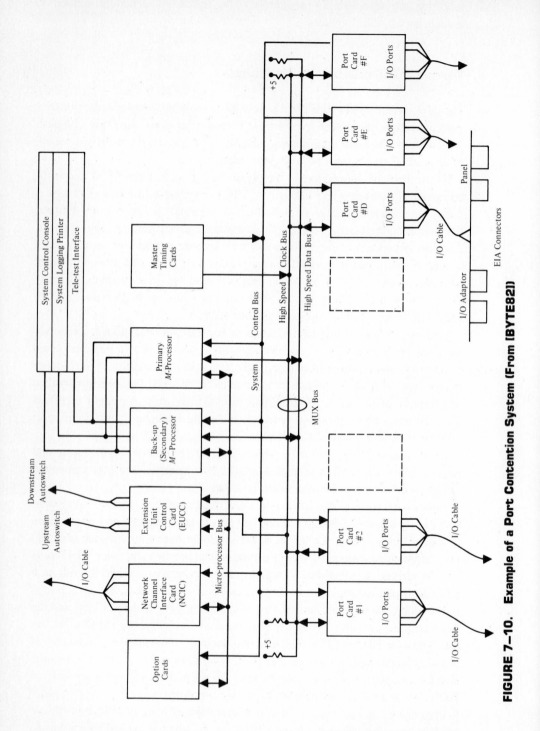

**FIGURE 7–10.  Example of a Port Contention System (From [BYTE82])**

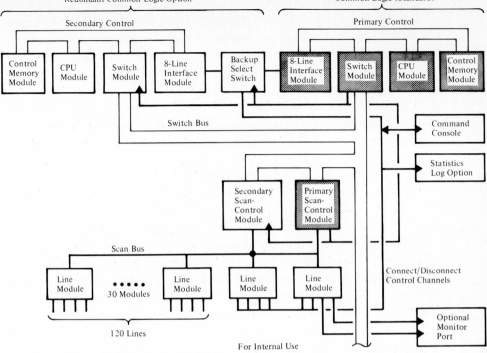

**FIGURE 7–11. Example of a Port Selection System (From [VONA80])**

slots that are directed to the proper port. Note the redundant architecture for reliability.

## Data Switches

There is little additional that need be said about these devices. No distinction is made between terminal lines and ports. The switch simply has a set of I/O lines and is capable of establishing connections between lines. Any or a combination of the digital switching techniques described in Section 7.2 may be used. Some or all of the functions described in this section may be provided.

## Switching Statistical Multiplexers

There is one device that is quite different from the other types that we have been discussing: the *switching statistical multiplexer* (StatMux). Unlike, the synchronous TDM techniques used in most digital switches, the switching StatMux uses asynchronous or statistical TDM. First, we review this concept. Then we look at the use of statistical TDM for switching.

## Statistical Multiplexers

In a synchronous time-division multiplexer, it is generally the case that many of the time slots in a frame are wasted. A typical application of synchronous TDM involves linking a number of terminals to a shared computer port. Even if all terminals are actively in use, most of the time there is no data transfer at any particular terminal.

The statistical multiplexer exploits this common property of data transmission by dynamically allocating time slots on demand. As with a synchronous multiplexer, the statistical multiplexer has a number of I/O lines on one side and a higher speed multiplexed line on the other. Each I/O line has a buffer associated with it. In the case of the statistical multiplexer, there are $n$ I/O lines, but only $k$, where $k < n$, time slots available on the TDM frame. For input, the function of the multiplexer is to scan the input buffers, collecting data until a frame is filled, and then send the frame. On output, the multiplexer receives a frame and distributes the slots of data to the appropriate output buffers.

Figure 7.12 contrasts statistical and synchronous TDM. Note that there is more overhead per slot for statistical TDM since each slot carries an address as well as data. Since data arrive from and are distributed to I/O lines unpredictably, the address information is required to assure proper delivery.

The principal advantage of a statistical multiplexer is that it makes more efficient use of the shared transmission line. For long-haul networks, where either a dial-up or leased line is used, cost is an important consideration. However, in the local network context, the line is likely to be owned by the

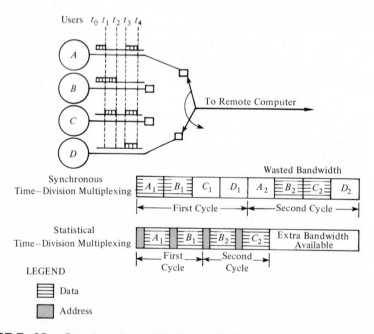

**FIGURE 7–12. Synchronous TDM Contrasted with Statistical TDM**

organization; hence a pure statistical multiplexer may not confer advantage for local networking.

On the other hand, the statistical multiplexer requires more elaborate address and control circuitry than does the synchronous TDM. Also, lines may experience blocking or queueing delays on a statistical multiplexer, whereas this does not happen on a synchronous TDM.

### Switching Applications

As mentioned, the statistical multiplexer, as such, may not confer any particular benefit in a local network context. However, a version of the multiplexer with switching capability is a low-cost alternative to the devices discussed earlier for modest local network requirements [SCHO81].

The switching multiplexer uses the same technique as a statistical multiplexer, with two additions:

- There may be more than one multiplexed line.
- There is sufficient intelligence to permit any form of routing through the multiplexer.

As with a statistical multiplexer, the switching multiplexer can provide a full-duplex connection between a line and a channel on a multiplexed line (usually referred to as a *trunk*). For line-to-trunk traffic, data are buffered and sent out in fixed-size chunks with an address appended. For trunk-to-line, each slot of incoming data is handled separately; the address is stripped off and the data chunk is routed to the appropriate output line.

This capability is not limited to trunk-line interaction. Two lines can be connected, with data exchanged between them, without addressing. Two channels on separate trunks can be connected; each slot of incoming data on a designated channel is routed, address and all, to the other trunk.

Figure 7.13 summarizes the connection possibilities of the switching multi-

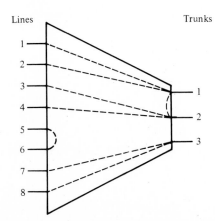

**FIGURE 7–13. Connection Possibilities in a Switching Statistical Multiplexer**

plexer. Statistical TDM frames are used on the trunks. Connected lines may be synchronous or asynchronous and of varying speeds. Some type of control unit is needed to control the routing.

Figure 7.14 is a conceptual architecture that suggests how a switching multiplexer might be implemented. There are a number of I/O logic units for the lines and trunks. Each unit is capable of receiving and buffering data and transferring it to a data store; on output, it can accept data from the data store and transmit. Areas of the data store serve as dedicated buffers for the I/O units. As data accumulate, they must be transferred to the appropriate I/O unit for transmission. This is done under control of the control unit, which uses information in the routing table to determine the routing.

The switching multiplexer can perform all of the data switching functions described in previous sections, although generally on a smaller scale. Preconfigured connections can be set up. The device can have sufficient intelligence to support on-demand port selection and port contention. A mixture of fixed and demand-assigned connections can be provided.

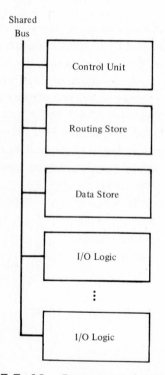

**FIGURE 7–14. Conceptual Architecture of a Switching Statistical Multiplexer**

# THE COMPUTERIZED BRANCH EXCHANGE

## Evolution of the CBX

The CBX is a marriage of two technologies: digital switching and telephone exchange systems. The forerunner of the CBX is the *private branch exchange* (PBX). A PBX is an on-premise facility, owned or leased by an organization, which interconnects the telephones within the facility and provides access to the public telephone system. Typically, a telephone user on the premises dials a three or four digit number to call another telephone on the premises, and dials one digit (usually 8 or 9) to get a dial tone for an "outside line," which allows the caller to dial a number in the same fashion as a residential user.

The original private exchanges were manual, with one or more operators at a switchboard required to make all connections. Back in the 1920s, these began to be replaced by automatic systems, called *private automatic branch exchanges* (PABX), which did not require attendant intervention to place a call. These "first-generation" systems used electromechanical technology and analog signaling. Data connections could be made via modems. That is, a user with a terminal, a telephone, and a modem or acoustic coupler in the office could dial up an on-site or remote number that reached another modem and exchange data.

The "second-generation" PBXs were introduced in the middle 1970s. These systems use electronic rather than electromagnetic technology and the internal switching is digital. Such a system is referred to as a digital PBX, or *computerized branch exchange* (CBX). These systems were designed primarily to handle analog voice traffic, with the codec function built into the switch so that digital switching could be used internally. The systems were also capable of handling digital data connections without the need of a modem.

The "third-generation" systems are touted as "integrated voice/data" systems, although the differences between third generation and upgraded second generation are rather blurred. Perhaps a better term is "improved digital PBX." Some of the characteristics of these systems that differ from those of earlier systems include:

- *The use of digital phones:* This permits integrated voice/data workstations.
- *Distributed architecture:* Multiple switches in a hierarchical or meshed configuration with distributed intelligence provides enhanced reliability.
- *Nonblocking configuration:* Typically, dedicated port assignments are used for all attached phones and devices.

Mention should be made of two systems that do not fall cleanly into the categories listed above. One is AT&T's Dimension PBX, which is not, as some people think, a digital PBX. Whereas digital PBXs use PCM digital voice signals, Dimension PBX uses a form of analog voice encoding known as pulse amplitude modulation (PAM). However, because PAM involves the use of discrete voltage pulses, TDM techniques can be used for switching.

Another AT&T offering is Centrex, in which the switching facility for a site may be located remotely, so as to serve a number of customers. The user, however, can still dial other local users with an extension number. Hence, Centrex gives the appearance of a PBX.

It is worthwhile to summarize the main reasons why the evolution described above has taken place. To the untrained eye, analog and digital PBXs would seem to offer about the same level of convenience. The analog PBX can handle telephone sets directly and uses modems to accommodate digital data devices; the digital PBX can handle digital data devices directly and uses codecs to accommodate telephone sets. Some of the advantages of the digital approach are

- *Digital technology:* By handling all internal signals digitally, the digital PBX can take advantage of low-cost LSI and VLSI components. Digital technology also lends itself more readily to software and firmware control.
- *Time-division multiplexing:* Digital signals lend themselves readily to TDM techniques, which provide efficient use of internal data paths, access to public TDM carriers, and TDM switching techniques, which are more cost effective than older, cross bar techniques.
- *Digital control signals:* Control signals are inherently digital and can easily be integrated into a digital transmission path via TDM. The signaling equipment is independent of the transmission medium.
- *Encryption:* This is more easily accommodated with digital signals.

## Telephone Call Processing Requirements

The characteristic that distinguishes the CBX from a digital switch is its ability to handle telephone connections. Freeman [FREE80] lists eight functions required for telephone call processing:

- Interconnection
- Control
- Attending
- Busy testing
- Alerting
- Information receiving
- Information transmitting
- Supervisory

The interconnection function encompasses three contingencies. The first contingency is a call originated by a station bound for another station on the CBX. The switching technologies that we have discussed are used in this context. The second contingency is a call originated by a CBX station bound for an external recipient. For this, the CBX must not only have access to an external trunk, but must perform internal switching to route the call from the user station to the trunk interface. The CBX also performs a line to trunk concentration function to avoid the expense of one external line per station. The third contingency is a call originated externally bound for a CBX station. Referred to as *direct inward dialing*, this allows an external caller to use the unique phone number of a CBX station to establish a call without going through an operator. This requires trunk to line expansion plus internal switching.

The control function includes, of course, the logic for setting up and tearing down a connection path. In addition, the control function serves to activate and control all other functions and to provide various management and utility services, such as logging, accounting, and configuration control.

The CBX must recognize a request for a connection; this is the attending function. The CBX then determines if the called party is available (busy testing) and, if so, alerts that party (alerting). The process of setting up the connection involves an exchange of information between the CBX and the called and calling parties. Note how dramatically this differs from the distributed packet-switching approach of LANs and HSLNs.

Finally, a supervisory function is needed to determine when a call is completed and the connection may be released, freeing the switching capacity and the two parties for future connections.

Let us look more closely at the sequence of events required to successfully complete a call. First, consider an internal call from extension 226 to extension 280. The following steps occur:

1. 226 goes off-hook (picks up the receiver). The control unit recognizes this condition.
2. The control unit finds an available digit receiver and sets up a circuit from 226 to the digit receiver. The control unit also sets up a circuit from a dial-tone generator to 226.
3. When the first digit is dialed, the dial-tone connection is released. The digit receiver accumulates dialed digits.
4. After the last digit is dialed, the connection to the digit receiver is released. The control unit examines the number for legitimacy. If it is not valid, the caller is informed by some means, such as connection to a rapid busy signal generator. Otherwise, the control unit then determines if 280 is busy. If so, 226 is connected to a busy-signal generator.
5. If 280 is free, the control unit sets up a connection between 226 and a ring-back-tone generator and a connection between 280 and a ringer.
6. When 280 answers by going off-hook, the ringing and ring-back connections are dropped and a connection is set up between 226 and 280.
7. When either 280 or 226 goes on-hook, the connection between them is dropped.

For outgoing calls, the following steps are required.

1–3. As above. In this case the caller will be dialing an access code number (e.g., the single digit 9) to request access to an outgoing trunk.

4. The control unit releases the connection to the digit receiver and finds a free trunk group and sends out an off-hook signal.

5. When a dial tone is returned from the central office, the control unit repeats steps 2 and 3.

6. The control unit releases the connection to the digit receiver and sends the number out to the trunk and makes a connection from the caller to the trunk.

7. When either the caller or the trunk signals on-hook, the connection between them is dropped.

There are variations on the foregoing sequence. For example, if the CBX performs least-cost routing, it will wait until the number is dialed and then select the appropriate trunk.

Finally, incoming calls, when direct inward dialing is supported, proceed as follows.

1. The control unit detects a trunk seizure signal from the central office and sends a start-dialing signal out on that trunk. It also sets up a path from the trunk to a digit receiver.

2. After the last digit is received, the control unit releases the path, examines the dialed number, and checks the called station for busy, in which case a busy signal is returned.

3. If the called number is free, the control unit sets up a ringing connection to the called number and a ring-back connection to the trunk. It monitors the called station for answer and the trunk for abandon.

4. When the called station goes off-hook, the ringing and ring-back connections are dropped and a connection is set up between the trunk and the called station.

5. When either the trunk or called station signals on-hook, the connection between them is dropped.

As you can see, the requirements for setting up a telephone connection are more complex than those for a data connection.


## Data Switching Requirements

The data switching requirements for a CBX are the same as those for a digital switch. Typically, a terminal user will be requesting connection to a computer port. The same issues of speed, asynchronous/synchronous, and calling technique arise.

There are several new wrinkles. The CBX may support a voice/data workstation with one twisted pair for the phone and two pairs for the terminal. In such arrangements, the destination port may be selected from the phone rather than the terminal or a keypad.

The CBX has the advantage of direct connect to outgoing telephone lines. The terminal user who wishes to access an external computer need not have a telephone and a modem; the CBX can provide the link-up service. Typically, the connection is to an outgoing analog voice line. To provide the proper service, the CBX maintains a pool of modems that can be used by any data device to communicate over the external lines.

The exact implementation of the modem pool depends on the architecture of the CBX, but some strange contortions may be required. Consider the case of a CBX whose switching capability consists of a TDM bus switch. Figure 7.15 illustrates this. A device wishing to communicate outside will be connected to an available modem in the pool. The modem produces analog signals which must be switched to an outgoing analog trunk. But the CBX switches only digital signals! Therefore, the modem output is routed to a codec, which digitizes the data and puts them back onto the TDM bus. They are then routed to a trunk interface, where the signal is converted back to analog and sent on its way. Whew!

The most important characteristic is the internal integration of data and digitized voice. The same switching mechanism is used for both. Therefore, both must conform to common slot size and timing conventions. This is a requirement not faced by the digital switch designer.

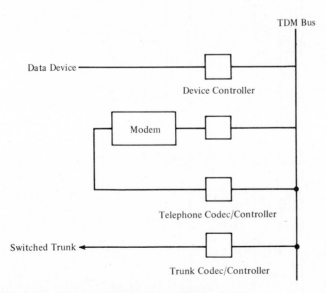

**FIGURE 7–15.  Use of a Modem in a CBX**

## CBX Architecture

A variety of architectures have been developed by CBX manufacturers. Since these are proprietary, the details are not generally known in most cases (but see [KASS79a]). In this section, we attempt to present the general architectural features common to all CBX systems.

### CBX Components

Figure 7.16 presents a generic CBX architecture. You should find it quite similar to the data switching architecture we have discussed. Indeed, since the requirements for the CBX are a superset of those for the data switch, a similar architecture is not surprising.

As always, the heart of the system is some kind of digital switching network. The switch is responsible for the manipulation and switching of time multiplexed digital signal streams, using the techniques described in Section 7.2. The digital switching network consists of some number of space and time switching stages. Many of the CBXs are not sufficiently large, in terms of lines or capacity, to require complex switching networks. Indeed, some have no network as such, but simply use a TDM bus switch.

Attached to the switch are a set of interface units, which provide access to/ from the outside world. Typically, an interface unit will perform a synchronous

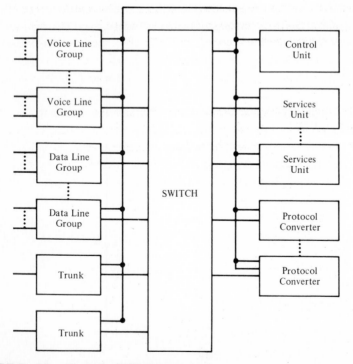

**FIGURE 7—16.  Generic CBX Architecture**

time-division multiplexing function in order to accommodate multiple incoming lines. On the other side, the unit requires two lines into the switch for full duplex operation.

It is important to understand that the interface unit is performing synchronous and not asynchronous TDM, even though connections are dynamically changing. On the input side, the unit performs a multiplex operation. Each incoming line is sampled at a specified rate. For $n$ incoming lines each of data rate $x$, the unit must achieve an input rate of $nx$. The incoming data are buffered and organized into chunks of time-slot size. Then, according to the timing dictated by the control unit, individual chunks are sent out into the switch at the internal CBX data rate, which may be in the range 50 to 500 Mbps. In a nonblocking switch, $n$ time slots are dedicated to the interface unit for transmission, whether or not they are used. In a blocking switch, time slots are assigned for the duration of a connection. In either case, the time-slot assignment is fixed for the duration of the connection, and synchronous TDM techniques may be used.

On the output side, the interface unit accepts data from the switch during designated time slots. In a nonblocking switch these may be dedicated (requiring more than a simple TDM bus switch), but are in any case fixed for the duration of the connection. Incoming data are demultiplexed, buffered, and presented to the appropriate output port at its data rate.

Several types of interface units are used. A data line group unit handles data devices, providing the functions described in Section 7.3. An analog voice line group handles a number of twisted-pair phone lines. The interface unit must include codecs for digital-to-analog (input) and analog-to-digital (output) conversion. A separate type of unit may be used for integrated digital voice/data workstation, which present digitized voice at 64 kbps and data at the same or a lower rate. The range of lines accommodated by interface units is typically 8 to 24.

In addition to multiplexing interface units that accommodate multiple lines, trunk interface units are used to connect to off-site locations. These may be analog voice trunks or digital trunks, which may carry either data or PCM voice. Whereas a line interface unit must multiplex incoming lines to place on the switch, and demultiplex switch traffic to send to the lines, the trunk unit must demultiplex and multiplex in both directions (see Figure 7.17). Consider an incoming digital line with $n$ channels of time-multiplexed data (the argument is the same for an analog trunk, which presents $n$ channels of frequency-multiplexed voice). These data must be demultiplexed and stored in a buffer of length $n$ units. Individual units of the buffer are then transmitted out to the switch at the designated time slots. Question: Why not pass the TDM stream directly from input to the bus, filling $n$ contiguous time slots? Actually, in a nonblocking dedicated port system, this is possible. But for a system with dynamic time-slot assignment, the incoming data must be buffered and sent out on time slots that vary as connections are made and broken.

The other boxes in Figure 7.16 can be explained briefly. The control unit

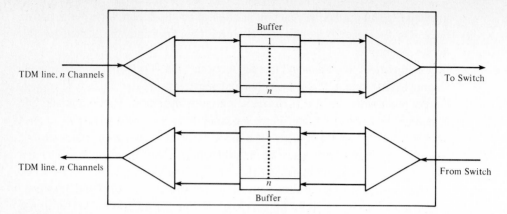

**FIGURE 7–17. Operation of a Trunk Interface Unit**

operates the digital switch and exchanges control signals with attached devices. For this purpose, a separate bus or other data path is used; control signals generally do not propagate through the switch itself. As part of this or a separate unit, network administration and control functions are implemented. Service units would include such things as tone and busy-signal generators and dialed-digit registers. Some CBX systems provide protocol convertors for connecting dissimilar lines. A connection is made from each line to the protocol convertor.

It should be noted that this generic architecture lends itself to a high degree of reliability. The failure of any interface unit means the loss of only a small number of lines. Key elements such as the control unit can be made redundant.

### Distributed Architecture

For reasons of efficiency and reliability, many CBX manufacturers offer distributed architectures for their larger systems. The CBX is organized into a central switch and one or more distributed modules, with coaxial or fiber optic cable between the central switch and the modules, in a 2-level hierarchical star topology.

The distributed modules off-load at least some of the central-switch processor's real-time work load (such as off-hook detection). The degree to which control intelligence is off-loaded varies. At one extreme, the modules may be replicas of the central switch, in which case they function almost autonomously with the exception of certain overall management and accounting functions. At the other extreme, the modules are as limited as possible.

A distributed architecture means that it will often be necessary to concatenate several connections to achieve a connection between two devices. Consider Figure 7.18. A connection is desired between lines a and b. In module A, a connection is established between line a and one channel on a TDM trunk to the central switch. In the central switch, that channel is connected to a channel on a TDM trunk to module B. In module B, that channel is connected to line b.

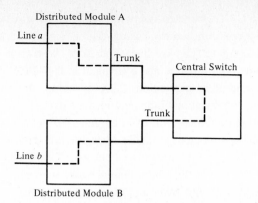

**FIGURE 7–18.   Circuit Establishment in a Distributed CBX**

There are several advantages to a distributed architecture:

- It permits growth beyond the practical size of a single digital switch.
- It provides better performance by off-loading of functions.
- It provides higher reliability: the loss of a single module need not disable the entire system.
- It reduces twisted-pair wiring distances.

**7.5**

## CBX VERSUS LAN

There is a clear overlap between the capabilities provided by a CBX system and a LAN. Both can support a large number and wide variety of digital devices. In order to choose between the two technologies, the potential customer should lay out all the mandatory and desirable features, and then compare the two based on a match against requirements and cost (this process is described in [DERF83]). In this section we compare briefly the two approaches, based on a checklist suggested in [PFIS82]. CBX and LAN can be compared in the following categories:

- Installation
- Reliability
- Data types
- Distance
- Speed
- Capacity
- Cost

The installation of the cable for a LAN in an already finished building is without question a time-consuming and expensive task. It is not out of bounds to have the wire costs of a LAN installation be 50% of the total! Consider, now, the requirements for a CBX. Phone connections require a two-wire (usually twisted-pair) connection. Data connections, using digital signaling, usually require two twisted pairs for a full-duplex line. Therefore, with many CBX systems, the user who wants both a phone and a terminal in the office requires three twisted-pair lines. The third-generation CBX systems often provide integrated digital voice/data workstations that require only two twisted pairs. Some vendors, using the ping-pong protocol, offer an integrated voice/data link consisting of a single 256-kbps twisted pair (128 kbps for full duplex voice, 128 kbps for full-duplex data). In any case, just about all existing office sites are wired with twisted pairs for distribution of traditional phone services. Further, PBXs are almost always installed with two pairs of wiring per outlet—one for backup. So most PBXs have a number of available spare twisted-pair lines. This could represent a tremendous savings compared to a LAN.

With respect to reliability, there are problems with both CBX and LAN systems. This topic is addressed in more detail in Chapter 12. Here, let us just say that the reliability problems of the LAN may be the more severe, contrary to the usual first impression. CBX systems can be made fully redundant, virtually eliminating network-wide failures. But it is easy to postulate situations that would disable all or a substantial part of a LAN.

Both the CBX and the LAN can adequately handle most digital data communications requirements. The CBX is superior for handling voice. The centralized control nature of the CBX is ideal for the variety of voice processing requirements in an office environment. Another type of transmission—video—can at present only be practically handled by a broadband LAN.

The distances achievable by the CBX and the LAN are about equal. With a distributed architecture, a CBX can easily span a multibuilding complex by locating a switching center in each building, thus matching the range achievable with a broadband LAN.

In terms of data rate, the LAN has an edge. Third-generation CBX systems generally support data up to a maximum of 64 kbps (some vendors have plans for rates of up to 256 kbps). A LAN can, with proper interfaces, accommodate attachments in the Mbps range. To many users, 64 kbps may appear to be equivalent to infinity. However, some of the newer workstations, with high-resolution graphics, require much higher data rates. Furthermore, file transfer operations can get severely bogged down at those lower rates.

Closely related to this is the question of capacity and here the picture is murkier. On its face, it would appear that the CBX has the edge. The total digital transfer capacity of a CBX can go up to about 500 Mbps (the data rate on a TDM bus, for example). Baseband bus and ring systems are far less, and even a broadband tops out at about 300 Mbps over a number of channels. However, the nature of the traffic must be taken into account. Most digital data traffic in the office is bursty in nature (terminal to host traffic). On a LAN, the network is utilized by a node only for the duration of the burst. But on a CBX, a node will consume a dedicated portion of the capacity for the duration of a connection.

Last on our checklist is the question of cost. For this, there is no definitive answer, partly because component costs are changing rapidly and partly because it is installation dependent. For what it's worth, Figure 3.6 summarizes the results of a 1981 study by the IEEE 802 committee. The study showed that baseband and broadband were very close in cost, with a small advantage to broadband in larger installations. The CBX turned out to be considerably cheaper. The chart suggests that for most applications, the CBX is the preferred alternative.

There is a final point of comparison that was not included in the checklist because it relates to detailed design strategy rather than the pros and cons of the two approaches. This point has to do with the nature of the network interface. In a circuit-switched system, the network is usually "transparent"; that is, two connected devices communicate as if they had a direct connection. In a packet-switched system, the issue of the protocol between the network and the attached device arises. Of course, with the introduction of protocol-conversion services on the CBX, the distinctions blur. In any case, it is to this issue that we turn next.

## 7.6

## RECOMMENDED READING

A good overview of digital switching concepts can be found in [DAVI73]. [SKAP79] provides a more detailed look. [HOBB81, Chap. 12]* provides a clear discussion of TSI and TMS.

[VONA80]* describes and discusses port selection and port contention devices. [SCHO81] describes the switching statistical multiplexer. A general survey of digital data switching devices can be found in [KANE80]*.

A very clear discussion of the PBX and CBX appears in [MART76, Chap. 22], which also lists and describes the large list of features and services found in a modern CBX. A good recent paper is [GOEL83]. The architecture of a CBX is discussed in [KASS79b]. Two papers that contrast the CBX and the LAN are [PFIS82]* and [RICH80]*.

## 7.7

## PROBLEMS

7.1 Demonstrate that there is a high probability of blocking in a two-stage switch.

7.2 Explain the following statement in Section 7.2: "The timings on the shorter bus are amenable to greater control because of the much shorter propagation delay.''

**7.3**  What is the magnitude of delay through a TSI stage?

**7.4**  For STS, give an example of blocking when the number of TSI units equals the number of incoming lines. What is the minimum number of TSI units for proper functioning (even in a blocking mode)?

**7.5**  In Figure 7.15, why is it not possible to route the digital data coming from the device directly to an outgoing trunk, where it will be converted to analog by the codec for transmission?

**7.6**  Assume that the velocity of propagation on a TDM bus is $0.7c$, its length is 10 m, and the data rate is 500 Mbps. How many bits should be transmitted in a time slot to achieve a bus efficiency of 99%?

**7.7**  Demonstrate that in a TSI data store at most only half of the memory is usefully occupied at any one time. Devise a means of reducing the TSI memory requirement while maintaining its nonblocking property.

**7.8**  Is it necessary to include address bits with each time slot in a statistical TDM stream? Is there a more efficient technique?

**7.9**  Justify the assertion in Section 7.2 that, for an STS network, the number of TSI units must be double the number of incoming and outgoing lines for nonblocking.

**7.10**  Reconsider Problem 3.6, but now assume that there is a central switching unit on floor 3 and a satellite switching unit on floor 6.

# The Network Interface

Previous chapters have looked at the capabilities and features of the various types of local networks, but little has been said of the devices that connect to those networks. The purpose of a local network is to provide a means of communication for the various attached devices. To realize this purpose, the interface between the network and attached devices must be such as to permit cooperative interaction. This section addresses the complexities implicit in that seemingly simple notion.

We began with a statement of the problem: the networking requirements for cooperative interaction. Then we consider the connection of digital devices to packet-switched networks, the common case for LANs and HSLNs; this is the area in which most of the complexity arises. The simpler issues relating to circuit-switched networks and to analog devices are then considered.

## 8.1

## THE REQUIREMENT

To understand the network interface requirement, let us first consider, from the computer vendor's point of view, how to provide a computer networking capability. Many vendors offer some sort of networking capability. Applications such as transaction processing, file transfer, electronic mail, and so on are available to run on a network of computers and intelligent terminals. The vendor supports these applications with a networking and communications software package. Examples are IBM's SNA and DEC's DECNET. For clarity in the following discussion, we will consider a generic package based on the OSI model; the principles apply equally well to other, proprietary architectures.

It is important to note that the OSI model does not provide an architecture for the *networking* of *multiple* computers; it is a model for the *communications* between *two* computers, based on a set of protocols. Networking requires not only communications protocols but network management, a naming facility, network services, and so on. These issues are addressed later. In this chapter we are concerned with the communications protocol implications of local networking.

Communications protocols, such as those compatible with the OSI model, do provide a basis for computer networking. Traditionally, this has been done in two ways, as depicted in Figure 8.1. A common vendor offering is a private network (Figure 8.1a). Computers are connected by point-to-point links, which can be local direct connects (a special case of "local network"!) or long-haul links, either dial-up or leased. Each node in the network can act both as an end point for executing applications and as a switch for passing along data. A layer 2 protocol, such as HDLC, is sufficient to provide connectivity; the network can be viewed as a set of computers hooked together by paired, point-to-point, layer 2 links. Any given computer supports more than one link by using more than one physical port, as indicated in the diagram.

This figure is a bit misleading in that it shows a link only at one protocol layer—layer 2. Of course, there is also a layer 1 link for each layer 2 link. Furthermore, the figure suggests that there will be peer communication at higher protocol layers. However, it would be possible with this configuration for a user to write a package for exchanging data between two machines that makes use of none of these higher-layer services; the user still needs a physical connection and link control logic. Layer 2, then, is the highest *required* layer for this configuration to work.

For a long-haul network, the private network configuration can be justified if there is either a very high volume of traffic, or a very low volume. With a high volume of traffic between nodes, the expense of dedicated (leased) lines is reasonable. With a low volume of traffic, dial-up lines are cost effective. Over some range between these two extremes the public or value-added network (VAN) provides the most cost-effective communications support for computer networking (Figure 8.1b). The VAN, discussed in Chapter 2, consists of switches and communication lines configured to provide connectivity among attached devices. The VAN provides, among others, two services that are relevant here:

• *Routing:* To send data, an attached device specifies the address of the destination device; the VAN is responsible for routing those data through the network to its destination.

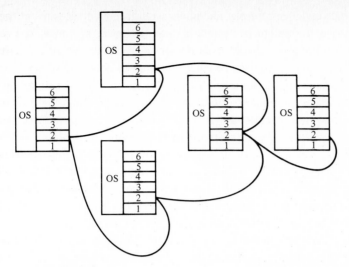

a. Private Network

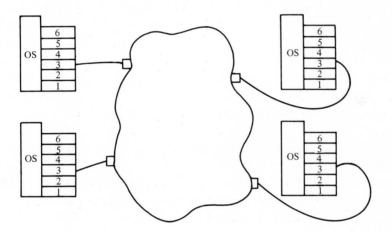

b. Public Network

**FIGURE 8–1. Approaches to Computer Networking.**

- *Multiplexing:* An attached device does not need one physical port for each device with which it may communicate. Rather, the VAN supports multiple virtual circuits multiplexed on a single physical line.

The reader will recognize these as functions requiring a layer 3 protocol. Typically, the X.25 standard is used. Most vendors who provide private networks can provide the same networking applications over a VAN. The discussion in Chapter 2 describes the mechanism by which this is accomplished.

Figure 8.1 thus serves to illustrate the network interface requirement. With a private network, the vendor's devices are directly connected to each other and the issue does not really arise. With a separate packet-switched communications network, the vendor must determine how to interface its devices to the network. The solution is to implement compatible layers 1 through 3, as with X.25.

A multiaccess local network does not fit neatly into either of the categories noted above. Devices are not attached by point-to-point links as in a private network; instead, a multipoint link exists. Neither is a local network a VAN, with a network of intermediate switching nodes. The problem for the computer vendor is how to integrate the local network into its communications and networking software. The alternatives for this integration are discussed below.

From the customer's point of view, the local network interface is also an important issue. Typically, a customer will acquire some new data processing equipment in addition to the local network. The customer probably also has existing equipment to be hooked into the network. The customer would also like the flexibility of acquiring future equipment of various types, possibly from various vendors. The problem, then, for the customer is to procure a local network whose interface accommodates a variety of equipment with little or no special software required for that equipment. What approach should the customer take?

## 8.2

## PACKET-SWITCHED INTERFACING

### Approaches to LAN/HSLN Attachment

Packet switching is used on both LANs and HSLNs. As we have seen, packet switching implies that the data to be sent over the network by a device are organized into packets which are sent through the network one at a time. Protocols must be used to specify the construction and exchanges of these packets. At a minimum for a local network, protocols at layers 1 and 2 are needed to control the multiaccess network communication (e.g., these layers would comprise the LLC, MAC, and physical functions specified by IEEE 802).

Thus all attached devices must share these common local network protocols. From a customer's point of view, this fact structures the ways in which devices attach to a LAN or HSLN into three alternatives, depicted in Figure 8.2:

- Homogeneous/single vendor approach
- "Standards" approach
- Standard network interface approach

A homogeneous network is one in which all equipment—network plus attached devices—is provided by a single vendor. All equipment shares a common set of networking and communications software. The vendor has integrated a local network capability into its product line. Customers need not concern themselves with details of protocols and interfaces.

Undoubtedly, many customers will adopt this approach. The single-vendor

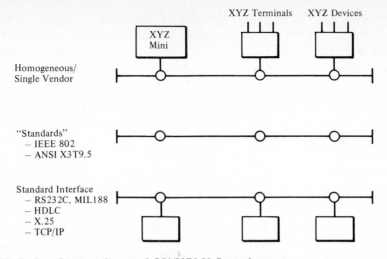

**FIGURE 8–2. Approaches to LAN/HSLN Attachment.**

system simplifies maintenance responsibility and provides an easy path for system evolution. On the other hand, the flexibility to obtain the best piece of equipment for a given task may be limited. Relying on a vendor, without consideration of their network architecture, to be able easily to accommodate foreign equipment is risky.

Another approach that a customer may take is to procure a local network that conforms to a standard and dictate that all equipment be compatible with that standard. The local network would consist of a transmission medium plus an expandable set of "attachment points." This approach, although attractive, has some problems. The IEEE standard for LANs is still a proposal as of this writing. Worse, from the point of view of the present discussion, the standard is loaded with options, so that two devices claiming to be "IEEE-compatible" may not be able to coexist on the same network. The ANSI standard for HSLN's is also still in draft form. And even when these standards do become final, there is little hope that incompatible systems will fade away.

The promise of local networks standards lies not in the solving of the interconnect problem. Standards offer the hope that the prospect of a mass market will lead to cheap silicon implementations of local network protocols. But the interconnect problem is an architectural issue, not a protocol issue.

Now consider a local network as consisting of not only a transmission medium, but also a set of intelligent devices that implement the local network protocols *and* provide an interface capability for device attachment. We will refer to this device as a *network interface unit* (NIU). The NIUs, collectively, control access to and communications across, the local network. Subscriber devices attach to the NIU through some standard communications or I/O interface. The details of the local network operation are hidden from the device.

The NIU architecture is commonly used by independent local network vendors (those who sell only networks, not the data processing equipment that uses the network). It holds out the promise that interface options provided by virtually all vendors for communications and I/O operation can be used to attach to a local network.

Next, we look at the workings of an NIU. Following that, we consider the architectural implications for networking.

## The Network Interface Unit

The NIU is a microprocessor-based device that acts as a communications controller to provide data transmission service to one or more attached devices. The NIU transforms the data rate and protocol of the subscriber device to that of the local network transmission medium and vice versa. Data on the medium are available to all attached devices, whose NIUs screen data for reception based on address. In general terms, the NIU performs the following functions:

- Accepts data from attached device.
- Buffers the data until medium access is achieved.
- Transmits data in addressed packets.
- Scans each packet on medium for own address.
- Reads packet into buffer.
- Transmits data to attached device at the proper data rate.

The hardware interface between the NIU and the attached device is typically a standard serial communications interface, such as RS-232-C. Almost all computers and terminals support this interface. For higher speed, a parallel interface, such as an I/O channel or direct memory access (DMA) interface can be provided. For example, a number of vendors offer an NIU interface directly into the UNIBUS of DEC's minicomputer line. Figure 8.3 gives a generic architecture for an NIU.

The NIU can either be an outboard or an inboard device. As an outboard device, the NIU is a stand-alone unit, which may have one or more serial communications ports for device attachment. High-speed parallel ports are also used. As an inboard device, the NIU is integrated into the chassis of the data processing device, such as a minicomputer or terminal. An inboard NIU generally consists of one or more printed-circuit boards attached to the device's bus.

From a customer's point of view, an NIU with standard interface options solves, at least at the electrical level, the interconnect problem. From a designer's point of view, the NIU is a useful architectural concept. Whether a network is homogeneous or not, and whether the interface provided to the local network is standard or not, there must be some distributed logic for controlling local network access. Conceptualizing this logic as an NIU clarifies some of the communications architectural issues associated with networking applications on a local network.

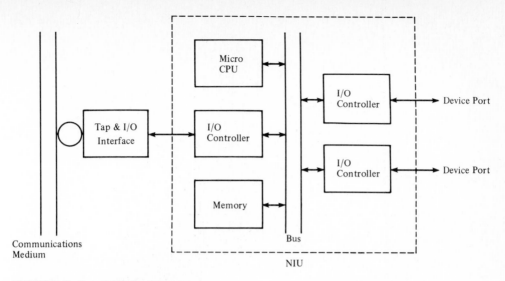

**FIGURE 8–3. NIU Architecture.**

In what follows, we treat the NIU as a distinct device. Recognize that this device could be so integrated into the attached device as to be indistinguishable. This does not affect the reasoning involved.

## THE DEVICE/NIU INTERFACE

### Modes of Attachment

Having introduced the concept of the NIU, we can now turn to the problem of integrating local network protocols into the communications software of a system. Figure 8.4 illustrates two approaches to this problem. Part *a* of this figure reminds us that OSI layers 1 and 2 are required to control access to the shared transmission medium. Each NIU attaches to the medium and implements these two layers; all the NIUs cooperate to communicate with each other.

To provide service to an attached device, the NIU can function as a gateway. A *gateway* is a device for connecting two systems that use different protocols: a protocol converter, if you like. In this case the NIU contains logic for communicating with the attached device using some protocol native to that device; the level of communication is at some layer *n* (Figure 8.4b). The NIU converts between that protocol and that of the local network.

Compare this architecture with Figure 2.15, which describes the VAN/PDN architecture. In that figure the level of communication between the DTE and DCE is at layer 3. The operation is as follows. The data that originate at the application layer, plus all the headers generated by layers 7 through 4, are

A LOCAL NETWORK PROTOCOLS

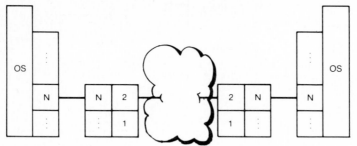

B THE NIU AS GATEWAY (PROTOCOL MODE)

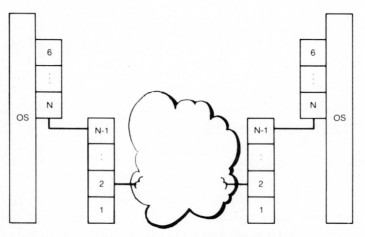

C THE NIU AS FRONT-END NETWORK PROCESSOR (INTERFACE MODE)

**FIGURE 8–4.  Communications Layers for Local Networks.**

treated as a unit of data by layer 3. Layer 3 has the responsibility of routing this data unit to the destination system. It does this by means of a protocol with the *local* DCE at layer 3. Of course, to transmit a layer 3 frame from DTE to DCE, a logical link (layer 2) over a physical link (layer 1) is needed. Hence the DTE-DCE conversation consists of protocols at layers 1, 2, and 3. Now, the DCE uses a different set of protocols to route the data unit through the network to the destination DCE, which in turn has a layer 1, 2, 3 protocol conversation with the destination DTE. The result is that a layer 4 packet has been routed from source to destination through gateways which convert the protocols up through layer 3.

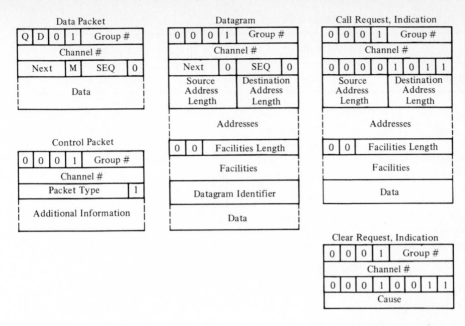

**FIGURE 8—5.  X.25 Layer 3 Formats.**

As an example, consider the X.25 standard. Figure 8.5 shows some of the layer 3 packet formats; a list of packet types is shown in Table 8.1. Figure 8.6 shows a typical sequence of events in a virtual call. The left-hand part of the figure shows the packets exchanged between user machine A and its DCE; the right-hand part shows the packets exchanged between user machine B and its DCE. The routing of packets between the DCEs is the responsibility of the internal logic of the network.

The sequence of events is as follows:

1. A requests a virtual circuit to B by sending a Call Request packet to its DCE. The packet includes a virtual circuit number (group, channel), as well as source and destination addresses. Future incoming and outgoing data transfers will be identified by the virtual circuit number.
2. B's DCE receives the call request and sends a Call Indication packet to B. This packet has the same format as the Call Request packet but a different virtual circuit number, selected by B's DCE from the set of locally unused numbers.
3. B indicates acceptance of the call by sending a Call Accepted packet specifying the same virtual circuit number as that of the Call Indication packet.

**TABLE 8.1   X.25 Layer 3 Packet Types**

| Packet Type | | Octet 3 Bits[a] | | | | | | | |
|---|---|---|---|---|---|---|---|---|---|
| From DCE to DTE | From DTE to DCE | 8 | 7 | 6 | 5 | 4 | 3 | 2 | 1 |
| *Call Setup and Clearing* | | | | | | | | | |
| Incoming call | Call request | 0 | 0 | 0 | 0 | 1 | 0 | 1 | 1 |
| Call connected | Call accepted | 0 | 0 | 0 | 0 | 1 | 1 | 1 | 1 |
| Clear indication | Clear request | 0 | 0 | 0 | 1 | 0 | 0 | 1 | 1 |
| DCE clear confirmation | DTE clear confirmation | 0 | 0 | 0 | 1 | 0 | 1 | 1 | 1 |
| *Data and Interrupt* | | | | | | | | | |
| DCE data | DTE data | × | × | × | × | × | × | × | 0 |
| DCE interrupt | DTE interrupt | 0 | 0 | 1 | 0 | 0 | 0 | 1 | 1 |
| DCE interrupt confirmation | DTE interrupt confirmation | 0 | 0 | 1 | 0 | 0 | 1 | 1 | 1 |
| *Datagram*[b] | | | | | | | | | |
| DCE datagram | DTE datagram | × | × | × | × | × | × | × | 0 |
| Datagram service signal | | × | × | × | × | × | × | × | 0 |
| *Flow Control and Reset* | | | | | | | | | |
| DCE RR (MODULO 8) | DTE RR (MODULO 8) | × | × | × | 0 | 0 | 0 | 0 | 1 |
| DCE RR (MODULO 128)[b] | DTE RR (MODULO 128)[b] | 0 | 0 | 0 | 0 | 0 | 0 | 0 | 1 |
| DCE RNR (MODULO 8) | DTE RNR (MODULO 8) | × | × | × | 0 | 0 | 1 | 0 | 1 |
| DCE RNR (MODULO 128)[b] | DTE RNR (MODULO 128)[b] | 0 | 0 | 0 | 0 | 0 | 1 | 0 | 1 |
| | DTE REJ (MODULO 8)[b] | × | × | × | 0 | 1 | 0 | 0 | 1 |
| | DTE REJ (MODULO 128)[b] | 0 | 0 | 0 | 0 | 1 | 0 | 0 | 1 |
| Reset indication | Reset request | 0 | 0 | 0 | 1 | 1 | 0 | 1 | 1 |
| DCE reset confirmation | DTE reset confirmation | 0 | 0 | 0 | 1 | 1 | 1 | 1 | 1 |
| *Restart* | | | | | | | | | |
| Restart indication | Restart request | 1 | 1 | 1 | 1 | 1 | 0 | 1 | 1 |
| DCE restart confirmation | DTE restart confirmation | 1 | 1 | 1 | 1 | 1 | 1 | 1 | 1 |
| *Diagnostic* | | | | | | | | | |
| Diagnostic[b] | | 1 | 1 | 1 | 1 | 0 | 0 | 0 | 1 |

[a]A bit indicated as "×" may be set to either "0" or "1."
[b]Not necessarily available on every network.
*Source:* CCITT X.25.

4. A receives a Call Connected packet with the same virtual circuit number as that of the Call Request packet.
5. A and B send Data and Control packets using their respective virtual circuit numbers.
6. A (or B) sends a Clear Request packet to terminate the virtual circuit and receives a local Clear Confirmation packet.
7.  B (or A) receives a Clear Indication packet and transmits a Clear Confirmation packet.

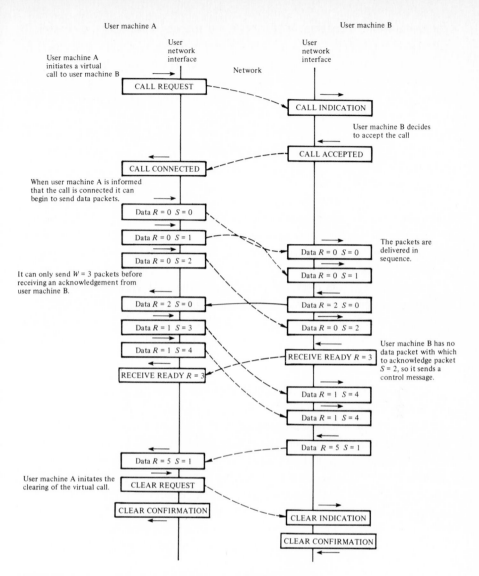

**FIGURE 8—6.  Sequence of Events: X.25 Protocol.**

We point out that this DTE–DCE interface is asymmetric. That is, only selected layer 3 protocol information is transferred end-to-end between subscriber DTEs. Much of the information, such as flow control and acknowledgment, has only local significance. (However, a 1980 revision allows some end-to-end significance as an option.) To be forwarded through the packet network, the DTE's data are encapsulated with the network's headers, which are only understood internally. The DTE–DCE layers 1 through 3 are replaced by those of the network.

Returning now to Figure 8.4, we see that the NIU can function instead as a front-end network processor (FNP). An FNP is a network processor that provides communications management services to an attached information processor. In contrast to a gateway, which *converts* from one set of protocols to another, the FNP *replaces* the protocols that might be found in the attached device. This is depicted in Figure 8.4c. The attached device contains layers 7 down through $n$. There is an $n/n$ - 1 interface to the NIU which contains layers $n$ - 1 to 1, with layers 2 and 1 being the local network protocols.

The typical host–FNP situation is one in which the host is a mainframe and the front end is a minicomputer. In that case, a common interface boundary is between session (5) and transport (4). This is a reasonable break: layers 1 through 4 can be thought of as "communications" management, responsible for managing physical and logical links and providing a reliable end-to-end transport service. Layers 5 and 6 can be thought of as "message management," responsible for maintaining a dialogue between end points and providing appropriate message formatting services. So the 5/4 break, although certainly not unique, is a logical one.

As an example, we consider a case where the FNP contains up through a DOD standard protocol called Transmission Control Protocol (TCP) [DARP81b]. TCP is essentially a layer 4 protocol, although it contains some features that ISO considers part of layer 5. This is a useful case to examine because DOD is funding experiments in the use of an NIU containing TCP as its upper layer [WOOD79].

The higher level/TCP interface is defined in Table 8.2 in the form of a set of primitives, much like the IEEE 802 LLC service specification summarized in Chapter 5. The interface provides for calls made by the TCP user to the TCP to OPEN or CLOSE a connection, to SEND or RECEIVE data, or to obtain STATUS about a connection. These calls would appear to the higher-layer software much like calls to an operating system, such as the calls to open, read/write, and close a file. For example, a host process wishing to establish a connection would use the OPEN command specifying an ID, called a local port, to identify the local end point, and another ID called the foreign socket, to identify the requested destination process. The active/passive flag indicates

**TABLE 8.2   User/TCP Interface**

---

*Format:* COMMAND-NAME (parameter-list) → returned-value

OPEN (local port, foreign socket, active/passive [,buffer size] [,timeout] [,precedence] [,security/compartment]) → local connection name
SEND (local connection name, buffer address, byte count, EOL flag, URGENT flag, [,timeout])
RECEIVE (local connection name, buffer address, byte count)
CLOSE (local connection name)
STATUS (local connection name) → status data block
ABORT (local connection name)

---

whether this is a positive request to establish the connection or merely an indication that the system is available and listening for a connection request. The remaining optional parameters specify certain characteristics of the connection. If and when a connection is made, TCP returns a value giving the local connection name. Semantically, this feature is similar to a procedure or function call that returns a value.

The remaining calls, or TCP commands, function in like manner. Now, if TCP is in a front end and the higher-layer software is in the host, some means of communicating the commands is needed. A common arrangement is for the front end to have a high-speed direct memory access (DMA) channel to the host. In that case, the host could place a command identifier plus parameters in a reserved area of memory, which would be read by the front end. If the front end and host are connected by a serial communication link, command plus parameters could be sent as a block of data across the link, using a layer 2 protocol.

Notice what is happening here. Consider the use of the SEND command by a session layer (layer 5) in the host. Layer 5 has some user data encapsulated in a layer 5 frame. The next logical step, as seen in Figure 2.11, is to wrap this up in a layer 4 (in this case, TCP) frame. To do this, the following steps occur.

1. The session layer creates a command string consisting of an identifier of SEND, plus its parameters, including the layer 5 frame.
2. This package is sent directly to the host's link layer, where it is wrapped in a layer 2 frame and sent to the front end.
3. The front end's layer 2 unwraps the layer 2 frame, and sends the command string to some server module, which may be part of the TCP package or separate.
4. The server module activates TCP with the SEND command.
5. TCP interprets the command, accesses the layer 5 frame, and wraps it in a layer 4 frame. The format of that frame is indicated in Table 8.3.

The TCP frame will subsequently acquire layer 3 and layer 2 fields and be sent out by the front end.

Now we are in a position to consider the various possible modes of attachment to an NIU. The following six modes can be considered.

- Layer 1 gateway
- Layer 2 gateway
- Layer 3 gateway
- Layer 3/2 FNP
- Layer 4/3 FNP
- Layer 5/4 FNP

These modes are depicted in Figure 8.7.

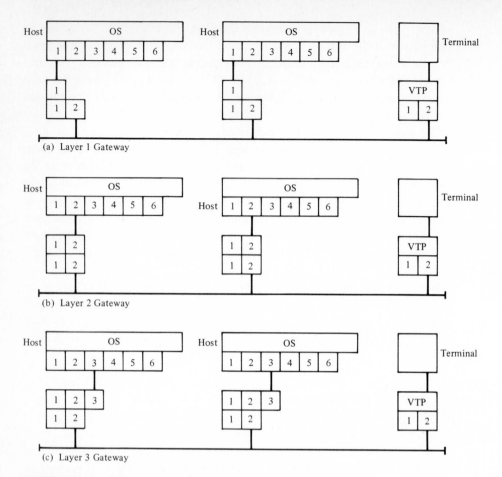

(a) Layer 1 Gateway

(b) Layer 2 Gateway

(c) Layer 3 Gateway

**FIGURE 8–7. Modes of Attachment to a LAN/HSLN.**

## The NIU as Gateway

### Layer 1 Gateway

This mode, which could be referred to as the transparent mode, permits protocol-compatible devices to communicate as if the NIUs and cable were not present. The NIU appears as a modem and provides signaling transparency. For example, for an RS-232C interface, when the originating device raises Request-to-Send to the originating NIU, the destination NIU raises Received-Line-Signal Detector (Carrier Detect) to the destination device. Data transfer is accomplished using buffering within the NIU. The transmitting NIU accumulates data from the transmitting device until either a buffer fills, a timer expires, or a control sequence is detected. The accumulated data are packaged in a frame and sent to the receiving NIU. The receiving NIU transmits the data to the receiving device.

Four parameters within each NIU control data transfer. These are: buffer size, time-out, control sequence(s), and destination address (NIU, SAP). At

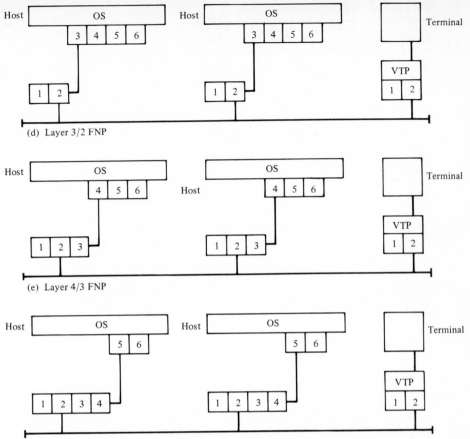

(d) Layer 3/2 FNP

(e) Layer 4/3 FNP

(f) Layer 5/4 FNP

**FIGURE 8–7. (continued)**

least the address parameter is variable and must be set using a control mode. For intelligent attached devices, a small I/O program would be needed to set NIU parameters. For dumb terminals, the associated NIU would have to provide a user interface (terminal handler) for setting parameters.

There is a lot of appeal in this approach. If the local network is truly transparent to the attached devices, any networking or communications capability that operates over traditional communications lines will operate over the local network with no modification.

Of course, this mode is not quite "transparent." There are two phases (this is true of all the modes): a control phase, for requesting a connection, and a data transfer phase. But the logic needed for the control phase is minor.

There are some disadvantages to this approach, particularly for synchronous communications. Chief among these is flow control. Flow control mechanisms for synchronous communication function at layer 2. If one device attached to the local network via its NIU is beginning to overrun the capacity of the destination device, the destination device can send, at layer 2, a message that

**TABLE 8.3 TCP Header Format***

| Name | Size (bits) | Purpose |
|---|---|---|
| Source port | 16 | Source port number |
| Destination port | 16 | Destination port number |
| Sequence number | 32 | Number of first octet in segment |
| Acknowledgment number | 32 | Piggyback sequence number |
| Data offset | 4 | Number of 32-bit words in header |
| Reserved | 6 | Future use |
| URG | 1 | Urgent pointer significant |
| ACK | 1 | Acknowledgment field significant |
| EOL | 1 | End of letter |
| RST | 1 | Reset the synchronization |
| SYN | 1 | Synchronize sequence numbers |
| FIN | 1 | No more data from sender |
| Window | 16 | Number of data octets sender is willing to receive |
| Checksum | 16 | Checksum of header plus data |
| Urgent pointer | 16 | Amount of data in segment that is urgent |
| Options | $8\times$ | Communicates special options |
| Padding | 0–7 | Ensures that header is a multiple of 32 bits long |

*Total length: 160 bits $+ 32n$; maximum data field length: 64K octets.

will halt or reduce the flow of data. However, if the attached device sends data to the NIU faster than it can be accepted, there is no way for the NIU to exert flow control on the attached device. A similar problem exists with error control. If an attached device fails to receive an acknowledgment to a frame, it does not know whether the fault is in the NIU or the destination device.

These problems are not fatal, but they do present difficulties to the designer.

### Layer 2 Gateway

In this mode, a layer 2 protocol is established between the attached device and the NIU. An example is HDLC.

As with a layer 1 gateway, there are two phases of communication: control and data transfer. For setting up a connection to some destination device, a dialogue is needed that is outside the layer 2 protocol. Again, this can be provided by a small I/O program. Once a connection is established, the layer 2 protocol would support data transfer.

This mode also presents a flow control problem. In this case, the NIU can exercise flow control over the attached device. However, the remote device has no means, *at layer 2*, of exercising flow control on the source device. Higher-layer protocols must be relied on in the two devices.

Another problem, common to both layer 1 and layer 2 protocols, is that the NIU does not support multiplexing. That is, for each logical connection to another device on the network, the attached device must have one physical connection to the network. This situation most closely resembles that of a private network using dial-up lines.

### Layer 3 Gateway

In this mode, the local network presents the appearance of a VAN. Typically, the NIU would provide the X.25 layer 3 protocol for attached intelligent devices. The advantage of this approach is that any networking capability that will work on an X.25 VAN will work on the local network. The X.25 layer 3 protocol provides a multiplexing capability so that multiple virtual circuits are supported over a single physical link.

In this mode, we at last get away from the necessity of a separate control dialogue. As the discussion above shows, and as we know from the specification of layer 3 functions in Chapter 2, the network layer functionality includes a connection request capability.

The X.25 interface is already offered by a number of LAN vendors. Because this is such a common means of connecting to a communications network, its use for local network is likely to become common.

## The NIU as Front-End Processor

### Layer 3/2 FNP

Figure 8.7d illustrates a layer 3/2 FNP mode. This is an attractive option that lends itself to a high-performance inboard NIU. The two layers needed to control the local network are in the NIU; all other layers are in the attached device. This configuration also provides high "visibility" for the local network. Software executing in the attached device can directly invoke layer 2 functions provided by the local network, such as broadcasting and priorities.

### Layer 4/3 FNP

This mode is illustrated in Figure 8.7e. Since this architecture is less clean than either the layer 3/2 or the layer 5/4, and since it offers no particular advantage, we do not pursue it here.

### Layer 5/4 FNP

In this mode, the NIU takes on the scope and characteristics of what is normally thought of as true FNP. All of the layers normally associated with communications management are implemented in the NIU; the higher message management layers are in the attached device. For communication between two devices that implement these higher layers, this approach works well.

One issue that arises is whether a mainframe should connect directly to the NIU, or through its own FNP. This will depend on the details of the systems involved. Typically, the FNP performs a variety of services for its mainframe, including not only message management, but logging and auditing functions, terminal management, and so on. A discussion of this point can be found in [STAC80] and [STAC81b].

## Summary

The discussion in this section has dealt with the issue of which communications architecture layers should reside in the NIU, and therefore be considered part of the local network service, and which should reside in the attached device. The choice will depend on a variety of factors, including cost and performance. As yet, there is little operational experience with most of these alternatives to guide us. Consequently, we can only close this section with a few preliminary observations.

The principal advantage of placing as many layers as possible in the NIU is that this makes the task of intelligent device attachment as easy as possible. The customer or user must be assured that the various devices on the network are compatible. By placing more of the communications functionality in the network, the scope of this task is reduced. On the other hand, placing as little functionality as possible in the network may increase the network's flexibility. Functions in the attached device can be tailored to achieve certain objectives in such areas as performance, priorities, and security.

## 8.4

# TERMINAL HANDLING FOR LANS

In the preceding section, the discussion focused on the requirements for attaching an intelligent device to a LAN or HSLN. Such devices implement the necessary communication layers and can communicate across a network as described in Chapter 2. For simplicity, we will refer to all such devices as hosts. But there are other devices that do not have the processing power to implement the OSI layers, such as dumb terminals, printers, and even limited-function intelligent terminals. We will refer to these devices generically as terminals.

A review of the material in Section 8.3 does not reveal how to accommodate terminals on a LAN. All of the approaches discussed assumed that some number of layers would be implemented in the attached device. How, then, to attach terminals?

Two general approaches are possible. The first is to treat terminal–host communication as fundamentally different from host–host communication. This approach can be explained using the concept of a secondary network, which is discussed next. The application of this concept in the local network context is then described. The second approach relies on the use of a virtual terminal protocol. This concept is defined, following which its use in the local network context is discussed.

## The Secondary Network

Let us refer to the kind of computer network we have discussed in Section 2.3 and previously in this chapter as a primary network. A primary network consists of the hardware and software required to interconnect applications executing within the OSI architecture. These include mainframes, FNPs, minicomputers, and intelligent terminals (generically, hosts). Typically, a mainframe will contain the higher-order layers (5, 6, 7), and all communications functions (layers 1 through 4) are off-loaded to an FNP. Minis and intelligent terminals typically contain all the OSI layers.

Within the OSI architecture, applications execute as modules sitting on top of the presentation layer (layer 6). Interconnection is logically achieved by means of a session established by session control (layer 5). To communicate with another application, an application requests that a session be established between a "logical port" attached to itself and a "logical port" attached to the other application. This service is provided by layer 5, which can establish both local and remote connections.

This mechanism works fine for devices containing all the software needed to implement the OSI layers. However, there are a number of devices, such as dumb terminals, printers, and so on (generically, terminals), which should be accessible over a network but which do not have the functionality of the various OSI layers. The secondary network consists of the hardware and software required to connect these devices to an OSI network. Whereas the primary network uses a 7-layer architecture, secondary connections use protocols tailored to the device in question.

Conceptually, we can think of these devices being serviced by application programs that act as gateways to the primary network. We will refer to these gateways as *secondary network servers* (SNS's). Since an SNS is an application, it can establish sessions with other applications over the primary network. A device such as a terminal local to a particular computer, connects directly to a local SNS and, through it, participates on the primary network.

These concepts are illustrated in Figure 8.8. Applications are represented as bubbles resting on layer 6. Sessions are represented by dashed lines. For example, consider the terminal T1 communicating with the SNS in minicomputer A. T1 could be directly connected to A or remotely via communications link or even by a network, as we will explain below. In any case, there is a connection between T1 and the SNS that does not use the OSI layers; this we refer to as a secondary network connection. Now, suppose that T1 is logged on to A via the SNS, and wishes to access an application on minicomputer B. The SNS, as an application, can invoke the communications functions of A to establish a session with the application on B; we refer to this as a primary network connection.

With this brief background, we now look at the use of the secondary network approach for local networks.

## Secondary Network Device Attachment

Each of the diagrams in Figure 8.7 indicates the connection of a terminal to the LAN via an NIU. To provide a secondary network connection from terminal to

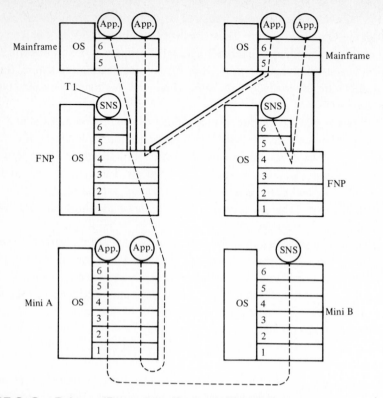

**FIGURE 8–8. Primary/Secondary Network Concepts.**

host, the NIU must allow the terminal user to request a connection to an SNS in a host (alternatively, a host could set up the connection). Data transfer must occur as if the terminal were directly connected to the host. Note that the local network medium is being used to support both primary (host-host) and secondary (terminal-host) network connections. As before, either a gateway or FNP mode of attachment can be used.

### Gateway Attachment

Recall that three modes of device attachment via gateway were described:

- Layer 1 gateway
- Layer 2 gateway
- Layer 3 gateway

The use of a layer 1 gateway for asynchronous or synchronous terminals is easily explained. As described in Section 8.3, the layer 1 gateway creates a transparent connection, appearing to function as simply a modem. A layer 2 gateway can be used for synchronous terminals only, since the NIU requires a layer 2 protocol with the attached device. Thus a synchronous terminal, using for example BISYNC or HDLC, could communicate over the network to an SNS in a host.

The layer 3 gateway is not so easily dealt with. Here the NIU requires protocol layers 1 through 3 in the attached device, but most terminals do not have layer 3. A way around this problem has been developed within the context of the X.25 standard, and this is described next.

As supplements to the X.25 standard, CCITT has developed a set of standards related to a facility known as a *packet assembler disassembler* (PAD). The PAD is designed to solve the two fundamental problems associated with the attachment of terminals to a network:

1. Many terminals are not capable of implementing the protocol layers for attaching in the same manner as a host. The PAD facility provides the intelligence for communicating with a host using the X.25 protocol.
2. There are differences among terminal types. The PAD facility provides a set of parameters to account for those differences. However, it only deals with asynchronous, start–stop terminals.

Three standards define the PAD facility:

- X.3: Describes the functions of the PAD and the parameters used to control its operation (Table 8.4).
- X.28: Describes the PAD–terminal protocol.
- X.29: Describes the PAD–host protocol.

Figure 8.9a indicates the architecture for use of the PAD. The terminal attached to the PAD sends characters one at a time. These are buffered in the PAD and then assembled into an X.25 packet, and sent through the network to the host. Host packets are received at the PAD, disassembled by stripping off the X.25 header, and passed to the terminal one character at a time. Simple commands between terminal and PAD (X.28), used to set parameters and establish virtual circuits, consist of character strings. Similar host–PAD control information (X.29) is transmitted in the data field of an X.25 packet, with a bit set in the X.25 header to indicate that this is control information.

### FNP Attachment

In the approaches just discussed, there were no new requirements placed on the NIUs to which hosts were attached. When the host–NIU interface is an FNP mode, however, the host NIU must be capable of distinguishing between primary and secondary connections, in order that data be routed properly.

First consider the layer 3/2 FNP, depicted in Figure 8.10a. The layer 3 software in the attached device contains logic for interfacing with the layer 2 software in the NIU. Further, there must be logic for routing incoming data to either layer 3 or an SNS module. The reason for this is that the local network serves as both a primary and a secondary network medium. Both terminals and computers connected to the local network can send data to a computer attached to the network. Hence incoming data must be routed either to the network layer, which will eventually pass the data up through session to a logical port, or

**TABLE 8.4   PAD Parameters (X.3 Standard)**

| Number | Indication | Selectable Values |
|--------|-----------|-------------------|
| 1 | Whether the terminal operator can escape from data transfer to PAD command state | 0: not allowed<br>1: allowed |
| 2 | Whether PAD echoes back characters received from terminal | 0: no echo<br>1: echo |
| 3 | Terminal characters that will trigger the sending of a partially full packet by the PAD | 0: only send full packets<br>1: carriage return<br>126: all control characters |
| 4 | Time-out value; PAD will stop assembly and send packet when value reached | 0: no time out<br>1–255: multiple of 50 ms |
| 5 | Whether PAD can exercise flow control over terminal output, using control characters | 0: not allowed<br>1: allowed |
| 6 | Whether PAD can send service signals (control information) to terminal | 0: not allowed<br>1: allowed |
| 7 | Action(s) taken by PAD on receipt of break signal from terminal | 0: nothing<br>1: interrupt<br>2: reset<br>4: send break to host<br>8: escape from data transfer<br>16: discard output |
| 8 | Whether PAD can disard host data intended for terminal | 0: not allowed<br>1: allowed |
| 9 | Number of padding characters to be inserted after carriage return | 0: determined by data rate<br>1–7: number of characters |
| 10 | Whether PAD inserts control characters to prevent terminal line overflow | 0: no<br>1–255: yes, line length |
| 11 | Terminal speed (bps) | 0: 110      8: 200<br>1: 134.5   9: 100<br>2: 300      10: 50 |
| 12 | Whether terminal can exercise flow control over PAD output, using control characters | 0: not allowed<br>1: allowed |

directly to an SNS. On the terminal side, the NIU can employ a simple layer 1 and 2 gateway for terminal attachment.

The situation for a layer 5/4 FNP mode is shown in Figure 8.10b. As before, the host NIU must distinguish between primary and secondary data. Incoming data are routed either to layer 5 or to an SNS. The layer 3 and 4 software in

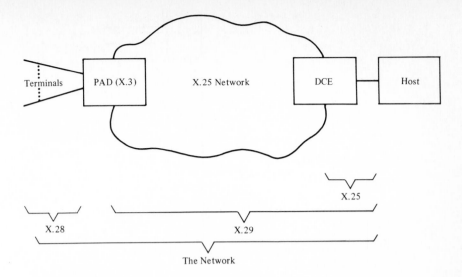

(a) Parameter-Defined Terminal

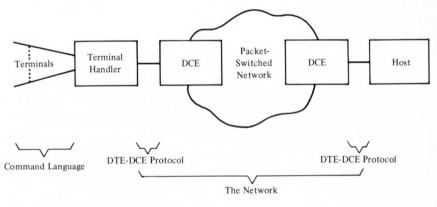

(b) Virtual Terminal Protocol

**FIGURE 8—9.  Two Views of Terminal-Network Architecture.**

the NIU must somehow be bypassed or it must somehow accommodate passing secondary network data packets without requiring a transport connection.

## Virtual Terminal Protocols

We have thus developed techniques for each mode of attachment for connecting terminals to packet-switched local networks so that they can effectively communicate with host devices. There is, however, a problem buried in this approach that relates to one of the advertised benefits of a local network. Specifically,

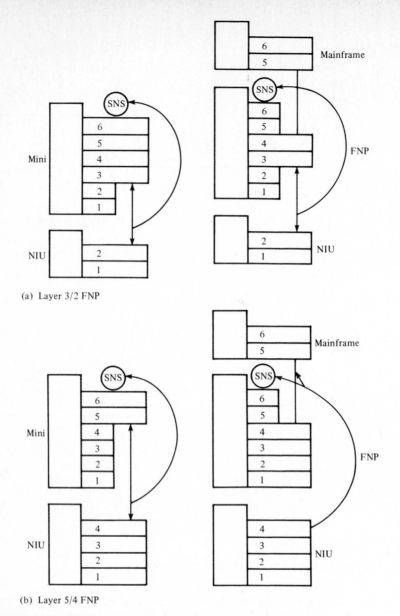

(a) Layer 3/2 FNP

(b) Layer 5/4 FNP

**FIGURE 8–10. Protocol Architectures for Local Networks.**

the local network user typically would like not to be locked in to a single vendor. The user would like to be able to procure hosts and terminals from a variety of vendors, but also to maintain complete connectivity.

What does this imply? Usually, in order to be able to use a terminal from one vendor with a host from another vendor, a special host software package must be built to accommodate the foreign terminal. Now consider a LAN with $N$ types of terminals and $M$ types of hosts. For complete connectivity, each host type must contain a package for handling each terminal type. In the worst case,

*MN* I/O packages must be developed. Furthermore, if a new type of host is acquired, it must be equipped with *N* new I/O packages. If a new type of terminal is acquired, each host must be equipped with a new I/O package, for a total of *M* new packages. This is not the type of situation designed to encourage multivendor LANs.

To solve this problem, a universal terminal protocol is needed—one that can handle all types of terminals. Such a thing exists today in name only: *virtual terminal protocol* (VTP). However, rudimentary versions do already exist. One is the X.28/X.29/X.3 protocol just described. Another is the TELNET protocol of ARPANET [DAVI77]. The true VTP is a fundamentally different and more flexible approach than the PAD concept. In this section we present a brief overview of VTP principles; more detail may be found in [DAY80], [DAY81], and [MAGN79].

As the name implies, the VTP is a protocol, a set of conventions for communication between peer entities. It includes the following functions:

- Providing the service of establishing and maintaining a connection between two application-level entities.
- Controlling a dialogue for negotiating the allowable actions to be performed across the connection.
- Creating and maintaining a data structure that represents the ''state'' of the terminal.
- Translating between actual terminal characteristics and a standardized representation.

The first two functions are in the nature of session control (layer 5); the latter two are presentation control (layer 6) functions. Figure 8.9 illustrates the difference in philosophy between this approach and that of the PAD. In the VTP approach, the terminal handler, which implements the terminal side of the protocol, is considered architecturally as a host attached to the network. Thus the protocol is end-to-end in terms of reliability, flow control, and so on. On the other hand, the X.29 standard is not a protocol as such. The PAD is considered part of the network, not a separate host. From the point of view of the host, the PAD facility is part of its local DCE's X.25 layer 3 functionality. Although the PAD concept affords an easily implemented capability, it does not provide the architectural base for a flexible terminal-handling facility.

The principal purpose of the VTP is to transform the characteristics of a real terminal into a standardized form or virtual terminal. Because of the wide differences in capabilities among terminals, it is unreasonable to attempt to develop a single virtual terminal type. Four classes of interest:

- *Scroll mode:* These are terminals with no local intelligence, including keyboard-printer and keyboard-display devices. Characters are transmitted as they are entered, and incoming characters are printed or displayed as they come in. On a display, as the screen fills, the top line is scrolled off.

- *Page mode:* These are keyboard-display terminals with a cursor-addressable character matrix display. Either user or host can modify random-accessed portions of the display. I/O can be a page at a time.
- *Form/data entry mode:* These are similar to page mode terminals, but allow definition of fixed and variable fields on the display. This permits a number of features, such as transmitting only the variable part, and defining field attributes to be used as validity checks.
- *Graphics mode:* These allow the creation of arbitrary two-dimensional patterns.

Little has yet been done for graphics mode, but a number of proposals exist for the first three modes. Table 8.5 is a proposed European standard defining the primitives or commands that can be used to control the terminal and the parameters that define the terminal.

For any VTP, there are basically four phases of operation:

- *Connection management:* includes session-layer-related functions, such as connection request and termination.

**TABLE 8.5  Parameters and Primitives for VTP**

| Primitives | Parameters |
|---|---|
| *Scroll Mode* | |
| Agree | Terminal class |
| Disagree | Line length |
| Request | Erase/overprint |
| Indicate | Dialogue mode |
| New line | Auxiliary data structure |
| Start of line | |
| Text segment | |
| Purge | |
| Asynchronous attention | |
| Synchronous attention | |
| *Paged Mode* | |
| Scroll mode primitives | Scroll mode parameters |
| Delete all | Page size |
| Position | |
| *Data Entry Terminal Mode* | |
| Paged mode primitives | Paged mode parameters |
| Attribute[a] | |
| Delete attribute | |
| Erase unprotected | |
| Next unprotected field | |

[a]Attributes are protected/unprotected fields, and three levels of display: nondisplay, normal, and intensified.
*Source:* [TANE81a].

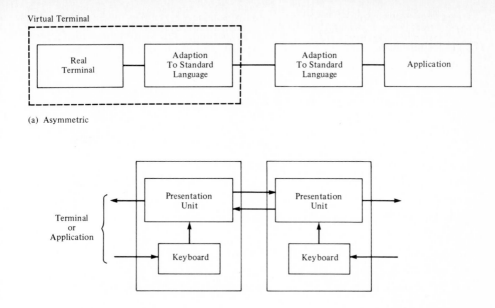

Virtual Terminal

(a) Asymmetric

(b) Symmetric

**FIGURE 8–11.   Virtual Terminal Protocol Models.**

- *Negotiation:* used to determine a mutually agreeable set of characteristics between the two correspondents.
- *Control:* exchange of control information and commands (e.g., defining the attributes of a field).
- *Data:* transfer of data between two correspondents.

Figure 8.11 shows two models for VTPs. In the asymmetric model, the virtual terminal is seen as a combination of the real terminal and the functions needed to adapt it to a standard language. On the other side is the host-resident application, which either "talks" VTP or must adapt its own representation to the standard language. A more general view is the symmetric one, which uses a shared presentation unit which represents the state of the virtual terminal. The presentation unit is implemented as a data structure that both sides, symmetrically, may read and update. Figure 8.12 is an example. The advantage of the symmetric view is that it permits terminal-to-terminal and even host-to-host, as well as terminal-to-host dialogue.

## The Terminal/NIU Interface

Again referring to Figure 8.7, possible LAN implementations of a VTP can be considered. In each case, terminals attach to the local network via an NIU which contains VTP. Thus, each NIU that supports terminals must have a VTP module plus the device-specific logic that adapts its terminal type to the virtual

```
type  field = record
          text: array [0 .. MaxText] of char;          {contents of the field}
          xposition: 0 .. MaxX;                         {horizontal position on screen}
          yposition: 0 .. MaxY;                         {vertical position on screen}
          size: 0 .. MaxSize;                           {size of the field}
          rendition: 0 .. MaxRendition;                 {color, intensity, etc.}
          adjustment: (left, right);                    {positioning of text within field}
          lcletters, ucletters, numbers, space, special: boolean;   {allowed input}
          protected, EntryRequired, MustFill: boolean
      end;
var   datastruct: record
          display: array [0 .. MaxField] of field;      {collection of fields}
          cursor: record x: 0 .. MaxText; y: 0 .. MaxField end;   {cursor position}
          TerminalType: (scroll, page, form);
          FlowMode: (alternating, FreeRunning);         {half or full duplex}
          turn: (mine, his);                            {who goes next (if half duplex)}
          state: (uninitialized, normal, interrupted)
      end;
```

**FIGURE 8–12.  VTP Data Structure (From [TANE81a])**

terminal type. On the host side, the VTP is a layer 6 or layer 5/6 protocol and
resides in the host.

Several implications of this approach are worthy of comment:

1. The advertised benefit of reduced implementation is achieved. The addition
   of a new terminal type requires the implementation of a single terminal
   handling routine, resident in the NIU. The addition of a new host type only
   requires that that host support VTP.
2. A common format for terminal-to-host traffic is used on the LAN. This
   facilitates auditing or eavesdropping by other network entities. For purposes
   of network management, this is a good thing, but there are privacy and
   security implications.
3. Somehow, the transport and session functions must be accommodated: These
   could be implemented in the terminal NIU, thus eliminating the use of the
   secondary network concept for terminals (although it may still be used for
   other devices, such as printers and disk controllers). Alternatively, the VTP
   in the host could be viewed as a type of secondary network server, reducing
   the processing demand placed on the terminal NIU.

## 8.5

## CIRCUIT-SWITCHED NETWORKS

The interface issues relating to circuit-switched local networks are far simpler
to deal with than those of packet-switched networks. With a circuit-switched
local network, such as a CBX, the mode of attachment is essentially transparent,
much like the layer 1 protocol mode discussed above.

As before, there are two phases of operation, a connection phase and a data
transfer phase. The data transfer phase uses synchronous TDM; thus no protocols
and no logic are required. As was mentioned, this is a truly transparent
connection.

For the connection phase, the main issue is the means by which the attached device requests a connection. For this discussion, it is useful to refer back to Figure 7.16, which indicates that each digital data device attaches to the network via some form of data line group. At least three means of connection establishment have been used.

1. Data devices typically connect via a twisted pair; therefore, near the data device, there must be a line driver to which the device attaches. This driver can include a simple keypad for selecting a destination.
2. Either the line driver or the data line group (more likely the latter) can contain the logic for conducting a simple dialogue with a terminal. In this case, the terminal user enters the connection request via the terminal.
3. The attached device (host) could contain a simple I/O program that generates connection requests in a form understandable to the network.

Regardless of the means, the switch architecture can support the private network configuration shown in Figure 8.1a. The local network connection would appear as a dial-up line to the attached device.

Finally, we mention the protocol converter featured in Figure 7.16. This facility acts as a gateway between devices with dissimilar protocols. It is used, for example, to convert between asynchronous ASCII terminals and the synchronous IBM 3270 protocol. In the future, this might be used to implement a VTP.

## 8.6

## ANALOG DEVICES

There are very few cases of analog device attachment to a local network to discuss. The most common is the telephone. Analog telephones are easily accommodated on a CBX that includes a codec in the line group (Figure 7.16). The other likely place to find analog devices is on a broadband network. As we have discussed, these networks easily accommodate video and audio attachments by dedicating channels for their use.

## 8.7

## RECOMMENDED READING

As yet, there is not much literature on this subject. [STAC80]* is perhaps the most systematic look at NIU interfaces for LANs; other articles of interest are [WOOD79]*, [LABA80], [WAY81] and [STAC81b]. A view of the issue for HSLNs is contained in [NESS81].

A readable description of X.3/X.28/X.29 is contained in [MART81a]. [DAY80] contains a good discussion of virtual terminal protocols.

## PROBLEMS

**8.1**   Consider Figure 8.7c. Assume that the host–NIU protocol is X.25 and the NIU–NIU protocol is IEEE 802. Describe, with an example, how the layer 3 X.25 protocol is converted to the LLC protocol for transmission over the network.

**8.2**   Repeat Problem 8.1, but now assume the ANS X3T9.5 link layer for NIU–NIU.

**8.3**   Consider Figure 8.7d. Assume that the host–NIU interface is IEEE-802 LLC. Describe, with an example, how the host layer 3 software makes use of the layer 2 services to transmit data to a destination host.

**8.4**   Repeat Problem 8.3, but now assume the ANS X3T9.5 interface.

**8.5**   Consider a layer 1 gateway being used by devices that communicate with a synchronous layer 2 protocol, such as HDLC or BISYNC. How is the NIU overflow problem handled?

**8.6**   Describe how a protocol converter in a digital switch architecture can be used to implement VTP.

**8.7**   In Figure 8.7f, the transport layer is in the NIU rather than the host and therefore part of the communications subnetwork. Since the transport layer is supposed to provide end-to-end reliability, is there cause for concern? Describe any potential problems and ways of attacking them.

# CHAPTER 9

# Network Performance: LAN/HSLN

This chapter has two objectives:

- To give the reader some insight into the factors that affect performance and the relative performance of various local network schemes.
- To present analytic techniques that can be used for network sizing and to obtain first approximations of network performance.

It is beyond the scope of this book to derive analytic expressions for all of the performance measures presented; that would require an entire book on local network performance. Further, this chapter can only sketch the techniques that would be useful to the analyst in approximating performance; for deeper study references to appropriate literature are provided.

Because of the distinctly different issues involved in packet-switched (LAN, HSLN) and circuit-switched (digital switch, CBX) networks, these are treated in separate chapters. This chapter begins by presenting some of the key performance considerations for LANs and HSLNs; the section serves to put the techniques and results presented subsequently into perspective. Separate sections present results for LAN and HSLN systems. Finally, the more difficult problem of end-to-end performance is broached.

# LAN/HSLN PERFORMANCE CONSIDERATIONS

The key characteristics of the LAN that structure the way its performance is analyzed are that there is a shared access medium, requiring a medium access control protocol, and that packet switching is used. HSLNs share these characteristics. It follows that the basic performance considerations, and the approaches to performance analysis, will be the same for both. With the above points in mind, this section explores these basic considerations. The section begins by defining the basic measures of performance, then looks at the key parameter for determining LAN/HSLN performance, known affectionately to devotees as *a*. Having been introduced to *a*, the reader is in a position to appreciate the interrelationship of the various factors that affect LAN/HSLN performance, which is the final topic.

The results that exist for the portion of performance within the local network boundary are summarized in subsequent sections. As we shall see, these results are best organized in terms of the medium access control protocol.

## Measures of Performance

Three measures of LAN and HSLN performance are commonly used:

- *D:* the delay that occurs between the time a packet or frame is ready for transmission from a node, and the completion of successful transmission.
- *S:* the throughput of the local network; the total rate of data being transmitted between nodes (carried load).
- *U:* the utilization of the local network medium; the fraction of total capacity being used.

These measures concern themselves with performance within the local network. How they relate to the overall performance of the network and attached devices is discussed later.

The parameter $S$ is often normalized and expressed as a fraction of capacity. For example, if over a period of 1 s, the sum of the successful data transfers between nodes is 1 Mb on a 10-Mbps channel, then $S = 0.1$. Thus $S$ can also be interpreted as utilization. The analysis is commonly done in terms of the total number of bits transferred, including overhead (headers, trailers) bits; the calculations are a bit easier, and this approach isolates performance effects due to the local network alone. One must work backward from this to determine effective throughput.

Results for $S$ and $D$ are generally plotted as a function of the offered load $G$, which is the actual load or traffic demand presented to the local network. Note that $S$ and $G$ differ. $S$ is the normalized rate of data packets successfully transmitted; $G$ is the total number of packets offered to the network; it includes control packets, such as tokens, and collisions, which are destroyed packets that must be retransmitted. $G$, too, is often expressed as a fraction of capacity. Intuitively, we would expect $D$ to increase with $G$: The more traffic competing for transmission time, the longer the delay for any individual transmission. $S$ should also increase with $G$, up to some saturation point, beyond which the network cannot handle more load.

Figure 9.1 shows the ideal situation: channel utilization increases to accommodate load up to an offered load equal to the full capacity of the system; then utilization remains at 100%. Of course, any overhead or inefficiency will cause performance to fall short of the goal. The depiction of $S$ versus $G$ is a reasonable one from the point of view of the network itself. It shows the behavior of the system based on the actual load on it. But from the point of view of the user or the attached device, it may seem strange. Why? Because the offered load includes not only original transmissions but also acknowledgments and, in the case of errors or collisions, retransmissions. The user may want to know the throughput and the delay characteristics as a function of the device-generated data to be put through the system—the "input load." Or if the network is the focus, the analyst may want to know what the offered load is given the input load. We will return to this discussion later.

The reader may also wonder about the importance of $U$. $D$ and $S$ are certainly of interest, but the efficiency or utilization of the channel may seem of minor importance. After all, local networks are advertised as having very high bandwidth and low cost compared to long-haul networks. Although it is true that utilization is of less importance for local compared to long-haul links, it is still worth considering. Local network capacity is not free, and demand has a tendency to expand to fill available capacity.

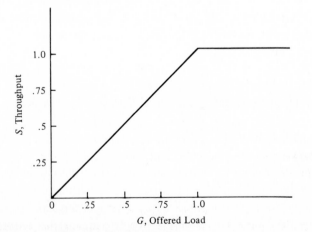

**FIGURE 9–1. Ideal channel utilization.**

**TABLE 9.1  Example of Relationships Among LAN/HSLN Measures of Performance[a,b]**

| I | S | G | D | U |
|------|------|------|--------|------|
| 100 | 100 | 101 | 0.0505 | 0.1 |
| 500 | 500 | 505 | 0.2525 | 0.5 |
| 990 | 990 | 1000 | 0.5 | 0.99 |
| 2000 | 990 | — | — | 0.99 |

[a]Capacity: 1000 frames/sec.
[b]I, input load (frames per second); S, throughput (frames per second); G, offered load (frames per second); D, delay (seconds); U, utilization (fraction of capacity).

In summary, we have introduced two additional parameters:

- $G$: the offered load to the local network; the total rate of data presented to the network for transmission.
- $I$: the input load; the rate of data generated by the stations attached to the local network.

Table 9.1 is a very simplified example to show the relationship between these parameters. Here we assume a network with a capacity of $C = 1000$ frames per second. For simplicity, $I$, $S$, and $G$ are expressed in frames per second. It is assumed that 1% of all transmitted frames are lost and must be repeated. Thus at an input $I = 100$ frames per second, on the average 1 frame per second will be repeated. Thus $S = 100$ and $G = 101$. Assume that the input load arrives in batches, once per second. Hence, on average, with $I = 100$, $D = 0.0505$ s. The utilization is defined as $S/C = 0.1$.

The next two entries are easily seen to be correct. Note that for $I = 990$, the entire capacity of the system is being used ($G = 1000$). If $I$ increases beyond this point, the system cannot keep up. Only 1000 frames per second will be transmitted. Thus $S$ remains at 990 and $U$ at 0.99. But $G$ and $D$ grow without bound as more and more backlog accumulates; there is no steady-state value. This pattern will become familiar as the chapter proceeds.

## The Effect of Propagation Delay and Transmission Rate

Recall from Figure 1.1 that local networks are distinguished from long-haul networks on the one hand, and multiprocessor systems on the other, by the data rate or bandwidth ($B$) employed and the distance ($d$) of the communications path. In fact, it is the product of these two terms, $B \times d$, that can be used to characterize local networks. Furthermore, as we shall see, this term, or cousins of it, is the single most important parameter for determining the performance of a local network. We shall see that a network's performance will be the same, for example, for both a 50-Mbps, 1 km bus and a 50-Gbps, 1-m bus (the latter might someday be used to interconnect Josephson diode computers).

A good way to visualize the meaning of $B \times d$ is to divide it by the propagation velocity of the medium, which is nearly constant among most media of interest. A good approximation for propagation velocity is about two-thirds of the speed of light, or $2 \times 10^8$ m/s. A dimensional analysis of the formula

$$\frac{Bd}{V}$$

shows this to be equal to the length of the transmission medium in bits, that is, the number of bits that may be in transit between two nodes an any one time.

We can see that this does indeed distinguish local networks from multiprocessor and long haul networks. Within a multiprocessor system, there are generally only a few bits in transit. For example, the latest IBM I/O channel offering operates at up to 24 Mbps over a distance of up to 120 m, which yields at most about 15 bits. Processor-to-processor communication within a single computer will typically involve fewer bits than that in transit. On the other hand, we saw in Chapter 6 that the bit length of a long-haul network can be hundreds of thousands of bits. In between, we have local networks. Several examples: a 500-m Ethernet system (10 Mbps) has a bit length of 25; both a 1-km HYPERchannel (50 Mbps) and a typical 5-km broadband LAN (5 Mbps) are about 250 bits long.

A useful way of looking at this is to consider the length of the medium as compared to the typical frame transmitted. Multiprocessor systems have very short bit lengths compared to frame length; long-haul nets have very long ones. Local networks generally are shorter than a frame up to about the same order of magnitude.

Intuitively, one can see that this will make a difference. Compare local networks to multiprocessor computers. Relatively speaking, things happen almost simultaneously in a multiprocessor system; when one component begins to transmit, the others know it almost immediately. For local networks, the relative time gap leads to all kinds of complications in the medium access control protocols, as we have seen. Compare long-haul networks to local networks. To have any hope of efficiency, the long-haul link must allow multiple frames to be in transit simultaneously. This places specific requirements on the link layer protocol, which must deal with a sequence of outstanding frames waiting to be acknowledged. LAN and HSLN protocols generally allow only one frame to be in transit at a time, or at the most a few for some ring protocols. Again, this affects the access protocol.

The length of the medium, expressed in bits, compared to the length of the typical frame is usually denoted by $a$:

$$a = \frac{\text{length of data path (in bits)}}{\text{length of frame}}$$

Some manipulation shows that

$$a = \frac{Bd}{VL}$$

where $L$ is the length of the frame. But $d/V$ is the propagation time on the medium (worst case), and $L/B$ is the time it takes a transmitter to get an entire frame out onto the medium. So

$$a = \frac{\text{propagation time}}{\text{transmission time}}$$

Typical values of $a$ range from about 0.01 to 0.1 for LANs and 0.01 to over 1 for HSLNs. Table 9.2 gives some sample values for a bus topology. In computing $a$, keep in mind that the maximum propagation time on a broadband network is double the length of the longest path from the headend, plus the delay, if any, at the headend. For baseband bus and ring networks, repeater delays must be included in propagation time.

The parameter $a$ determines an upper bound on the utilization of a local network. Consider a perfectly efficient access mechanism that allows only one transmission at a time. As soon as one transmission is over, another node begins transmitting. Furthermore, the transmission is pure data—no overhead bits. (*Note*: These conditions are very close to being met in a digital switch but not, alas, in LANs and HSLNs.) What is the maximum possible utilization of the network? It can be expressed as the ratio of total throughput of the system to the capacity or bandwidth:

$$\begin{aligned} U &= \frac{\text{throughput}}{B} \\ &= \frac{L/(\text{propagation} + \text{transmission time})}{B} \\ &= \frac{L/(d/V + L/B)}{B} \\ &= \frac{1}{1 + a} \end{aligned} \tag{9.1}$$

So, utilization varies inversely with $a$. This can be grasped intuitively by studying Figure 9.2. This figure shows a baseband bus with two stations as far apart as possible (worst case) that take turns sending frames. If we normalize time such that the frame transmission time $= 1$, then the sequence of events can be expressed as follows.

1. A station begins transmission at $t_o$.
2. Reception begins at $t_o + a$.
3. Transmission is completed at $t_o + 1$.
4. Reception ends at $t_o + 1 + a$.
5. The other station begins transmitting.

**TABLE 9-2   Values of _a_**

| Data Rate (Mbps) | Packet Size (bits) | Cable length (km) | _a_ |
|---|---|---|---|
| 1 | 100 | 1 | 0.05 |
| 1 | 1,000 | 10 | 0.05 |
| 1 | 100 | 10 | 0.5 |
| 10 | 100 | 1 | 0.5 |
| 10 | 1,000 | 1 | 0.05 |
| 10 | 1,000 | 10 | 0.5 |
| 10 | 10,000 | 10 | 0.05 |
| 50 | 10,000 | 1 | 0.025 |
| 50 | 100 | 1 | 2.5 |

Event 2 occurs *after* event 3 if $a > 1.0$. In any case the total time for one "turn" is $1 + a$, but the transmission time is only 1, for a utilization of $1/(1 + a)$.

The same effect can be seen to apply to a ring network in Figure 9.3. Here we assume that one station transmits and then waits to receive its own transmission before any other station transmits. The identical sequence of events outlined above applies.

Equation (9.1) is plotted in Figure 9.4. The implications for throughput are shown in Figure 9.5.

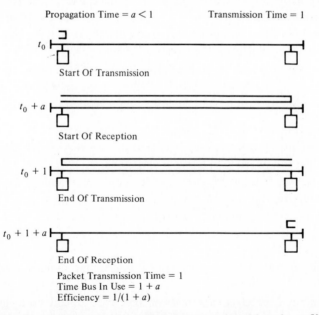

FIGURE 9—2a.   Effect of _a_ on utilization: baseband bus ($a < 1$).

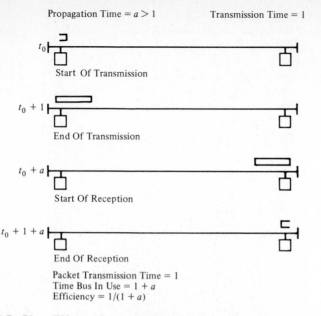

Propagation Time $= a > 1$       Transmission Time $= 1$

$t_0$    Start Of Transmission

$t_0 + 1$    End Of Transmission

$t_0 + a$    Start Of Reception

$t_0 + 1 + a$    End Of Reception

Packet Transmission Time $= 1$
Time Bus In Use $= 1 + a$
Efficiency $= 1/(1 + a)$

**FIGURE 9–2b.**   **Effect of *a* on utilization: baseband bus (*a* > 1).**

So we can say that an upper bound on the utilization or efficiency of a LAN or HSLN is $1/(1 + a)$, regardless of the medium access protocol used. Two caveats: First, this assumes that the maximum propagation time is incurred on each transmission. Second, it assumes that only one transmission may occur at a time. These assumptions are not always true; nevertheless, the formula $1/(1 + a)$ is almost always a valid upper bound, because the overhead of the medium access protocol more than makes up for the lack of validity of these assumptions.

The overhead is unavoidable. Frames must include address and synchronization bits. There is administrative overhead for controlling the protocol. In addition, there are forms of overhead peculiar to one or more of the protocols. We highlight these briefly for the most important protocols:

- *Contention protocols (ALOHA, S-ALOHA, CSMA, CSMA/CD):* time wasted due to collisions; need for acknowledgment frames. S-ALOHA requires that slot size equal transmission plus maximum propagation time.
- *Collision avoidance:* time spent waiting to see if other stations have data to send; acknowledgment frames.
- *Token bus:* token transmission; acknowledgment frames.
- *Token ring:* time waiting for token if intervening stations have no data to send.
- *Slotted ring:* time waiting for empty slot if intervening stations have no data to send.
- *Register insertion:* delay at each node of time equal to address length. From

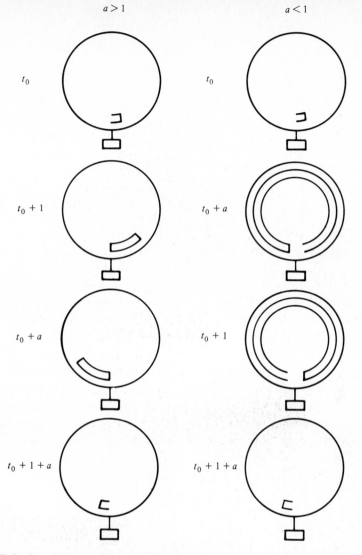

**FIGURE 9–3. Effect of _a_ on utilization: ring.**

the point of view of a single station, the propagation time and hence _a_ may increase due to insertion of registers on the ring.

- _Explicit reservation:_ reservation transmission, acknowledgments.
- _Implicit reservation:_ overhead of protocol used to establish reservation, acknowledgments.

There are two distinct effects here. One is that the efficiency or utilization of a channel decreases as _a_ increases. This, of course, affects throughput. The other effect is that the overhead attributable to a protocol wastes bandwidth and

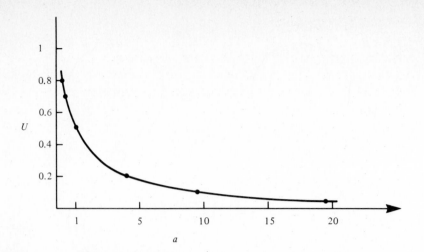

**FIGURE 9–4. Utilization as a function of _a_.**

hence reduces effective utilization and effective throughput. By and large, we can think of these two effects as independent and additive. However, we shall see that, for contention protocols, there is a strong interaction such that the overhead of these protocols increases as a function of _a_.

In any case, it would seem desirable to keep _a_ as low as possible. Looking back to the defining formula, for a fixed network _a_ can be reduced by increasing frame size. This will only be useful if the length of messages produced by a station is an integral multiple of the frame size (excluding overhead bits). Otherwise, the large frame size is itself a source of waste. Furthermore, a large frame size increases the delay for other stations. This lead us to the next topic: the various factors that affect LAN/HSLN performance.

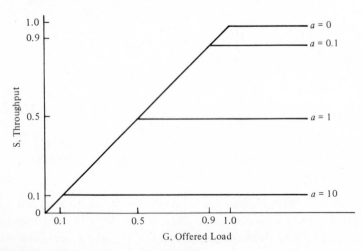

**FIGURE 9–5. Effect of _a_ on throughput.**

## Factors That Affect Performance

We list here those factors that affect the performance of a LAN or a HSLN. We are concerned here with that part which is independent of the attached devices—those factors that are exclusively under the control of the local network designer. The chief factors are:

- Bandwidth
- Propagation delay
- Number of bits per frame
- Local network protocol
- Offered load
- Number of stations

The first three terms have already been discussed; they determine the value of $a$.

Next are the local network protocols: physical, medium access, and link. The physical layer is not likely to be much of a factor; generally, it can keep up with transmissions and receptions with little delay. The link layer will add some overhead bits to each frame and some administrative overhead, such as virtual circuit management and acknowledgments. This area has not been studied much, and is best considered as part of the end-to-end performance problem discussed in Section 9.4. This leaves the medium access layer, which can have a significant effect on network performance. Sections 9.2 and 9.3 are devoted to this topic.

We can think of the first three factors listed above as characterizing the network; they are generally treated as constants or givens. The local network protocol is the focus of the design effort—the choice that must be made. The next two factors, offered load and the number of stations, are generally treated as the independent variables. The analyst is concerned with determining performance as a function of these two variables. Note that these two variables must be treated separately. Certainly, it is true that for a fixed offered load per station, the total offered load increases as the number of stations increase. The same increase could be achieved by keeping the number of stations fixed but increasing the offered load per station. However, as we shall see, the network performance will be different for these two cases.

One factor that was not listed above: the error rate of the channel. An error in a frame transmission necessitates a retransmission. Because the error rates on local networks are so low, this is not likely to be a significant factor.

## 9.2

## LAN PERFORMANCE

A considerable amount of work has been done on the analysis of the performance of various LAN protocols for bus/tree and ring. This section will limit itself to summarizing the results for the protocols discussed in Chapter 5, those protocols that are most common for LANs.

We begin by presenting an easily-used technique for quickly establishing bounds on performance. Often, this back-of-the-envelope approach is adequate for system sizing.

Next, comparison of the three protocols being standardized by IEEE 802 is presented. These three protocols are likely to dominate the United States market, at least, and an insight into their comparative performance is needed.

We then look more closely at contention protocols and devote more time here to the derivation of results. This process should give the reader a feeling for the assumptions that must be made and the limitations of the results. More time is spent on the contention protocols because we wish to understand their inherent instability. As we shall see, the basis of this instability is a positive feedback mechanism that behaves poorly under heavy load.

Finally, we revisit token ring and view it in context with the other two common ring protocols: register insertion and slotted ring.

## Bounds on Performance

The purpose of this section is to present a remarkably simple technique for determining bounds on the performance of an LAN. Although a considerable amount of work has been done on developing detailed analytic and simulation models of the performance of various LAN protocols, much of this work is suspect because of the restrictive assumptions made. Furthermore, even if the models were valid, they provide a level of resolution not needed by the local network designer.

A commonsense argument should clarify this point. In any LAN or HSLN, there are three regions of operation, based on the magnitude of the offered load:

- A region of low delay through the network, where the capacity is more than adequate to handle the load offered.
- A region of high delay, where the network becomes a bottleneck. In this region, relatively more time is spent controlling access to the network and less in actual data transmission compared to the low-delay region.
- A region of unbounded delay, where the offered load exceeds the total capacity of the system.

This last region is easily identified. For example, consider the following network:

- Capacity = 1 Mbps
- Number of stations = 1000
- Frame size = 1000 bits

If, on average, each station generates data at a rate exceeding 1 frame per second, then the total offered load exceeds 1 Mbps. The delay at each station will build up and up without bound.

The third region is clearly to be avoided. But almost always, the designer will wish to avoid the second region as well. The second region implies an inefficient use of the network. Further, a sudden surge of data while in the second region would cause corresponding increases in the already high delay. In the first region, the network is not a bottleneck and, as we will discuss in Section 9.4, will contribute typically only a small amount to the end-to-end delay.

Thus the crucial question is: What region will the network operate in, based on projected load and network characteristics? The third region is easily identified and avoided; it is the boundary between the first two regions that must be identified. If the network operates below that boundary, it should not cause a communications bottleneck. If it operates above the boundary, there is reason for concern and perhaps redesign. Further, because traffic estimates are unlikely to be precise, it is often not necessary to know exactly where that boundary is—a good approximation is adequate.

With the above points in mind, we present a technique for estimating performance bounds, based on the approach taken by the IEEE 802 committee [ARTH81, ARTH82, STUC83]. To begin, let us ignore the medium access control protocol and develop bounds for throughput and delay as a function of the number of active stations. Four quantities are needed:

- $T_{idle}$ = the mean time that a station is idle between transmission attempts: the station has no messages awaiting transmission.
- $T_{msg}$ = the time required to transmit a message once medium access is gained.
- $T_{delay}$ = the mean delay from the time a station has a packet to transmit until completion of transmission; includes queueing time and transmission time.
- THRU = mean total throughput on the network of messages per unit time.

We assume that there are $N$ active stations, each with the same load-generating requirements. To find an upper bound on total throughput, consider the ideal case in which there is no queueing delay: Each station transmits when it is ready. Hence each station alternates between idle and transmission with a throughput of $1/(T_{idle} + T_{msg})$. The maximum possible throughput is just the summation of the throughputs of all $N$ stations:

$$\text{THRU} \leq \frac{N}{T_{idle} + T_{msg}} \tag{9.2}$$

This upper bound increases as $N$ increases, but is only reasonable up to the point of the raw capacity of the network, which can be expressed

$$\text{THRU} \leq \frac{1}{T_{msg}} \tag{9.3}$$

The breakpoint between these two bounds occurs at

$$\frac{N}{T_{idle} + T_{msg}} = \frac{1}{T_{msg}}$$

$$N = \frac{T_{idle} + T_{msg}}{T_{msg}} \tag{9.4}$$

This breakpoint defines two regions of operation. With the number of stations below the breakpoint, the system is not generating enough load to utilize fully system capacity. However, above the breakpoint, the network is saturated: It is fully utilized and is not able to satisfy the demands of the attached stations.

To see the reasonableness of this breakpoint, consider that the capacity of the network is $1/T_{msg}$. For example, if it takes 1 μs to transmit a message, the data rate is $10^6$ messages per second. The amount of traffic being generated by $N$ stations is $N/(T_{idle} + T_{msg})$. If the traffic exceeds the networks capacity, messages get backlogged and delay increases. Note also that traffic increases either by increasing the number of stations ($N$) or increasing the rate at which stations transmit messages (reduce $T_{idle}$).

These same considerations allow us to place a lower bound on delay. Clearly,

$$T_{delay} \geq T_{msg} \tag{9.5}$$

Now, consider that at any load the following relationship holds:

$$\text{THRU} = \frac{N}{T_{idle} + T_{delay}} \tag{9.6}$$

since $1/(T_{idle} + T_{delay})$ is the throughput of each station. Combining (9.3) and 9.6) we have

$$T_{delay} \geq NT_{msg} - T_{idle}$$

The breakpoint calculation, combining (9.5) and the equation above yields the same result as before (see Figure 9.6). Keep in mind that these bounds are asymptotes of the true delay and throughput curves. The breakpoint delimits two regions. Below the breakpoint, capacity is underutilized and delay is low. Above the breakpoint, capacity saturates and delay blows up. In actuality, the changes are gradual rather than abrupt.

Bounds on the other side are easily found. The delay would be maximized if all $N$ stations had a message to transmit simultaneously:

$$T_{delay} \leq NT_{msg}$$

Combining with equation (9.6) gives us

$$\text{THRU} \geq \frac{N}{T_{idle} + NT_{msg}}$$

These bounds give one a rough idea of the behavior of a system. It allows one

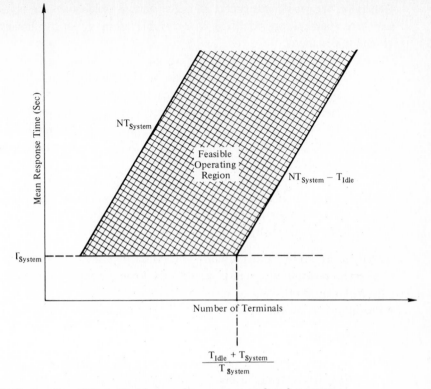

**FIGURE 9–6. Feasible operating region, zero-overhead system.**

to do a simple back-of-the-envelope calculation to determine if a proposed system is within reasonable bounds. If the answer is no, much analysis and grief may be saved. If yes, the analyst must dig deeper.

Two examples, from [STUC83], should clarify the use of these equations. First, consider a workstation attached to a 1-Mbps local network that generates, on average, three messages per minute, with messages averaging 500 bits. With message transmission time equal to 500 μs, the mean idle time is 19.5 s. The breakpoint number of station is, roughly,

$$N = \frac{20}{500 \times 10^{-6}} = 40,000 \text{ stations}$$

If the number of stations is much less than this, say 1000, congestion should not be a problem. If it is much more, say 100,000, congestion may be a problem.

Second, consider a set of stations that generate PCM digitized voice packets on a 10-Mbps local network. Data are generated at the rate of 64 kbps. For 0.1-s packets, we have a transmission time per packet of 640 μs. Thus

$$N = \frac{0.1}{640 \times 10^{-6}} = 156 \text{ stations}$$

Generally, we would not expect all voice stations (telephones) to be active at one time; perhaps one-fourth is a reasonable estimate, so the breakpoint is around 600 stations.

Note that in both these examples, we have very quickly arrived at a first-order sizing of the system with no knowledge of the protocol. All that is needed is the load generated per station and the capacity of the network.

The calculations above are based on a system with no overhead. They provide bounds for a system with perfect scheduling. One way to account for overhead is to replace $T_{msg}$ with $T_{sys}$, where the latter quantity includes an estimate of the overhead per packet. This is done in Figure 9.6.

A more accurate, though still rough handle on performance can be had by considering the protocol involved. We develop the results for token passing. A similar analysis can be found in [HAYE81]. This protocol, for bus or ring, has the following characteristics:

- Stations are given the opportunity to transmit in a fixed cyclical sequence.
- At each opportunity, a station may transmit one message.
- Frames may be of fixed or variable length.
- Preemption is not allowed.

Some additional terms are needed:

- $R(K)$ = mean throughput rate (messages/second) of station $K$
- $T_{over}$ = total overhead (seconds) in one cycle of the $N$ stations
- $C$ = duration (seconds) of a cycle
- UTIL$(K)$ = utilization of the network due to station $K$.

Let us begin by assuming that each station always has messages to transmit; the system is never idle. The fraction of time that the network is busy handling requests from station $K$ is just

$$\text{UTIL}(K) = R(K)\,T_{msg}(K)$$

To keep up with the work, the system must not be presented with a load greater than its capacity:

$$\sum_{K=1}^{N} \text{UTIL}(K) = \sum_{K=1}^{N} R(K)T_{msg}(K) \le 1$$

Now consider the overhead in the system, which is the time during a cycle required to pass the token and perform other maintenance functions. Clearly,

$$C = T_{over} + \sum_{K=1}^{N} T_{msg}(K)$$

From this we can deduce that

$$R(K) = \frac{1}{C} = \frac{1}{T_{over} + \sum\limits_{K=1}^{N} T_{msg}(K)}$$

Now, let us assume that the medium is always busy but that some stations may be idle. This line of reasoning will lead us to the desired bounds on throughput and delay. Since we assume that the network is never idle, the fraction of time the system spends on overhead and transmission must sum to unity:

$$\frac{T_{\text{over}}}{C} + \sum_{K=1}^{N} R(K)T_{\text{msg}}(K) = 1$$

Thus

$$C = \frac{T_{\text{over}}}{1 - \sum_{K=1}^{N} R(K)T_{\text{msg}}(K)}$$

Note that the duration of a cycle is proportional to the overhead; doubling the mean overhead time should double the cycle time for a fixed load. This result may not be intuitively obvious; the reader is advised to work out a few examples.

With $C$ known, we can place an upper bound on the throughput of any one source:

$$R(J) \leq \frac{1}{C} = \frac{1 - \sum_{K=1}^{N} R(K)T_{\text{msg}}(K)}{T_{\text{over}}} \tag{9.7}$$

Now let us assume that all sources are identical: $R(K) = R$, $T_{\text{msg}}(K) = T_{\text{msg}}$. Then (9.7) reduces to

$$R \leq \frac{1 - NRT_{\text{msg}}}{T_{\text{over}}}$$

Solving for $R$:

$$R \leq \frac{1}{T_{\text{over}} + NT_{\text{msg}}}$$

But, by definition, $R = 1/(T_{\text{delay}} + T_{\text{idle}})$, so we can express:

$$T_{\text{delay}} = \frac{1}{R} - T_{\text{idle}}$$

$$T_{\text{delay}} \geq T_{\text{over}} + NT_{\text{msg}} - T_{\text{idle}}$$

In practice, $T_{\text{over}}$ may consist of some fixed amount of time $C_0$ for each cycle plus an amount $C_1$ for each station that receives the token. These numbers will differ for token ring and token bus:

$$T_{\text{delay}} \geq C_0 + N(T_{\text{msg}} + C_1) - T_{\text{idle}}$$

We also have the inequality of (9.5) and can solve for the breakpoint:

$$N = \frac{T_{\text{msg}} + T_{\text{idle}} - C_0}{T_{\text{msg}} + C_1} \tag{9.8}$$

Figure 9.7 depicts the delay-station plot, showing the two regions. Note that the slope of the line in the heavily loaded region is $T_{\text{msg}} + C_1$.

A similar analysis can be carried out for CSMA/CD. Figure 9.8 is a comparison developed in [ARTH82]. The absolute positions of the various policies depend on specific assumptions about overhead and, in the case of CSMA/CD, the value of $a$. But the relative positions are generally true: under lightly loaded conditions CSMA/CD has a shorter delay time, but the protocol breaks down more rapidly under increasing load.

## Comparative Performance of Token Passing and CSMA/CD

The purpose of this section is to give the reader some insight into the relative performance of the most important LAN protocols: CSMA/CD, token bus, and token ring. We begin with a simplified model which highlights the main points of comparison. Following this, a careful analysis performed by the IEEE 802 committee is reported.

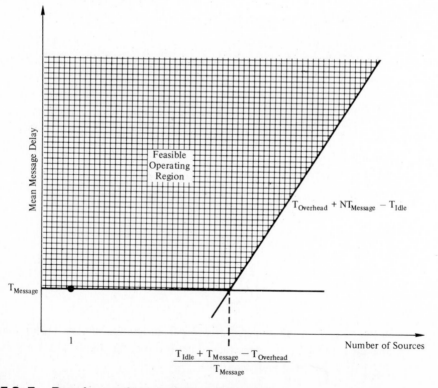

**FIGURE 9–7.  Bounds on token-passing performance.**

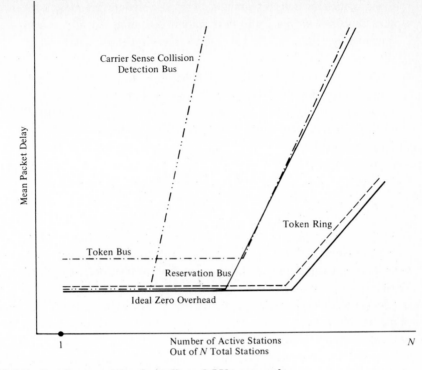

**FIGURE 9–8. Comparative bounds on LAN protocols.**

For the model, we assume a local network with $N$ stations. Our purpose is to estimate the maximum throughput achievable on the LAN. For this purpose, we assume that each station is always prepared to send a frame.

First, let us consider token ring. Time on the ring will alternate between data-frame transmission and token passing. Refer to a single instance of a data frame followed by a token as a cycle and define:

- $C$ = average time for one cycle
- $DF$ = average time to transmit a data frame
- $TF$ = average time to pass a token

It should be clear that the average cycle rate is just $1/C = 1/(DF + TF)$. Intuitively,

$$S = \frac{DF}{DF + TF} \tag{9.9}$$

That is, the throughput, normalized to system capacity, is just the fraction of time that is spent transmitting data.

Refer now to Figure 9.3; time is normalized such that frame transmission time equals 1 and propagation time equals $a$. For the case of $a < 1$, a station transmits a frame at time $t_o$, receives the leading edge of its own frame at $t_o +$

$a$, and completes transmission at $t_o + 1$. The station then emits a token, which takes time $a/N$ to reach the next station (assuming equally spaced stations). Thus one cycle takes $1 + a/N$ and the transmission time is 1. So $S = 1/(1 + a/N)$.

For $a > 1$, the reasoning is slightly different. A station transmits at $t_o$, completes transmission at $t_o + 1$, and receives the leading edge of its frame at $t_o + a$. At that point, it is free to emit a token, which takes a time $a/N$ to reach the next station. The cycle time is therefore $a + a/N$ and $S = 1/[a(1 + 1/N)]$. Summarizing,

$$\text{Token:} \quad S = \begin{cases} \dfrac{1}{1 + a/N} & a < 1 \\[3mm] \dfrac{1}{a(1 + 1/N)} & a > 1 \end{cases} \tag{9.10}$$

The reasoning above applies equally well to token bus, where we assume that the logical ordering is the same as the physical ordering and that token-passing time is therefore $a/N$.

For CSMA/CD, we base our approach on a derivation in [METC76]. Consider time on the medium to be organized into slots whose length is twice the end-to-end propagation delay. This is a convenient way to view the activity on the medium; the slot time is the maximum time, from the start of transmission, required to detect a collision. Again, assume that there are $N$ active stations, each generating the same load. The load can be expressed as the probability that a station has a frame to transmit during any slot.

Time on the medium consists of two types of intervals. First is a transmission interval, which lasts $1/2a$ slots. Second is a contention interval, which is a sequence of slots with either a collision or no transmission in each slot. The throughput is just the proportion of time spent in transmission intervals [similar to the reasoning for equation (9.9)].

To determine the average length of a contention interval, we begin by computing $A$, the probability that exactly one station attempts a transmission in a slot and therefore acquires the medium. This is just the binomial probability that any one station attempts to transmit and the others do not:

$$A = \binom{N}{1} p^1 (1 - p)^{N-1}$$

$$= Np(1 - p)^{N-1}$$

This function takes on a maximum over $p$ when $p = 1/N$:

$$A = \left(1 - \frac{1}{N}\right)^{N-1}$$

Why are we interested in the maximum? Well, we want to calculate the maximum utilization of the medium. It should be clear that this will be achieved if we maximize the probability of successful seizure of the medium. This says that the following rule should be enforced: During periods of heavy usage, a station should restrain its offered load to $1/N$. On the other hand, during periods of light usage, maximum utilization cannot be achieved because $G$ is too low; this region is not of interest here.

Now we can estimate the mean length of a contention interval, $w$, in slots:

$$E[w] = \sum_{i=1}^{\infty} i \cdot \Pr\,[i \text{ slots in a row with a collision or no}$$

$$\text{transmission followed by a slot with one transmission]}$$

$$= \sum_{i=1}^{\infty} i(1 - A)^i A$$

The summation converges to

$$E[w] = \frac{1 - A}{A}$$

We can now determine the maximum utilization, which is just the length of a transmission interval as a proportion of a cycle consisting of a transmission and a contention interval.

$$\text{CSMA/CD:} \quad S = \frac{1/2a}{1/2a + \dfrac{1 - A}{A}} = \frac{1}{1 + 2a\dfrac{1 - A}{A}} \tag{9.11}$$

Figure 9.9 shows normalized throughput as a function of $a$ for various values of $N$ and for both token passing and CSMA/CD. For both protocols, throughput declines as $a$ increases. This is to be expected. But the dramatic difference between the two protocols is seen in Figure 9.10, which shows throughput as a function of $N$. Token-passing performance actually improves as a function of $N$, because less time is spent in token passing. Conversely, the performance of CSMA/CD decreases because of the increased likelihood of collision or no transmission.

It is interesting to note the asymptotic value of $S$ as $N$ increases. For token:

$$\text{Token:} \quad \lim_{N \to \infty} S = \begin{cases} 1 & a < 1 \\[2mm] \dfrac{1}{a} & a > 1 \end{cases}$$

For CSMA/CD, we need to know that $\lim_{N \to \infty}(1 - 1/N)^{N-1} = 1/e$. Then

$$\text{CSMA/CD:} \quad \lim_{N \to \infty} S = \frac{1}{1 + 3.44a}$$

Continuing this example, it is relatively easy to derive an expression for delay for token passing. Once a station (station 1) transmits, it must wait for the following events to occur before it can transmit again:

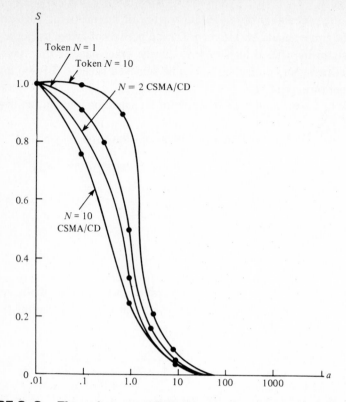

**FIGURE 9—9.** Throughput as a function of *a* for token-passing and CSMA/CD.

- Station 1 transmits token to station 2.
- Station 2 transmits data frame.
- Station 2 transmits token to station 3.
- Station 3 transmits data frame.

      •

      •

      •

      •

- Station $N-1$ transmits token to station $N$.
- Station $N$ transmits data frame.
- Station $N$ transmits token to station 1.

Thus the delay consists of $(N-1)$ cycles plus $a/N$, the token passing time. We have

$$Token: \quad D = \begin{cases} N + a - 1 & a < 1 \\ aN & a > 1 \end{cases} \qquad (9.12)$$

Thus, delay increases linearly with load, and for a fixed number of stations delay is constant and finite even if all stations always have something to send.

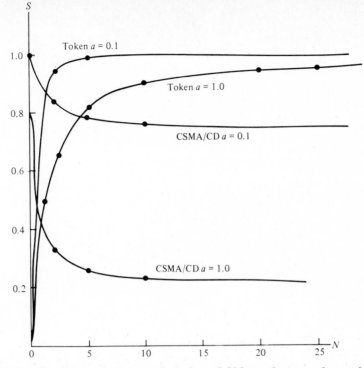

**FIGURE 9–10.  Throughput as a function of *N* for token-passing and CSMA/CD.**

The delay for CSMA/CD is more difficult to express and depends on the exact nature of the protocol (persistence, retry policy). In general, we can say that the delay grows without bound as the system becomes saturated. As *N* increases, there are more collisions and longer contention intervals. Individual frames must make more attempts to achieve successful transmission. We explore this behavior further in the next section.

We now report the results of a deeper analysis done for the IEEE 802 committee [ARTH81, ARTH82]. A similar analysis is also reported in [BUX81]. The analysis is based on considering not only mean values but second moments of delay and message length. Two cases of message arrival statistics are employed. In the first, only 1 station out of 100 has messages to transmit, and is always ready to transmit. In such a case, one would hope that the network would not be the bottleneck, but could easily keep up with one station. In the second case, 100 stations out of 100 always have messages to transmit. This represents an extreme of congestion and one would expect that the network may be a bottleneck.

The results are shown in Figure 9.11. It shows the actual data transmission rate versus the transmission speed on a 2-km bus. Note that the abscissa is not offered load but the actual capacity of the medium. The 1 station or 100 stations provide enough input to utilize the network fully. Hence these plots are a

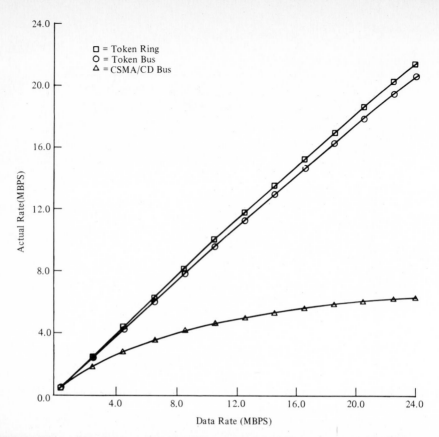

**FIGURE 9–11a. Maximum potential data rate for LAN protocols: 2000 bits per packet; 100 stations active out of 100 stations total.**

measure of maximum potential utilization. Three systems are examined: token ring with a 1-bit latency per station, token bus, and CSMA/CD. The analysis yields the following conclusions:

- For the given parameters, the smaller the mean frame length, the greater the difference in maximum mean throughput rate between token passing and CSMA/CD. This reflects the strong dependence of CSMA/CD on $a$.
- Token ring is the least sensitive to work load.
- CSMA/CD offers the shortest delay under light load, while it is most sensitive under heavy load to the work load.

Note also that in the case of a single station transmitting, token bus is significantly less efficient than the other two protocols. This is so because the assumption is made that the propagation delay is longer than for token ring, and that the delay in token processing is greater than for token ring.

Another phenomenon of interest is seen most clearly in Figure 9.11b. For a CSMA/CD system under these conditions, the maximum effective throughput at 5 Mbps is only about 1.25 Mbps. If the expected load is, say 0.75 Mbps,

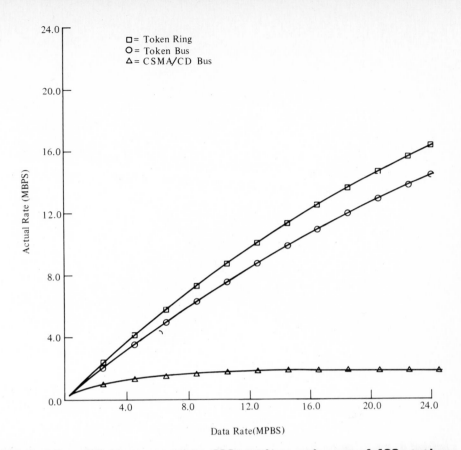

**FIGURE 9–11b.  500 bits per packet; 100 stations active out of 100 stations total.**

this configuration may be perfectly adequate. If, however, the load is expected to grow to 2 Mbps, raising the network data rate to 10 Mbps or even 20 Mbps will not accommodate the increase! The same conclusion, less precisely, can be drawn from the example presented at the beginning of this section.

As with all the other results presented in this chapter, these depend on the nature of the assumptions made and do not reflect accurately the nature of the real-world work load. Nevertheless, they show in a striking manner the nature of the instability of CSMA/CD and the ability of token ring and token bus to continue to perform well in the face of overload conditions.

## The Behavior of Contention Protocols

The preceding section revealed that CSMA/CD performs less well than token-passing under increasing load or increasing *a*. This is characteristic of all contention protocols. In this section we explore this subject in more detail, for

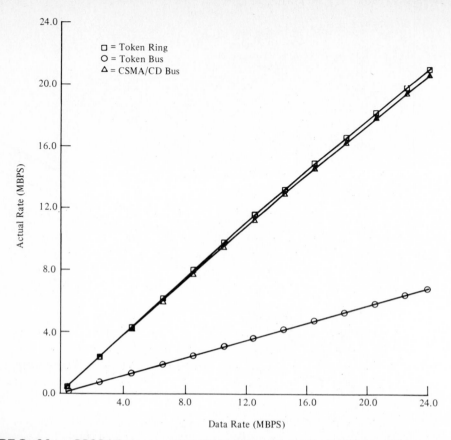

**FIGURE 9–11c.   2000 bits per packet; 1 station active out of 100 stations total.**

the interested reader. To do this, we present results based on the assumption that there are an infinite number of stations. This may strike the reader as an absurd tactic, but, in fact, it leads to analytically tractable equations that are, up to a point, very close to reality. We will define that point shortly. For now, we state the infinite-source assumption precisely: There are an infinite number of stations, each generating an infinitely small rate of frames such that the total number of frames generated per unit time is finite.

The following additional assumptions are made:

1. All frames are of constant length. In general, such frames give better average throughput and delay performance than do variable length frames. In some analyses, an exponential distribution of frame length is used.
2. The channel is noise-free.
3. Frames do not collect at individual stations; that is, a station transmits each frame before the next arrives, hence $I = S$. This assumption weakens at higher loads, where stations are faced with increasing delays for each packet.

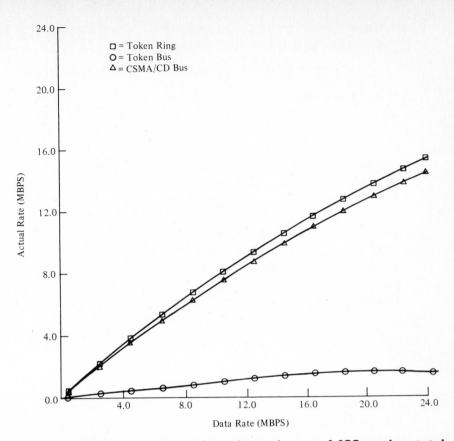

**FIGURE 9–11d.   500 bits per packet; 1 station active out of 100 stations total.**

4. *G*, the offered load, is Poisson distributed.
5. For CSMA/CD, no time is lost for carrier sense and collision detection.

These assumptions do not reflect accurately any actual system. For example, higher-order moments or even the entire probability distribution of frame length or *G* may be needed for accurate results. These assumptions do provide analytic tractability, enabling the development of closed-form expressions for performance. Thus they provide a common basis for comparing a number of protocols and they allow the development of results that give insight into the behavior of systems. In the following discussion, we shall cite simulation and measurement studies that indicate that these insights are valid.

Let us look first at the simplest contention protocol, pure ALOHA. Traffic, of course, is generated as so many frames per second. It is convenient to normalize this to the frame transmission time; then we can view *S* as the number of frames generated per frame time. Since the capacity of the channel is one frame per frame time, *S* also has the usual meaning of throughput as a fraction of capacity.

The total traffic on the channel will consist of new frames plus frames that must be retransmitted because of collision:

$$G = S + \text{(number of retransmitted frames per unit time)}$$

Now, a frame must be retransmitted if it suffers a collision. Thus we can express the rate of retransmissions as $G \cdot \text{Pr}[\text{individual frame suffers a collision}]$. Note that we must use $G$ rather than $S$ in this expression. To determine the probability of collision, consider as a worst case, two stations, A and B, as far apart as possible on a bus (i.e., a normalized distance $a$, as in Figure 9.2). A frame transmitted by station A will suffer a collision if B begins transmission prior to A but within a time $1 + a$ of the beginning of A's transmission, or if B begins transmission after A within a time period $1 + a$ of the beginning of A's transmission. Thus the vulnerable period is of length $2(1 + a)$.

We have assumed that $G$ is Poisson distributed. For a Poisson process with rate $\lambda$, the probability of an arrival in a period of time $t$ is $1 - e^{-\lambda t}$. Thus, the probability of an arrival during the vulnerable period is $1 - e^{-2(1+a)G}$. Therefore, we have

$$G = S + G[1 - e^{-2(1+a)G}]$$

So

$$ALOHA: \quad S = Ge^{-2(1+a)G} \qquad (9.13)$$

This derivation assumes that $G$ is Poisson, which is not the case even for $I$ Poisson. However, studies indicate that this is a good approximation [SCHW77]. Also, deeper analysis indicates that the infinite population assumption results closely approximate finite population results at reasonably small numbers—say, 50 or more stations [KLEI76]. This is also true for CSMA and CSMA/CD systems [TOBA80a, TOBA82].

Another way of deriving (9.13) is to note that $S/G$ is the fraction of offered frames that are transmitted successfully, which is just the probability that for each frame, no additional frames arrive during the vulnerable period, which is $e^{-2(1+a)G}$.

Throughput for slotted ALOHA is also easily calculated. All frames begin transmission on a slot boundary. Thus the number of frames that are transmitted during a slot time is equal to the number that was generated during the previous slot and await transmission. To avoid collisions between frames in adjacent slots, the slot length must equal frame transmission time plus propagation delay (i.e., $1 + a$). Thus the probability that an individual frame suffers collision is $1 - e^{-(1+a)G}$. Thus we have:

$$S\text{-}ALOHA: \quad S = Ge^{-(1+a)G} \qquad (9.14)$$

Differentiating (9.13) and (9.14) with respect to $G$, we have that the maximum possible values for $S$ are $1/[2e(1 + a)]$ and $1/[e(1 + a)]$ respectively. These results differ from those reported in previous accounts of local network performance [TROP81, FRAN81], which ignore $a$ and have $S = Ge^{-2G}$ for ALOHA and $S = Ge^{-G}$ for slotted ALOHA. The discrepancy arises because these formulas were originally derived for satellite channels, for which they are valid, but are often compared with CSMA-type protocols which are derived for local networks (e.g., [TOBA80b]). The results, which correspond to $a = 0$, are plotted in Figure 9.12. For small values of $a$ ($a \leq 0.01$), these figures are adequate; but for comparison with CSMA protocols, equations (9.13) and (9.14) should be used.

Figure 9.12 provides insight into the nature of the instability problem with contention protocols. As offered load increases, so does throughput until, beyond its maximum value, throughput actually declines as $G$ increases. This is because there is an increased frequency of collisions: more frames are offered, but fewer successfully escape collision. Worse, this situation may persist even if the input to the system drops to zero! Consider: For high $G$, virtually all offered frames are retransmissions and virtually none get through. So, even if no new frames are generated, the system will remain occupied in an unsuccessful attempt to clear the backlog; the effective capacity of the system is virtually zero. Thus, even in a moderately loaded system, a temporary burst of work could move the network into the high-collision region permanently. This type of instability is not possible with the noncontention protocols.

Delay is more difficult to calculate, but the following reasoning gives a good approximation. We define delay as the time interval from when a node is ready to transmit a frame until when it is successfully received. This delay is simply the sum of queueing delay, propagation delay, and transmission time. In ALOHA, the queueing delay is 0; that is, a node transmits immediately when it has a frame to transmit. However, because of collisions, we may consider the queueing delay time to be the total time consumed prior to successful transmission (i.e., the total time spent in unsuccessful transmissions). To get at this, we need to know the expected number of transmissions per frame. A little

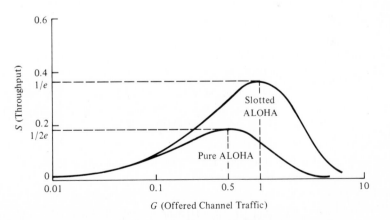

**FIGURE 9–12. Performance of ALOHA, S-ALOHA with $a$ = 0.**

thought shows that this is simply $G/S$. So the expected number of retransmissions per frame is just $G/S - 1 = e^{2(1+a)G} - 1$. The delay $D$, can then be expressed as

$$D = [e^{2(1+a)G} - 1] \, \delta + a + 1$$

where $\delta$ is the average delay for one retransmission. A common algorithm used for ALOHA is to retransmit after a time selected from a uniform distribution of from 1 to $K$ frame-transmission times. This minimizes repeated collisions. The average delay is then $(K + 1)/2$. To this, we must add the amount of time a station must wait to determine that its frame was unsuccessful. This is just the time it would take to complete a transmission $(1 + a)$ plus the time it would take for the receiver to generate an acknowledgment $(w)$ plus the propagation time for the acknowledgment to reach the station $(a)$. For simplicity, we assume that acknowledgment packets do no suffer collisions. Thus:

$$ALOHA: \qquad D = [e^{2(1+a)G} - 1]\left(1 + 2a + w + \frac{K + 1}{2}\right) + a + 1 \qquad (9.15)$$

For S-ALOHA, a similar reasoning obtains. The main difference now is that there is a delay, averaging half a slot time between the time a node is ready to send a frame and the time the next slot begins:

$$S\text{-}ALOHA: \qquad D = [e^{(1+a)G} - 1]\left(1 + 2a + w + \frac{K + 1}{2}\right)$$
$$+ 1.5a + 1.5 \qquad (9.16)$$

These formulas confirm the instability of contention-based protocols under heavy load. As the rate of new frames increases, so does the number of collisions. We can see that both the number of collisions and the average delay grow exponentially with $G$. Thus there is not only a trade-off between throughput $(S)$ and delay $(D)$, but a third factor enters the trade-off: stability. Figure 9.13 illustrates this point. Figure 9.13a shows that delay increases exponentially with offered load. But Figure 9.13b is perhaps more meaningful. It shows that delay increases with throughput up to the maximum possible throughput. Beyond that point, although throughput declines because of increased numbers of collisions, the delay continues to rise.

It is worth pondering Figures 9.12 and 9.13 to get a better feeling for the behavior of contention channels. Recall that we mentioned that both $S$ and $G$ are "derived" parameters, and what we would really like to estimate is the actual traffic generated by network devices, the "input load" $I$. As long as the input load is less than the maximum potential throughput, $\text{Max}_G(S)$, then $I = S$. That is, the throughput of the system equals the input load. Therefore, all packets get through. However, if $I > \text{Max}_G(S)$, Figures 9.12 and 9.13 no longer apply. The system cannot transmit frames as fast as they arrive. The result: if

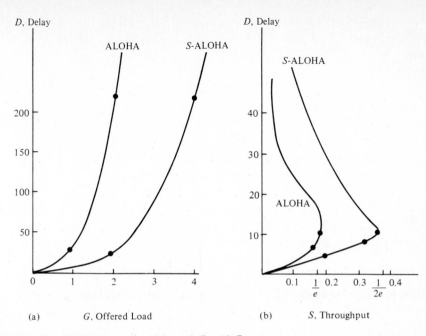

(a)        $G$, Offered Load           (b)       $S$, Throughput

**FIGURE 9–13.**    **Delay as a function of $G$ and $S$.**

$I$ remains above the threshold indefinitely, then $D$ goes to infinity, $S$ goes to zero, and $G$ grows without bound.

Figure 9.13b shows that, for a given value of $S$, there are two possible values of $D$. How can this be? In both cases, $I = S$, and the system is transmitting all input frames. The explanation is as follows: As the input, $I = S$, approaches the saturation point, the stochastic nature of the input will eventually lead to a period of a high rate of collisions, resulting in decreased throughput and higher frame delays.

Finally, we mention that these results depend critically on the assumptions made. For example, if there is only one station transmitting, then the achievable throughput is 1.0, not 0.18 or 0.37. Indeed, with a single user at a high data rate and a set of others users at very low data rates, utilization approaching 1 can be achieved. However, the delay encountered by the other users is significantly longer than in the homogeneous case. In general, the more unbalanced the source rates, the higher the throughput [KLEI76].

We now turn to the CSMA protocols. A similar line of reasoning can be used to derive closed-form analytic results as is done with ALOHA and S-ALOHA. Perhaps the clearest derivations can be found in [LABA78]. The same or similar results can be found in [KLEI75], [KLEI76], [SCHW77], [HERR79], [TOBA80a], [TOBA82], and [HEYM82].

Figure 9.14 compares the various contention protocols for $a = 0.01$ and 0.05. Note the dramatic improvement in throughput of the various CSMA

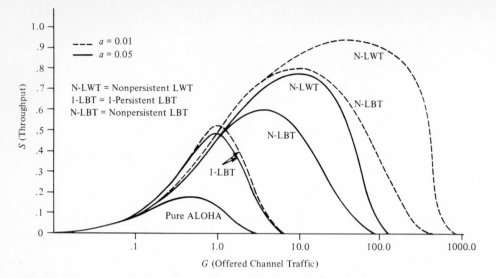

**FIGURE 9–14.  Throughput for variation contention protocols.**

schemes over ALOHA. Also note the decline in performance for increased $a$. This is seen more clearly in Figure 9.15. As expected, the performance of all CSMA schemes declines with $a$ since the period of vulnerability grows. For high enough values of $a$, say 0.5 to 1.0, they approach S-ALOHA. At these values, neither the carrier sense nor the collision detection are of much use. Thus the distributed reservation protocol for HSLNs in Chapter 6 does not suffer by using S-ALOHA rather than CSMA to contend for reservations.

Figure 9.16 shows delay as a function of throughput. As can be seen, CSMA/CD offers significant delay and throughput improvements over CSMA at $a = 0.05$. As $a$ increases, these protocols converge with each other and with S-ALOHA.

One of the critical assumptions used in deriving all these results is that the number of sources is infinite. The validity of the assumption can be seen in Figure 9.10. Note that for small values of $a$, the efficiency of the system with a finite number of stations differs little from that achieved as the number of stations grows to infinity. For larger values of $a$, the differences are more marked. The figure shows that the infinite-population assumption underestimates efficiency but is still a good approximation.

A second assumption that is unrealistic is that of fixed frame sizes. While a local network could enforce fixed frame sizes, this is clearly inefficient if the messages are of variable length. One common situation is to have one long frame size for file transfer and a shorter size for interactive traffic and acknowledgments. Now, as frame length decreases, $a$ increases, so if all frames were short, then the utilization would be less than if all frames were long. Presumably, with a mixture of the two traffic types, the efficiency would be somewhere in between. This has been shown to be the case in [TOBA80a].

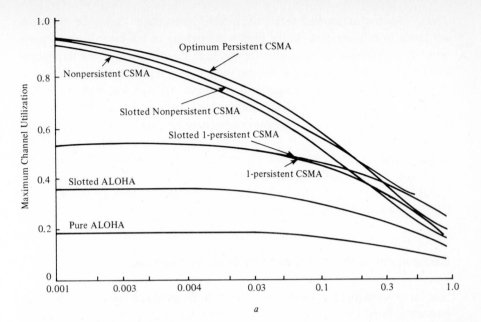

**FIGURE 9–15.  Maximum channel utilization for various contention protocols.**

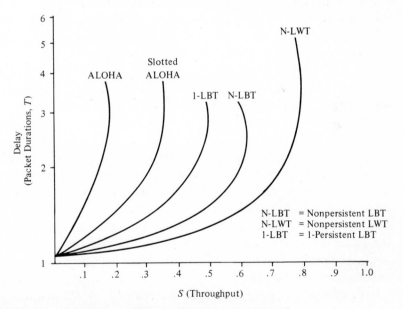

**FIGURE 9–16.  Delay for various contention protocols.**

The analysis also showed that only a small percentage of longer frames is sufficient to achieve close to the higher throughput of the case of long frames only. However, this increased throughput is to the detriment of the throughput and delay characteristics of the shorter frames. In effect, they are crowded out.

A final point about the foregoing derivations: All represent analytic models of local network performance. Greater validity can be achieved through simulation, where some of the assumptions may be relaxed, and through actual performance measurement. In general, these efforts tend to confirm the validity of the analytic models. Although not entirely accurate, these models provide a good feel for the behavior of the network. Interested readers may consult [LABA78, SHOC80a, MARA82, AIME79, OREI82]. A general discussion of CSMA/CD modeling techniques is contained in [ROUN83].

## Comparative Performance of Ring Protocols

It is far more difficult to do a comparative performance of the three major ring protocols than the comparison of bus and token ring protocols. The results depend critically on a number of parameters unique to each protocol. For example:

- *Token ring:* size of token, token processing time
- *Slotted ring:* slot size, overhead bits per slot
- *Register insertion:* register size

Thus it is difficult to do a comparison, and although there have been a number of studies on each one of the techniques [TROP81, PENN79], few have attempted pairwise comparisons, much less a three-way analysis. Given this unfortunate situation, this section will merely attempt to summarize the most significant comparative studies.

The most systematic work in this area has been done by Liu and his associates [LIU78, LIU82, HILA82]. Liu made comparisons based on analytic models developed by others for token ring, slotted ring, and CSMA/CD, plus his own formulations for register insertion. He then obtained very good corroboration from simulation studies.

Figure 9.17 summarizes the results. They are based on the assumption that $a = 0.005$ and that register insertion ring frames are removed by the destination station, whereas slotted ring and token ring frames are removed by the source station. This is clearly an unfair comparison, since register insertion, under this scheme, does not include acknowledgments, but token ring and slotted ring do. The figures do show that slotted ring is the poorest performer, and that register insertion can carry a load greater than 1.0. This is because the protocol permits multiple frames to circulate.

Bux performed an analysis comparing token ring, slotted ring, and CSMA/

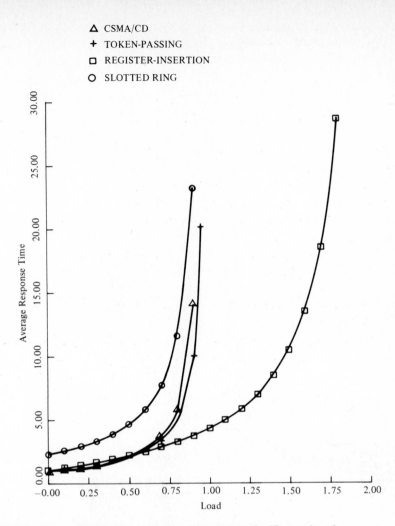

**FIGURE 9–17a.   Delay for various ring protocols (6 stations).**

CD [BUX82]. This careful analysis produced several important conclusions. First, the delay-throughput performance of token ring versus CSMA/CD confirms our earlier discussion. That is, token ring suffers greater delay than CSMA/CD does at light load but less delay and stable throughput at heavy loads. Further, token ring has superior delay characteristics to slotted ring. The poorer performance of slotted ring seems to have two causes: (1) the relative overhead in the small slots of a slotted ring is very high, and (2) the time needed to pass empty slots around the ring to guarantee fair bandwidth is significant. Bux also reports several positive features of slotted ring: (1) the expected delay for a message is proportional to length (i.e., shorter packets get better service than

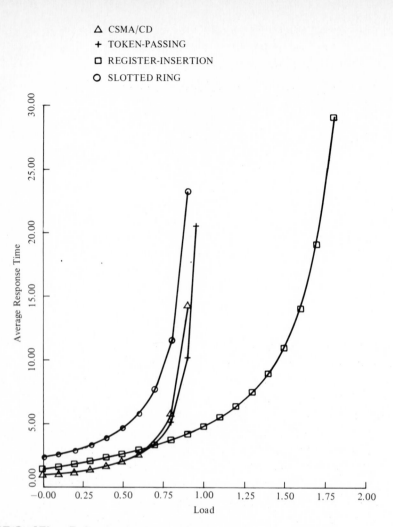

△ CSMA/CD
+ TOKEN-PASSING
□ REGISTER-INSERTION
○ SLOTTED RING

**FIGURE 9–17b. Delay for various ring protocols (20 stations).**

long ones), and (2) overall mean delay is independent of packet length distribution. Bux has recently extended his analysis to include register insertion [BUX83], achieving results comparable to Liu's.

Another study of token ring versus slotted ring is reported in [CHEN82]. Cheng's results confirm those of Bux; that is, the delay of slotted ring exceeds that of token ring. Interestingly, Cheng also showed that the performance of the ring improves as the number of slots increases at least to equal the number of nodes. However, for local area networks, which typically have $a < 1$, a multiple-slot ring is achieved only by having very small slots or artificial delays. With smaller slots, the overhead is proportionally greater.

Finally, we mention a study reported in [YU81], which also concluded that insertion ring had shorter delays than token ring. In this study, Yu looked at a ring with a data rate of 100 Mbps over a 5-km distance. The distribution of packet size was assumed to be bimodal, with half having a length of 4 Kbytes and half with a length of 100 bytes. Thus the value of $a$, using average packet size, was about 0.125.

It is difficult to draw conclusions from the efforts made so far. The slotted ring seems to be the least desirable over a broad range of parameter values, owing to the considerable overhead associated with each small packet. For example, the Cambridge ring, which is the most widely available ring commercially in Europe, uses a 37 bit slot with only 16 data bits! The designers of the Cambridge ring originally started out with register insertion but rejected it for slotted ring. The sole reason seems to have been reliability: a fault developing in a shift register can disrupt the entire ring [WILK79].

As between token ring and register insertion, the evidence suggests that at least for some sets of parameter values, register insertion gives superior delay performance. Interestingly, there seems to be no commercially available register insertion product with the exception of the IBM Series 1 loop, where performance is not an issue. On the other hand, token ring in the United States, with a boost from IEEE 802 and IBM, and slotted ring in Europe, where many firms have licensed the Cambridge slotted ring, seem destined to dominate the marketplace.

The primary advantage of register insertion is the potentially high utilization it can achieve. In contrast with token ring, multiple stations can be transmitting at a time. Further, a station can transmit as soon as a gap opens up on the ring; it need not wait for a token. On the other hand, the propagation time around the ring is not constant, but depends on the amount of traffic.

A final point in comparing token ring and register insertion. Under light loads, register insertion operates more efficiently, resulting in slightly less delay. However, both systems perform adequately. Our real interest is under heavy load. A typical LAN will have $a < 1$, usually $a << 1$, so that a transmitting station on a token ring will append a token to the end of its packet. Under heavy load, a nearby station will be able to use the token. Thus almost 100% utilization is achieved, and there is no particular advantage to register insertion.

## 9.3

## HSLN PERFORMANCE

Although little or no modeling of the ANS protocol has been done, there has been extensive work on modeling the similar HYPERchannel protocol. In this section we summarize some of these results. Keep in mind that, in contrast to the ANS protocol, HYPERchannel has built-in priorities. That is, the station with the earliest time position always has the first opportunity to transmit, on down to the station with the last opportunity and hence the lowest priority.

Perhaps the most work in this area has been done by Franta and his associates

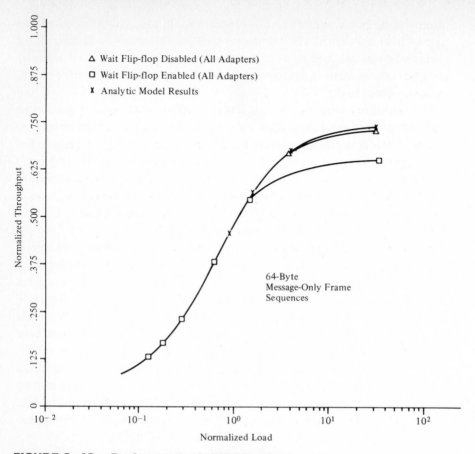

**FIGURE 9–18. Performance of HYPERchannel.**

at the University of Minnesota [CHLA80a, CHLA80b, CHRI81, FRAN80, FRAN82]. Similar results have also been reported in [BURK79] and [SPAN81]. The group first developed an analytic model representing a HYPERchannel system as a closed finite source queueing system, such that once a transmission request was generated by an NIU, no additional requests by that NIU are generated until the outstanding request is transmitted. Subsequently, a simulation model was developed and, finally, some actual performance measures were taken. Happily, the three approaches agree closely. Figure 9.18 shows the measured results for a 6-node, 1000-ft system. The results are for 4 Kbyte packets, so *a* is about 0.002. The results show that the protocol is stable in the sense that throughput does not deteriorate as load increases.

The figures include a curve for the enabling of a wait flip-flop, which functions in the same manner as the wait flag for ANS X3T9.5. Surprisingly, performance degrades with the use of the wait flip-flop. The reason is that the use of this mechanism increases the frequency with which the HYPERchannel contention interval occurs. Thus there are more collisions and poorer performance. Because the ANS protocol does not have a contention interval, the use of a wait flag should have only a minor effect on performance.

A set of simulation studies of HYPERchannel have been performed at Lawrence Livermore Laboratories [DONN79, WATS80, WATS82]. These results are in close agreement with those of Franta's group. The Livermore group extended its studies to include modeling of the link layer with the interesting result that, as with CSMA/CD, HYPERchannel performance degrades under high load. The cause of this phenomenon is that, at layer 2, a HYPERchannel NIU will lock out receptions while attempting to establish a connection for transmission. This can lead to a condition approaching deadlock, and the degradation of throughput. This result points out the importance of viewing local network performance in the context of the entire network.

Finally, we mention a simulation study done at MITRE [KATK81a, KATK81b]. Again, the results were similar to those quoted above. The authors also modeled performance including layer 2 functions and found that the effective achievable data transmission rate was only 6.18 Mbps. This emphasizes the importance of not equating end-to-end throughput with raw data rate.

All of these results, by and large, are applicable to the ANS X3T9.5 protocol. One would expect this protocol to do somewhat better because of the lack of collisions.

**9.4**

## END-TO-END PERFORMANCE

So far, we have been concerned with the throughput and delay performance for transmitting packets over an LAN or HSLN. Some useful insights have been gained and techniques developed for estimating that performance. Alas, this is of no concern to the local network user. The user is concerned with *end-to-end* performance. Examples:

- Two hosts regularly exchange large files. What is the end-to-end throughput rate during file transfer?
- A user at a terminal is querying a data base on a host. What is the delay from the end of query entry to the beginning of response?

Consider the steps involved in sending data from one host to another. In general terms, we have:

1. Process in source host initiates transfer.
2. Host system software transfers data to NIU.
3. Source NIU transfers data to destination NIU.
4. Destination NIU transfers data to destination host.
5. Host system software accepts data, notifies destination process.
6. Destination process accepts data.

Each of these steps involves some processing and the use of a resource potentially shared by others. What we have discussed so far, and the focus of virtually all local network performance studies, is step 3.

To get a handle on end-to-end performance, the analyst must model the NIU, the host–NIU link, and the host, as well as the NIU–NIU link. This requires the development of computer system performance models. Although these techniques have been around for a while, one of the few attempts to apply these principles systematically to local network performance has been undertaken by a group at CONTEL Information Systems [LISS81, MAGL80, MAGL81a, MAGL82, MITC81]. We summarize their approach in this section.

The discussion will be with reference to Figure 9.19. As mentioned earlier, the total delay, say, from the time a message is generated at node A by some application until it reaches node B, is just the sum of the delays encountered at each step. Each such step can be modeled using queueing theory. A queueing situation arises when a "customer" arrives at a service facility and, finding it busy, is forced to wait. The delay incurred by a customer is just the time spent waiting in the queue plus the time for service. The delay depends on the pattern of arriving traffic and the characteristics of the server. Table 9.3 summarizes some simple results. Results for more complex cases may be found in [MART67].

The system depicted in Figure 9.19 consists of a set of single-server queueing systems in tandem, that is, the output of one queue is the input to the next. In the general case, it is a complex task to characterize the behavior of this system, and closed form analytic solutions do not exist. However, there is a theorem (Jackson's theorem) which states that under certain conditions, each node in the network of queues can be treated independently. Thus the delay at each queue can be calculated separately and summed to give an overall figure. The assumptions [JACK63]:

- Work arrives from outside the system with a Poisson distribution.
- Exponential service time at each node with first-come, first served policy.

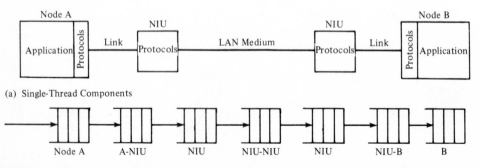

(a) Single-Thread Components

(b) Queueing Model

**FIGURE 9–19.   End-to-end local network performance model.**

**TABLE 9.3  Isolated Queues**

Parameters
  $w$ = mean number of items waiting for service (not including items being served)
  $q$ = mean number of items in system (waiting and being served)
  $t_w$ = mean time item spends waiting for service
  $t_q$ = mean time item spends in system, waiting and being served
  $\rho$ = utilization: fraction of time a servicer is busy
  $S$ = mean service time for an item

Assumptions: Poisson arrivals with parameter $\lambda$, exponential service times

$$w = \frac{\rho2}{1 - \rho}$$

$$q = \frac{\rho}{1 - \rho}$$

$$t_w = \frac{\rho S}{1 - \rho}$$

$$t_q = \frac{S}{1 - \rho}$$

$$\rho = \lambda S$$

---

• No saturated queues: queues are large enough to hold the maximum number of waiting customers.

There is some evidence that networks of the type we are discussing, which may violate these assumptions, are nevertheless closely approximated by the decomposition approach [MAGL81b]. Furthermore, the assumption of exponential service time usually results in upper bounds to delays; thus the analysis will give conservative estimates.

Solving for total delay is thus computationally simple. Starting with the first queue, and given an arrival rate $\lambda$, the delay at that step is determined. As long as $\rho = \lambda S \leq 1$, the queue is stable and the output rate is equal to the input rate. This now becomes the input to the second stage, and so on. For a stable system, we must have

$$\lambda \leq \frac{1}{\text{Max } [S_i]}$$

This represents the maximum achievable throughput. As long as this condition is satisfied, the total delay for a message over $N$ stages is simply

$$D = \sum_{i=1}^{N} D_i$$

Now, let us begin with the first stage, node A. Node A must perform a number of tasks related to the passing of a message, including applications processing and the processing for the various protocol layers. These tasks may have various priorities with pre-emptive interrupts allowed. For each class of task, the queueing equation is

$$
t_{qj} = \frac{1}{1 - \sum\limits_{i=1}^{j-1} \rho_i} \left[ \frac{\sum\limits_{i=1}^{j} \rho_i S_i}{1 - \sum\limits_{i=1}^{j} \rho_i} + S_j \right]
$$

Where $\rho_i = \lambda_i S_i$.

To solve this equation, we need values for the $\lambda_i$ and $S_i$. The $\lambda_i$ depend on the rate at which messages are generated; this should become clear in the example below. The $S_i$ can be approximated by estimating the execution path length of each service routine and dividing by the effective instruction per second rate of the processor. Since other activities, such as disk I/O may be handled by the processor, its raw instruction execution rate needs to be modified by some overhead factor.

The next delay encountered is the communications link between node A and its NIU. This delay will depend on the nature of the interface. As an example consider a half-duplex line with a given interface transfer rate. Here there are two classes of arrivals for a single server: node-to-NIU and NIU-to-node traffic. The $\lambda_i$ ($i = 1, 2$) depend on the rate at which messages arrive for transmission across the link. The service time in either direction ($S_1, S_2$) is just the average message length divided by the data rate. It is easy to see that, assuming no priorities,

$$
\rho = \lambda_1 S_1 + \lambda_2 S_2
$$

$$
S = \frac{\rho}{\lambda_1 + \lambda_2}
$$

where $S$ is the overall average service time. Then

$$
\begin{aligned}
t_{qj} &= t_w + S_j \\
&= \frac{\rho S}{1 - \rho} + S_j \qquad j = 1, 2
\end{aligned}
$$

The NIU is the next source of delay and may be modeled in the same fashion as node A. Next comes the local network itself. The delay at this stage depends on the topology (ring, bus, or tree) and the medium access protocol. Sections 9.2 and 9.3 are devoted to developing results in this area. The remainder of the steps are symmetric with those already discussed and need not be described.

Two refinements to the model above: First, an NIU often has multiple ports. Hence the arrival rate of work at an NIU consists of the rates from multiple hosts. This must be taken into account. Second, the node-NIU link may be multiplexed so that arrivals are from multiple remote nodes.

As an example, we consider an analysis reported in [MITC81]. In this example, node A is a host and node B an intelligent workstation. Within node A, there is some application program exchanging messages with the workstation. There are five main classes of activities associated with the application. We assume that these are serviced by the host on a preemptive resume basis. The activities, in descending order of priority:

1. *Link-in:* link level functions for messages inbound from the NIU.
2. *Link-out:* link level functions for messages outbound to the NIU.
3. *Protocols-in:* higher level protocol functions for inbound messages.
4. *Protocols-out:* higher level protocol functions for outbound messages.
5. *Application:* application processing.

The host/NIU interface is assumed to have an effective transfer rate of 800 kbps, while the workstation/NIU interface is 9.6 kbps. This would be the case for integrated host NIU and a stand-alone terminal NIU.

The NIU is assumed to implement up through the transport layer with the following priorities:

1. Network link-in
2. Node link-in
3. Network link-out
4. Node link-out
5. Higher-layer protocols

Finally, a nonpersistent CSMA/CD bus system operating at 1.544 Mbps is assumed.

The results are summarized in Table 9.4, which shows that, within the moderate utilization range of the bus, the bus contributes only 5% of the delay. The implication, confirmed by the other studies referenced earlier, is that the effect of the topology and medium access control on overall delay is negligible until the medium approaches saturation. In Section 9.2, we outlined a quick and simple means of estimating the saturation point. It is clearly desirable to operate below that point and, while operating below that point, only a rough approximation of the delay due to the medium will suffice.

Nevertheless, we have devoted considerable space to looking at the performance of various topology/MAC approaches. This is so because the saturation points for different approaches are different. But it needs to be pointed out that beyond the determination of a saturation point, the focus of activity should be the broader end-to-end delay issue.

This section has touched only briefly on the techniques for end-to-end delay analysis. The interested reader is referred to [MART67], [SAUE81], [KOBA78], and [IBM71].

## TABLE 9.4   End-to-End Delay, CSMA/CD Network

*Traffic parameters*
  Arrival rate: 0.017 message per second
  Aggregate load: 100,000 bps

*CSMA/CD parameters*
  Propagation: 30 µs
  Retransmission interval: 5

*MSG lengths*
  Input: 800 characters
  Output: 12,000 characters

*I/F Transfer rates*
  Host 800,000 bps
  Workstation: 9600 bps

*Protocol path-length parameters*
  Node protocols
    Send: 12,000 instructions
    Receive: 12,000 instructions

  Node access link layer
    Send: 75 instructions
    Receive: 75 instructions

  Network access link layer
    Send: 75 instructions
    Receive: 75 instructions

  TCP/IP: 12,000

  Multiprogram level: 32

*Processor capacities*
  Host: 1.100 MIPS
  BIU: 0.615 MIPS
  Workstation: 0.115 MIPS

Host application program path length: 50,000 instructions
Cable utilization: 0.0565
Total normalized traffic, including retransmissions: 0.06

### Delay Categories

| Throughput | Response | Host | HI/F | WI/F | HBIU | WBIU | W/S | Cable |
|---|---|---|---|---|---|---|---|---|
| 0.50 | 2.0066 | 0.04 | 0.01 | 0.84 | 0.01 | 0.02 | 0.02 | 0.05 |
| 1.00 | 2.0252 | 0.04 | 0.01 | 0.84 | 0.01 | 0.02 | 0.02 | 0.05 |
| 1.50 | 2.0444 | 0.04 | 0.01 | 0.84 | 0.01 | 0.02 | 0.02 | 0.05 |
| 2.00 | 2.0645 | 0.04 | 0.01 | 0.84 | 0.01 | 0.02 | 0.02 | 0.05 |
| 2.50 | 2.0853 | 0.04 | 0.01 | 0.83 | 0.02 | 0.02 | 0.02 | 0.05 |
| 3.00 | 2.1071 | 0.04 | 0.01 | 0.83 | 0.02 | 0.02 | 0.02 | 0.05 |
| 3.50 | 2.1298 | 0.04 | 0.01 | 0.83 | 0.02 | 0.02 | 0.02 | 0.05 |
| 4.00 | 2.1536 | 0.04 | 0.01 | 0.83 | 0.02 | 0.02 | 0.02 | 0.05 |
| 4.50 | 2.1785 | 0.05 | 0.01 | 0.83 | 0.02 | 0.02 | 0.02 | 0.05 |
| 5.00 | 2.2047 | 0.05 | 0.01 | 0.83 | 0.02 | 0.02 | 0.02 | 0.05 |
| 5.50 | 2.2324 | 0.05 | 0.01 | 0.83 | 0.02 | 0.02 | 0.02 | 0.05 |
| 6.00 | 2.2616 | 0.05 | 0.01 | 0.82 | 0.03 | 0.02 | 0.02 | 0.05 |
| 6.50 | 2.2927 | 0.05 | 0.01 | 0.82 | 0.03 | 0.02 | 0.02 | 0.05 |
| 7.00 | 2.3259 | 0.05 | 0.01 | 0.82 | 0.03 | 0.02 | 0.02 | 0.05 |
| 7.50 | 2.3615 | 0.06 | 0.01 | 0.82 | 0.03 | 0.01 | 0.02 | 0.05 |
| 8.00 | 2.4001 | 0.06 | 0.01 | 0.81 | 0.03 | 0.01 | 0.03 | 0.05 |
| 8.50 | 2.4424 | 0.06 | 0.01 | 0.81 | 0.03 | 0.01 | 0.03 | 0.05 |
| 9.00 | 2.4892 | 0.06 | 0.01 | 0.80 | 0.04 | 0.01 | 0.03 | 0.05 |
| 9.50 | 2.5423 | 0.07 | 0.01 | 0.79 | 0.04 | 0.01 | 0.03 | 0.05 |
| 10.00 | 2.6041 | 0.07 | 0.01 | 0.78 | 0.05 | 0.01 | 0.03 | 0.05 |

*Source:* [MITC81].

## RECOMMENDED READING

[STUC83]* summarizes the techniques discussed in Section 9.2 to obtain quick estimates of the bounds on performance. It also presents the results of the analysis referred to in that section. [KLEI76] discusses most of the contention protocols and contains an excellent exposition on computer system modeling. [TOBA80b] is a much-referenced summary of most of the infinite-source-assumption work on contention protocols. [LIU82]* analyzes the performance of the various ring protocols. [TROP81] is a thorough survey of LAN/HSLN performance studies up to 1981. An interesting case study of end-to-end performance is [MITC81]*.

## PROBLEMS

**9.1** Equation (9.1) is valid for token ring and baseband bus. What is an equivalent expression for
   **a.** Broadband bus?
   **b.** Slotted ring?
   **c.** Register insertion ring?
   **d.** Broadband tree (use several different configurations)?

**9.2** Develop a display similar to Figure 9.6 that shows throughput as a function of $N$.

**9.3** Derive equations similar to (9.10) and (9.11) for the case where there are two types of frames, one 10 times as long as the other, that are transmitted with equal probability by each station.

**9.4** Consider a 10-Mbps, 1-km bus, with $N$ stations and frame-size $= F$. Determine throughput and delay for token bus and throughput for CSMA/CD:
   **a.** $N = 10, F = 1000$
   **b.** $N = 100, F = 1000$
   **c.** $N = 10, F = 10,000$
   **d.** $N = 100, F = 10,000$

**9.5** Compare equations (9.1), (9.10), and (9.11). Under what circumstances does the throughput for the latter two equations exceed the theoretical maximum of (9.1)? Explain.

**9.6** For the graphs in Figure 9.11, determine $a$ and comment on the results.

**9.7** Demonstrate that the number of stations and offered load affect performance independently for the following protocols.
   **a.** CSMA/CD.
   **b.** Collision avoidance.
   **c.** Token bus.

**d.** Token ring.

**e.** Slotted ring.

**f.** Register insertion.

**g.** Reservation.

**9.8** Consider a S-ALOHA system with a finite number of stations $N$ and $a = 0$. The offered load from each station is $G_i$, the throughput $S_i$. Derive an equation for $S$ as a function of $G_i$. Assume that the $G_i$ are identical; what is the equation for $S$? Verify that this approaches $Ge^{-G}$ as $N \to \infty$. Above what value of $N$ is the difference negligible?

**9.9** Demonstrate that CSMA/CD is biased toward long transmissions.

**9.10** Show that, for $a = 0$, the following relationship holds for 1-persistent CSMA

$$S = \frac{G(1 + G)e^{-G}}{G + e^{-G}}$$

**9.11** The performance of CSMA/CD depends on whether the collision detection is performed at the same site as the transmission (baseband) or at a time later whose average is $a$ (broadband). What would you expect the relative performance to be?

**9.12** Let $T_{msg}(K) = 0.1$ s and $T_{over} = 0.1$ s for a 50-station token system. Assume that all stations always have something to transmit. Compute $C$, $R(K)$, and UTIL$(K)$. What is the percent overhead? Now let $T_{over} = 0.2$. What is the percent overhead?

**9.13** Consider the conditions extant at the end of Problem 9.12. Assume that individual stations may be busy or idle. What is the cycle time $C$? Now halve the overhead $(T_{over} = 0.1)$. What is the cycle time $C$?

**9.14** For equation (9.7), let the number of stations be two. Plot $R(2)$ versus $R(1)$ and show the admissible mean throughput rates. Interpret the result in terms of relative static priority policies.

**9.15** Do an asymptotic breakpoint analysis for CSMA/CD.

**9.16** Equations (9.10) and (9.12) are valid for token ring and for token baseband bus. What are equivalent equations for broadband bus?

# CHAPTER 10

# Network Performance: Digital Switch/CBX

The nature of the performance questions and the analytic approach are markedly different for circuit-switched systems compared to packet-switched systems. Packet-switched systems allocate their capacity using asynchronous TDM. Thus each packet that arrives for service will experience a variable amount of delay depending on the load on the system and the nature of the protocol. Further, packets in a stream of packets from a source may experience different amounts of delay, and the throughput for that source is variable.

In contrast, a circuit-switched system uses synchronous TDM. When a circuit is established between two stations, a constant amount of bandwidth is dedicated to that circuit. There are no delays other than the propagation delay through the switch, and the throughput is a fixed amount equal to the provided data rate. These values are of no analytic interest. Rather, the performance questions have to do with system sizing and availability.

Consider a switch with $L$ attached stations and a capacity to handle $N$ simultaneous circuits. For a space-division switch, that capacity is just the maximum number of simultaneous independent paths. For a time-division switch, capacity is determined by the internal speed of the switch. Example: For a TDM bus switch, it is just the effective bus data rate (less overhead) divided by the individual circuit data rate. Now, if $L > N/2$, the system is blocking. The fundamental performance questions we wish to ask are:

- What is the degree of blocking, that is, what is the probability that a connection request will be blocked, given $L$ and $N$? Alternatively, what capacity ($N$) is needed given $L$ to achieve a certain upper bound on the probability of blocking?
- If blocked calls are queued for service, what is the average delay? Alternatively, what capacity is needed to achieve a certain average delay?

For a nonblocking switch, of course, these questions do not arise. In fact, insofar as the switch itself is concerned, there are no performance questions to analyze! The only question is one of cost: Is it worth it to provide sufficient capacity so that blocking never occurs?

These questions certainly do arise for a blocking switch. They are also relevant in a different context. Recall that a common service provided by a digital switch or CBX is port contention. For this service, on a nonblocking switch, the questions above apply, with $L$ the number of terminals, $N$ the number of host ports, and $L > N$.

Both the blocking switch and port contention on a nonblocking switch are examples of multiserver queueing problems, and solution approaches will be presented in this chapter. A more complex case is a port contention service provided on a blocking switch. Either the switch or the port contention group could be the bottleneck. As a first approximation, one can treat the problems separately and size the system based on which component is the bottleneck.

The analytic techniques for addressing the issues raised above were developed for telephone switching exchanges. They are equally applicable to CBX and digital switch networks. In the next section we introduce the principles of telephone traffic analysis. Following that we present some formulas that have been developed for calculating key traffic variables.

## 10.1

## CIRCUIT-SWITCHING TRAFFIC CONCEPTS

Two parameters determine the amount of load presented to a switch:

- $\lambda$: the mean rate of calls (connection requests) attempted per unit time
- $h$: the mean holding time per successful call

The basic measure of traffic is the traffic intensity, expressed in a dimensionless unit, the *erlang*:

$$A = \lambda h$$

$A$ can be interpreted from several points of view. It is, in effect, a normalized version of $\lambda$: $A$ equals the average number of calls arriving during the average holding period. We can view the switch as a queueing system, where the number of servers $N$ is equal to the circuit capacity of a switch or to the number of host ports of a port contention unit. A moment's thought should reveal that $A$ is related to the queueing system utilization, $\rho$, by $A = \rho N$. Thus, $A$ is a measure of the average number of circuits or servers required. For example, if the calling rate averages 20 calls per minute, and the average holding time is 3 minutes, then $A = 60$. We would expect, say, a switch with a capacity of 120 circuits to be about half utilized. A switch of capacity 50 would clearly be inadequate. A capacity of 60 represents a lower bound. Because of the fluctuations around the mean rate $A$, this capacity would at times be inadequate.

To clarify these concepts, consider Figure 10.1, which shows the pattern of activity on a switch of capacity 10 circuits over a period of 1 hour. The rate of calls, per minute, is 97/60. The average holding time per call, in minutes, is 294/97. Thus $A = (97/60) (294/97) = 4.9$ erlangs. Another way of viewing this parameter is that $A$ is the mean number of calls in progress. Thus, on the average, 4.9 circuits are engaged.

The latter interpretation is, however, true only for a nonblocking switch. The parameter $\lambda$ was defined as the rate of calls attempted; hence $A$ is a measure of offered traffic, not carried traffic. We will introduce a measure for carried traffic in the next section.

Typically, a blocking system is sized to deal with some peak level of traffic intensity. It is generally thought unreasonable to size for the highest surge of traffic anticipated; rather, the common practice is to size the system to meet the average rate encountered during a busy hour. The busy hour is the 60-minute period during the day when the traffic is highest in the long run. CCITT recommends taking the average of the busy hour traffic on the 30 busiest days of the year, called the "mean busy hour traffic" and using that quantity to size a system. The North American standard is to take the average of the 10 busiest

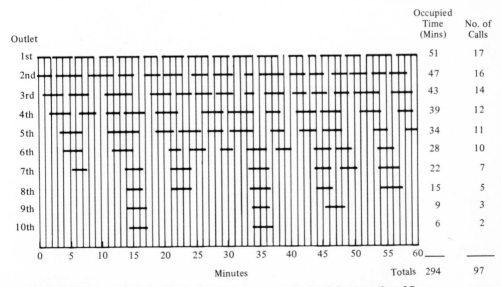

**FIGURE 10–1.  Distribution of traffic on a switch with capacity 10.**

days. Of course, these are typically measurements of carried rather than offered traffic and can only be used to estimate the true load.

The parameter $A$, as a measure of busy-hour traffic, serves as input to a traffic model. The model is used to answer questions such as those posed in the introduction to this chapter. There are two key factors that determine the nature of the model:

- The manner in which blocked calls are handled.
- The number of traffic sources.

We elaborate on these concepts briefly in this section. The next section discusses techniques for employing these models.

Blocked calls may be handled in one of two ways. First, the switch can put the blocked call in a queue awaiting a free circuit; this is referred to as *lost calls delayed* (LCD), although in fact the call is not lost. Second, the switch can simply reject the call. This in turn leads to two assumptions about the action of the user. If the user hangs up and waits some random time interval before reattempting a call, this is known as *lost calls cleared* (LCC). If the user repeatedly attempts calling, it is known as *lost call held* (LCH). In the present content, LCH is of little interest; we will focus on LCD and LCC.

The second key element of a traffic model is whether the number of sources is assumed infinite or finite. This difference can be seen in Figure 10.2. For an infinite source model, there is assumed to be a fixed arrival rate. For the finite source case, the arrival rate will depend on the number of sources already

INFINITE SOURCE

(a) Lost Calls Cleared

(b) Lost Calls Delayed

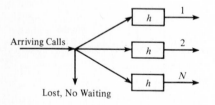

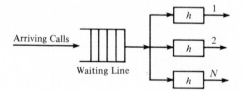

FINITE SOURCE

(c) Lost Calls Cleared

(d) Lost Calls Delayed

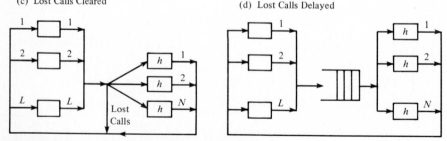

**FIGURE 10–2.  Multiserver queueing models.**

engaged. Thus, if each of $L$ sources generates calls at a rate $\lambda/L$, then, when the switch is unoccupied, the arrival rate is $\lambda$. However, if there are $K$ sources occupied at time $t$, then the instantaneous arrival rate at that time is $\lambda(L - K)/L$. Infinite source models are easier to deal with. The infinite source assumption is reasonable when the number of sources is at least 5 to 10 times the capacity of the system.

## 10.2

## MULTISERVER MODELS

We are now ready to turn to the use of the various traffic models for system sizing. For each of the four models of Figure 10.2, formulas have been derived for the quantities of interest. These are summarized in Table 10.1. These formulas are based on the following assumptions:

- Poisson arrivals.
- Exponential holding time [not needed for formula (a)].
- Equal traffic intensity per source.
- Calls served in order of arrival (for delay calculations).

Even with these assumptions, it can be seen that the formulas involve lengthy summations. In earlier days, much of the work of traffic theorists lay in simplifying assumptions to the point that the equations could be calculated at all. The results were and are published in tables [FRAN76]. Clearly, the tendency would be to misuse the available tables in situations whose assumptions did not fit any of the tables. The problem is now alleviated with the use of the computer. Nevertheless, the tabular results are still useful for quick and rough sizing.

Several parameters in Table 10.1 warrant comment. For LCC systems, $P$ is the probability that a call request will be cleared or lost. It is the ratio of calls unable to obtain service to the total call requests; in telephone traffic, it is also called grade of service. For LCD systems, an arriving call will be delayed rather than cleared. $P(>0)$ is the probability that a call request will find the switch fully utilized and be delayed. $P(>t)$ is the probability that *any* call request will be delayed by an amount greater than $t$, whereas $P_2(>t)$ is the probability that a call that is delayed will be delayed by an amount greater than $t$.

### Infinite Sources, Lost Calls Cleared

The simplest equation is for an infinite sources, LCC model. The key parameter of interest here is the probability of loss, or grade of service. Values in the range 0.01 to 0.001 are generally considered quite good.

The equation for infinite source, LCC, known as *Erlang B*, is easily programmed, as shown in Figure 10.3a. Given the offered load and number of

## TABLE 10.1 Traffic Formulas[a]

**(a) Infinite sources, lost calls cleared:**

$$P = \frac{\dfrac{A^N}{N!}}{\displaystyle\sum_{x=0}^{N} \dfrac{A^x}{x!}}$$

**(c) Infinite sources, lost calls delayed:**

$$P(>0) = \frac{\dfrac{A^N}{N!} \dfrac{N}{N-A}}{\displaystyle\sum_{x=0}^{N-1} \dfrac{A^x}{x!} + \dfrac{A^N}{N!} \dfrac{N}{N-A}}$$

The probability of delay greater than $t$ is

$$P(>t) = P(>0)\, e^{-(N-A)T}$$

where $T = t/h$ is expressed as a multiple of the average holding time.

The average delay $D_1$ on all calls is

$$D_1 = P(>0)\, \frac{h}{N-A}$$

The average delay $D_2$ on calls delayed is

$$D_2 = \frac{h}{N-A}$$

The probability of delay greater than $t$, on calls delayed is

$$P_2(>t) = e^{-(N-A)T}$$

**(b) Finite sources, lost calls cleared:**

$$P = \frac{\left(\dfrac{L-1}{N}\right) M^N}{\displaystyle\sum_{x=0}^{N}\left(\dfrac{L-1}{x}\right) M^x}$$

$$\text{for}\quad \left(\frac{L-1}{N}\right) = \frac{(L-1)!}{N!(L-1-N)!};$$

$$\left(\frac{L-1}{x}\right) = \frac{(L-1)!}{x!(L-1-x)!}$$

$$M = \frac{A}{L - A(1-P)}$$

**(d) Finite sources, lost calls delayed:**

$$P(>0) = \frac{\displaystyle\sum_{x=N}^{L} \dfrac{L!}{N!}\dfrac{M^x}{(L-x)!N^{x-N}}}{\displaystyle\sum_{x=0}^{N-1}\left(\dfrac{L}{x}\right)M^x + \sum_{x=N}^{L} \dfrac{L!}{N!}\dfrac{M^x}{(L-x)!N^{x-N}}}$$

$$\text{for}\quad \left(\frac{L}{x}\right) = \frac{L!}{x!\,(L-x)!}$$

$$M = \frac{A}{L+1-A(1-P)} \approx \frac{A}{L+1-A}$$

---

[a] $A$ = offered traffic, Erlangs
$N$ = number of servers
$L$ = number of sources
$h$ = mean holding time
$P$ = probability of loss (blocking, delay)
$P(>0)$ = probability of delay greater than 0
$P(>t)$ = probability of delay greater than t
$D_1$ = mean delay, all calls
$D_2$ = mean delay, delayed calls

servers, the probability of blocking can be calculated. More often, the inverse problem is of interest: determining the amount of traffic that can be handled by a given capacity to produce a given grade of service. Another inverse problem is to determine the capacity required to handle a given amount of traffic at a given grade of service. For both these problems, tables or suitable trial-and-error programs are needed. Table 10.2 is an extract from such tables. Figure 10.4 plots the probability of loss as a function of offered load with the number of servers as a parameter.

```
10 PRINT "THIS IS ERLANG-B, BY L.F.GOELLER,9-29-78."
20 PRINT "ERLANG-B SHOWS TRAFFIC ON EACH TRUNK."
30 INPUT "TRAFFIC OFFERED GROUP = ",A
40 LET N=O: LET T=1: LET T1=1: LET O=A: LET Z=10
50 PRINT "   N      OFRD  CRD     TOT    G/S"
60 LET N=N+1: LET T=T*A/N: LET T1=T1+T: LET P=T/T1
70 LET L=A*P: LET S=A-L: LET C=O-L
80 PRINT #31;N;%9F4;O;%6F4;C;%8F4;S;%6F4;P
90 LET O=L: IF P<.001 THEN 110
91 IF N<Z THEN 60
100 STOP : LET Z=Z+10: PRINT "OFFERED TRAFFIC WAS ",A: GOTO 50
110 END
```

(a) Input is offered load. Output shows carried load (TOT) and grade of service for given capacity (N). Output also shows incremental contribution of each additional circuit.

```
10 PRINT "ERLANG-C CALCULATES DELAY."
20 INPUT "TRAFFIC IN ERLANGS OFFERED GROUP=",A
30 PRINT "  N    P       D1      D2     Q1     Q2";
31 PRINT "    P8  P4   P2   P1   PP"
40 LET N=1: LET T=1: LET T1=1
50 IF N<=A THEN 120
60 LET T2=T*(A/N)*(N/(N-A)): LET P=T2/(T1+T2)
70 LET D2=1/(n-A): LET D1=P*D2: LET Q2=A*D2: LET Q1=P*Q2
80 LET P8=P/EXP(.125/D2): LET P4=P/EXP(.25/D2)
90 LET P2=P/EXP(.5/D2): LET P1=P/EXP(1/D2)
91 LET P0=P/EXP(2/D2)
100 PRINT %3I;N;%6F4;P;%7F2;D1;D2;Q1;Q2;%4F2;P8;P4;P2;P1;P0
110 IF P<.02 THEN 130
120 LET T=T*A/N: LET T1=T1+T: LET N=N+1: GOTO 50
130 STOP
```

(b) Input is offered load. Output shows, for capacity (N), probability of delay (P), mean delay on all calls (D1) and delayed calls (D2), mean queue length overall (Q1) and when all servers are busy (P2), and probability of delay greater than an eighth, quarter, half, one, and two holding times (P8, P4, P2, P1, PP).

**FIGURE 10–3.  Programs for Erlang B and Erlang C (From [GOEL79]).**

Two important points can be noted from the table:

- A larger capacity system is more efficient than a smaller capacity one for a given grade of service.
- A larger capacity system is more susceptible to reduction of the grade of service.

To illustrate the first point, consider two switches, each with a capacity of 10 circuits. They have a joint capacity of 20 circuits and can handle an offered

**TABLE 10.2  Erlang B Table**

| Number of Circuits | Capacity (erlangs) for Grade of Service of: | | | |
| --- | --- | --- | --- | --- |
| | 0.01 (1/100) | 0.005 (1/200) | 0.002 (1/500) | 0.001 (1/1000) |
| 1 | 0.01 | 0.005 | 0.002 | 0.001 |
| 4 | 0.87 | 0.70 | 0.53 | 0.43 |
| 5 | 1.36 | 1.13 | 0.90 | 0.76 |
| 10 | 4.46 | 3.96 | 3.43 | 3.09 |
| 20 | 12.03 | 11.10 | 10.07 | 9.41 |
| 24 | 15.27 | 14.21 | 13.01 | 12.24 |
| 40 | 29.0 | 27.3 | 25.7 | 24.5 |
| 70 | 56.1 | 53.7 | 51.0 | 49.2 |
| 100 | 84.1 | 80.9 | 77.4 | 75.2 |

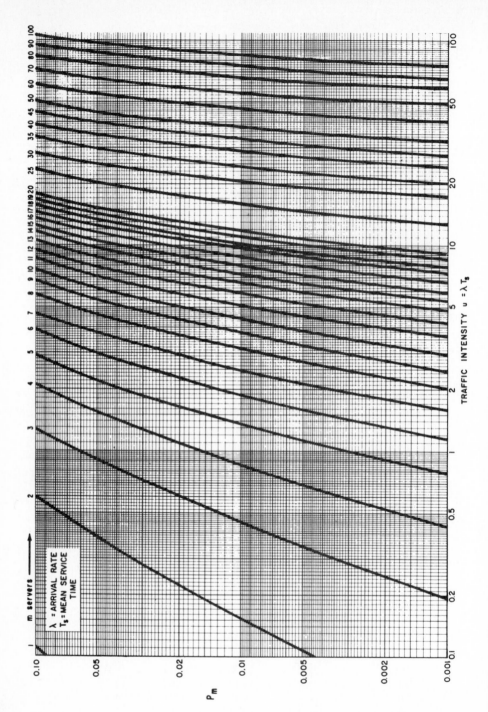

**FIGURE 10—4.** Probability of loss for infinite sources, LCC systems.

NETWORK PERFORMANCE

traffic intensity of 6.86 for a grade of service of 0.002. However, a single switch of capacity 20 circuits, will handle 10.07 erlangs at a grade of service of 0.002. To illustrate the second point, consider a switch of capacity 10 circuits giving a grade of service of 0.002 for a load of 3.43 erlangs. A 30% increase in traffic reduces the grade of service to 0.01. However, for a switch of capacity 70 circuits, only a 10% increase in traffic reduces the grade of service from 0.002 to 0.01.

Of course, all of the discussion above deals with offered traffic. If sizing is being done on the basis of system measurement, all that we are likely to have is carried traffic. Figure 10.5 is a program for Erlang B which accepts carried traffic as input and then performs a seeking algorithm to work backward to offered traffic. This program reflects the relationship between carried traffic $C$ and offered traffic:

$$C = A(1 - P)$$

For small values of $P$, it can be seen that $A$ is a good approximation of $C$.

```
 10 PRINT "THIS IS CARRIED, BY L. F. GOELLER, 7-8-79"
 20 PRINT "CARRIED RELATES CARRIED TRAFFIC IN GROUP"
 30 PRINT "TO OFFERED TRAFFIC AND TRAFFIC ON EACH LINE."
 40 INPUT "TRAFFIC IN ERLANGS CARRIED BY GROUP = ",K
 80 INPUT "PERCENT RECALL= ",R
 90 INPUT "PERCENT OVERFLOW TO TOLL =",X
100 IF R+X<=100 THEN 120
110 PRINT "TRY AGAIN": GOTO 80
120 LET X=X/100: LET R=R/100: LET D=1-R-X
130 INPUT "CALL HOLDING TIME IN MINUTES+",M1
140 LET A=K
150 INPUT "NUMBER OF LINES IN GROUP =",W: LET I=1: LET Y=1
160 IF M1*K*W=0 THEN 600
170 IF W>K THEN 190
180 PRINT "TOO FEW LINES. TRY AGAIN.": GOTO 150
190 PRINT
200 PRINT " N      OFRD    CRD     TOT    G/S"
210 LET T=1: LET T1=1
220 FOR N=1 TO W
230    LET T=T*A/N: LET T1=T1+T: LET P=T/T1
240 NEXT N
250 LET L=A*P: LET S=A-L
260 LET Y=S-K: IF ABS (Y)<.0001 THEN 300
270 IF Y<0 THEN 290
280 LET A=A-I: LET I=I/10
290 LET A=A+I: GOTO 210
300 LET T=1: LET T1=1: LET O=A
310 FOR N=1 TO W
320    LET T=T*A/N: LET T1=T1+T: LET P=T/T1
330    LET L=A*P: LET S=A-L: LET C=O-L
350    PRINT %3I;N;%9F3;O;%6F3;C;%8F3;S;%6F3;P
360    LET O=L
370 NEXT N
380 STOP
390 LET R1=R*L: LET X1=X*L: LET D1=D*L: LET F=A-R1
410 LET M=60/M1: LET F1=F*M: LET R2=R1*M
430 LET X2=X1*M: LET D2=D1*M: LET A1=A*M: LET K1=K*M
470 PRINT "FIRST ATTEMPT HOURS, CALLS =";%9F2;F;F1
480 PRINT "OFFERED HOURS, CALLS        =";%9F2;A;A1
490 PRINT "CARRIED HOURS, CALLS        =";%9F2;K;K1
500 PRINT "RECALLING  HOURS, CALLS     =";%9F2;R1;R2
510 PRINT "TOLL OVERFLOW HOURS, CALLS  =";%9F2;X1;X2
520 PRINT "DEAD HOURS, CALLS           =";%9F2;D1;D2
530 PRINT
540 STOP : GOTO 140
550 REM: FOR HARD COPY OUTPUT, CHANGE 190 PRINT TO
560 REM: 190 PRINT: SET OF="SOL2"
570 REM: CHANGE 380 STOP TO 380 PRINT
580 REM: CHANGE 540 STOP: GOTO 140 TO
590 REM: 540 SET OF=#00: STOP: GOTO 140
600 END
```

(c) Input is carried traffic, capacity, holding time, and retry policy (LCC: Recall=0, Overflow=100; LCH: Recall=100, Overflow=0). Output is offered traffic and grade of service.

**FIGURE 10–5. Erlang B program with carried traffic as input (From [GOEL79]).**

## Finite Sources, Lost Calls Cleared

In reality, of course, the number of sources is not infinite but finite, and equation (b) of Table 10.1, known as *Engset*, applies. This is a more complex formula and, because of the extra parameter $L$, the tables are more unwieldy than for Erlang B. In many cases, the infinite source assumption will suffice.

To get a handle on the relative size of the difference between finite and infinite source assumptions, let us compare two systems. One is infinite source with a calling rate of $\lambda$; the other is a finite source with a calling rate per source of $\lambda/L$. We then have

$$A_\infty = \lambda h$$

$$A_L = \frac{\lambda}{L}(L - n)h = \lambda h\left(1 - \frac{n}{L}\right) \geq \lambda h\left(1 - \frac{N}{L}\right)$$

where $A_\infty$ = offered traffic, infinite source case

$\quad\quad A_L$ = offered traffic, $L$ sources

$\quad\quad n$ = number of sources currently engaged in a call

The inequality results from the fact that the number of sources engaged cannot exceed the total capacity $N$ of the system.

We have

$$A_\infty > A_L \geq A_\infty\left(1 - \frac{N}{L}\right)$$

Thus, for $L$ much larger than $N$, $A_\infty$ is a good approximation of $A_L$.

This conclusion is confirmed by Table 10.3, which shows that as the number of sources gets large compared to capacity, the effective capacity approaches the value for the infinite source case. Note that as the probability of loss decreases, the approximation becomes relatively less accurate. You should also

**TABLE 10.3  Lost Calls Cleared, Finite and Infinite Sources (Number of Servers = 10)**

| Number of Sources | Offered Load (Effective Capacity) | | |
|---|---|---|---|
| | $p = 0.005$ | $p = 0.01$ | $p = 0.05$ |
| ∞ | 3.96 | 4.46 | 6.22 |
| 50 | 4.16 | 4.64 | 6.4 |
| 25 | 4.6 | 5.1 | 6.81 |
| 20 | 4.81 | 5.32 | 7.06 |
| 15 | 5.27 | 5.78 | 7.41 |
| 12 | 5.97 | 6.47 | 8.02 |
| 10 | 10 | 10 | 10 |

be able to deduce from this table that the probability of loss is always less for a finite system than for a similar system with an infinite source. Thus the infinite source model will give conservative estimates for sizing.

## Lost Calls Delayed

When queueing is allowed, the designer may be interested more in the delay characteristics than the blocking characteristics of the switch. Table 10.1c shows several formulas for the infinite source, LCD case. The designer might be interested in the probability of any delay (*Erlang C* formula), the probability of a delay greater than a given amount, or the mean value of delay. A BASIC program for calculation is shown in Figure 10.3b.

The probability of delay, the probability of delay greater than a given amount, and the average delay on all offered calls are complex functions of $A$ and $N$ and can be solved only with the aid of a computer or the appropriate tables. Fortunately, the average delay and the probability of delay greater than a given amount, *for calls that are delayed*, are easily calculated and of some interest.

As an example, consider this problem: What is the load that can be offered to a switch of capacity 1500 with a mean holding time of 1000 s, if the fraction of delayed calls waiting longer than 1 minute is not to exceed 10%? Thus we have $N = 1500$, $h = 1000$, $T = t/h = 60/1000 = 0.06$, and $P_2(> 60) = 0.1$. Substituting, we have

$$\ln (0.1) = -(1500 - A)(0.06)$$

Solving for $A$ yields $A = 1462$. Thus, for these requirements, the load on the system may be very near to the total capacity.

Our next example makes use of Figure 10.6, which shows the probability of delay for infinite source, lost calls delayed. Consider a switch with capacity 20 that experiences an average call holding time of 5 minutes. If the load on the system is 16 erlangs, what is the fraction of all calls that will be delayed greater than 2.5 minutes? First, we need the fraction of calls that will be delayed at all. From Figure 10.6, with $A = 16$ and $N = 20$, we have that $P(>0)$ is approximately 0.25. Then

$$P(>2.5) = P(>0)e^{-(N-A)t/h}$$
$$= 0.25e^{-(20-16)(2.5/5)}$$
$$= 0.03$$

The average delay on calls delayed is $h/(N - A) = 1.25$ minutes. The average delay for all calls is $P(>0) \cdot 1.25 = 0.31$ minute.

Table 10.1d shows the formula for finite source, lost calls delayed. This is the most complicated analytically, and the infinite source case should be used for a first approximation.

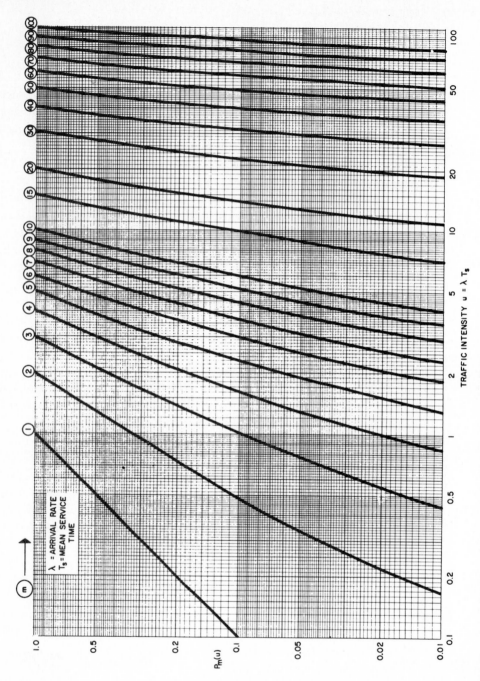

FIGURE 10—6. Probability of delay for infinite sources, LCD systems.

NETWORK PERFORMANCE

## Summary

Using either tables or computer programs, the equations of Table 10.1 can be used in a variety of ways. For infinite sources, LCC, there are three variables: $P$, $N$, and $A$ (which can be determined from $\lambda$ and $h$). Given any two variables, one can solve for the third. Example questions:

- Given a measured value of $P$ for a particular $N$, how much must $N$ be increased to reduce $P$ to a given level?
- Given $\lambda$, $h$ and a desired value for $P$, what capacity ($N$) is required?

For infinite source, lost calls delayed, there is the additional parameter, the delay. As before, among the variables $P(>0)$, $N$, and $A$, given any two the third can be found. To determine $D$, $h$ must be known.

The same considerations apply for the finite-source case (LCC or LCD). In this case, a fixed $L$ is used, and then the same types of problems can be addressed.

**10.3**

---

## RECOMMENDED READING

A good introduction to the queueing theory underlying the concepts of this chapter can be found in [MART72]. A more thorough but still readable discussion is [IBM71]. One of the best textbooks on queueing theory, and one of the few that deals with the teletraffic concepts of this chapter is [COOP81]. A discussion that relates queueing theory directly to the problems of circuit-switching traffic is [BECK77]. [FRAN76] contains tables for all of the formulas presented in this book. The latter two publications are available from an organization with the unlikely name of Lee's abc of the Telephone, Box 537, Geneva, IL 60134.

Other books with useful accounts of the circuit-switched traffic problem are [JOLL68], [INOS79], and [SHAR82].

**10.4**

---

## PROBLEMS

**10.1** Using Figure 10.4, answer the following questions:
   **a.** Assume that the measured probability of loss is 0.05 for a system with capacity 10. How much must the capacity be increased to reduce the probability of loss to 0.005?
   **b.** The expected arrival rate of calls is 5 per minute, with an expected holding time of 2 minutes. What capacity switch is needed to give a probability of loss of 0.01?

**10.2**    A switch of capacity 25 is handling an offered load of 15 erlangs. If the load is increased by 100%, how much must the capacity be increased to maintain the same grade of service? Use the infinite sources, LCC model.

**10.3**    A switch of capacity 20 has been engineered for a probability of delay of 0.1. The average holding time, however, turns out to be 20% greater than anticipated. Assuming infinite sources, what is the actual probability of delay?

**10.4**    What capacity switch is required to handle 230 calls per hour with a probability of delay of no greater than 0.5? Assume that the average holding time is 100 s. Now add the additional requirement that the probability of a delay greater than 100 s, for all calls, should be no more than 0.05. Is the capacity just calculated adequate? If not, what capacity is needed?

**10.5**    Why is a switch considered blocking for $L > N/2$, but a port contention unit is blocking for $L > N$?

**10.6**    The probability of loss for LCC systems, also known as call congestion, is the probability that an arriving call will find all circuits busy. Another quantity, the blocking probability, also known as time congestion, is the probability that, at an arbitrary time, all circuits are busy. Are these quantities the same for the infinite source case? For the finite source case? Answer using commonsense arguments, without mathematics.

**10.7**    For infinite source, lost calls cleared, derive an expression for the number of lost calls per unit time.

# CHAPTER 11

# Internetworking

In many, perhaps most, cases a local network will not be an isolated entity. An organization may have more than one type of local network at a given site, to satisfy a spectrum of needs. An organization may have local networks at various sites and need them to be interconnected for central control or distributed information exchange. And an organization may need to provide a connection for one or more terminals and hosts on a local network to other computing resources.

This chapter looks at the range of issues involved in connecting a local network to other networks. This is commonly termed *internetworking*. The term *catenet* is sometimes used to refer to multiple networks connected together.

## 11.1

## HOMOGENEOUS LOCAL NETWORKS

The simplest kind of multiple local network is one involving homogeneous local networks. Such networks exhibit the same interface to attached devices and generally use the same internal protocol for medium access.

A simple example of this principle is the repeater used on baseband networks. However, this is not a true multiple network system. The repeater is merely used to extend the length of the baseband cable. It amplifies and retransmits all signals, including collisions. Thus, the system behaves, from virtually all points of view, as a single network.

A system with truly separate but homogeneous networks requires a bridge to connect them. This concept was introduced in Chapter 4 as a means of linking multiple rings.

A bridge, in essence, consists of two NIUs linked together. To summarize again the main functions of a bridge, consider a connection between networks A and B. The bridge must do the following:

- Read all frames transmitted on A, and accept those addressed to B.
- Using the medium access control protocol for B, retransmit the frames onto B.
- Do the same for B-to-A traffic.

In addition to these basic functions, there are some interesting design considerations.

1. The bridge makes no modifications to the content or format of the frames it receives, nor does it encapsulate them with an additional header. If any modifications or additions are made, we are dealing with a more complex device: a gateway. This is discussed in later sections.
2. Despite item 1, the bridge can be conceived internally as using another protocol. Figure 11.1 shows a bridge consisting of two NIUs connected by a point-to-point link, which might be an HDLC link. For purposes of crossing that link, one or more LAN frames will be wrapped in an HDLC frame.
3. The bridge should contain enough buffer space to meet peak demands. Over a short period of time, frames may arrive faster than they can be retransmitted.
4. The bridge must contain addressing and routing intelligence. At a minimum,

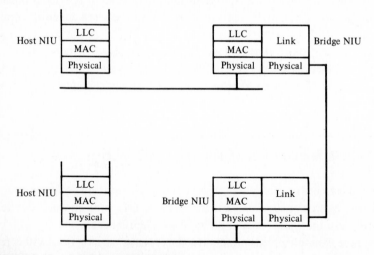

**FIGURE 11–1.  LAN-to-LAN Bridge.**

the bridge must know which addresses are on each network in order to know which frames to pass. Further, there may be more than two networks in a sort of cascade configuration. The bridge must be able to pass along frames addressed for networks further on.

5. A bridge may connect more than two networks. This was discussed in Chapter 4.

Having described this rather simple device, we should address the subject of why bridges are used. The principal reasons are:

- *Reliability:* The danger in connecting all data processing devices in an organization to one network is that a fault on the network disables all communications. By using bridges, the network can be partitioned into self-contained units.
- *Performance:* In general, performance on a LAN or HSLN declines with an increase in the number of stations or the length of the medium. A number of smaller networks will give improved performance if devices can be clustered so that intranetwork traffic significantly exceeds internetwork traffic.
- *Security:* A bridge architecture can enhance network security. This topic is explored in Chapter 12.
- *Convenience:* It may simply be more convenient to have multiple networks. For example, if a broadband local network is to be installed in two buildings separated by a highway, it may be far easier to use a microwave point-to-point bridge link than to attempt to string coaxial cable between the two buildings.
- *Geographic coverage:* A corporation may install homogeneous LAN systems in a number of cities and wish them to function as a single integrated network. Bridges with the architecture of Figure 11.1 can be used to link widely separated networks.

All of the discussion above is with reference to packet-switched local networks. For circuit-switched local networks, the function of a bridge is not needed. A hierarchical star configuration still acts as a single network, but exhibits the advantages listed above for multiple homogeneous networks.

**11.2**

## HYBRID LOCAL NETWORKS

From the discussions in Chapters 1 and 3, it should be evident that the three kinds of local networks (LAN, HSLN, CBX) have different and complementary strengths. In some locations, a mixture of two or three types may best serve the needs of an organization.

For example, all telephones, low-speed terminals, and microcomputers could attach to a CBX. This arrangement takes advantage of the low attachment cost of the CBX for devices that do not have high data rate requirements. Most minicomputers and some higher-speed peripherals could be attached to a LAN. Finally, mainframes and mass storage devices could be connected via HSLN.

We have already outlined reasons for each of these types of networks. But it should be clear that connections across types might also be needed. Terminals and personal computers attached to a CBX may wish access to applications performed on the minicomputers or to data controlled by a mainframe, and so on.

Figure 11.2 shows a possible hybrid local network architecture. We briefly

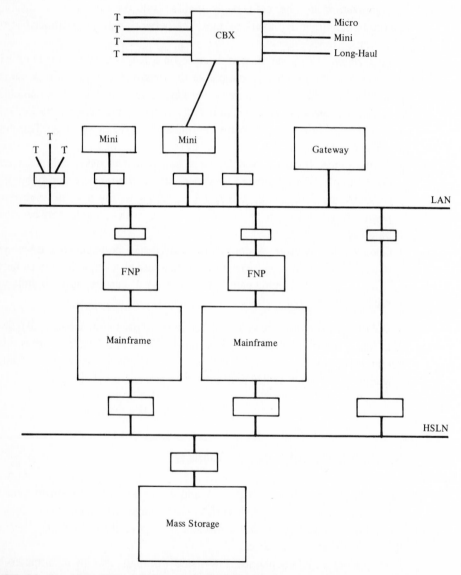

**FIGURE 11–2. Hybrid Local Network Architecture.**

**INTERNETWORKING**

discuss each of the connections depicted. First, a CBX could attach directly to a LAN via one or more NIU ports. A terminal wishing to connect to some LAN device would first request an NIU connection and then access the LAN as if directly connected. A nice feature of this link is that the CBX, through its trunk access to the long-haul telecommunications network, can provide a connection for remote terminals to dial in to the LAN.

Another possible CBX–LAN link is via I/O ports of a host machine connected to the LAN. If the CBX–host links are dedicated to a single logical connection, the CBX is providing a port contention service. If the CBX provides a protocol server for some multiplex protocol like X.25, then the CBX–host link can handle multiple logical connections. The CBX is now acting as a terminal concentrator. This link could be established either to a LAN host which has a time-sharing application, or to a front-end processor to a mainframe.

Next, consider LAN–HSLN connections. The traffic to be handled over this connection falls into two general categories: interactive and file transfer. One example of interactive traffic is a terminal attached to the LAN (directly or via CBX–NIU link) that wants to use a time-sharing application on a mainframe. Another example is a process on a LAN host needing to query a mainframe data base for an item of data. This type of traffic typically involves rather short messages. It is clear that this kind of traffic should be kept off the HSLN, which performs best with long packets. The proper connection is to have the mainframe's front-end processor (FNP) connect directly to the LAN. The FNP is designed for exactly this type of traffic.

File transfer traffic can be handled differently. An example: a data entry application is run on a LAN host. Periodically, files are to be transferred to a mainframe's mass storage for archiving. This type of traffic could go directly over an NIU–NIU link. This link may not quite be a bridge, since the LAN and HSLN may use different frame formats, but it would not be much more complex than that.

Finally, long-haul links can be handled in two ways. Some simple requirements, such as remote terminal access, can be met with the CBX connection to long-haul circuit switched networks. Other applications can be met via a gateway to packet-switched networks. The gateway could be a host or NIU attached to the LAN. This is the function usually referred to as internetworking, and is the subject of the remainder of this chapter.

## 11.3

# PRINCIPLES OF INTERNETWORKING

## Requirements

Up until now, we have discussed instances in which the differences among networks were small. Now let us consider the more general problem of connecting a local network to outside resources. For now, let us limit ourselves to LANs; the principles for HSLNs are the same, and the protocol issues we are discussing do not apply to CBXs. For LAN connection, we can distinguish a number of cases:

1. *LAN-to-LAN:* A user or application process on one LAN desires access to a user or application process on another. The possibilities include:
   a. Point-to-point link, homogeneous networks. For example, a corporation might procure a LAN for each of its main offices from a single vendor.
   b. Network link, homogeneous networks. As above, but it is found more feasible to connect through a network (e.g., an X.25 long-haul packet-switched network).
   c. Point-to-point link, heterogeneous networks. An organization may have two LANs, in the same location, or separated, from different vendors.
   d. Network link, heterogeneous networks. As above, but linked by a packet-switched network.
2. *LAN-to-network:* In this case, some or all LAN subscribers need access to services available on a long-haul network (e.g., a data base or information utility available through a packet-switched network). Two possibilities are:
   a. Host-to-network link. Each host (or terminal) that requires a network link establishes one independent of the LAN.
   b. LAN-to-network link. As a service, the LAN establishes a link to the long-haul network which may be multiplexed to provide access for multiple hosts.

Of these six cases, three are of no real interest as problems in internetworking. Case 1a can be handled with a bridge. The two halves of the bridge maintain a layer 2 point-to-point link. Case 1b is also solved by a bridge, with a special adaptation to handle the long-haul network protocol. For example, consider two LANs connected via an X.25 network. The bridge on LAN A accepts frames as before. Now, it wraps that frame in a layer 3 packet and transmits it to the bridge at LAN B, which unwraps the frame and inserts it into LAN B. For this purpose, a virtual circuit may be maintained between the two bridges. This mechanism is actually a form of gateway, but one so simple and specialized that a generalized solution is not required. Case 2a does not involve internet-working at all! Each host on the LAN is responsible for its own link to the long-haul network and for implementing the protocols of that network; the LAN is not involved.

The remaining three cases require some kind of logic or protocol beyond that needed for intranetwork routing and delivery. This logic can be considered to reside in a gateway. Figure 11.3 depicts these three cases. It can be seen (or will be seen) that these three cases are fundamentally the same. The internet-working requirements are the same for all these cases. In essence, we wish to permit process-to-process communication across more than one network.

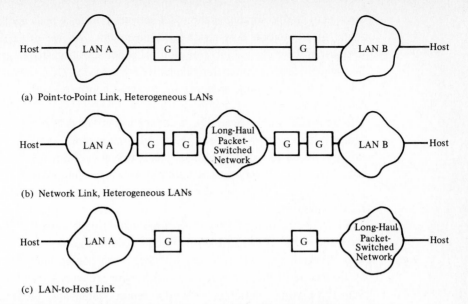

(a) Point-to-Point Link, Heterogeneous LANs

(b) Network Link, Heterogeneous LANs

(c) LAN-to-Host Link

**FIGURE 11–3. Local Network Internetworking Requirements.**

Before turning to the architectural approaches to providing the service of Figure 11.3, we list some of the requirements on the internetworking facility. These include:

1. Provide a link between networks. At minimum, a physical and link control connection is needed.
2. Provide for the routing and delivery of data between processes on different networks.
3. Provide an accounting service that keeps track of the use of the various networks and gateways and maintains status information.
4. Provide the services listed above in such a way as not to require modifications to the networking architecture of any of the attached networks. This means that the internetworking facility must accommodate a number of differences among networks. These include:
   a. Different addressing schemes. The networks may use different end point names and addresses and directory maintenance schemes. Some form of global network addressing must be provided, as well as a directory service.
   b. Different maximum packet size. Packets from one network may have to be broken up into smaller pieces for another. This process is referred to as fragmentation.
   c. Different network interfaces. For purposes of this discussion, we will assume that the interface is at layer 3, such as is found in an X.25 network. This assumption is a reasonable one since layers 1 through 3

are specific to the communications subnetwork, while layers 4 and above relate to end-to-end host process considerations. As we discussed in Chapter 8, there are a number of protocol residency alternatives between host and NIU for LANs. In this chapter we use the DTE, DCE terminology for the communications architecture, to avoid confusion with the host–NIU architecture.

d. Different time-outs. Generally, a connection-oriented transport service will await an acknowledgment until a time-out expires, at which time it will retransmit its segment of data. Generally, longer times are required for successful delivery across multiple networks. Internetwork timing procedures must allow successful transmission that avoids unnecessary retransmissions.

e. Error recovery. Intranetwork procedures may provide anything from no error recovery up to reliable end-to-end (within the network) service. The internetwork service should not depend on nor be interfered with by the nature of the individual network's error recovery capability.

f. Status reporting. Different networks report status and performance differently. Yet it must be possible for the internetworking facility to provide such information on internetworking activity to interested and authorized processes.

g. Routing techniques. Intranetwork routing may depend on fault detection and congestion control techniques peculiar to each network. The internetworking facility must be able to coordinate these to adaptively route data between DTEs on different networks.

h. Access control. Each network will have its own user access control techniques. These must be invoked by the internetwork facility as needed. Further, a separate internetwork access control technique may be required.

i. Connection, connectionless. Individual networks may provide connection-oriented (e.g., virtual circuit) or connectionless (datagram) service. The internetwork service should not depend on the nature of the connection service for the individual networks.

## Architectural Approaches

We have seen that some kind of gateway function is needed to interconnect networks. The key issue in designing such a gateway deals with the communications architecture that is used. There are essentially two dimensions that determine this architecture:

- The nature of the interface.
- The nature of the transmission service.

There are two choices for the interface: two networks interface at either the DCE or DTE level. An interface at the DCE level implies, at minimum, that the networks have a common network access interface (e.g. X.25). It does not necessarily imply that the networks have the same internal protocols; if they do, the gateway reduces to a bridge. In any case, there is a standardized format for packets entering and leaving each network. The principal advantage of this approach is that, with the exception of an expanded address space, the hosts are not aware that there are multiple networks. If the system is designed properly, no changes need be made in the host software. If two hosts can connect over a single network, they can connect via multiple networks with the same network access interface.

If it is not possible to standardize the network access interface, some form of protocol translation, or at least manipulation, is needed. At the worst, a specialized gateway for each pair of networks must be constructed. A better approach, as we shall see, is to standardize the objects that pass between networks.

The other dimension for characterizing internetwork architecture is the nature of the transmission service, which can be either end to end or network by network. The end-to-end approach assumes that all networks offer at least an unreliable datagram service; that is, if a sequence of packets is sent from one host to another on the same network, some but not necessarily all will get through, and there may be duplications and reordering of the sequence. The transmission across multiple networks requires a common end-to-end protocol for providing reliable end-to-end service. In the network-by-network approach, the technique is to provide reliable service within each network and then to string together individual network segments across multiple networks.

Table 11.1 lists possible realizations of the four architectures that result from the 2 × 2 combination of interface and transmission service. Two of these combinations are of little interest here. The only type of approach that seems to fit neatly into the end-to-end DCE-level architecture is a configuration of multiple homogeneous networks connected by bridges. The bridge is certainly a DCE device, and whatever end-to-end protocol is used by the networks is automatically carried across networks. To see this, consider two hosts, A and B, on different LANs. When a packet is sent by A to B, the LLC layer of A's NIU constructs a frame with the destination address of B's NIU, *not* the bridge's NIU. Thus a connection-oriented service at the LLC or higher layer is carried transparently through the bridge.

**TABLE 11.1  Alternative Internetworking Approaches**

|  | DTE Level | DCE Level |
|---|---|---|
| **Network-by-Network** | Protocol translator | X.75 |
| **End-to-End** | Internet protocol (IP) | Bridge |

The other architecture of little interest here is network-by-network DTE level. In this case, we are dealing with networks that have no common network access interface and no common end-to-end protocol. The only way to achieve internetworking is for each gateway to be a true protocol translator between its two attached networks. This is an exercise in special-purpose software and is not pursued further.

The two remaining architectures are represented by radically different approaches taken by standards organizations. An example of a network-by-network DCE-level architecture is the X.75 standard, designed as an extension to X.25. X.75 specifies a protocol for exchange of packets between networks to allow a series of intranetwork X.25 virtual circuits to be strung together. To two hosts on different networks, it appears that they have a single virtual circuit connecting them. In fact, the virtual circuits terminate at the DCE gateways, which maintain the status information required to connect separate virtual circuits.

The end-to-end DTE-level architecture is implemented using a protocol above the network layer, called *Internet Protocol* (IP). IP was initially developed for ARPANET and has been standardized by the Defense Department. A very similar IP standard has been developed by the National Bureau of Standards. As was mentioned in Chapter 2, IP is a layer that fits between layers 3 and 4. It provides a datagram service between hosts. Figure 11.4 depicts its operation for data exchange between host A on a LAN and host B on a LAN through a long-haul packet-switched network. The data to be sent by A are encapsulated in a datagram with an IP header specifying a global network address (host B). This datagram is then encapsulated with the LAN protocol and sent to a gateway that strips off the LAN header. The datagram is then encapsulated with the X.25 protocol and transmitted across the network to a gateway. The gateway strips off the X.25 fields and recovers the datagram, which is then wrapped in LAN headers and sent to B. If a connection-oriented service is required, A and B must share a common layer 4 protocol.

Table 11.2 compares IP and X.75 on a number of features. Because IP places no significant restrictions on internal network protocols, it is the more flexible approach and seems the most appropriate for local networks. In the remainder of this section, we will elaborate on the design and operation of a multiple-network system using IP gateways. In Section 11.4, IP and other internetwork protocols of interest are described.

## Operation of an IP Catenet

To begin, we describe briefly the sequence of steps involved in sending a datagram between two hosts on different networks. This is followed by a more detailed discussion of the design issues involved.

The process starts in the sending host. The host wants to send an IP datagram to a host in another network. The IP module in the host constructs the datagram

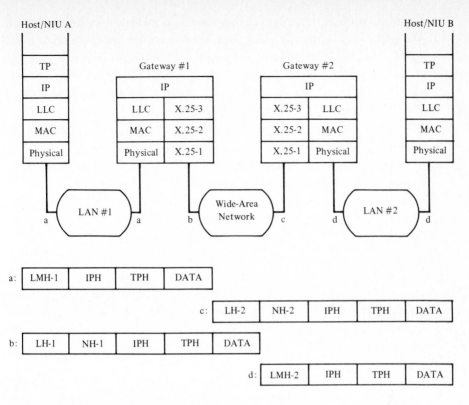

LMH-*i* : Combined LLC and MAC header for LAN i
LH-*j* : Link Header (X.25 Layer 2) for DTE = Gateway *j*
NH-*k* : Network Header (X.25 Layer 3) for DTE = Gateway k
IPH : Internet Protocol Header
TPH : Transport Protocol Header

**FIGURE 11—4. Message Encapsulation: IP Approach.**

with a global network address and recognizes that the destination is on another network. So the first step is to send the datagram to a gateway (example: Host A to gateway 1 in Figure 11.4). To do this, the IP module appends to the IP datagram a header appropriate to the network that contains the address of the gateway. For example, for an X.25 network, a layer 3 packet is formed by the IP module to be sent to the gateway.

**TABLE 11.2 Comparative Features of IP and X.75**

| IP | X.75 |
|---|---|
| DTE gateway | DCE gateway |
| Datagram service | Virtual circuit service |
| Gateway must know IP and two network access interfaces | Gateway must maintain state information about all virtual circuits |
| Adaptive routing | Fixed routing |
| All hosts must have IP and may need common layer 4 | All networks must be X.25 |

Next, the packet travels through the network to the gateway, which receives it via a DCE–DTE protocol. The gateway unwraps the packet to recover the original datagram. The gateway analyzes the IP header to determine whether this datagram contains control information intended for the gateway, or data intended for a host farther on. In the latter instance, the gateway must make a routing decision. There are four possibilities:

1. The destination host is attached directly to one of the networks to which the gateway is attached. This is referred to as "directly connected."
2. The destination host is on a network which has a gateway that directly connects to this gateway. This is known as a "neighbor gateway."
3. To reach the destination host, more than one additional gateway must be traversed. This is known as a "multiple-hop" situation.
4. The gateway does not know the destination address.

In case 4, the gateway returns an error message to the source of the datagram. For cases 1 through 3, the gateway must select the appropriate route for the data, and insert them into the appropriate network with the appropriate address. For case 1, the address is the destination host address. For cases 2 and 3, the address is a gateway address. Remember, we are speaking here of a lower layer address, usually a layer 3 address or, in the case of local networks, a layer 2 address.

Before actually sending data, however, the gateway may need to fragment the datagram to accommodate a smaller packet size. Each fragment becomes an independent IP datagram. Each new datagram is wrapped in a lower layer packet for transmission. The gateway then queues each packet for transmission. It may also enforce a maximum queue-length size for each network to which it attaches to avoid having a slow network penalize a faster one. In any case, once the queue limit is reached, additional datagrams are simply dropped.

The process described above continues through zero or more gateways until the datagram reaches the destination host. As with a gateway, the destination host recovers the IP datagram from its network wrapping. If fragmentation has occurred, the IP module in the destination host buffers the incoming data until the original data field is reassembled. It then passes this block of data to a higher layer. The higher layer (e.g., TCP) is responsible for the proper sequencing of a stream of datagrams and for end-to-end error and flow control.

With that thumbnail sketch of the operation of an IP-controlled catenet, we can now go back and examine some design issues in greater detail. These are:

- Addressing
- Routing
- Fragmentation and reassembly

### Addressing

A distinction is generally made among names, addresses, and routes [SHOC78]. A name specifies what an object is, an address specifies where it is, and a route indicates how to get there. The distinction between names and addresses can be a useful concept, but it is also an arbitrary one. For a single network, an application program uses a name to identify a referent (process, host); the host translates the name into an address understood by the network; and the network may utilize a route to reach the referent.

In a catenet, the distinction is less clear. Applications continue to use names and individual networks continue to use addresses and, if necessary, routes. To transfer data through a gateway, two entities must be identified: the destination network and the destination host. The gateway requires a network address in order to perform its function. This address can be specified in a number of ways:

• The application can refer to a network by a unique number; in effect, the name and address are the same.
• The internet logic in the host can translate a network name into a network address.
• A global host addressing scheme can be used. That is, there is a unique identifier for each host in the catenet. For routing purposes, each gateway would need to derive network addresses from host addresses.

Surprisingly, the latter technique has been proposed by the developers of Ethernet [DALA81]. They recommend a 48-bit host address. This is an address space sufficient to accommodate over $10^{14}$ unique referents, so it is likely to be sufficient for the foreseeable future. The primary advantages of this approach are that it permits hosts to move from one network to another and that it allows address recognition at the host to be "hardwired." The main disadvantages are that some central facility must manage the assignment of names and that unnecessarily long address fields must be carried across multiple networks. Given the proliferation of local networks, this unique address approach does not seem feasible.

So, typically, a gateway will receive an internet packet with a referent in the form Net.Host, where Net is a network address. The identifier Host is usually *both* a name and an address. To the higher-layer software in the host that generated the packet, Host is an address, translated from an application-level name. However, when it comes time for a gateway to deliver a datagram to a host on an attached network, Host must be translated into a layer 3 or 2 network address. This is so because different networks will have different address field lengths. Hence, Host is treated as a name by the gateway.

The referent Net.Host can be considered a two-level hierarchical identifier of a host in the catenet. The Ethernet developers have proposed a third level of addressing to identify, at the internet level, an individual service access port (SAP) at a host [BOGG80, DALA82]. Thus the internet identifier would be of the form Net.Host.SAP. With this identifier, an internet protocol can be viewed as process to process rather than host to host. With SAP in the internet layer, the internet protocol is responsible for multiplexing and demultiplexing datagrams for software modules that use the internet service. The advantage of this approach is that the next-higher layer could be simplified, a useful feature for small microprocessor devices. There are some problems in this approach, particularly when local networks are involved, where there is likely to be a proliferation of host types. Perhaps the most significant problem relates to the use of "well-known" ports, which allow ready access to common services. For example, TCP port 23 is the remote login service. Devices not using TCP, but using some other higher-level protocol, would have other well-known ports. If ports were implemented as SAPs at the IP level, the assignment of well-known ports would have to be centralized. For a further discussion, see [CLAR82].

Several other features of addressing that are important when local networks are involved should be mentioned. One feature that is particularly useful is the support of multicasting and broadcasting within the IP layer. Table 11.3 depicts the possible combinations. A multicast address specifies a group of hosts to which a message is to be sent. A group can be defined on a specific network or scattered over a number of networks. A broadcast address specifies all hosts on a network. A message can be broadcast to all hosts on one network or all hosts on all networks.

Another feature that may be useful for attaching local networks to catenets is the concept of a "hidden network," i.e., a network that appears as a single DTE to another network on the catanet. With a proliferation of local networks, it seems unreasonable that all of the hosts on a local network must be known to the catenet. Thus the entire network would have a single internet Host identifier, and a gateway at the attachment point would have to translate this into one of a number of specific local network host identifiers. A simple technique for doing this on an X.25 network is described in Section 11.4.

Finally, an important service that must somehow be provided in the catenet is a directory service. The host software must be able to determine the Net.Host identifier of a desired destination. One or more directory servers are needed, which themselves are well known. Each server would contain part or all of a name/address directory for catenet hosts.

**TABLE 11.3  Internet Multicasting and Broadcasting**

| Destination | Network Address | Host Address |
| --- | --- | --- |
| Specific host | Specific | Specific |
| Multicast | | |
|   Directed | Specific | Group |
|   Global | All | Group |
| Broadcast | | |
|   Directed | Specific | All |
|   Global | All | All |

*Source:* [DALA82].

**TABLE 11.4  INTERNET Routing Table for the BBN gateway**

| Network Name | Net Address | Route[a] |
|---|---|---|
| SATNET | 4 | Directly connected |
| ARPANET | 10 | Directly connected |
| BBN-NET | 3 | 1 hop via RCC 10.3.0.72 (ARPANET 3/72) |
| PURDUE-COMPUTER SCIENCE | 192.5.1 | 2 hops via PURDUE 10.2.0.37 (ARPANET 2/37) |
| INTELPOST | 43 | 2 hops via MILLS 10.3.0.17 (ARPANET 3/17) |
| DECNET-TEST | 38 | 3 hops via MILLS 10.3.0.17 (ARPANET 3/17) |
| WIDEBAND | 28 | 3 hops via RCC 10.3.0.72 (ARPANET 3/72) |
| BBN-PACKET RADIO | 1 | 2 hops via RCC 10.3.0.72 (ARPANET 3/72) |
| DCN-COMSAT | 29 | 1 hop via MILLS 10.3.0.17 (ARPANET 3/17) |
| FIBERNET | 24 | 3 hops via RCC 10.3.0.72 (ARPANET 3/72) |
| BRAGG-PACKET RADIO | 9 | 1 hop via BRAGG 10.0.0.38 (ARPANET 0/38) |
| CLARK NET | 8 | 2 hops via MILLS 10.3.0.17 (ARPANET 3/17) |
| LCSNET | 18 | 1 hop via MIT-LCS 10.0.0.77 (ARPANET 0/77) |
| BBN-TERMINAL CONCENTRATOR | 192.1.2 | 3 hops via RCC 10.3.0.72 (ARPANET 3/72) |
| BBN-JERICHO | 192.1.3 | 3 hops via RCC 10.3.0.72 (ARPANET 3/72) |
| UCLNET | 11 | 1 hop via UCL 4.0.0.60 (SATNET 60) |
| RSRE-NULL | 35 | 1 hop via UCL 4.0.0.60 (SATNET 60) |
| RSRE-PPSN | 25 | 2 hops via UCL 4.0.0.60 (SATNET 60) |
| SAN FRANCISCO-PACKET RADIO-2 | 6 | 1 hop via C3PO 10.1.0.51 (ARPANET 1/51) |

[a]Names and acronyms identify gateways in the INTERNET system.
*Source:* [SHEL82].

## Routing

Routing is generally accomplished by maintaining a routing table in each host and gateway that gives, for each possible destination network, the next gateway to which the IP datagram should be sent.

Table 11.4 shows the routing table for the BBN gateway, which is part of the DARPA catenet. If a network is directly connected, it is so indicated. Otherwise, the datagram must be directed through one or more gateways (one or more hops). The table indicates the identity of the next gateway on the route (which must share a common network with this gateway or host) and the number of hops to the destination.

The routing table may be static or dynamic. A static table, however, could contain alternate routes if a gateway is unavailable. A dynamic table is more flexible in responding both to error and congestion situations. In the DARPA catenet, for example, when a gateway goes down, all of its neighbors will send out a status report, allowing other gateways and hosts to update their routing tables. A similar scheme can be used to control congestion. This latter is particularly important because of the mismatch in capacity between local and long-haul networks. The interested reader may consult [DARP81c], which specifies a variety of internet control messages used to facilitate routing. Routing tables may also be used to support other internet services, such as security and priority.

### Fragmentation and Reassembly

To avoid fixing the maximum size of a packet, a constraint that is unfavorable to CSMA/CD LANs and HSLNs, fragmentation must be done at the IP level by gateways.

Both DOD and NBS specify an efficient technique for IP fragmentation. The technique requires the following fields in the datagram header:

- ID
- Length
- Offset
- More flag.

The ID is some means of uniquely identifying a host-originated datagram. In IP, it consists of the source and destination addresses, an identifier of the protocol layer that generated the datagram, and a sequence number supplied by that protocol layer. The Length is the length of the data field in octets, and the Offset is the position of a fragment in the original datagram in multiples of 64 bits.

The source host IP layer creates a datagram with Length equal to the entire length of the data field, with Offset = 0, and the More Flag reset. To fragment a long packet, an IP module in a gateway performs the following tasks:

1. Creates two new datagrams and copies the header fields of the incoming datagram into both.
2. Divides the data into two approximately equal portions along a 64-bit boundary, placing one portion in each new datagram. The first portion must be a multiple of 64 bits.
3. Sets the Length field of the first datagram to the length of the inserted data, and sets the More Flag. The Offset field is unchanged.
4. Sets the Length field of the second datagram to the length of the inserted data, and adds the length of the first data portion divided by eight to the Offset field. The More Flag remains the same.

Table 11.5 gives an example. The procedure can be generalized to an *n*-way split.

To reassemble a datagram, there must be sufficient buffer space at the reassembly point. As fragments with the same ID arrive, their data fields are inserted in the proper position in the buffer until the entire datagram is reassembled, which is achieved when a contiguous set of data exists starting with an Offset of zero and ending with data from a fragment with a reset More Flag. Typically, reassembly is done at the host, to avoid burdening gateways

**TABLE 11.5   Fragmentation Example**

| Original Datagram | First Fragment | Second Fragment |
|---|---|---|
| Length = 472 | Length = 240 | Length = 232 |
| Offset = 0 | Offset = 0 | Offset = 30 |
| More = 0 | More = 1 | More = 0 |

with unnecessarily large buffer space and to permit fragments to arrive via different routes. However, as mentioned, it is an advantage in certain local networks to make the packet size as large as possible. Therefore, it might be a good design decision to dictate reassembly of datagrams entering a local network.

## 11.4

## INTERNETWORK PROTOCOLS

In this section we review three approaches for defining internet protocols. The first makes use of an additional protocol layer that fits between layers 3 and 4 of the OSI model. The second is designed for use in connecting X.25 networks. The third is not an internet protocol as such, but a means for local networks to make use of an X.25 long-haul network for internetting.

### IP

The Internet Protocol (IP) is the name given to a protocol standard developed by DOD [DARP81a] and by NBS [NBS80a, NBS81a]. The two protocols exhibit only minor differences; both are an outgrowth of the Internet Protocol developed for ARPANET [POST81]. The following description is based on the NBS standard; differences with DOD are pointed out where appropriate.

As before, the protocol can be specified in three parts:

- The interface with a higher layer (e.g., DOD's TCP, NBS's TP), specifying the services that IP provides.
- The IP protocol, specifying host-gateway and gateway-gateway interaction.
- The interface with a lower layer, specifying required services.

#### IP Protocol

IP is best explained by beginning with the protocol between IP modules, which is defined with reference to the IP header format (Table 11.6). The header is largely self-explanatory. Some clarifying remarks:

- *Lifetime:* In NBS-IP, this field indicates the maximum number of gateways

**TABLE 11.6  IP Header Format**

| Name | Size (bits) | Purpose |
|------|-------------|---------|
| Version | 4 | Version of protocol |
| IHL | 4 | Header length in 32-bit words |
| Grade of service | 8 | Specify priority, reliability, and delay parameter |
| Data unit length | 16 | Length of datagram in octets |
| Identifier | 16 | Unique for protocol, source, destination |
| Flags | 3 | Includes more flag |
| Fragment offset | 13 | Offset of fragment in 64-bit units |
| Lifetime | 8 | Number of allowed hops |
| User protocol | 8 | Protocol layer that invoked IP |
| Header checksum | 16 | Applies to header only |
| Source address | 64 | 16-bit net, 48-bit host |
| Destination address | 64 | 16-bit net, 48-bit host |
| Options | Variable | Specifies additional services |
| Padding | Variable | Ensures that header ends on 32-bit boundary |

that a datagram may visit. It is used to prevent endlessly circulating datagrams. DOD specifies this field in units of seconds, for the same purpose, and also to permit reassembly to be aborted at timeout.

- *Checksum:* This is computed at each gateway.
- *Address:* The DOD address fields are 32 bits long, and the allocation of bits to network and host addresses is variable.
- *Options:* The only NBS option defined so far is a security field to indicate the security level of the datagram. In addition, DOD defines: Source Routing, which allows the source host to dictate the routing; Record Route, used to trace the route a datagram takes; Internet Timestamp.

### IP Services

IP provides a connectionless data transfer service to IP users (e.g., TCP, TP) in hosts attached to networks of the catenet. Three primitives are defined at the user–IP interface. The DATA.request primitive is used to request transmission of a data unit. DATA.indication is used by IP to notify a user of the arrival of a data unit. Finally, an ERROR primitive may be used to notify a user of failure to deliver a datagram. This service is not assumed to be reliable; that is, there is no guarantee that errors will be reported.

The formats for the three primitives:

- DATA.request (source-network, source-host, destination-network, destination-host, user-protocol, grade-of-service, data-unit-identifier, data-unit-lifetime, options, data).
- DATA.indication (source-network, source-host, destination-network, destination-host, user-protocol, grade-of-service, options, data).

- ERROR (source-network, source-host, destination-network, destination-host, user-protocol, data-unit-identifier, error-location, error-type).

It is easy to see how these primitives can be mapped into the IP header format. The DOD specification is less formal but similar to the NBS one. It does not specify an error primitive and has a RECEIVE primitive, instead of DATA.indication, which must be invoked by the user to indicate a readiness to receive data from a particular host.

### IP-Network Interface

IP is designed to operate in a catenet consisting of diverse individual networks. Therefore, only a minimum level of service is expected and the requirement is only for an unreliable datagram service. The IP layer in a host or gateway may choose to take advantage of a higher level of service if it is available on a particular network. For example, two gateways on the same X.25 network may choose to maintain a virtual circuit between them if they expect to exchange a lot of traffic.

The specific format and content of the IP-network primitives will depend on the nature of the network interface. Thus the IP layer in each host and gateway must be tailored to the network or networks to which it is attached. NBS specifies the following minimum service:

- DATA.request [source-host, destination-host, user-protocol (internet), grade-of-service, options, data].
- DATA.indication [destination-host, user-protocol (internet), data].

The source and destination host fields specify the correspondent IP entities attached to this network. The user protocol needs to be specified to indicate to the destination host that this packet contains an internet datagram. This allows purely intranetwork traffic to avoid the overhead of an IP header. The grade-of-service and options parameters are passed down from the IP user, and the data field is the IP datagram. Note that the destination host is not assumed to be able to use any but the most essential parameters.

# X.75

The X.75 standard was developed by CCITT as a supplement to X.25. It is designed for use between public X.25 networks and is not likely to be used or even allowed as an interface between public and private networks. However, it could also be used to connect a collection of private X.25 networks in a catenet that does not include public networks.

Figure 11.5 depicts the principle of X.75. As shown, X.25 specifies an interface between host equipment (DTE) and user equipment (DCE) that encompasses layers 1 through 3 and permits the set up, maintenance, and

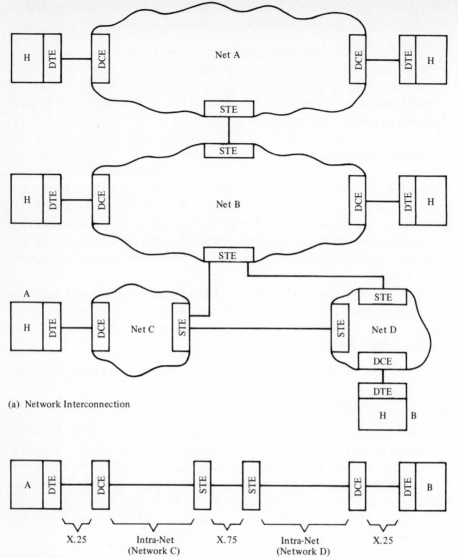

(a) Network Interconnection

(b) Protocols

**FIGURE 11–5.  Interconnection of X.25 Networks via X.75.**

termination of virtual circuits between two DTEs. X.75 specifies signal terminating equipment (STE) that act as DCE-level gateways to connect two X.25
networks.

The interconnection of X.25 networks via X.75 provides a DTE–DTE virtual
circuit as a connected series of virtual circuits:

- DCE to STE (intranetwork)
- STE to STE (internetwork)
- 0 or more:

- •• STE to STE (intranetwork)
- •• STE to STE (internetwork)
- • STE to DCE

Each section is a distinct entity with a separate virtual circuit, and separate flow control and error control.

From the point of view of the DTE, however, it merely sees an enlarged X.25 network; X.75 is invisible. The DTE–DCE interface is still defined by X.25. As before, intranetwork protocols are undefined. The internetwork STE–STE interface is defined by X.75.

The transmission of a packet between two hosts can be explained with reference to Figure 11.5b. Host A sends an X.25 data packet to its DCE with the virtual circuit number (group, channel) that it associates with a connection to B. This packet is transmitted via network C to an STE. The STE uses the same format (Figure 11.6b), but modifies the virtual circuit number and flow control information for the appropriate STE–STE virtual circuit. The receiving STE then sends the packet to B's DCE, which presents a packet to B with the virtual circuit number that B associates with a connection to A. Three important points about this process:

- • There is no encapsulation by the STEs. The same layer 3 header format is reused.
- • There is no end-to-end protocol. As in a single X.25 network, all information has local significance only.
- • Because of the 12-bit field, an STE–STE internet link can handle a maximum of 4096 connections.

Call Request and Clear Request are handled step by step but must propagate end to end. Routing information must exist within DCEs and STEs to accomplish

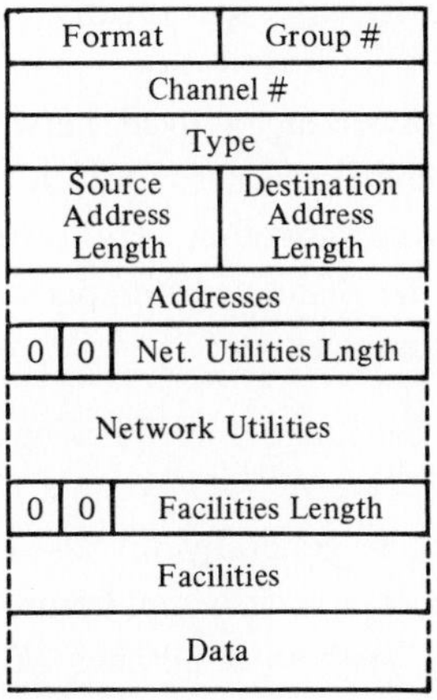

| Format | Group # |
|---|---|
| Channel # | |
| Type | |
| Source Address Length | Destination Address Length |
| Addresses | |
| 0 0 Net. Utilities Lngth | |
| Network Utilities | |
| 0 0 Facilities Length | |
| Facilities | |
| Data | |

(a) Control

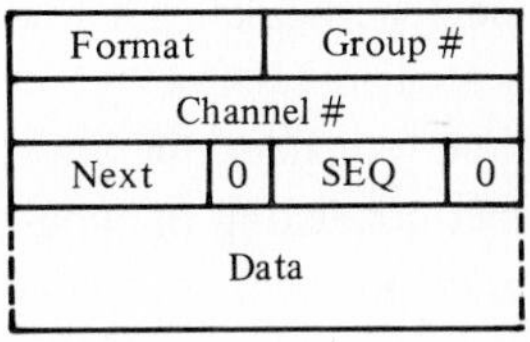

| Format | Group # |
|---|---|
| Channel # | |
| Next 0 SEQ 0 | |
| Data | |

(b) Data

FIGURE 11–6.  X.75 Formats.

this. For example, a CALL REQUEST packet from A triggers the set up of a DCE–STE virtual circuit. Using the X.75 control packet format, which differs from X.25 only in the addition of a network-level utilities field, an STE–STE virtual circuit is set up between networks C and D. The CALL REQUEST packet then propagates to B's DCE, setting up another virtual circuit. Finally, a CALL INDICATION packet is delivered to B. The same procedure is used for CALL ACCEPTED and CLEAR REQUEST packets.

### X.25 Gateway

Brief mention should be made of another way in which X.25 can be used to provide internet service to a local network [GRAN83]. Assume that we have a local network which provides an X.25 interface via NIU, and we desire to hook this into a public X.25 network. A gateway could be provided that functions as a DTE on the public network. All CALL REQUEST packets from local network hosts addressed to public network hosts would be routed to the gateway. The gateway would serve to terminate a local network virtual circuit and set up a virtual circuit on the public network. From the point of view of the public network, the entire local network appears as a single DTE. Up to 4096 simultaneous connections can be accommodated.

## 11.5

## REMARKS

Much of the material of this chapter, particularly in Sections 11.3 and 11.4, has dealt in general with the issues of internetworking, without specific reference to local networks. This section includes some remarks specifically concerned with local networks.

First, consider the most general case of connecting a local network to a catanet consisting of long-haul networks and other local networks. A common internet protocol is needed to bind these networks together. The difficulty in doing so in a cost-effective way stems from the distinct differences between local and long-haul networks. The two key differences are:

- *Speed:* Local network links are typically in the range 1 to 50 Mbps. Long-haul links are often 56 kbps or less.
- *Outstanding packets:* The local network link is generally direct—no intermediate switches—and fast enough that one packet is delivered before another is sent out. On a long-haul network, there may be a number of packets outstanding between two hosts.

Let us consider these differences in the context of the IP protocol. With IP, packets may arrive out of order—either because multiple routes are used or because a packet is damaged or destroyed. It is assumed that a higher-layer protocol (TCP, TP) will buffer the packets and pass them on in correct order. This places a burden on local network hosts heretofore not required.

Next, consider that with IP both error and flow control may be handled simply by discarding packets. The upper layer is expected to exercise end-to-end flow control and to recover from errors via the sequence number mechanism. Because of the mismatch in speed between local and long-haul networks, effective hop-by-hop flow control is vital. If a local network floods a long haul gateway, which simply discards the overflow, a positive feedback mechanism may arise, in which the local network sends new packets to the gateway and retransmits old ones. Alternatives:

- The gateway–host IP over a local net could be expanded to include some specific form of flow control. The simplest form would be that a local network host would wait for a positive acknowledgment to each packet before transmitting the next. Alternatively, a sliding-window protocol could be used.
- The gateway could send control packets to each local network host advising it of the degree of congestion in the next network.

Thus problems relating to sequencing, error control, and flow control indicate that IP as it stands is not ideal for bringing local networks into the catanet. In looking at this problem it is useful to consider IP and the next-higher layer as a unit, since together they provide a complete internet transport service. With this viewpoint, a number of alternatives are suggested in [WARN80]. Warner considers TCP as the next-higher layer, but the alternatives have more general applicability:

1. Implement TCP/IP in every host, using TCP as the intranetwork transport protocol. This has the virtue of simplicity, but it places an unnecessary processing and header length overhead on intranetwork traffic.
2. Use TCP/IP for long haul, and a separate transport protocol for intranetwork in each host. If, for example, the local network provides IEEE-802 LLC, then the intranet transport protocol can be very streamlined. This approach achieves good utilization of both local and long-haul links. However, it requires two layer 4 modules in each host, and it does not solve the flow control problem.
3. Terminate TCP/IP at the gateway. Intranetwork traffic, including host-to-gateway, would use the local network's transport protocol. The gateway would translate this to the long-haul TCP and string together two transport connections.
4. Implement a subset of TCP for intranetwork traffic. This approach has been taken by Warner and also investigated by MITRE [HOLM81], who have placed a streamlined TCP/IP,  with a combined header length of 192 bits (down from 320), in the NIU.

Options 2 and 4 seem to be the most desirable. Both attempt to tailor the protocol to the needs of the particular network while providing a uniform protocol for all networks. With either approach, the local network gateway should be augmented in two ways. First, one of the flow control mechanisms mentioned earlier should be implemented. Second, reassembly of fragmented packets should be possible at the gateway. This is particularly important for CSMA networks, where short packets lead to inefficiency.

For certain kinds of ring networks, however, option 3 may be desirable. Consider that the minimum length of an IP header is 160 bits, and that of TCP is 160, for a total of 320 bits. For slotted ring, and perhaps register insertion, this is an unacceptable header overhead. Also, option 3 may be preferred from the point of view of the catanet because it limits the number of hosts and networks which must be known centrally.

Despite its problems, however, IP is the best approach for the general case. It provides the flexibility required to interconnect multiple networks of various types.

In special cases, other approaches may be considered. For connecting a single local network that offers an X.25 interface to a public X.25 network, the X.25 gateway is an effective approach. To connect multiple local networks, which may be different internally but which all offer X.25, a private X.75 network is attractive. The packet header on a data packet is a mere 24 bits for X.25/X.75. Finally, for homogeneous local networks, nothing more than a bridge is needed.

## 11.6

## RECOMMENDED READING

The best overall discussion of internetworking is [CERF78]. A comparison of X.75 and IP can be found in [POST80]. A good general discussion of IP is presented in [NBS80a]. Other useful discussions: [DRIV79], [POST81], and [SHEL82].

For local networks, a specific discussion can be found in [WAIN82]*. [WARN80]* lists some of the problems of including local networks in an IP catanet. [DALA82]* is a readable and thorough discussion of the Ethernet approach. [SUNS79] is an interesting checklist of design issues.

## 11.7

## PROBLEMS

**11.1** Consider a token-passing local network configured as a single system with $N$ stations or two systems with $N/2$ stations each connected by a bridge. Assume no delay at the bridge other than medium access delay. Do a breakpoint analysis of the type of Chapter 9 to show the relative delay characteristics of the two configurations as a function of the percentage of internetwork traffic.

**11.2** Discuss the protocol architecture implications of the various hybrid network connections described in Section 11.2.

**11.3** Describe a mechanism for implementing the hidden network (see Section 11.3) using TCP/IP.

**11.4** Because of fragmentation, an IP datagram can arrive in pieces, not necessarily in the right order. The IP layer at the receiving host must accumulate these fragments until the original datagram is reconstituted.

    **a.** Consider that the IP layer creates a buffer for assembling the datagram. As assembly proceeds the buffer will consist of data and ''holes'' between the data. Describe an algorithm for reassembly based on this concept.

    **b.** For the algorithm above, it is necessary to keep track of the holes. Describe a simple mechanism for doing this.

**11.5** For the X.25 gateway (Section 11.4), how are CALL REQUEST packets from public network to local network accommodated?

# Local Network Design
# Issues

In this chapter we look at three important local network design issues. The first, and most complex, is that of network control. It is safe to say that more networks have come to grief because of inadequacies in network control than from any other problem.

Next, we look at the reliability, availability, and survivability of local networks. On the whole, local networks are rather reliable systems. However, the cost of a complete network failure to an organization is likely to be high, so this is an important area to address.

Finally, we look at the area of security. The requirements in this area vary widely from one installation to the next, but the same basic principles can be used in all cases.

All of these topics relate not just to local networks but to computer networks as well, and each is worthy of book-length treatment. All that we will attempt in this chapter is to introduce the concepts and then focus on some design issues of particular interest in the context of local networks.

## NETWORK CONTROL

A computer network is a complex system that cannot create or run itself. The manager of the network must be able to configure the network, monitor its status, react to failures and overloads, and plan intelligently for future growth.

We begin by looking at and defining the overall concept of network management, which encompasses a host of human and automated tasks designed to support the network manager. These principles apply whether the network is local or not. We then focus on those aspects of network control that are unique to local networks, looking in turn at the distinctive requirements of packet-switched and circuit-switched networks. Finally, we show how these concepts relate to the somewhat different concept of computer network control.

### Network Management

Network management is a broad concept that encompasses those tasks, human and automated, that "support" the creation, operation, and evolution of a network. The word support is used advisedly. Network management does not encompass the actual managerial function of controlling the development and ongoing use of a system, nor the disciplines required to actually develop and modify the system. Rather, it is the "glue" or infrastructure of techniques and procedures that assure the proper operation of a system (see [STAL80]).

In this section, we review briefly the key elements of network management. We use this to set the context for the discussion that follows, which focuses on some network control features for local networks.

Network management encompasses the following functions or disciplines:

- Operations
- Administration
- Maintenance
- Configuration management
- Documentation/training
- Data base management
- Planning
- Security

A brief discussion follows. A more thorough treatment, using somewhat different categories, can be found in [FREE82].

Operations management is responsible for the day-to-day operation of the network. A key element of operations is the status of the network, including traffic and performance status, active devices, and accounting and billing information. It should be possible to monitor response time performance, locate bottlenecks, and record information for later analysis and for customer or user accounting.

Administration deals with managing the use of the network. This includes such things as system generation, assigning user passwords, managing resource and file access, and billing users.

Maintenance is that key function which assures that the network continues to operate. It involves, first, detecting and reporting problems. Once a problem is known, it must be isolated to determine the cause. Finally, the problem must be resolved. Many of the detection and even isolation functions can be automated. Nevertheless, much of the maintenance activity is a human task. Maintenance management can support this task with a data base of events and network characteristics and components, and some automated capabilities for determining problem resolution.

The three functions discussed so far can, at least partially, be supported by a *network control center* (NCC). The following subsections will describe desirable attributes of an NCC. Before that, however, we briefly summarize the remaining network management functions.

The primary objective of configuration management (CM) is the effective management of a system's life cycle and its evolving configuration. CM identifies hardware and software components of the system at an appropriate level for control—not so aggregated that the specific functions are not visible, and not so disaggregated as to create an overwhelming amount of detail. CM tracks each component through the system life cycle, documenting and controlling any changes, and ensuring that the overall system retains its integrity and conforms to requirements. CM also maintains information on the status of each system component.

The documentation/training function is responsible for educational functions, including CAI, and for developing and maintaining documentation. Data base management provides the capability for a network management data base. Planning is responsible for ongoing requirements analysis and configuration change planning. Security is responsible for prevention and detection of unauthorized network access.

This capsule summary should give the reader some idea of the tremendous scope of network management. We narrow our focus now to those aspects of network management that can be implemented in a local network control center.

## The Network Control Center: LAN/HSLN

In many LANs and HSLNs, a network control center (NCC) is provided. Typically, this device attaches to the network through an NIU and consists of a keyboard/screen interface and a microcomputer. Except for the smallest networks (fewer than 10 to 20 NIUs), an NCC is vital. It supports key operations, administration, and maintenance functions. The need for an automated set of functions with an operator interface for controlling the complexities of a network is beyond doubt. For a good discussion of some of the problems of networking, the reader is referred to [WILE82]. In this section we list some of the important NCC functions; their value should become clear as the discussion proceeds.

All of the functions of an NCC involve observation, active control, or a combination of the two. They fall into three categories:

• Configuration functions
• Monitoring functions
• Fault isolation

### NCC Configuration Functions

One of the principal functions of an NCC is to control the link layer connections between NIU ports or service access points. A connection can be set up in one of two ways. First, the link layer protocol in the NIU can issue a connection request to another NIU, either in response to higher-layer software or a terminal user command. These could be referred to as "switched connections." Second, the NCC could set up a permanent connection between two NIUs.

The operation of the permanent connection is simple. The NCC sets parameters in the NIU indicating that all data received from a particular attached device are to be routed to a designated destination address. As the NIU receives the data, they are wrapped in a link layer frame with the appropriate destination address and transmitted. The NCC can also, under operator command, break a connection (permanent or switched). Another useful feature is being able to designate a backup or alternate address to be used in case the primary destination fails to respond.

A related NCC function is that of directory management. The NCC can maintain a name/address table that allows users to request a connection by name. Thus network resources can be identified by an operator-specified symbolic name rather than a fixed address. A resource may be any device or service—terminals, hosts, peripherals, application programs, or utility programs. For example, a user at a terminal who wishes to use the accounts payable package could request it with LOGON ACCTSP. This gives the operator, via the NCC, the ability to move applications around (for load balancing or because a host is down). The directory is kept at the NCC, but portions or all of it can also be down-line loaded to NIUs to reduce the network traffic required for directory look-up. An example of a directory service is described in [BASS80].

The NCC can also control the operation of the NIUs. The NCC could have the ability to shut down and start up NIUs and to set NIU parameters. For example, an NIU may be restricted to a certain set of NIUs or destination names that it can communicate with. This is a simple means of setting up a type of security system. Assuming that the MAC protocol supports it, NIUs can be assigned priorities.

## NCC Monitoring Functions

A second important set of functions that can be performed by an NCC is that of network monitoring. This activity falls into three categories: performance monitoring, network status, and accounting.

Performance monitoring encompasses three components: performance measurement, which is the actual gathering of statistics about network traffic and timing; performance analysis, which consists of software for reducing and presenting the data; and synthetic traffic generation, which permits the network to be observed under a controlled load. One obvious motivation for a performance monitoring facility is that it can be used to validate analytic and simulation models of LAN/HSLN performance. This is of interest to researchers and designers. But performance monitoring has a key operational role as well. It allows the network manager to assess the current status of the network, to locate bottlenecks and other problems, and to plan for future growth.

Table 12.1 lists the types of measurements reported at one local network facility [AMER82, AMER83] and gives some idea of the kind of measurements

**TABLE 12.1  Performance Measurement Reports**

| Name | Variables | Description |
|------|-----------|-------------|
| Host communication matrix | Source × destination | (Number, %) of (packets, data packets, data bytes) |
| Group communication matrix | Source × destination | As above, consolidated into address groups |
| Packet type histogram | Packet type | (Number, %) of (packets, original packets) by type |
| Data packet size histogram | Packet size | (Number, %) of data packets by data byte length |
| Throughput-utilization distribution | Source | (Total bytes, data bytes) transmitted |
| Packet interarrival time histogram | Interarrival time | Time between consecutive carrier (network busy) signals |
| Channel acquisition delay histogram | NIU acquisition delay | (Number, %) of packets delayed at NIU by given amount |
| Communication delay histogram | Packet delay | Time from original packet ready at source to receipt |
| Collision count histogram | Number of collisions | Number of packets by number of collisions |
| Transmission count histogram | Number of transmissions | Number of packets by transmission attempts |

*Source:* [AMER82].

that are of interest. Amer lists some examples of the types of questions that can be answered with these reports. Questions concerning possible errors or inefficiencies include:

- Is traffic evenly distributed among the network users or are there source–destination pairs with unusually heavy traffic?
- What is the percentage of each type of packet? Are some packet types of unusually high frequency, indicating an error or an inefficient protocol?
- What is the distribution of data packet sizes? Are variable size data packets worth the additional overhead or would fixed size packets suffice?
- What are the channel acquisition and communication delay distributions? Are these times excessive?
- Are collisions a factor in getting packets transmitted, indicating possible faulty hardware or protocols?
- What is the information utilization and throughput? How do the information statistics compare with the channel statistics?

A second area has to do with increasing traffic load and varying packet sizes:

- What is the effect of traffic load on utilization, throughput, and time delays? When, if ever, does traffic load start to degrade system performance?
- Defining a stable network as one whose utilization is a nondecreasing function of traffic load, what is the trade off among stability, throughput, and delay?
- What is the maximum capacity of the channel under normal operating conditions? How many active users are necessary to reach this maximum?
- Do larger packets increase or decrease throughput and delay?
- How does constant packet size affect utilization and delay?

These areas are certainly of interest to the network manager. Other questions of concern have to do with response time and throughput by user class and determining how much growth the network can absorb before certain performance thresholds are crossed.

Because of the broadcast nature of LANs and HSLNs, many of the measurement data can be collected passively at the NCC, without perturbing the network. The NCC's NIU can be programmed to accept all packets, regardless of destination address. For a heavily loaded network, this may not be possible, and a sampling scheme must be used. A local network containing bridges presents some problem; one collection point per segment is required. On a ring, passive monitoring will catch all packets only if they are removed at the source rather than the destination.

However, not all information can be centrally collected. To get end-to-end measures, even within the local network, would require knowing the time of arrival of packets from devices to the NIUs. A number of protocol-specific measures cannot be centrally collected. For example, for CSMA/CD, the following measures are of interest:

- Mean amount of time an NIU defers before transmitting.
- Number of collisions by source NIU.
- Mean number of collisions per packet.

All of these measures require some collection capability at the NIUs. From time to time, the NIUs can send the collected data to the NCC. Unfortunately, this technique increases the complexity of the NIU and requires overhead communication.

A second major area of NCC monitoring is that of network status. The NCC keeps track of which NIUs are currently activated and the connections that exist. This information is displayed to the operator on request.

Finally, the NCC can support some accounting and billing functions. This can be done on either a device or user basis. For the latter, the NCC must be aware of the identity of network users. This topic is addressed in Section 12.3.

### NCC Fault Isolation Functions

The NCC can continuously monitor the network to detect faults and, to the extent possible, narrow the fault down to a single component or small group of components.

This topic is explored in Section 12.2. Here we mention two common techniques for fault isolation. The NCC can periodically poll each NIU, requesting that it return a status packet. Alternatively, each NIU can be required to periodically and automatically (without poll) emit a status packet. When an NIU fault is detected, the NCC can alert the operator and also attempt to disable the NIU so that it does not interfere with the network.

An example of an NCC used for fault isolation is reported in [CHRI78].

## The Network Control Center: CBX/Digital Switch

The functions that can be performed by an NCC for a CBX or digital switch are similar to those for a LAN or HSLN. Again, the NCC will have a keyboard/screen interface. For a switch, however, the NCC intelligence is not stand-alone but integrated into the control unit of the switch.

As before, we can organize the functions into configuration, monitoring, and fault isolation.

### NCC Configuration Functions

When a new line or set of lines is added to a switch, its parameters must be defined, unless the switch is capable of handling only one kind of input. This can be done via the NCC. Examples of parameters include data rate, code (e.g., ASCII), and whether echo-back is required. These parameters would generally be the same for all lines terminating in one physical group (see Figure 7.16).

Logical groups may also be defined and parameterized. A good example of this is a port contention group. A common name must be defined. In addition, there might be a permission list, restricting access to a designated set of terminal lines. If queueing is permitted, the queue size must be defined. Other parameters, such as priorities and maximum holding time, can be included.

For switches that do not have a user port selection capability, the NCC must be used to actually configure the network (i.e., set up the connections between devices). This is generally done at system generation time and changed only occasionally. Connections can be one to one, or many to many as for port contention. In either case, the user need not (and cannot) select a port—it is done automatically.

The NCC can also dynamically force and break connections. An example of the use of the break command is to release a connection when a device has been abandoned but not turned off. The NCC should also be able to close a queue to a port (i.e., not allow any new calls to queue) and to clear a queue. This action can be used to prepare a resource to be disabled and tested.

### NCC Monitoring Functions

As with a packet-switched local network, certain traffic statistics are of interest for a circuit-switched network. The parameters differ, though. Examples:

- Number of calls (connection requests) by user, user group.
- Mean connection time.
- Calls lost.
- Queue statistics: queue length, queueing time, number of queue overflows.

These statistics give the network manager a good indication of utilization and enable informed planning for future growth.

For accounting and billing purposes, more detailed information is needed, particularly if the switch has a trunk to the long-haul network. A measurement process referred to in the PBX world as *call detail recording* (CDR) is used. CDR records all pertinent information related to all calls placed by individual stations or user groups. For each call the record would include calling extension (address), called extension, date, time, and duration.

Finally, the NCC monitoring function includes status reporting. Summary information would include current number of connections and queue sizes. More detailed data may also be displayable. For example, for each data line, the NCC could provide:

- Enabled/disabled
- Connection status (idle, service, ringing, connected)
- Group membership
- Data rate
- Device type
- Echo/non-echo
- ASCII/non-ASCII
- Originate-only, answer-only, or both

### NCC Fault Isolation Functions

The NCC can report the status of lines, to include a line that is supposed to be active but fails to respond to a connection request. In addition, the NCC should be able to put individual devices in loop-back mode and test the device by sending a stream of data and comparing that to returned data.

### Computer Network Control

We close this section with a word about what local network control is not. It is not a capability for controlling the operation of a computer network. What we have been talking about so far may be referred to as communications network control. In contrast, computer network control encompasses activities at all layers of the OSI model.

Figure 12.1 is a depiction of computer network control. A *node management workstation* (NMW) exists at the application level. Each layer includes a supervisory part that interfaces with the node management workstation. The NMW executes supervisory and control functions and retrieves information collected in each layer. In addition, as an application, the NMW can establish sessions with NMWs in other nodes.

For computer network control two other elements are needed:

- *One or more storage facilities:* These can be used by NMWs, either locally or remotely to store data.
- *One or more operator interface modules:* These can be used by an operator to control the NMWs.

Examples of computer network control actions:

- Enabling/disabling network objects (paths, virtual circuits, nodes, communication links).
- Gathering statistics on objects.
- Inquiring current status of objects.
- Running tests through network.

Thus, although there may be some overlap, the responsibilities of communications network control and computer network control are distinct. It is possible, at least in a homogeneous network, to merge the two facilities. But for now, it is likely that the local network manager will need two NCCs and two operator interfaces.

## 12.2

## RELIABILITY, AVAILABILITY, SURVIVABILITY

The purpose of this section is to introduce the reader to the concepts of reliability, availability, and survivability (RAS) as they relate to local networks. A detailed

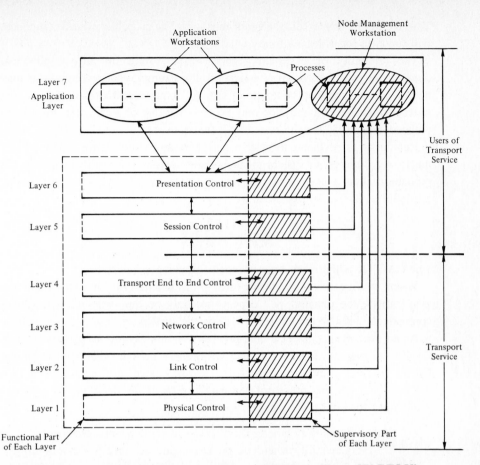

**FIGURE 12–1.    Network Control within an OSI Node (From [ELDE82]).**

look at this topic, which would draw extensively on mathematical analysis and electrical engineering, is beyond the scope of this book. This brief discussion merely attempts to raise some architectural issues specifically related to local networks.

## Basic Concepts

We begin by introducing the basic concepts of interest. This discussion is based on [KATZ78].

Reliability is the probability that a system or component will perform its specified function for a specified time under specified conditions. Component failure is expressed by the *mean time between failures* (MTBF). Typically, it is assumed that the "up" time for a component is exponentially distributed:

$$\Pr[T < t] = 1 - e^{-\lambda t}$$

Thus the MTBF is $1/\lambda$, and the variance is $1/\lambda^2$. The probability that a component will function for at least a time $t$ is $e^{-\lambda t}$.

The reliability of a system depends on the reliability of its individual components plus the system organization. For example, some components may be redundant, such that the failure of just one component does not affect system operation. Or the configuration may be such that loss of a component results in reduced capability, but the system still functions.

Reliability is pertinent to system designers and maintenance engineers. Of much more interest to system managers and users is availability, which is the probability that a system or component is available at a given time $t$. The availability, $A$, can be expressed as

$$A = \frac{\text{MTBF}}{\text{MTBF} + \text{MTTR}}$$

where MTTR is the mean time to repair following a failure.

When dealing with the availability of a function or service (functional availability), the quantity will depend not only on the availability of system components but also the expected load on the system.

As an example, consider a dual-processor system. Nonpeak periods account for 40% of requests for service, and during those periods, either processor can handle the load. During peak periods, both processors are required to handle the full load, but one processor can handle 80% of the peak load. Functional availability for the system can be expressed as:

$$A_F = (\text{Capability when one processor is up}) \cdot \Pr[1 \text{ processor up}]$$
$$+ (\text{Capability when two processors are up}) \cdot \Pr[2 \text{ processors up}]$$

The probability that both processors are up is $A^2$, where $A$ is the availability of either processor. The probability of just one processor up is $A(1 - A) + (1 - A)A = 2A - 2A^2$. Using a value for $A$ of 0.9, and recalling that one processor is sufficient for nonpeak loads, we have

$$A_F(\text{nonpeak}) = (1.0)(0.18) + (1.0)(0.81) = 0.99$$

and, for peak periods

$$A_F(\text{peak}) = (0.8)(0.18) + (1.0)(0.81) = 0.954$$

Overall functional availability, then, is

$$A_F = 0.6A_F(\text{peak}) + 0.4A_F(\text{nonpeak}) = 0.9684$$

Thus, on the average, about 97% of requests for service can be handled by the system.

Finally, survivability is the probability that a function or service is available after a specified subset of components or systems become unavailable.

With these concepts in mind, we can now turn to the RAS concerns for local networks. Generally, two types of problems can disrupt communications. The first is transmission errors. Typically, the error rates on local network media are very low, on the order of $10^{-8}$ to $10^{-11}$. This type of error is handled by the various protocol layers and need not concern us here.

The second kind of problem is component failure or malfunction, which is the problem that relates to RAS. We can categorize these components into network components and attached devices. We are not interested, in this section, in attached device failures. An attached device failure should not cause the loss of the entire network—only the function or service offered by that device is lost. Of course, if the device performs a network-critical role, such as a network access logon server, its loss could indeed cripple the network. But this is an application-related problem and will not be examined here.

Which leaves us with RAS concerns related to local network component failure, a topic to which we now turn.

## Broadband Networks

The advantage of a broadband network is its tremendous capacity and flexibility. A great number and variety of devices dispersed over a large area can be supported on a single network. This advantage is also the most serious danger of a broadband system: loss of the network can be catastrophic. Such vulnerability is unacceptable in most organizations. Hence the architecture of the local network must overcome the inherent weakness of broadband.

Four elements of the local network need to be addressed:

1. *Headend:* This is a "single point of failure." Loss of the headend means loss of the entire network.
2. *Transmission medium:* The transmission medium consists of standard CATV cable, taps, splitters, and amplifiers. These components are highly reliable, with a typical mean time between failures (MTBF) of 18 years for amplifiers and 30 to 40 years for all other components [COOP82]. It is, however, possible for a failure to occur due to accidental or deliberate physical trauma. Also, because amplifiers draw power from the cable itself, loss of power supply can disable the cable.
3. *Network interface unit:* The NIU presents less of an availability and survivability problem than the headend or medium. In general, malfunction of an NIU does not affect the network as a whole; it merely denies access to the attached device or devices. There is, however, one way in which NIU failure can affect the entire network: jamming. If an NIU remains in a transmit mode, the affected channel or channels are useless.
4. *Network control center:* The NCC also presents a relatively minor availability problem. The NCC is actually not required during steady-state operation of the network for most systems. Individual NIUs are capable of making and breaking connections and exchanging data.

Let us now look briefly at measures that can be taken to improve broadband RAS.

### Headend

The passive headend used in the dual-cable configuration is simply a length of cable joining the two portions of the system. It is as reliable as the rest of the transmission medium, treated below.

For a midsplit system, failure of the frequency converter, an active component, causes failure of the entire network. A hot backup can be supplied that can override the primary converter and control the cable. Care must be taken to assure that a malfunctioning backup does not seize control from a functioning primary converter. Schematically, the configuration is depicted in Figure 12.2.

### Transmission Medium

The next area of concern is the cable itself. An obvious means to improve reliability is by providing a backup cable (in the case of a dual cable, a dual backup cable is required). Each NIU could have two cable ports for connecting to the two cables. When a fault is detected on the primary cable, the NCC could use the backup cable to send a message to each NIU, instructing it to use the backup cable for future transmissions.

If there is a component failure, such as a tap or amplifier, the backup cable architecture is a good solution. However, the scheme seems less reliable as a means of recovering from physical cable damage. As a practical matter, the backup cable must be located near the primary cable along its entire length. This enables the NIUs to be attached to both cables with a reasonable amount of drop cable. Consequently, any physical damage sustained by the primary may also affect the backup cable.

An alternative or supplementary measure is the use of addressable taps [WILL81]. The NCC can probe the quality of the line by sending control signals

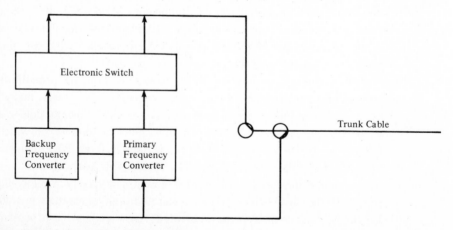

**FIGURE 12–2.  Redundant Head End.**

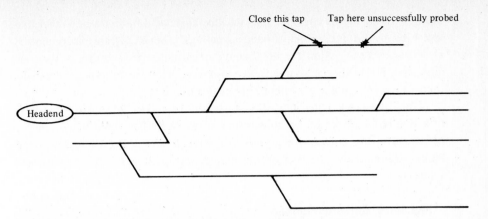

**FIGURE 12–3. Use of Addressable Taps for Fault Isolation.**

to successive taps. The signal instructs the tap to return a signal which is compared with a stored value of expected magnitude. For a dual-cable system, the tap must merely be able to open and close, passing signals in an open state and returning them ("loop-back") in a closed state. For midsplit systems, the tap must be more complex, capable of accepting a control signal on one frequency and transmitting one on another frequency.

When a fault is isolated, the NCC can send another control signal to a tap, causing the tap to shut off the part of the cable beyond it. The tap selected should be the one just inbound of the tap that was unsuccessfully probed (see Figure 12.3). In this way, damage to the cable will affect only those stations downstream from the fault (away from the headend). The effectiveness of this measure can be increased by using a heavily branched topology rather than a single linear bus. Obviously, if damage occurs on the main trunk near the headend, the entire network will be lost.

Other than the headend, the only active CATV components are the amplifiers. Parallel redundant amplifiers can be used, with only a modest increase in attenuation.

Despite all these measures, a network manager or user can have legitimate concern about the availability of a large local network. A simple, effective measure is to partition the network into subnetworks joined by bridges and point-to-point links. Each subnetwork would have its own headend and perhaps its own NCC.

### Network Interface Units

As mentioned above, a typical NIU failure affects only the attached device or devices. However, some failure in logic could cause an NIU to transmit excessively, jamming the channel. Other problems: A transmitter malfunction could produce distorted signals; a receiver failure would interfere with CSMA protocols.

To guard against the most serious problem, jamming, addressable taps can again be used. In this case, the taps must be signaled on a frequency other than that used by the NIUs (out-of-band signaling). The NCC can experimentally close taps, starting with the most remote ones, until the jamming is shut out. This also pinpoints the source of the problem. The use of subnetworks also limits the havoc that a streaming NIU can cause.

To detect more benign failures, it is useful for the NCC to monitor the status of active NIUs. This can be done in two ways. All NIUs could be required to periodically (e.g., once every second) emit a status packet addressed to the NCC. Alternatively, the NCC could periodically poll each NIU, requesting a status packet.

### Network Control Center

Because of the lesser availability concerns associated with the NCC, it is reasonable to take no measures to enhance its reliability. However, a hot backup, in the same spirit as that for the headend, could be used. The backup NCC would connect to the cable via an independent NIU and would monitor all cable activity without transmitting. If it detected an NCC failure, it would instruct the NCC's NIU to shut down and would then seize control of the network.

Another simple measure to enhance NCC availability is to connect it to the LAN via two separate NIUs. Then, failure of a single NIU will not cause the loss of the NCC.

### Baseband Bus Networks

The architecture of a baseband bus network entails fewer availability concerns compared to broadband. Referring back to Figure 4.3, the baseband bus has no active components (headend, amplifiers) and for large networks consists of segments connected by repeaters. Hence there is less likelihood of failure and the failure can easily be confined to a single segment.

To assure this confinement, repeaters should contain sufficient intelligence not to transmit from a cable that is being jammed. Another measure, as in broadband, is the use of multiple cables. This is, in fact, often done with HSLNs (Figure 6.10).

NIU and NCC concerns are the same as for broadband LANs and can be treated in the same fashion.

### Ring Networks

The subject of ring reliability was addressed initially in Section 4.2. It was pointed out that the loss of a single link or repeater on a simple ring can result in the loss of the entire network. Measures for overcoming this inherent reliability problem were depicted in Figure 4.11 and are summarized here:

**LOCAL NETWORK DESIGN ISSUES**

- Ring wiring concentrators make it easy to isolate a fault and also to close a bypass relay to remove the problem.
- Multiple rings connected by bridges reduce the impact of a ring failure.

With the addition of some intelligence to the ring wiring concentrators [referred to as an active wiring concentrator (AWC)], fault recovery can be automated and availability improved [DIXO82, ANDR82]. First, we require that each repeater generate network timing signals on its outbound link when there is no message to send. Thus failure of a link or repeater is immediately known to the next repeater on the link by the loss of input signal. This station can then generate a beacon frame to inform downstream stations of the outage. The beacon frame includes the station's address, to identify the location of the problem. Within an AWC subring, the AWC intelligence or station is the last downstream station. When the beacon frame reaches the AWC station, the AWC can identify the failed lobe (repeater plus links) and remove it by closing a bypass switch.

The procedure above works for all repeaters and for all links except those between AWCs. To recover from an inter-AWC link failure, a backup ring that connects the AWCs and circulates in the opposite direction to the primary ring is used. Figure 12.4 illustrates the architecture. As an example, the circled numbers relate to the following events.

1. The link between AWC2 and AWC1 fails.
2. Ring station 1 detects loss of input and transmits a beacon frame.
3. The AWC1 station receives the frame and determines that the failure is upstream from ring station 1.
4. Assuming that the failure is in the link from AWC1 to ring station 1, AWC1 bypasses that lobe.
5. Ring station 2 now detects loss of input and transmits a beacon frame.
6. AWC1 now assumes that the problem is upstream.
7. AWC1 opens the bypass, reinserting ring station 1, and connects the backup segment from AWC3. This action breaks the flow of timing signals from AWC1 to AWC2 on the backup ring.
8. AWC2 detects the loss of timing signals and switches the primary ring flow from its own AWC ring station to the backup segment leading to AWC3.

These actions isolate the AWC2–AWC1 link fault and restore a closed ring.

In the configuration of Figure 12.4, the backup links are not used except when a failure occurs. A number of proposals have appeared which would use the backup or secondary links not only to increase availability but to improve throughput. The group at Ohio State [WOLF78] developed an enhancement to their register insertion ring, called Distributed Double Loop Computer Network (DDLCN), by providing two links between repeaters, one in each direction (Figure 12.5a). Traffic can be carried in either direction. If a fault occurs, stations on both sides can wrap around so that incoming data are repeated back

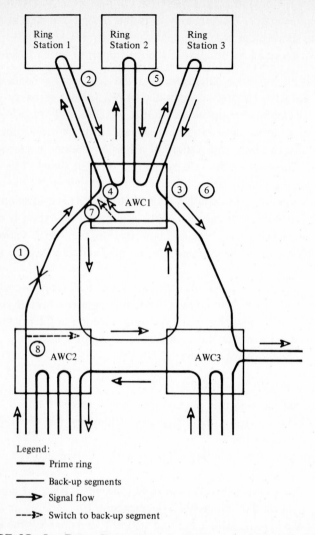

Legend:

—— Prime ring

—— Back-up segments

—▷ Signal flow

---▷ Switch to back-up segment

**FIGURE 12—4. Reconfiguration of a Ring with Wiring Concentrators.**

out in the direction they came from. Another double-loop network, called daisy chain loop, was proposed [GRNA80]. Here, the backup links connect every other node (Figure 12.5b). This network was shown to be superior to DDLCN in both reliability and performance in both the fault-free and fault modes of operation.

It should be intuitively clear that the delay performance of the daisy chain is superior to DDLCN. For example, for the 15-node rings illustrated, the maximum number of "hops" for DDLCN is 7, whereas for the daisy chain, it is 6. Also, intuitively, reliability is improved because there are more alternative paths in the daisy chain.

Further improvement can be had by increasing the length of the backward

(a) 15-node Distributed Double Loop Network

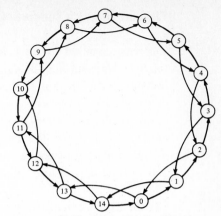

(b) 15-node Daisy-Chain Loop Network

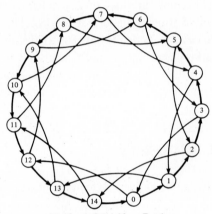

(c) 15-node Optimal Loop Topology

**FIGURE 12–5. Double-Loop Configurations.**

hop to $h = |\sqrt{N}|$, i.e. the largest integer less than or equal to $\sqrt{N}$ (for DDLCN $h = 1$; for daisy chain, $h = 2$). Figure 12.5c shows this architecture for a 15-station ring. It has been shown that this value of $h$ is optimal, both in terms of throughput and availability [RAGH81].

Of course, all of these double loop arrangements require more complexity and intelligence in the repeater, which now has two incoming and two outgoing links and must make a routing decision on each host transmission. A simpler scheme would be to have a separate and independent backup ring, analogous to the technique for bus and tree topologies. This falls midway between single ring and the integrated dual ring in both reliability and complexity.

Finally, we mention that NCC and NIU (excluding repeater) concerns are the same as for bus/tree LANs and can be treated in the same fashion.

## Digital Switch Networks

The most common approach to improving the availability of a digital switch is the use of redundancy, as illustrated in Figure 7.11. With the exception of the individual line cards, all of the components of the switch can be made redundant: power supply, processor, and special-purpose features such as a protocol convertor. Backup battery capability is usually provided to take over automatically in the event of power failure.

The primary processor is responsible for monitoring all devices for failure and running diagnostics. When a failure is detected, the failed component is disabled so that it will not interfere with switch operation, and an operator is alerted. The backup processor maintains a duplicate of all current status and connection data and continually exchanges monitor information with the primary. Should the backup detect a failure in the primary processor, it disables the primary and assumes control.

With this architecture, the loss of any single component other than a line card will cause no disruption or loss of service. The loss of a line card affects only the attached devices, typically only 8 or 16 devices. This loss is immediately reported and card replacement normally takes only a few minutes.

Availability is further improved in the hierarchical star architecture (Figure 7.18) if each of the switches is capable of independent operation.

## 12.3

## NETWORK SECURITY

Network security can be defined as the protection of network resources against unauthorized disclosure, modification, utilization, restriction, or destruction [CHAM80]. Security has long been an object of concern and study for both data processing systems and communications facilities. With computer networks, these concerns are combined. And for local networks, the problems may be most acute.

Consider a full-capacity local network, with direct terminal access to the network and data files and applications distributed among a variety of processors. The local network may also provide access to and from long-haul communications and be part of a catanet. The complexity of the task of providing security in such an environment is clear.

The subject is a broad one, and encompasses physical and administrative controls as well as automated ones. In this section we confine ourselves to considerations of automated security controls and focus attention on three areas of specific concern for local networks:

- Access control
- Encryption
- Multilevel security

More general discussions of computer network security can be found in [WOOD83c] and [DENN79].

## Access Controls

The purpose of access controls is to ensure that only authorized users have access to the system and its individual resources and that access to and modification of particular portions of data is limited to authorized individuals and programs.

Figure 12.6 depicts, generically, the measures taken to control access in a data processing system. They fall into two categories: first, those associated with the user or groups of users and, second, those associated with the data. In what follows, we elaborate on these concepts and extend them to the local networking environment.

The control of access by user is referred to as authentication. A quite common example of this on a time-sharing system is the user logon, which requires both a user id and a password. The system will only allow a user to logon if that user's id is known to the system and if the user knows the password associated by the system with that id. This id/password system is a notoriously unreliable method of access control. Users can forget their passwords, and accidentally or intentionally reveal their password. Also, the id/password file is subject to penetration attempts.

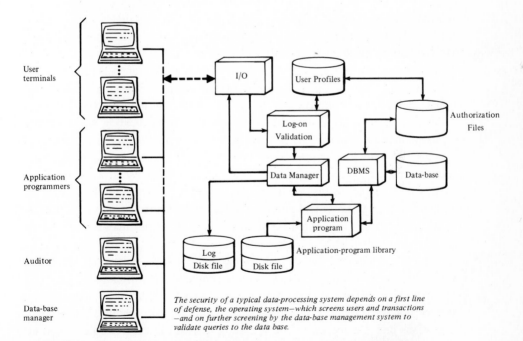

The security of a typical data-processing system depends on a first line of defense, the operating system—which screens users and transactions—and on further screening by the data-base management system to validate queries to the data base.

**FIGURE 12–6. Data Processing System Security (From [BERN82]).**

No cost-effective method of overcoming this problem exists. Exotic techniques such as voiceprints, fingerprints, and hand geometry analysis may be foolproof but are at present prohibitively expensive. Simple measures that can be taken now are to change passwords frequently and to maintain multiple tight measures of security over the id/password directory. One additional measure that is cost effective is to associate id's with terminals rather than users and hard wire the code into the terminal. This changes an administrative/software security problem into a physical security problem. However, if it is desirable to allow one-to-many and/or many-to-one relationships between users and terminals, this technique is ineffective.

The problem of authentication is compounded over a multiaccess medium LAN or HSLN. The logon dialogue must take place over the communications medium and eavesdropping is a potential threat. One approach to protection would be to certify that each NIU (except those of the NCC) can capture only data addressed to it. This is no easy task, as we discuss below. Another approach is to encrypt the id/password data. This is described below.

User and user group authentication can be either centralized or distributed. In a centralized approach the network provides a logon service, which we can think of as being associated with the NCC. In the case of a LAN or HSLN, this could be accomplished by setting up a connection between each inactive NIU and the NCC's NIU. When a user activates an NIU, the initial connection is automatically to the NCC. After a successful logon, the NCC then establishes a connection between the requesting NIU and the requested destination address. When this connection is terminated, the original user–NCC connection is reestablished. A similar technique would be used in a digital switch. A data port off-hook condition would result in a connection to a logon server; after authentication, the request connection would be made.

Distributed authentication treats the network as a transparent communication link, and the usual logon procedure is carried out by the destination host. Of course, the security concerns for multiaccess media must still be addressed.

In fact, in many local networks, two levels of authentication will probably be used. Individual hosts may be provided with a logon facility to protect host-specific resources and applications. In addition, the network as a whole may have protection to restrict network access to authorized users. This two-level facility is desirable for the common case, currently, in which the local network connects disparate hosts and simply provides a convenient means of terminal-host access. Future integrated networks (in the OSI sense) may require only a network-level scheme.

Following successful authentication, the user has been granted access to one or a set of hosts and/or processes. This is generally not sufficient for a system that includes sensitive data in its data base. Through the authentication procedure, a user can be identified together with a profile that specifies permissible operations and file accesses. The operating system can enforce rules based on the user profile. The data base management system, however, must control access to specific portions of records. For example, it may be permissible for anyone in administration to obtain a list of company personnel, but only selected individuals may have access to salary information. The issue is more than just one of level of detail. Whereas the operating system may grant a user permission to access a file or use an application, following which there are no further security checks, the data base management system must make a decision on each individual access attempt. That decision will depend not only on the user's identity but also on the specific parts of the record being accessed, and even on the information already divulged to the user.

A general model of access control as exercised by a data base management system is that of an access matrix (Table 12.2). One axis of the table consists of identified subjects that may attempt data access. Typically, this list will consist of individual users or user groups, although access could be controlled for terminals, hosts, or processes instead of or in addition to users. The other axis lists the objects that may be accessed. At the greatest level of detail, objects may be individual data fields. More aggregate groupings, such as records, record types, or even the entire data base may also be objects in the matrix. Each entry in the matrix indicates the access rights of that subject for that object.

In practice, an access matrix is usually sparse, and is implemented by decomposition in one of two ways. The matrix may be decomposed by columns, yielding access control lists. Thus for each object, an access control list lists users and their permitted access opportunities. Decomposition by rows yields capability tickets. A capability ticket specifies authorized objects and operations

**TABLE 12.2  Data Base Access Matrix**

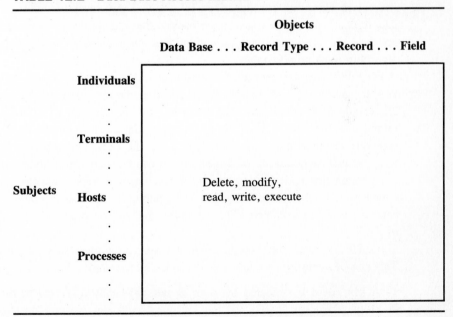

|  |  | Objects |
|---|---|---|
|  |  | Data Base . . . Record Type . . . Record . . . Field |
| **Subjects** | **Individuals** · · · **Terminals** · · · **Hosts** · · · **Processes** · · · | Delete, modify, read, write, execute |

for a user. Each user has a number of tickets and may be authorized to loan or give them to others. Because tickets may be dispersed around the system, they present a greater security problem than access control lists.

Network considerations for access control parallel those for authentication. Encryption may be needed to provide secure communications on a LAN or HSLN. Typically, access control is decentralized, that is, controlled by host-based data base management systems. However, if a network data base server exists on a LAN or HSLN, access control becomes a network service.

## Encryption

In the preceding section we referred to one of the major security risks on LANs and HSLNs, which use a multiaccess medium—the risk of eavesdropping. Eavesdropping can be accomplished by programming an NIU to accept packets other than those addressed to it or by physically tapping into the medium. One countermeasure that, properly used, is very effective is to encrypt the data in each packet (i.e., send the data in code).

A number of schemes for encryption have been proposed; good discussions can be found in [KENT81] and [POPE79]. In this section we describe two techniques that are good candidates for local network use.

The first of these, the Data Encryption Standard (DES), developed by the National Bureau of Standards, is based on a conventional encryption scheme (Figure 12.7a). In this scheme, the original data (plaintext) is transformed into a bit or character pattern in code by means of a cipher. The cipher is an encryption algorithm parameterized by a key. Upon reception, the encrypted data (ciphertext) can be transformed back to the original if the cipher algorithm and key are known at the destination. For this process to work, the cipher algorithm must be reversible.

For DES, data are encrypted in 64-bit blocks using a 56-bit key. Using the key, the 64-bit input is transformed in a series of steps involving transposition and exclusive-or operations. The result is a 64-bit output in which each bit of output is a function of each bit of the input and each bit of the key. At the receiver, the plaintext is recovered by using the same key and reversing the steps. A precise definition of this algorithm can be found in [TANE81a].

Although this code is theoretically breakable, it is hoped that the time and expense required is prohibitive. For most purposes, the risk of code breaking can be considered to be zero. The risk in this method has to do with management of the keys.

For DES to work, the two parties to the connection must have the same key. This can be achieved in a number of ways. For two nodes A and B:

1. A key could be selected by A or B and physically delivered to the other party.

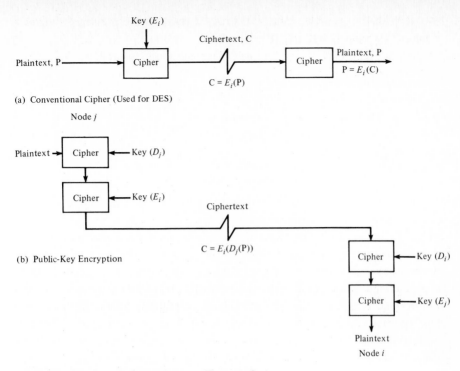

Key ($E_i$)

Plaintext, P

Cipher

Ciphertext, C

$C = E_i(P)$

Cipher

Plaintext, P

$P = E_i(C)$

(a) Conventional Cipher (Used for DES)

Node $j$

Plaintext

Cipher — Key ($D_j$)

Cipher — Key ($E_i$)

Ciphertext

$C = E_i(D_j(P))$

(b) Public-Key Encryption

Cipher — Key ($D_i$)

Cipher — Key ($E_j$)

Plaintext

Node $i$

**FIGURE 12–7.  Approaches to Encryption.**

2. A third party could select the key and physically deliver it to A and B.
3. If A and B have previously and recently used a key, one party could transmit the new key to the other, encrypted using the old key.
4. If A and B each have an encrypted connection to a third party C, C could deliver a key on the encrypted links to A and B.

This last course is the most attractive and could be handled from a host facility or the NCC. Of course, the keys used for A and B to communicate with C would have to be distributed by some means.

A clever means has been devised for transmitting keys securely without benefit of encryption! This technique, known as public-key encryption [DIFF76], is illustrated in Figure 12.7b. Until this technique was developed in 1976, it was assumed that the key had to be kept secret. To overcome that problem, a different design for the cipher is needed. For DES and like algorithms, the key used for encryption and decryption is the same. This is not a necessary condition. The encryption/ decryption can be accomplished by a pair of keys which create transformations that are the inverse of each other.

Now, if a cipher algorithm is chosen so that the encryption key, E, and the decryption key, D, differ and it is effectively impossible for D to be derived from E, the following technique will work.

1. Each node in the system publishes its encryption key, E, by placing it in a public register or file.

2. If B wishes to send a message P to A, it encrypts the message using A's public key, transmitting $E_A(P)$.

3. A applies its private decryption key to recover the message $P = D_A(E_A(P))$.

A further refinement is needed. Since anyone can transmit a message to A using A's public key, a means is needed to prevent imposters. This is accomplished by having a sender B encrypt the message or at least a source address field using its secret key $D_B$, and then encrypt using A's public key, sending out C $= E_A(D_B(P))$. On the other end, the receiver A first uses its private key and then uses B's public key on at least an address field to recover $P = E_B(D_A(C))$ $= E_B(D_A(E_A(D_B(P))))$.

With this technique any two stations can at any time set up a secure connection without a prior secret distribution of keys.

Finally, we mention that with either of the approaches described above, encryption can be end-to-end or link-oriented. End-to-end encryption is handled by the processes at each end of a session. Encryption becomes a presentation-layer function. This approach allows a certain flexibility but increases the burden on hosts and is not well suited to terminals, particularly dumb terminals. The other approach is to encrypt at the link level. Thus the data plus all headers except the layer 2 header are encrypted. This is a most convenient choice for LANs and HSLNs. The encryption capability can be incorporated into the NIU. The cost of this is reasonable: DES chips can be had for less than $50.

## Multilevel Security

The techniques that we have discussed so far have been concerned primarily with security as it relates to the individual user. A somewhat different but widely applicable requirement is to protect data or resources on the basis of levels of security. This is commonly found in the military, where information is unclassified (U), confidential (C), secret (S), top secret (TS), or beyond. Discussions of the military multilevel security problem in the context of LANs can be found in [SHIR82] and [GILL82].

Of course, the concept of multilevel is equally applicable in other areas, where information can be organized into gross categories and users can be granted clearances to access certain categories of data. For example, the highest level of security might be for strategic corporate planning documents and data, accessible by only corporate officers and their staff. Next might come sensitive financial and personnel data, accessible only by administration personnel. And so on.

When multiple categories or levels of data are defined, the requirement is referred to as one of multilevel security. The requirement is in two parts and is simply stated. A multilevel secure system must enforce:

• *No read up:* A subject can only read an object of less or equal security level.

- *No write down:* A subject can only write into an object of greater or equal security level.

These two rules, if properly enforced, provide multilevel security. For a data processing system, the approach that has been taken, and been the object of much research and development, is based on the reference monitor or security kernel concept [ANDE72]. The approach is depicted in Figure 12.8. The reference monitor controls the access of subjects to objects on the basis of security parameters of the subject and object. The reference monitor enforces the security rules (no read up, no write down) and has the following properties:

- *Complete mediation:* The security rules are enforced on every access, not just, for example, when a file is opened.
- *Isolation:* The reference monitor and data base are protected from unauthorized modification.
- *Verifiability:* The reference monitor's correctness must be provable; thus it must be small, simple, and easy to understand.

For a single data processing system, these are stiff requirements, and it is only recently that cost-effective solutions have begun to emerge. Systems that have a verified reference monitor are referred to as "trusted" or "secure" systems. There are two principal difficulties in developing a trusted computer. The first is due to the requirement for complete mediation. Every access to data within main memory and on peripheral storage must be mediated. Pure software

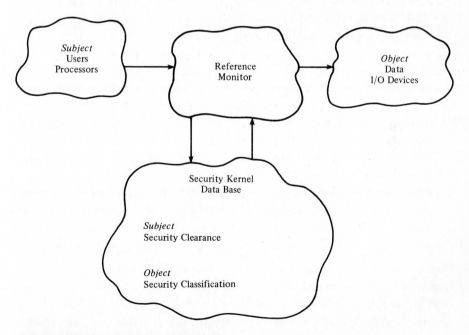

**FIGURE 12–8. Reference Monitor.**

implementations impose too high a performance penalty to be practical; the solution must be at least partly in hardware or firmware. The second difficulty is in the area of verifiability. It is no easy task to prove that a piece of hardware and an operating system are correct.

With this background, we now turn to the problem of multilevel security on a local network. It should be clear as the discussion proceeds that digital switches introduce no new problems or solutions and that LANs and HSLNs can be treated identically. For convenience, we will refer only to LANs in the following discussion.

### Overview

Figure 12.9a illustrates the problem: hosts and terminals at different security levels exist. To compound this situation, multilevel trusted hosts are part of the environment. With no modification to the LAN, those systems cannot be connected as shown. There are a number of approaches to correct this condition.

1. *Physical separation (Figure 12.9b):* The security problem disappears if the various LANs are kept in separate areas and protected at their designated security levels. This approach, however, negates most of the benefits of the LAN. Connectivity is drastically limited. Security requirements permit data to be passed upward (from a lower to a higher classification area), but this approach does not facilitate such data transfer.
2. *Bandwidth separation (Figure 12.9c):* With a broadband cable, each classification level could be assigned a separate channel. Cross-channel traffic could then be supported by a multilevel secure host. This approach requires the use of a trusted multilevel host.
3. *Encryption (not shown):* As the subject of much recent research, this is a promising approach. Each NIU would require encryption capability, and there needs to be a trusted facility for distributing keys to end points requesting a connection. This method may ultimately gain wide acceptance.
4. *Trusted hosts (Figure 12.9d):* Liberal use of trusted host machines (Guards) could satisfy the security requirement. If the trusted host were a minicomputer, mainframes could be connected by a trusted front end. Terminals would have to interface to the network via a trusted host.
5. *Trusted NIU (Figure 12.10):* The trusted NIU (TIU) is an NIU that provides the reference monitor capability. As we shall see, it is a remarkably simple device.

Of the options listed, 1 is impractical and 2 is not very flexible and is limited to broadband LANs. Options 3 and 4 have promise, but their cost effectiveness has yet to be demonstrated. The TIU concept, which has been funded by DOD and is the subject of ongoing research [SIDH82a, SIDH82b, GASS82] is a promising and apparently cost-effective approach. It is to this topic that we now turn.

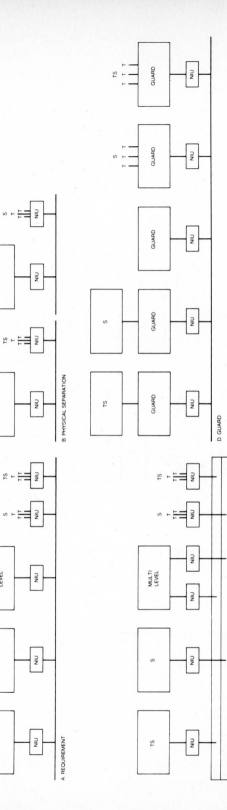

FIGURE 12–9. LAN/HSLN Security Approaches.

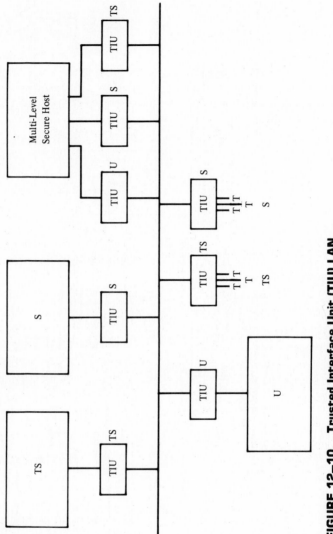

**FIGURE 12–10.   Trusted Interface Unit (TIU) LAN.**

## The Trusted Interface Unit

The Trusted Interface Unit (TIU) performs all the functions of an ordinary NIU. In addition, it is designed to operate at an assigned security level. Two other functions are required:

- The TIU will label each frame that it transmits with its security level.
- The TIU will accept only frames that are labeled with its own or a lesser security level.

Figure 12.10 depicts the architecture that can be supported by TIUs. Single-level hosts at a given security level connect to the LAN via a TIU of the same level. The TIU assures that the host receives only data up to the classification that it is permitted. All data transmitted by the host are labeled by the TIU with its security level, thereby ensuring that no end point of a lower classification level can receive the data.

As with hosts, terminals are also connected via TIUs. All terminals connected to the same TIU must operate at the same level.

A multilevel trusted host could connect to the LAN through a number of TIUs at various security levels. Each TIU is trusted to operate at its own security level. The trusted host is trusted to handle the communication ports to the various TIUs, again each at its own appropriate level.

Note that unclassified devices require a TIU operating at the unclassified level, not a simple NIU. The filtering function is most important for unclassified devices.

The use of TIUs requires modification to the LAN's layer 2 protocol. An additional field must be added for the security label.

The TIU approach is an attractive one because of the relative ease of building a trusted NIU. The performance penalty is slight; only a small amount of additional processing per packet is required. And compared to a general-purpose computer, the TIU is simple enough for one to feel encouraged about the verification process.

## Refinements

The previous section discusses, in general terms, the architecture of a multilevel secure LAN, based on a TIU implementation. Several refinements make this a more flexible capability.

- *Variable-level TIU:* This TIU would have a manual switch enabling an operator to select a security level other than the maximum one allowed for the TIU. Thus a terminal or host could operate at different security levels at different times. This could be a significant convenience.
- *Multilevel TIU:* A multilevel TIU would allow a multilevel trusted host to connect to the LAN through a single TIU. The multilevel TIU would trust its host to label data appropriately for transmission. For reception, the TIU would pass all data up to the host's maximum level.

- *Subnetworks:* In a multilevel environment, the cable and all TIUs must be physically protected to the highest security level of the LAN. However, it may not be practical or desirable to protect all attached devices to that level. One solution is to break the network into subnetworks that are physically separate and protected to various levels (Figure 12.11). Each subnetwork could be multilevel and physically protected to its highest level. Subnetworks would then connect by trusted bridges with encryption devices. Consider host A in Figure 12.11. While physically protected to secret, host A may run at an unclassified level, and at that level can communicate with host B on the unclassified network, which may be in another room or building. To prepare for such a connection, host A must be "sanitized" of all classified data, and its TIU adjusted to unclassified.

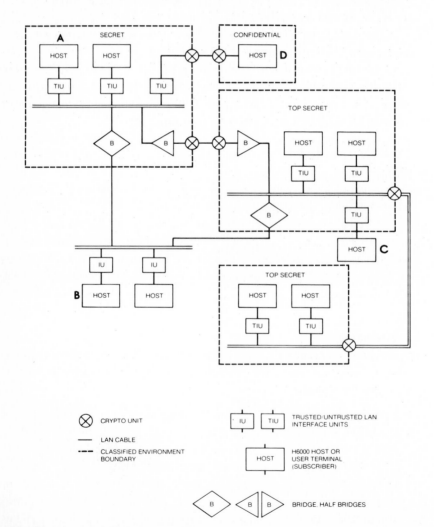

**FIGURE 12–11. Full Multilevel LAN.**

## RECOMMENDED READING

The issue of local network control is addressed in [ELDE82], where it is unfortunately referred to as local network management. Elden presents a conceptual framework for an integrated computer–communications network control system. Another view is found in [NBS81b]. Examples of commercially available NCCs are discussed in [CHRI78], [BASS80], and [MATS82]. A good example of a measurement facility is described in [AMER82]*.

Approaches to enhancing reliability and availability of bus/tree LANs are discussed in [BASS80]. A more detailed description for broadband may be found in [WILL81]*. For rings, a good discussion can be found in [SALT79]. The AWC approach is described in [ANDR82]*. [RAND78] is a good general discussion of computer reliability.

A good discussion of computer network security, covering all of the topics in Section 12.3, can be found in [KENT81]. [GASS82]* presents the TIU concept.

A more general discussion of LAN design issues is presented in [STAC81a]*.

## PROBLEMS

**12.1** Give some examples of useful applications of permanent link layer connections.

**12.2** List useful protocol-specific performance measures for the following protocols. Indicate whether collection can be centralized or must be distributed.
   **a.** Token bus.
   **b.** Collision avoidance (ANS X3T9.5).
   **c.** Token ring.
   **d.** Slotted ring.
   **e.** Register insertion.
   **f.** Distributed reservation.

**12.3** For centrally collected measurement data, there is a timing bias due to the propagation delay of the medium. Give examples of performance measures that are (are not) affected by this bias.

**12.4** Consider a system consisting of $N$ identical units, only $M$ of which are required for the system to function. Derive an expression for the availability of the system.

**12.5** Consider a ring network with the following parameters:

$N$ = number of nodes/repeaters
$h$ = skip distance in the backward direction

$d_{ij}$ = shortest hop distance from node $i$ to node $j$

$d$ = diameter = $Max_{ij}[d_{ij}]$

Note that for DDLCN, $d = |N/2|$, and for daisy chain, $d = |N/3| + 1$.

a. For the general case, derive an expression for $d$ as a function of $N$ and $h$. Show that $d$ is minimum for $h = |\sqrt{N}|$.

b. Assuming that the transfer of data between each combination of stations is equally likely, we have that the average number of hops is

$$K = \frac{1}{N} \sum_{i=0}^{N-1} \left[ \frac{1}{N-1} \sum_{j=0}^{N-1} d_{ij} \right]$$

$$= \frac{1}{N-1} \sum_{j=0}^{N-1} d_{ij} \qquad \text{for arbitrary } i$$

Solve for $K$ as a function of $N$, $h$. What is $K$ for DDLCN? For daisy chain? For $h = |\sqrt{N}|$? Show that $K$ is minimum for $h = |\sqrt{N}|$.

c. A measure of reliability is the number of alternate routes between the two farthest nodes on the network. There is exactly one forward route and a number of backward routes consisting of $b = |N/(h + 1)|$ backward hops and $(h - 1)$ forward hops; there are different routes depending on the different combination of forward and backward hops in the sequence. Derive an expression of the number of routes, $R$, as a function of $N$ and $h$. What is $R$ for DDLCN? For daisy chain? For $h = |\sqrt{N}|$? Show that $R$ is a minimum for $h = |\sqrt{N}|$.

12.6    In Figure 12.11, host C is in an unclassified environment connected to a LAN in a TS facility. Why must its TIU be inside the TS facility? Why is host D connected to its TIU via encryption devices whereas host C is not?

12.7    List and describe some potential security and penetration problems with the TIU concept.

# GLOSSARY

**ALOHA.**  A medium access control technique for multiple access transmission media. A station transmits whenever it has data to send. Unacknowledged transmissions are repeated.

**AMPLIFIER.**  An analog device designed to compensate for the loss in a section of transmission medium. It increases the signal strength of an analog signal over a range of frequencies.

**BANDWIDTH.**  Refers to a relative range of frequencies, that is, the difference between the highest and lowest frequencies transmitted. For example, the bandwidth of a TV channel is 6 MHz.

**BASEBAND.**  Transmission of signals without modulation. In a baseband local network, digital signals (1's and 0's) are inserted directly onto the cable as voltage pulses. The entire spectrum of the cable is consumed by the signal. This scheme does not allow frequency-division multiplexing.

**BRIDGE.**  A device that links two homogeneous packet-switched local networks. It accepts all packets from each network addressed to devices on the other, buffers them, and retransmits them to the other network.

**BROADBAND.**  The use of coaxial cable for providing data transfer by means of analog or radio-frequency signals. Digital signals are passed through a modem and transmitted over one of the frequency bands of the cable.

**BUS.** A topology in which stations are attached to a shared transmission medium. The transmission medium is a linear cable; transmissions propagate the length of the medium, and are received by all stations.

**CATENET.** A collection of packet-switched networks that are connected together via gateways.

**CATV.** Community Antenna Television. CATV cable is used for broadband local networks.

**CIRCUIT SWITCHING.** A method of communicating in which a dedicated communications path is established between two devices through one or more intermediate switching nodes. Unlike packet switching, digital data are sent as a continuous stream of bits. Bandwidth is guaranteed, and delay is essentially limited to propagation time. The telephone system uses circuit switching.

**COAXIAL CABLE.** An electromagnetic transmission medium consisting of a center conductor and an outer, concentric conductor.

**CODEC.** Coder–decoder. Transforms analog voice into a digital bit stream (coder), and digital signals into analog voice (decoder) using pulse code modulation (PCM).

**COLLISION.** A condition in which two packets are being transmitted over a medium at the same time. Their interference makes both unintelligible.

**COMPUTERIZED BRANCH EXCHANGE (CBX).** A local network based on the digital private branch exchange architecture. Provides an integrated voice/data switching service.

**CONTENTION.** The condition when two or more stations attempt to use the same channel at the same time.

**CRC.** Cyclic Redundancy Check. A numeric value derived from the bits in a message. The transmitting station calculates a number that is attached to the message. The receiving station performs the same calculation. If the results differ, then one or more bits are in error.

**CSMA.** Carrier Sense Multiple Access. A medium access control technique for multiple-access transmission media. A station wishing to transmit first senses the medium and transmits only if the medium is idle.

**CSMA/CD.** Carrier Sense Multiple Access with Collision Detection. A refinement of CSMA in which a station ceases transmission if it detects a collision.

**DATAGRAM.** A packet switching service in which packets (datagrams) are independently routed and may arrive out of order. The datagram is self-contained, and carries a complete address. Delivery confirmation is provided by higher level protocols.

**DCE.** Data Circuit-Terminating Equipment. A generic name for network-owned devices that provided a network attachment point for user devices.

**DIGITAL SWITCH.** A star topology local network. Usually refers to a system that handles only data but not voice.

**DTE.**  Data Terminal Equipment. A generic name for user-owned devices or stations that attach to a network.

**DUAL CABLE.**  A type of broadband cable system in which two separate cables are used: one for transmission and one for reception.

**FIBER OPTIC WAVEGUIDE.**  A thin filament of glass or other transparent material through which a signal-encoded light beam may be transmitted by means of total internal reflection.

**FRAME.**  A group of bits that includes data plus one or more addresses. Generally refers to a link layer (layer 2) protocol.

**FREQUENCY-AGILE MODEM.**  A modem used on some broadband systems which can shift frequencies in order to communicate with stations in different dedicated bands.

**FREQUENCY CONVERTER.**  In midsplit broadband cable systems, the device at the headend which translates between the transmitting and receiving frequencies. Also known as a frequency translator or a central retransmission facility.

**FREQUENCY-DIVISION MULTIPLEXING (FDM).**  A technique for combining multiple signals on one circuit by separating them in frequency.

**FSK.**  Frequency-Shift Keying. A digital-to-analog modulation technique in which two different frequencies are used to represent 1's and 0's.

**GATEWAY.**  A device that connects two systems, especially if the systems use different protocols. For example, a gateway is needed to connect two independent local networks, or to connect a local network to a long-haul network.

**GRADE OF SERVICE.**  For a circuit-switched system, the probability that, during a specified period of peak traffic, an offered call will fail to find an available circuit.

**HEADEND.**  The end point of a broadband bus or tree network. Transmission from a station is toward the headend. Reception by a station is from the headend.

**HIGH-SPEED LOCAL NETWORK (HSLN).**  A local network designed to provide high throughput between expensive, high-speed devices, such as mainframes and mass storage devices.

**HOST.**  The collection of hardware and software which attaches to a network and uses that network to provide interprocess communication and user services.

**HYBRID LOCAL NETWORK.**  An integrated local network consisting of more than one type of local network (LAN, HSLN, CBX).

**IEEE 802.**  A committee of IEEE organized to produce a LAN standard.

**INBOUND PATH.**  On a broadband LAN, the transmission path used by stations to transmit packets toward the headend.

**INFRARED.**  Electromagnetic waves whose frequency range is above that of microwave and below the visible spectrum: $3 \times 10^{11}$ to $4 \times 10^{14}$ Hz.

**INJECTION LASER DIODE (ILD).**   A solid state device that works on the laser principle to produce a light source for a fiber optic waveguide.

**INTERNETWORKING.**   Communication among devices across multiple networks.

**LASER.**   Electromagnetic source capable of producing infrared and visible light.

**LIGHT-EMITTING DIODE (LED).**   A solid-state device that emits light when a current is applied. Used as a light source for a fiber optic waveguide.

**LISTEN BEFORE TALK (LBT).**   Same as Carrier-Sense Multiple Access (CSMA).

**LISTEN WHILE TALK (LWT).**   Same as Carrier-Sense Multiple Access with Collision Detection (CSMA/CD).

**LOCAL AREA NETWORK (LAN).**   A general-purpose local network that can serve a variety of devices. Typically used for terminals, microcomputers, and minicomputers.

**LOCAL NETWORK.**   A communications network that provides interconnection of a variety of data communicating devices within a small area.

**MANCHESTER ENCODING.**   A digital signaling technique in which there is a transition in the middle of each bit time. A 1 is encoded with a high level during the first half of the bit time; a 0 is encoded with a low level during the first half of the bit time.

**MEDIUM ACCESS CONTROL (MAC).**   For bus, tree, and ring topologies, the method of determining which device has access to the transmission medium at any time. CSMA/CD and token are common access methods.

**MESSAGE SWITCHING.**   A switching technique using a message store and forward system. No dedicated path is established. Rather, each message contains a destination address and is passed from source to destination through intermediate nodes. At each node, the entire message is received, stored briefly, and then passed on to the next node.

**MICROWAVE.**   Electromagnetic waves in the frequency range 1 to 30 GHz.

**MIDSPLIT.**   A type of broadband cable system in which the available frequencies are split into two groups: one for transmission (5 to 116 MHz) and one for reception (168 to 300 MHz). Requires a frequency converter.

**MODEM.**   Modulator/Demodulator. Transforms a digital bit stream into an analog signal (modulator) and vice versa (demodulator). The analog signal may be sent over telephone lines, or could be radio frequencies or lightwaves.

**NETWORK CONTROL CENTER.**   The operator interface to software that observes and controls the activities in a network.

**NETWORK MANAGEMENT.**   A set of human and automated tasks that support the creation, operation, and evolution of a network.

**NONBLOCKING NETWORK.**   A circuit-switched network in which there is always at least one available path between any pair of idle end points regardless of the number of end points already connected.

**OPTICAL FIBER.** A lightwave transmission medium. Supports very high bandwidth.

**OUTBOUND PATH.** On a broadband LAN, the transmission path used by stations to receive packets coming from the headend.

**PACKET.** A group of bits that includes data plus source and destination addresses. Generally refers to a network layer (layer 3) protocol.

**PACKET SWITCHING.** A method of transmitting messages through a communications network, in which long messages are subdivided into short packets. The packets are then transmitted as in message switching. Usually, packet switching is more efficient and rapid than message switching.

**PASSIVE HEADEND.** A device that connects the two broadband cables of a dual cable system. It does not provide frequency translation.

**PBX.** Private Branch Exchange. A telephone exchange on the user's premises. Provides a switching facility for telephones on extension lines within the building and access to the public telephone network. May be manual (PMBX) or automatic (PABX). A digital PBX that also handles data devices without modems is called a CBX.

**PCM.** Pulse Code Modulation. A common method for digitizing voice. The bandwidth required for a single digitized voice channel is 64 kbps.

**PROPAGATION DELAY.** The delay between the time a signal enters a channel and the time it is received.

**PROTOCOL.** A set of rules governing the exchange of data between two entities.

**REGISTER INSERTION RING.** A medium access control technique for rings. Each station contains a register that can temporarily hold a circulating packet. A station may transmit whenever there is a gap on the ring and, if necessary, hold an oncoming packet until it has completed transmission.

**REPEATER.** A device that receives data on one communication link and transmits it, bit by bit, on another link as fast as it is received, without buffering. An integral part of the ring topology. Used to connect linear segments in a baseband bus local network.

**RING.** A topology in which stations are attached to repeaters connected in a closed loop. Data are transmitted in one direction around the ring, and can be read by all attached stations.

**RING WIRING CONCENTRATOR.** A site through which pass the links between repeaters, for all or a portion of a ring.

**SLOTTED ALOHA.** A medium access control technique for multiple-access transmission media. The technique is the same as ALOHA, except that packets must be transmitted in well-defined time slots.

**SLOTTED RING.** A medium access control technique for rings. The ring is divided into slots, which may be designated empty or full. A station may transmit whenever an empty slot goes by, by marking it full and inserting a packet into the slot.

**SPACE-DIVISION SWITCHING.** A circuit-switching technique in which each connection through the switch takes a physically separate and dedicated path.

**SPECTRUM.** Refers to an absolute range of frequencies. For example, the spectrum of CATV cable is now about 5 Hz to 400 MHz.

**SPLITTER.** Analog device for dividing one input into two outputs and combining two outputs into one input. Used to achieve tree topology on broadband CATV networks.

**STAR.** A topology in which all stations are connected to a central switch. Two stations communicate via circuit switching.

**STATISTICAL TIME-DIVISION MULTIPLEXING.** A method of TDM in which time slots on a shared transmission line are allocated to I/O channels on demand.

**SYNCHRONOUS TIME-DIVISION MULTIPLEXING.** A method of TDM in which time slots on a shared transmission line are assigned to I/O channels on a fixed, predetermined basis.

**TAP.** An analog device that permits signals to be inserted or removed from a twisted pair or coax cable.

**TDM BUS SWITCHING.** A form of time-division switching in which time slots are used to transfer data over a shared bus between transmitter and receiver.

**TERMINAL.** A collection of hardware and possibly software which provides a direct user interface to a network.

**TERMINATOR.** An electrical resistance at the end of a cable which serves to absorb the signal on the line.

**TIME-DIVISION MULTIPLEXING (TDM).** A technique for combining multiple signals on one circuit by separating them in time.

**TIME-DIVISION SWITCHING.** A circuit-switching technique in which time slots in a time-multiplexed stream of data are manipulated to pass data from an input to an output.

**TIME-MULTIPLEXED SWITCHING (TMS).** A form of space-division switching in which each input line is a TDM stream. The switching configuration may change for each time slot.

**TIME-SLOT INTERCHANGE (TSI).** The interchange of time slots within a time-division multiplexed stream.

**TOKEN BUS.** A medium access control technique for bus/tree. Stations form a logical ring, around which a token is passed. A station receiving the token may transmit data, and then must pass the token on to the next station in the ring.

**TOKEN RING.** A medium access control technique for rings. A token circulates around the ring. A station may transmit by seizing the token, inserting a packet onto the ring, and then retransmitting the token.

**TOPOLOGY.** The structure, consisting of paths and switches, that provides the communications interconnection among nodes of a network.

**TRANSCEIVER.**   A device that both transmits and receives.

**TRANSCEIVER CABLE.**   A four-pair cable that connects the transceiver in a baseband coax LAN to the controller.

**TRANSMISSION MEDIUM.**   The physical path between transmitters and receivers in a communications network.

**TREE.**   A topology in which stations are attached to a shared transmission medium. The transmission medium is a branching cable emanating from a headend, with no closed circuits. Transmissions propagate throughout all branches of the tree, and are received by all stations.

**TWISTED PAIR.**   An electromagnetic transmission medium consisting of two insulated wires arranged in a regular spiral pattern.

**VIRTUAL CIRCUIT.**   A packet-switching service in which a connection (virtual circuit) is established between two stations at the start of transmission. All packets follow the same route, need not carry a complete address, and arrive in sequence.

# REFERENCES

ABRA70 Abramson, N. "The ALOHA System—Another Alternative for Computer Communications." *Proceedings, Fall Joint Computer Conference*, 1970.

AIME79 Aimes, G. T., and Lazowska, E. D. "The Behavior of Ethernet-like Computer Communications Networks." *Proceedings, Seventh Symposium on Operating Systems Principles*, 1979.

ALLA82 Allan, R. "Local-area Networks Spur Moves to Standardize Data Communications Among Computers and Peripherals." *Electronic Design*, December 23, 1982.

AMER82 Amer, P. D. "A Measurement Center for the NBS Local Area Computer Network." *IEEE Transactions on Computers*, August, 1982.

AMER83 Amer, P. D.; Rosenthal, R.; and Toense, R. "Measuring a Local Network's Performance." *Data Communications*, April, 1983.

ANDE72 Anderson, J. P. *Computer Security Technology Planning Study*. Electronic Systems Division, Hanscom Field, Bedford, MA, Report ESD-TR-73-51, October, 1972.

ANDR82 Andrews, D. W., and Schultz, G.D. "A Token-Ring Architecture for Local Area Networks: An Update." *Proceedings, COMPCON Fall 82*, IEEE, 1982.

ANSI82 American National Standards Institute. *Draft, Proposed American National Standard Local Distributed Data Interface*. May, 1982.

ARCH81  Architecture Technology Corp. "Special Report: Network Systems Corporation, HYPERchannel." *LocalNetter*, November, 1981.

ARCH82  Architecture Technology Corp. "Special Report: AMTEL Messenger II. A Power Line Local Network Based Product." *LocalNetter*, February, 1982.

ARTH81  Arthurs, E., and Stuck, B. W. "A Theoretical Performance Analysis of Polling and Carrier Sense Collision Detection Communication Systems." *Proceedings, Seventh Data Communications Symposium*, 1981.

ARTH82  Arthurs, E.; Stuck, B. W.; Bux, W.; Marathe, M.; Hawe, W.; Phinney, T.; Rosenthel, R; and Tarasou, V. *IEEE Project 802 Local Area Network Standards, Traffic Handling Characteristics Committee Report*. IEEE, June, 1982.

BARC81  Barcomb, D. *Office Automation: A Survey of Tools and Technology*. Bedford, MA: Digital Press, 1981.

BASS80  Bass, C.; Kennedy, J. S.; and Davidson, J. M. "Local Network Gives New Flexibility to Distributed Processing." *Electronics*, September 25, 1980.

BECK77  Beckmann, P. *Elementary Queueing Theory and Telephone Traffic*. Geneva, IL: Lee's abc of the Telephone, 1977.

BELL82  Bell Telephone Laboratories. *Transmission Systems for Communications*, 1982.

BERN82  Bernhard, R. "Breaching System Security." *IEEE Spectrum*, June, 1982.

BERT80  Bertine, H. U. "Physical Level Protocols." *IEEE Transactions on Communications*, April, 1980.

BIND75  Binder, R. "A Dynamic Packet Switching System for Satellite Broadcast Channels." *Proceedings of the ICC*, 1975.

BOGG80  Boggs, D. R.; Shoch, J. F.; Taft, E. A.; and Metcalfe, R. M. "Pup: An Internetwork Architecture." *IEEE Transactions on Communications*, April, 1980.

BOSE81  Bosen, R. "A Low-Speed Local Net for Under $100 per Station." *Data Communications*, December, 1981.

BURK79  Burke, R. G. "Eliminating Conflicts on a Contention Channel." *Proceedings, Fourth Local Computer Network Conference*, 1979.

BUX81  Bux, W. "Local-Area Subnetworks: A Performance Comparison." *IEEE Transactions on Communications*, October, 1981.

BUX82  Bux, W.; Closs, F.; Janson, P. A.; Kummerle, K.; Miller, H. R.; and Rothauser, H. "A Local-Area Communication Network Based on a Reliable Token Ring System." *Proceedings, International Symposium on Local Computer Networks*, 1982.

BUX83  Bux, W., and Schlatter, M. "An Approximate Method for the Performance Analysis of Buffer Insertion Rings." *IEEE Transactions on Communications*, January 1983.

BYTE82  Bytex Corporation. *Autoswitch User Manual*. 1982.

CARL80  Carlson, D. E. "Bit-Oriented Data Link Control Procedures." *IEEE Transactions on Communications*, April, 1980.

CELA82  Celano, J. "Crossing Public Property: Infrared Link and Alternative Approaches for Connecting a High Speed Local Area Network." *Proceedings, Computer Networking Symposium*, 1982.

CERF78  Cerf, V. G., and Kristein, P. T. "Issues in Packet-Network Interconnection." *Proceedings of the IEEE*, November, 1978.

CHAM80  Champine, G. A.; Coop, R. D.; and Heinselman, R. C. *Distributed Computer Systems: Impact on Management, Design, and Analysis*. New York: North-Holland, 1980.

CHEN82 Cheng, W. *Performance Evaluation of Token Control Networks*. Ph.D. thesis, University of Illinois at Urbana-Champaign, 1982.

CHLA80a Chlamtac, I., and Franta, W. R. "Message-Based Priority Access to Local Networks." *Computer Communications*, April, 1980.

CHLA80b Chlamtac, I.; Franta, W. R.; Patton, P. C.; and Wells, B. "Performance Issues in Back-End Storage Networks." *Computer*, February, 1980.

CHOU83a Chou, W., ed. *Computer Communications, Vol. I: Principles*. Englewood Cliffs, NJ: Prentice-Hall, 1983.

CHOU83b Chou, W., ed. *Computer Communications, Vol. II*. Englewood Cliffs, NJ: Prentice-Hall, 1983.

CHRI78 Christensen, G. S. "Network Monitor Unit." *Proceedings, Third Conference on Local Computer Networking*, 1978.

CHRI79 Christensen, G. S. "Links Between Computer-Room Networks." *Telecommunications*, February, 1979.

CHRI81 Christensen, G. S., and Franta, W. K. "Design and Analysis of the Access Protocol for HYPERchannel Networks." *Proceedings, Third USA–Japan Computer Conference*, 1981.

CHU82 Chu, W. W.; Haller, W.; and Leung, K. K. "A Contention Based Channel Reservation Protocol for High Speed Local Networks." *Proceedings, Seventh Conference on Local Computer Networks*, 1982.

CLAN82 Clancy, G. J. et al. "The IEEE 802 Committee States Its Case Concerning Its Local Network Standards Efforts." *Data Communications*, April, 1982.

CLAR78 Clark, D. D.; Pogran, K. T.; and Reed, D. P. "An Introduction to Local Area Networks." *Proceedings of the IEEE*, November, 1978.

CLAR82 Clark, D. D. "Names, Addresses, Ports, and Routes." *Internet Protocol Implementation Guide*. Menlo Park, CA: SRI International, August, 1982.

COOP81 Cooper, R. B. *Introduction to Queueing Theory*. New York: North Holland, 1981.

COOP82 Cooper, E. "13 Often-Asked Questions About Broadband." *Data Communications*, April, 1982.

COOP83 Cooper, E., and Edholm, P. K. "Design Issues in Broadband Local Networks." *Data Communications*, February, 1983.

COTT79 Cotton, I. W. "Technologies for Local Area Computer Networks." *Proceedings, Local Area Communications Network Symposium*, 1979.

CROC83 Crochiere, R. E., and Flanagan, J. L. "Current Perspectives in Digital Speech." *IEEE Communications Magazine*, January, 1983.

CROW73 Crowther, W.; Rettberg, R.; Walden, D.; Orenstein, S.; and Heart, F. "A System for Broadcast Communication: Reservation ALOHA." *Proceedings, Sixth Hawaii International System Science Conference*, 1973.

CUNN80 Cunningham, J. E. *Cable Television*. Indianapolis: Howard W. Sams, 1980.

DAHO83 Dahod, A. M. "Local Network Standards: No Utopia." *Data Communications*, March, 1983.

DALA81 Dalal, Y. K., and Printis, R. S. "48-Bit Absolute Internet and Ethernet Host Numbers." *Proceedings, Seventh Data Communications Symposium*, 1981.

DALA82 Dalal, Y. K. "Use of Multiple Networks in the Xerox Network System." *Computer*, October, 1982.

DARP81a Defense Advanced Research Projects Agency. *Internet Protocol*. RFC: 791, September, 1981.

DARP81b Defense Advanced Research Projects Agency. *Transmission Control Protocol*. RFC: 793, September, 1981.

DARP81c Defense Advanced Research Projects Agency. *Internet Control Message Protocol*. RFC: 792, September, 1981.

DAVI73 Davies, D. W., and Barber, D. L. *Communication Networks for Computers*. New York: Wiley, 1973.

DAVI77 Davidson, J.; Hathaway, W.; Postel, J.; Mimno, N.; Thomas, R.; and Walden, D. "The ARPANET Telnet Protocol: Its Purpose, Principles, Implementation, and Impact on Host Operating System Design." *Proceedings, Fifth Data Communications Symposium*, 1977.

DAY80 Day, J. "Terminal Protocols." *IEEE Transactions on Communications*, April, 1980.

DAY81 Day, J. "Terminal, File Transfer, and Remote Job Protocols for Heterogeneous Computer Networks." In *Protocols and Techniques for Data Communication Networks*, edited by F. F. Kuo, Englewood Cliffs, NJ: Prentice-Hall, 1981.

DENN79 Denning, D. E., and Denning, P. J. "Data Security." *Computing Surveys*, September, 1979.

DERF83 Derfler, F., and Stallings, W. *A Manager's Guide to Local Networks*. Englewood Cliffs, NJ: Prentice-Hall/Spectrum, 1983.

DIFF76 Diffie, W., and Hellman, M. E. "New Directions in Cryptography." *IEEE Transactions on Information Theory*, November, 1976.

DIGI80 Digital Equipment Corp.; Intel. Corp.; and Xerox Corp. *The Ethernet: A Local Area Network Data Link Layer and Physical Layer Specifications*. September 30, 1980.

DINE80 Dineson, M. A., and Picazo, J. J. "Broadband Technology Magnifies Local Network Capability." *Data Communications*, February, 1980.

DINE81 Dineson, M. A. "Broadband Local Networks Enhance Communication Design." *EDN*, March 4, 1981.

DIXO82 Dixon, R. C. "Ring Network Topology for Local Data Communications." *Proceedings, COMPCON Fall 82*, IEEE, 1982.

DOLL78 Doll, D. R. *Data Communications: Facilities, Networks, and System Design*. New York: Wiley, 1980.

DONN79 Donnelly, J. E., and Yeh, J. W. "Interaction Between Protocol Levels in a Prioritized CSMA Broadcast Network." *Computer Networks*, March, 1979.

DRIV79 Driver, H. H.; Hopewell, H. L; and Iaquinto, J. F. "How the Gateway Regulates Information Flow." *Data Communications*, September, 1979.

EDN82 EDN Magazine. "Credibility Problems Could Block LAN Growth." *EDN*, September 1, 1982.

ELDE82 Elden, W. L. "Local Area Network Management." In [IEEE82].

FARM69 Farmer, W. D., and Newhall, E. E. "An Experimental Distributed Switching System to Handle Bursty Computer Traffic." *Proceedings, ACM Symposium on Problems in the Optimization of Data Communications*, 1969.

FLEM79 Fleming, P. *Principles of Switching*. Geneva, IL: Lee's abc of the Telephone, 1979.

FOLT81 Folts, H. C. "Coming of Age: A Long-Awaited Standard for Heterogeneous Nets." *Data Communications*, January, 1981.

FRAN76 Frankel, T. *Tables for Traffic Management and Design*. Geneva, IL: Lee's abc of the Telephone, 1976.

FRAN80 Franta, W. R., and Bilodeau, M. B. "Analysis of a Prioritized CSMA Protocol Based on Staggered Delays." *Acta Informatica*, June, 1980.

FRAN81 Franta, W. R., and Chlamtec, I. *Local Networks*. Lexington, MA: Lexington Books, 1981.

FRAN82 Franta, W. R., and Heath, J. R. *Performance of HYPERchannel Networks: Parameters, Measurements, Models, and Analysis*. University of Minnesota, Computer Science Department, Technical Report 82-3, January, 1982.

FREE80 Freeman, R. L. *Telecommunication System Engineering*. New York: Wiley, 1980.

FREE81 Freeman, R. L. *Telecommunication Transmission Handbook*. New York: Wiley, 1981.

FREE82 Freeman, R. B. "Net Management Choices: Sidestream or Mainstream." *Data Communications*, August, 1982.

GASS82 Gasser, M., and Sidhu, D. P. "A Multilevel Secure Local Area Network." *Proceedings, IEEE Symposium on Security and Privacy*, 1982.

GILL82 Gilligan, J. M., and Vasak, J. M. "A Generic Security Architecture for Distributed Systems." *Proceedings, Seventh Conference on Local Computer Networks*, 1982.

GOEL79 Goeller, L. F. "Programs for Traffic Calculation." *Business Communications Review*, May-June, 1979.

GOEL83 Goeller, L. F., and Goldston, J. A. "The ABCs of the PBX." *Datamation*, April, 1983.

GORD79 Gordon, R. L.; Farr, W. W.; and Levine, P. "Ringnet: A Packet Switched Local Network with Decentralized Control." *Proceedings, Fourth Conference on Local Computer Networks*, 1979.

GRAN83 Grant, A.; Hutchison, D.; and Shepherd, W. "A Gateway for Linking Local Area Networks and X.25 Networks." *Proceedings, SIGCOMM 83 Symposium*, 1983.

GRAU82 Graube, M. "Local Area Nets: A Pair of Standards." *IEEE Spectrum*, June, 1982.

GRNA80 Grnarov, A.; Kleinrock, L.; and Gerla, M. "A Highly Reliable Distributed Loop Network Architecture." *Proceedings, International Symposium on Fault-Tolerant Computing*, 1980.

HAFN74 Hafner, E. R.; Nenadal, Z.; and Tschanz, M. "A Digital Loop Communications System." *IEEE Transactions on Communications*, June, 1974.

HAHN81 Hahn, M., and Belanger, P. "Network Minimizes Overhead of Small Computers." *Electronics*, August 25, 1981.

HANS81 Hanson, K.; Chou, W.; and Nilsson, A. "Integration of Voice, Data, and Image Traffic in a Wideband Local Network." *Proceedings, Computer Networking Symposium*, 1981.

HAYE81 Hayes, J. F. "Local Distribution in Computer Communications." *IEEE Communications Magazine*, March, 1981.

HERR79 Herr, D. E., and Nute, C. T. "Modeling the Effects of Packet Truncation on the Throughput of CSMA Networks." *Proceedings, Computer Networking Symposium*, 1979.

HEYM82 Heyman, D. P. "An Analysis of the Carrier-Sense Multiple-Access Protocol." *Bell System Technical Journal*, October, 1982.

HEYW81 Heywood, P. "The Cambridge Ring Is Still Making the Rounds." *Data Communications*, July, 1981.

HILA82 Hilal, W., and Liu, M. T. "Analysis and Simulation of the Register-Insertion Protocol." *Proceedings, Computer Networking Symposium*, 1982.

HOBB81 Hobbs, M. *Modern Communications Switching Systems*. Blue Ridge Summit, PA: TAB Books, 1981.

HOHN80 Hohn, W. C. "The Control Data Loosely Coupled Network Lower Level Protocols." *Proceedings, National Computer Conference*, 1980.

HOLM81 Holmgren, S. F. *Evaluation of TCP/IP in a Local Network*. MITRE Working Paper 81WOO568, September 30, 1981.

HOPK77 Hopkins, G. T. *A Bus Communications System*. MITRE Technical Report MTR-3515, 1977.

HOPK79 Hopkins, G. T. "Multimode Communications on the MITRENET." *Proceedings, Local Area Communications Network Symposium*, 1979.

HOPK80 Hopkins, G. T., and Wagner, P. E. *Multiple Access Digital Communications System*. U.S. Patent 4,210,780, July 1, 1980.

HOPK82 Hopkins, G. T., and Meisner, N. B. "Choosing Between Broadband and Baseband Local Networks." *Mini-Micro Systems*, June, 1982.

HOPP77 Hopper, A. "Data Ring at Computer Laboratory, University of Cambridge." In *Local Area Networking*. National Bureau of Standards Publication 500-31, 1977.

IBM71 IBM Corp. *Analysis of Some Queueing Models in Real-Time Systems*. GF20-0007, 1971.

IBM82 IBM Corp. *IBM Series/1 Local Communications Controller Feature Description*. GA34-0142-2, 1982.

IEEE82 Institute for Electrical and Electronic Engineers. *IEEE Project 802, Local Network Standards, Draft C*. May 17, 1982.

ILC82 ILC Data Device Corp. *MIL-STD-1553 Designer's Guide*. 1982.

INOS79 Inose, H. *An Introduction to Digital Integrated Communications Systems*. Tokyo: University of Tokyo Press, 1979.

ITT75 International Telephone and Telegraph Corp. *Reference Data for Radio Engineers*, Indianapolis: Howard W. Sams, 1975.

JACK63 Jackson, J. R. "Job Shop-like Queueing Systems." *Management Sciences*, 1963.

JACO78 Jacobs, I.; Binder, R.; and Hoversten, E. "General Purpose Packet Satellite Networks." *Proceedings of the IEEE*, November, 1978.

JAJS83 Jajszczyk, A. "On Nonblocking Switching Networks Composed of Digital Symmetrical Matrices." *IEEE Transactions on Communications*, January, 1983.

JOEL77 Joel, A. E. "What Is Telecommunications Circuit Switching?" *Proceedings of the IEEE*, September, 1977.

JOEL79a Joel, A. E. "Circuit Switching: Unique Architecture and Applications." *Computer*, June, 1979.

JOEL79b Joel, A. E. "Digital Switching—How it Has Developed." *IEEE Transactions on Communications*, July, 1979.

JOLL68 Jolley, E. H. *Introduction to Telephony and Telegraphy*. New York: Hart, 1968.

JONE83 Jones, J. R. "Consider Fiber Optics for Local Network Designs." *EDN*, March 3, 1983.

KANA79 Kanakia, H., and Thomasian, A. "A Comparative Study of Access Control Mechanisms in Loop Networks." *Proceedings, Fourth Conference on Local Computer Networks*, 1979.

KANE80 Kane, D. A. "Data Communications Network Switching Methods," *Computer Design*, April, 1980.

KARP82 Karp, P. M., and Socher, I. D. "Designing Local-Area Networks." *Mini-Micro Systems*, April, 1982.

KASS79a Kasson, J. M. "The Rolm Computerized Branch Exchange: An Advanced Digital PBX." *Computer*, June, 1979.

KASS79b Kasson, J. M. "Survey of Digital PBX Design." *IEEE Transactions on Communications*, July, 1979.

KATK81a Katkin, R. D., and Sprung, J. G. "Simulating a Cable Bus Network in a Multicomputer and Large-Scale Application Environment." *Proceedings, Sixth Conference on Local Computer Networks*, 1981.

KATK81b Katkin, R. D., and Sprung, J. G. *Application of Local Bus Network Technology to the Evolution of Large Multi-computer Systems*. MITRE Technical Report MTR-81W290, November, 1981.

KATZ78 Katzan, H. *An Introduction to Distributed Data Processing*. New York: Petrocelli Books, 1978.

KENT81 Kent, S. T. "Security in Computer Networks." In *Protocols and Techniques for Data Communication Networks*, edited by F.F. Kuo. Englewood Cliffs, NJ: Prentice-Hall, 1981.

KILL82 Killen, M. "The Microcomputer Connection to Local Networks." *Data Communications*, December, 1982.

KLEE82 Klee, K.; Verity, J. W.; and Johnson, J. "Battle of the Networkers." *Datamation*, March, 1982.

KLEI75 Kleinrock, L., and Tobagi, F. A. "Packet Switching in Radio Channels: Part I: Carrier Sense Multiple-Access Modes and Their Throughput-Delay Characteristics." *IEEE Transactions on Communications*, December, 1975.

KLEI76 Kleinrock, L. *Queueing Systems, Vol. II: Computer Applications*. New York: Wiley, 1976.

KOBA78 Kobayashi, K. *Modeling and Analysis: An Introduction to System Performance and Evaluation Methodology*. Reading, MA: Addison-Wesley, 1978.

KRUT81 Krutsch, T. E. "A User Speaks Out: Broadband or Baseband for Local Nets?" *Data Communications*, December, 1981.

KUO80 Kuo, F. F., and Chu, W. W. *On the Impact of High Speed Local Networks upon Distributed Computer Architectures*. National Bureau of Standards Report ICST/LANP-80-1, September, 1980.

LABA78 LaBarre, C. E. *Analytic and Simulation Results for CSMA Contention Protocols*. MITRE Technical Report MTR-3672, 1978.

LABA80 LaBarre, C. E. *Communications Protocols and Local Broadcast Networks*. MITRE Technical Report MTR-3899, February, 1980.

LEVY82 Levy, W. A., and Mehl, H. F. "Local Area Networks." Series in *Mini-Micro Systems*, February, March, July, 1982.

LISS81 Lissack, T.; Maglaris, B.; and Chin, H. "Impact of Microprocessor Architecture on Local Network Interface Adapters." *Proceedings, Conference on Local Networks and Office Automation Systems*, 1981.

LIU78 Liu, M. T. "Distributed Loop Computer Networks." In *Advances in Computers, Vol. 17*. New York: Academic Press, 1978.

LIU82 Liu, M. T.; Hilal, W.; and Groomes, B. H. "Performance Evaluation of Channel Access Protocols for Local Computer Networks." *Proceedings, COMPCON 82 Fall*, 1982.

LUCZ78 Luczak, E. C. "Global Bus Computer Communication Techniques." *Proceedings, Computer Network Symposium*, 1978.

MAGL80 Maglaris, B., and Lissack, T. "An Integrated Broadband Local Network Architecture." *Proceedings, Fifth Conference on Local Computer Networks*, 1980.

MAGL81a Maglaris, B.; Lissack, T.; and Austin, M. "End-to-End Delay Analysis on Local Area Networks: An Office Building Scenario." *Proceedings, National Telecommunications Conference*, 1981.

MAGL81b Maglaris, B., and Lissack, T. "Queueing Model for Local Network Interface Adapters." *Technical Report*, Network Analysis Corporation, 1981.

MAGL82 Maglaris, B., and Lissack, T. "Performance Evaluation of Interface Units for Broadcast Local Area Networks." *Proceedings, COMPCON Fall 82*, 1982.

MAGN79 Magnee, F.; Endrizzi, A.; and Day, J. "A Survey of Terminal Protocols." *Computer Networks*, November, 1979.

MALO81 Malone, J. "The Microcomputer Connection to Local Networks." *Data Communications*, December, 1981.

MAND82 Mandelkern, D. "Rugged Local Network Follows Military Aircraft Standard." *Electronics*, April 7, 1982.

MARA82 Marathe, M., and Hawe, B. "Predicted Capacity of Ethernet in a University Environment." *Proceedings, SOUTHCON 82*, 1982.

MARK78 Mark, J. W. "Global Scheduling Approach to Conflict-Free Multiaccess via a Data Bus." *IEEE Transactions on Communications*, September, 1978.

MARK82 Markov, J. D., and Strole, N. C. "Token-Ring Local Area Networks: A Perspective." *Proceedings, COMPCON FALL 82*, IEEE, 1982.

MART67 Martin, J. *Design of Real-Time Computer Systems*. Englewood Cliffs, NJ: Prentice-Hall, 1967.

MART72 Martin, J. *Systems Analysis for Data Transmission*. Englewood Cliffs, NJ: Prentice-Hall, 1972.

MART76 Martin, J. *Telecommunications and the Computer, 2nd Ed*. Englewood Cliffs, NJ: Prentice-Hall, 1976.

MART81a Martin, J. *Computer Networks and Distributed Processing*. Englewood Cliffs, NJ: Prentice-Hall, 1981.

MART81b Martin, J. *Design and Strategy for Distributed Data Processing*. Englewood Cliffs, NJ: Prentice-Hall, 1981.

MATS82 Matsukane, E. "Network Administration and Control System for a Broadband Local Area Communications Network." *Proceedings, COMPCON FALL 82*, 1982.

MCNA82 McNamara, J. E. *Technical Aspects of Data Communication*. Bedford, MA: Digital Press, 1982.

METC76 Metcalfe, R. M., and Boggs, D. R. "Ethernet: Distributed Packet Switching for Local Computer Networks." *Communications of the ACM*, July, 1976.

METC77 Metcalfe, R. M.; Boggs, D. R.; Thacker, C. P.; and Lampson, B. W. "Multipoint Data Communication System with Collision Detection." *U.S. Patent* 4,063,220, 1977.

MIER82 Mier, E. E. "High-Level Protocols, Standards, and the OSI Reference Model." *Data Communications*, July, 1982.

MILL82 Miller, C. K., and Thompson, D. M. "Making a Case for Token Passing in Local Networks." *Data Communications*, March, 1982.

MITC81 Mitchell, L. C. "A Methodology for Predicting End-to-End Responsiveness in a Local Area Network." *Proceedings, Computer Networking Symposium*, 1981.

MOKH81 Mokhoff, N. "Communications: Fiber Optics." *IEEE Spectrum*, January, 1981.

MYER82 Myers, W. "Toward a Local Network Standard." *IEEE Micro*, August, 1982.

NBS80a National Bureau of Standards. *Features of Internetwork Protocol*. ICST/HLNP-80-8, July, 1980.

NBS80b National Bureau of Standards. *Features of the Transport and Session Protocols*. ICST/HLNP-80-1, March, 1980.

NBS81a National Bureau of Standards. *Specification of the Internetwork Protocol*. ICST/HLNP-81-6, May, 1981.

NBS81b National Bureau of Standards. *A Look at Network Management*. Report ICST/LANP-82-1, October, 1981.

NBS82 National Bureau of Standards. "Announcement of Plans to Propose a Federal Information Processing Standard for High Speed Channel Interface." *Federal Register*, October 5, 1982.

NESS81 Nessett, D. M. *HYPERchannel Architecture: A Case Study of Some Inadequacies in the ISO OSI Reference Model*. Lawrence Livermore Laboratory Report UCRL-53139, April, 1981.

OREI82 O'Reilly, P. J.; Hammond, J. L.; Schalg, J. H.; and Murray, D. N. "Design of an Emulation Facility for Performance Studies of CSMA-Type Local Networks." *Proceedings, Seventh Conference on Local Computer Networks*, 1982.

PARK83a Parker, R., and Shapiro, S. "Untangling Local Area Networks." *Computer Design*, March, 1983.

PARK83b Parker, R. "Committees Push to Standardize Disk I/O." *Computer Design*, March, 1983.

PENN79 Penny, B. K., and Baghdadi, A. A. "Survey of Computer Communications Loop Networks." *Computer Communications*, August and October, 1979.

PFIS82 Pfister, G. M., and O'Brien, B. V. "Comparing the CBX to the Local Network—and the Winner Is?" *Data Communications*, July, 1982.

PIER72 Pierce, J. R. "Network for Block Switches of Data." *Bell System Technical Journal*, July/August, 1972.

POPE79 Popek, G. J., and Kline, C. S. "Encryption and Secure Computer Networks." *Computing Surveys*, December, 1979.

POST80 Postel, J. B. "Internetwork Protocol Approaches." *IEEE Transactions on Communications*, April, 1980.

POST81 Postel, J. B.; Sunshine, C. A.; and Cihen, D. "The ARPA Internet Protocol." *Computer Networks*, 1981.

POUZ78 Pouzin, L., and Zimmermann, H. "A Tutorial on Protocols." *Proceedings of the IEEE*, November, 1978.

PROT82 Protunotarios, E. N.; Sykas, E. P.; and Apostolopoulos, T. K. "Hybrid Protocols for Contention Resolution in Local Area Networks." *Proceedings, Seventh Conference on Local Computer Networks*, 1982.

RAGH81 Raghavendra, C. S., and Gerla, M. "Optimal Loop Topologies for Distributed Systems." *Proceedings, Seventh Data Communications Symposium*, 1981.

RAND78 Randell, B.; Lee, P. A.; and TreLeaven, P. C. "Reliability Issues in Computing System Design." *Computing Surveys*, June, 1978.

RAUC82 Rauch-Hindin, W. "IBM's Local Network Scheme." *Data Communications*, May, 1982.

RAUC83 Rauch-Hindin, W. B. "Upper-Level Network Protocols." *Electronic Design*, March 3, 1983.

RAWS78 Rawson, E. G., and Metcalfe, R. M. "Fibernet: Multimode Optical Fibers for Local Computer Networks." *IEEE Transactions on Communications*, July, 1978.

RAWS79 Rawson, E. G. "Application of Fiber Optics to Local Networks." *Proceedings, Local Area Communications Network Symposium*, 1979.

REAM75 Reames, C. C., and Liu, M. T. "A Loop Network for Simultaneous Transmission of Variable-Length Messages." *Proceedings, Second Annual Symposium on Computer Architecture*, 1975.

RICH80 Richer, J.; Steiner, M.; and Sengoku, M. "Office Communications and the Digital PBX." *Computer Networks*, December, 1980.

ROBE73 Roberts, L. G. "Dynamic Allocation of Satellite Capacity Through Packet Reservation." *Proceedings, National Computer Conference*, 1973.

ROBE75 Roberts, L. G. "ALOHA Packet System With and Without Slots and Capture." *Computer Communications Review*, April, 1975.

ROMA77 Roman, G. S. *The Design of Broadband Coaxial Cable Networks for Multimode Communications*. MITRE Technical Report MTR-3527, 1977.

ROSE82 Rosenthal, R., ed. *The Selection of Local Area Computer Networks*. National Bureau of Standards Special Publication 500-96, November, 1982.

ROUN83 Rounds, F. "Use Modeling Techniques to Estimate Local-net Success." *EDN*, April 14, 1983.

RUSH82 Rush, J. R. "Microwave Links Add Flexibility to Local Networks." *Electronics*, January 13, 1982.

SALT79 Saltzer, J. H., and Pogran, K. T. "A Star-Shaped Ring Network with High Maintainability." *Proceedings, Local Area Communications Network Symposium*, 1979.

SALT81 Saltzer, J. H., and Clark, D. D. "Why a Ring?" *Proceedings, Seventh Data Communications Symposium*, ACM, 1981.

SALW83 Salwen, H. "In Praise of Ring Architecture for Local Area Networks." *Computer Design*, March, 1983.

SAND82 Sanders, L. "Interfacing with a Military Data-Comm Bus." *Electronic Design*, August 5, 1982.

SAUE81 Sauer, C. H., and Chandy, K. M. *Computer Systems Performance Modeling*. Englewood Cliffs, NJ: Prentice-Hall, 1981.

SCHO81 Scholl, T. H. "The New Breed—Switching Muxes." *Data Communications*, June, 1981.

SCHW77 Schwartz, M. *Computer-Communication Network Design and Analysis*. Englewood Cliffs, N.J.: Prentice-Hall, 1977.

SCHW82 Schwartz, J., and Melling, W.P. "Sharing Logic and Work." *Datamation*, November, 1982.

SEAM82 Seaman, J. "Local Networks: Making the Right Connection." *Computer Decisions*, June, 1982.

SHAR82 Sharma, R. L.; Sousa, P. T.; and Ingle, A. D. *Network Systems: Modeling, Analysis, and Design*. New York: Van Nostrand Reinhold, 1982.

SHEL82 Sheltzer, A.; Hinden, R.; and Brescia, M. "Connecting Different Types of Networks with Gateways." *Data Communications*, August, 1982.

SHIR82 Shirey, R. W. "Security in Local Area Networks." *Proceedings, Computer Networking Symposium*, 1982.

SHOC78 Shoch, J. F. "Internetwork Naming, Addressing, and Routing." *Proceedings, COMPCON 78*, 1978.

SHOC80a Shoch, J. F., and Hupp, J. A. "Measured Performance of an Ethernet Local Network." *Communications of the ACM*, December, 1980.

SHOC80b Shoch, J. F. *An Annotated Bibliography on Local Computer Networks*. Xerox Palo Alto Research Center, April, 1980.

SHOC82 Shoch, J. F.; Dala, Y. K.; and Redell, D. D. "Evolution of the Ethernet Local Computer Network." *Computer*, August, 1982.

SIDH82a Sidhu, D. P., and Gasser, M. *Design for a Multilevel Secure Local Area Network*. MITRE Technical Report MTR-8702, March, 1982.

SIDH82b Sidhu, D. P. "A Local Area Network Design for Military Applications." *Proceedings, Seventh Conference on Local Computer Networks*, 1982.

SKAP79 Skaperda, N. J. "Some Architectural Alternatives in the Design of a Digital Switch." *IEEE Transactions on Communications*, July, 1979.

SPAN81 Spaniol, O. "Analysis and Performance Evaluation of HYPERchannel Access Protocols." *Performance Evaluation*, 1981.

STAC80 Stack, T. R., and Dillencourt, K. A. "Protocols for Local Area Networks." *Proceedings, NBS Symposium on Computer Network Protocols*, 1980.

STAC81a Stack, T. R., and Dillencourt, K. A. "Functional Description of a Value-Added Local Area Network." *Proceedings, Computer Networking Symposium*, 1981.

STAC81b Stack, T. "LAN Protocol Residency Alternatives for IBM Mainframe Open System Interconnection." *Technical Report*, Network Analysis Corporation, 1981.

STAH82 Stahlman, M. "Inside Wang's Local Net Architecture."*Data Communications*, January, 1982.

STAL80 Stallings, W. "A Matrix Management Approach to System Development." *Proceedings, Nineteenth Annual NBS-ACM Technical Symposium*, June 19,1980.

STAL83a Stallings, W. *Tutorial: Local Network Technology*. Silver Spring, MD: IEEE Computer Society Press, 1983.

STAL83b Stallings, W. "Local Network Overview." *Signal Magazine*, January, 1983.

STAL83c Stallings, W. "Local Networks." *Scientific American*, to appear.

STAL84 Stallings, W. *Data and Computer Communications*. Macmillan, forthcoming.

STIE81 Steiglitz, M. "Local Network Access Tradeoffs." *Computer Design*, October, 1981.

STUC83 Stuck, B. "Which Local Net Bus Access Is Most Sensitive to Traffic Congestion?" *Data Communications*, January, 1983.

SUDA83 Suda, T.; Miyahara, H.; and Hasegawa, T. "Performance Evaluation of an Integrated Access Scheme in a Satellite Communication Channel." *IEEE Journal on Selected Areas in Communications*, January, 1983.

SUNS79 Sunshine, C. "Network Interconnection." *Proceedings of Local Area Communications Network Symposium*, 1979.

TANE81a Tanenbaum, A. S. *Computer Networks*. Englewood Cliffs, NJ: Prentice-Hall, 1981.

TANE81b Tanenbaum, A.S. "Network Protocols." *Computing Surveys*, December, 1981.

THOR80 Thornton, J. E. "Back-End Network Approaches." *Computer*, February, 1980.

THUR79 Thurber, K. J., and Freeman, H. A. "Architecture Considerations for Local Computer Networks." *Proceedings, First International Conference on Distributed Computer Systems*, 1979. (Reprinted in [THUR81].)

THUR81 Thurber, K. J., and Freeman, H. A., eds. *Tutorial: Local Computer Networks*. 2nd. ed. Silver Spring, MD: IEEE Computer Society Press, 1981.

TOBA80a Tobagi, F. A., and Hunt, V. B. "Performance Analysis of Carrier Sense Multiple Access with Collision Detection." *Computer Networks*, October/November, 1980.

TOBA80b Togabi, F. A. "Multiaccess Protocols in Packet Communication Systems." *IEEE Transactions on Communications*, April, 1980.

TOBA82 Tobagi, F. A. "Distributions of Packet Delay and Interdeparture Time in Slotted ALOHA and Carrier Sense Multiple Access." *Journal of the ACM*, October, 1982.

TROP81 Tropper, C. *Local Computer Network Technologies*. New York: Academic Press, 1981.

VONA80 Vonarx, M. "Controlling the Mushrooming Communications Net." *Data Communications*, June, 1980.

WAIN82 Wainwright, P. F. "Internetworking and Addressing for Local Networks." In [IEEE82].

WARN80 Warner, C. "Connecting Local Networks to Long-Haul Networks: Issues in Protocol Design." *Proceedings, Fifth Conference on Local Computer Networks*, 1980.

WATS80 Watson, W. B. "Simulation Study of the Configuration Dependent Performance of a Prioritized, CSMA Broadcast Network." *Proceedings, Fifth Conference on Local Computer Networks*, 1980.

WATS82 Watson, W. B. "Validation of a Discrete Event Computer Model of Network Systems Corporation's HYPERchannel." *Proceedings, Seventh Conference on Local Computer Networks*, 1982.

WAY81 Way, D. "Build a Local Network on Proven Software." *Data Communications*, December, 1982.

WILE82 Wiley, J. M. "Achilles' Heels of Modern Networking: A User's Lament." *Data Communications*, April, 1982.

WILK79 Wilkes, M. V., and Wheeler, D. J. "The Cambridge Digital Communication Ring." *Proceedings, Local Area Communications Network Symposium*, 1979.

WILL73 Willard, D. "MITRIX: A Sophisticated Digital Cable Communications System." *Proceedings, National Telecommunications Conference*, 1973.

WILL81 Willard, D. G. "Reliability/Availability of Wideband Local Communication Networks." *Computer Design*, August, 1981.

WILL82 Williams, D. G. "Industrial Controller Joins the MIL-STD-1553 Bus." *Electronic Design*, October 14, 1982.

WOLF78 Wolf, J. J., and Liu, M. T. "A Distributed Double-Loop Computer Network." *Proceedings, Seventh Texas Conference of Computing Systems*, 1978.

WOOD79 Wood, D. C.; Holmgren, S. F.; and Skelton, A. P. "A Cable-Bus Protocol Architecture." *Proceedings, Sixth Data Communications Symposium*, 1979.

WOOD83a Wood, D. C. "Local Networks." In [CHOU83b].

WOOD83b Wood, D. C. "Computer Networks." In [CHOU83b].

WOOD83c Wood, H. M., and Cotton, I. W. "Security in Computer Communications Systems." In [CHOU83a].

YU81  Yu, P. S. *Interconnection Structures of Backend Storage Networks*. IBM Technical Report RC 9165, December, 1981.

ZIMM80 Zimmermann, H. "OSI Reference Model—The ISO Model of Architecture for Open System Interconnection." *IEEE Transactions on Communications*, April, 1980.

# INDEX

Public data network (PDN), 35
Public-key encryption, 341
Pulse amplitude modulation (PAM), 191–192
Pulse code modulation (PCM), 22–24
Pure ALOHA, 112

Quarantining, 49
Queueing theory, 272, 273, 291

R-ALOHA, 158, 159
Radio-frequency (RF) signals, 75, 76
Random access techniques, 112
RAS. *See* Reliability, availability, survivability
Recovery, 49
Register insertion, 102, 128–130, 240–241, 266
 performance, 266, 268, 269
Register insertion ring, 333
Reliability, 326–327
 *See also* Reliability, availability, survivability
Reliability, availability, survivability (RAS), 326–336
 baseband networks, 332
 basic concepts, 327–329
 broadband networks, 329–332
 digital switch networks, 336
 ring networks, 332–335
Repeaters, 56, 293–294
 in ring topology LANs, 88–90
Reponse windows, 121
Resynchronization timer (RT), 154
Ring bridge, 99
Ring topology, 56, 88–95
 access control, 102, 128–136
  comparison of methods, 266–269
  register insertion, 128–130
  slotted ring, 131–132
  token ring, 132–136
 benefits, 90–91
 description, 88–90
 internetworking, 316
 problems, 91–92
 reliability concerns, 332–335
 star-ring, 93–95
 transmission media and, 68
Ring wiring concentrator, 93
Routing in IP catanet, 307–308
RT (resynchronization timer), 157

S-ALOHA, 113, 114, 241, 263, 264
SAP. *See* Service access point
Satellite networks, 158, 159
SATNET, 159
SDLC, 27
Secondary network, 221
 device attachment, 221–225
Secondary station, 44
Security, 336–348

access controls, 337–340
 encryption, 340–242
 multilevel, 342–348
SEL (digital selectors), 181
Selective repeat technique, 46
Semantics, 37
SEQ field, 45
SEQ/NEXT technique, 46
Sequencing, 32
Service access point (SAP), 39, 100, 105, 106, 140, 304, 305
Session, 49
Session layer, 42, 49
Signaling, defined, 16
Signals, 15–16
 defined, 15–16
Single-channel broadband systems, 60, 75, 85–86, 143–146
Sliding-window protocol, 46
Slotted ALOHA, 113, 114, 158, 159, 161, 241, 263, 264
Slotted ring, 102, 128, 131–132, 240
 performance, 266–269
SNA, 204
Space-division switching, 171–174
Split configuration, 82
Split systems, 82
Splitters, 83
Splitting, 41
Star-ring architecture, 92–95
Star topology, 55, 169–171
 transmission media and, 68
Start code, 26
Stations, 28
Statistical multiplexer, 188–189
Status reporting, 322, 324, 325
Stop code, 26
Store-and-forward message system, 30
Subnetworks, 348
Subsplit system, 82
Supervisory frames, 45, 47
Survivability, 328–329
 *See also* Reliability, availability, survivability (RAS)
Switching statistical multiplexer, 183, 187–190
Switching techniques, 27–36
 circuit switching, 28–29
 comparison of methods, 33–35
 for local networks, 36
 message switching, 30–31
 packet switching, 31–33
SYNC (synchronization character), 27
Synchronization character (SYNC), 27
Synchronous time-division multiplexing (TDM), 25, 170, 174–177
Synchronous transmission, 26–27, 183, 184
Syntax, 37

Syntax selection, 49

Taps, 83
TCP (Transmission Control Protocol), 49, 214–215
TDM. *See* Time-division multiplexing
TELENET, 33
Telephone systems, 12, 191
  call processing requirements, 192–194
  traffic, 279–291
    circuit-switching concepts, 280–283
    multiserver models, 283–290
TELNET protocol, 227
Terminal/port oriented switches, 183, 185–187
Terminals, 220
  handling for LANs, 220–230
Text compression, 49
Time-divisioin multiplexing (TDM), 24–26, 102, 170, 174–177, 192
Time-division switching, 174–182
Time-multiplexed switching (TMS), 174, 180–182
Time-slot interchange (TSI), 174, 177–179
Timing, 37
TIU (Trusted NIU), 344–348
TMS (time-multiplexed switching), 174, 180, 182
Token bus access control, 102, 111, 112, 119–124, 140, 240
  vs. CSMA/CD, 124–126
  description, 119–120
  IEEE 802, 120–124
  performance, 250–257
Token ring access control, 102, 128, 132–136, 140, 240, 266
  description, 132–134
  IEEE 802 standard, 134–136
  performance, 250–257, 266–269
  token maintenance, 136
T1 carrier, 25
Topology, 53–57
  bus, 56–57
  choice of, 57
  defined, 53
  ring, 56
  star, 55, 169–171
  transmission media and, 67–68
  tree, 56–57
  *See also* Local area networks
TP (Transport Protocol), 49
Traffic analysis
  concepts, 280–283
  models, 283–290
Trailer, 40
Transaction server, 50

Transmission, defined, 16
Transmission Control Protocol (TCP), 49, 214–215
Transmission media, 57–67
  choice, of 66–67
  coaxial cable, 60–62
  defined, 57
  line-of-sight, 65–66
  optical fiber cable, 62–65
  reliability concerns, 329, 330–331
  topology and, 67–68
  twisted pair, 59–60
Transmission rate, 236–242
Transmit state, 90
Transparent mode, 216
Transport layer, 42, 48–49
Transport Protocol (TP), 49
Tree topology, 56–57
  headend, 81
  transmission media and, 68
  *See also* Bus/tree networks
Trunk, 189
Trunk cable, 83
TSI (time-slot interchange), 174, 177–179
Twin pair, 184
Trusted network interface unit (TIU), 344–348
Twisted-pair, 16, 58, 59–60, 67
  in baseband systems, 75, 79–80
  topology and, 67, 68
TYMNET, 33

Unallocated frames, 127
University of Minnesota, 270
Unnumbered frames, 45, 47
Upward multiplexing, 41

Value-added network (VAN), 35, 204–205
Van (value-added network), 35, 204–205
Virtual circuit, 31–33, 99, 105
Virtual terminal protocols (VTP), 49, 225–230
  classes, 221–228
  functions, 227
  LAN implementations, 229–230
  phases of operation, 228–229
Voice data, 16–17, 22
Voice signals, multiplexing, 24
VTP. *See* Virtual terminal protocols

Wavelength division multiplexing, 64
WF (arbiter wait flag), 154

Xerox, 111
X.25 standard, 302, 303, 306, 309, 311–314, 316
X.75 standard, 302, 303, 311–314, 316